THE MANGA GUIDE™ TO
DATABASES

MANA TAKAHASHI
SHOKO AZUMA
TREND-PRO CO., LTD.

Ohmsha

no starch press

THE MANGA GUIDE TO DATABASES. Copyright © 2009 by Mana Takahashi and TREND-PRO Co., Ltd.

The Manga Guide to Databases is a translation of the Japanese original, *Manga de Wakaru Database*, published by Ohmsha, Ltd. of Tokyo, Japan. © 2004 by Mana Takahashi and TREND-PRO Co., Ltd.

This English edition is co-published by No Starch Press, Inc. and Ohmsha, Ltd.

11 10 09   2 3 4 5 6 7 8 9

ISBN-10: 1-59327-190-5
ISBN-13: 978-1-59327-190-9

Publisher: William Pollock
Author: Mana Takahashi
Illustrator: Shoko Azuma
Producer: TREND-PRO Co., Ltd.
Production Editor: Megan Dunchak
Developmental Editor: Tyler Ortman
Technical Reviewers: Baron Schwartz and Peter MacIntyre
Compositor: Riley Hoffman
Proofreader: Cristina Chan
Indexer: Sarah Schott

For information on book distributors or translations from the English edition, please contact No Starch Press, Inc.
No Starch Press, Inc.
555 De Haro Street, Suite 250, San Francisco, CA 94107
phone: 415.863.9900; fax: 415.863.9950; info@nostarch.com; http://www.nostarch.com/

Library of Congress Cataloging-in-Publication Data

Takahashi, Mana.
  The Manga guide to databases / Mana Takahashi, Shoko Azuma, and Trend-pro Co. -- 1st ed.
      p. cm.
  Includes index.
  ISBN-13: 978-1-59327-190-9
  ISBN-10: 1-59327-190-5
 1. Database management--Comic books, strips, etc. 2. Database management--Caricatures and cartoons. 3. SQL
(Computer program language)--Comic books, strips, etc. 4. SQL (Computer program language)--Caricatures and
cartoons. I. Azuma, Shoko, 1974- II. Trend-pro Co. III. Title.
  QA76.9.D3T34 2009
  005.75'65--dc22
                                                    2008046159

Contents

PREFACE

Databases are a crucial part of nearly all computer-based business systems. Some readers of this book may be considering introducing databases into their routine work. Others may have to actually develop real database-based business systems. The database is the technology that supports these systems behind the scenes, and its true nature is difficult to understand.

This book is designed so that readers will be able to learn the basics about databases through a manga story. At the end of each chapter, practice exercises are provided for confirmation and expanding the knowledge you've obtained. Each chapter is designed so that readers can gain an understanding of database technology while confirming how much they understand the contents.

The structure of this book is as follows.

Chapter 1 describes why we use databases. Why is a database necessary? What kind of difficulties will you have if you do not use a database? You will learn the background information that using a database requires.

Chapter 2 provides basic terminology. You'll learn about various database models and other terms relating to databases.

Chapter 3 explains how to design a database, specifically, a relational database, the most common kind.

Chapter 4 covers SQL, a language used to manage relational databases. Using SQL allows you to easily manage your data.

Chapter 5 explains the structure of the database system. Since a database is a system through which many people share data, you will learn how it can do so safely.

Chapter 6 provides descriptions of database applications. You'll learn how Web-based and other types of database systems are used.

This book was published thanks to the joint efforts of many people: Shoko Azuma for cartoons, TREND-PRO for production, and Ohmsha for planning, editing, and marketing. I extend my deep gratitude to all those concerned.

I hope that this book is helpful to all readers.

MANA TAKAHASHI

1
What Is a Database?

3

HMM...

I WONDER IF IT IS INEFFECTIVE TO MANAGE ALL THE DATA ON A DEPARTMENTAL BASIS.

IT WAS SUCH A HEADACHE WHEN THE PRICE OF APPLES WENT UP THE OTHER DAY.

PRINCESS RURUNA!!

BANG!

OH, IT'S YOU, CAIN. WHAT'S UP?

I HAVE A PRESENT FROM THE KING.

FROM MY FATHER?!

IF MY PARENTS WERE STILL IN THE CASTLE, THIS WOULD NOT BE HAPPENING...!

PRINCESS?

...SOME TIME AGO...

DO YOU HAVE TO GO?

SHAKE SHAKE

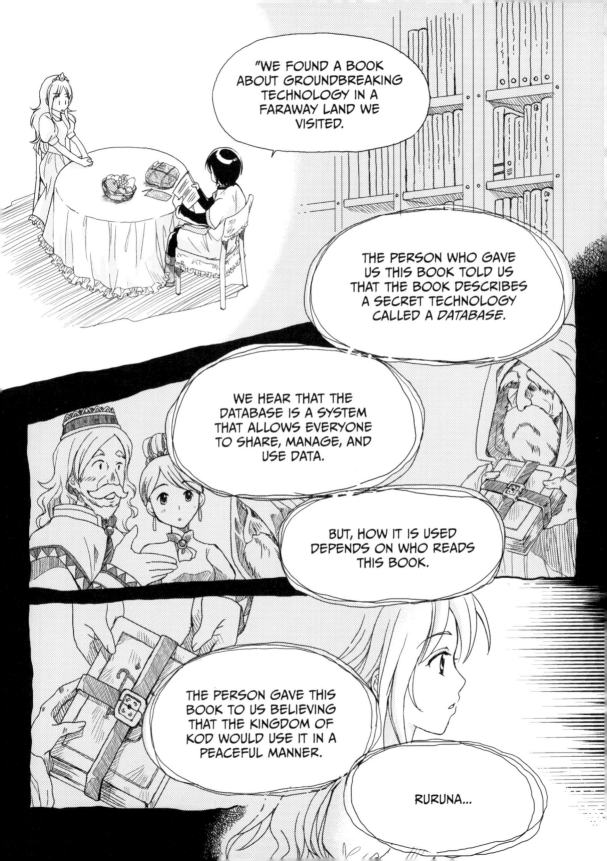

WHaT's UP In THE KInGDOM?

The Kingdom of Kod currently uses a file-based system to manage its data. But it seems that the current system has a few problems. What are they, in particular? Let's look at the system in detail.

The Kingdom currently has three departments: the Merchandise Department, the Overseas Business Department, and the Export Department. The Merchandise Department keeps track of all fruit produced in the country, the Overseas Business Department manages the foreign countries that are the Kingdom's business partners, and the Export Department keeps records of the amount of fruit the Kingdom exports.

DATA IS DUPLICATED

Princess Ruruna isn't satisfied with the current system. But why not? Each department in the Kingdom manages data independently. For example, the Merchandise Department and the Export Department each create files to manage fruit data. Therefore, data is duplicated needlessly across the departments. Each department must enter the data, store the data, then print receipts for confirmation, all of which is a waste. In addition, data trapped in one particular department is never shared effectively with the other departments.

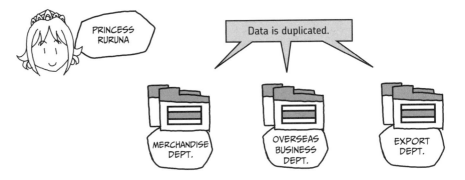

But that's not all. The system also creates problems when someone needs to change the data. For example, let's assume that the price of apples changes. To deal with this, Princess Ruruna must notify every department individually that the price of apples has changed. Isn't that inconvenient?

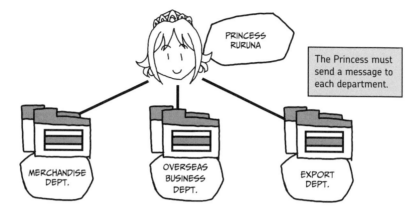

DATA CAN CONFLICT

It may seem easy enough to notify each department that the price of apples has changed, but it can create a new set of problems. Let's say that Princess Ruruna does notify the three departments that the price of apples has changed. However, the Overseas Business Department may forget to change the price, or the Export Department might change the price to 300G instead of 120G. These kinds of errors result in conflicting data between departments, which causes the content of the file systems to differ from the conditions of the real world. What a pain!

MERCHANDISE DEPARTMENT

Product name	Unit price	
Melon	800G	
Strawberry	150G	
Apple	120G	
Lemon	200G	

OVERSEAS BUSINESS DEPARTMENT

Product name	Unit price	
Melon	800G	
Strawberry	150G	
Apple	100G	
Lemon	200G	

EXPORT DEPARTMENT

Product name	Unit price	
Melon	800G	
Strawberry	150G	
Apple	300G	
Lemon	200G	

DATA IS DIFFICULT TO UPDATE

The current system not only creates conflicting data, but it also makes it difficult to respond to changes in business. For example, let's say that the King wants to launch a new Tourism Department. When a tour guide conducts a tour of the orchards and discusses the King-dom's fruit sales, the guide will want to use the most up-to-date sales figures.

But, unfortunately, the current system does not necessarily allow the departments to access each other's data, since the files are kept independently. To manage a new tourism business, Princess Ruruna will have to make copies of all the relevant files for the Tourism Department!

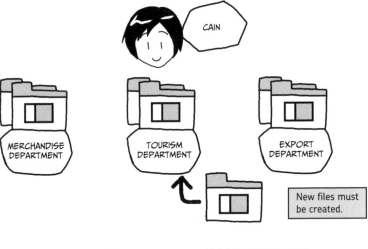

FILE FOR MERCHANDISE DEPT.

Product name	Unit price	
Melon	800G	
Strawberry	150G	
Apple	120G	
Lemon	200G	

FILE FOR TOURISM DEPT.

Product name	Unit price	
Melon	800G	
Strawberry	150G	
Apple	120G	
Lemon	200G	

This, in turn, increases the amount of duplicated data created when a new department starts. Considering these weaknesses, the current system is not efficient. It makes it difficult to start new projects and respond to environmental changes.

a Database—that's our solution!

Well, why is this system so inefficient? The problems all stem from separate and independent data management. What should Ruruna and Cain do? That's right—they should create a database! They must unify the management of data for the entire Kingdom. I will show you how to do this in the next chapter.

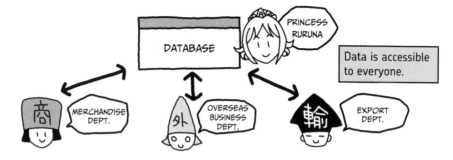

Uniform data management ensures that each department has the correct information, because each department sends a query to a single source of data. What an efficient system it is! It prevents data conflicts, and it also eliminates duplicated data, allowing for easy introduction and integration of new departments.

HOW TO USE A DATABASE

To introduce and operate a database, you must understand its unique challenges. First, the database will be used by many people, so you'll need a way for them to easily input and extract data. It needs to be a method that is easy for everybody to use.

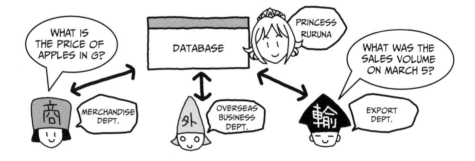

The new system also presents some risks—for example, it may make it possible for users to steal or overwrite important information like salary data, which is confidential and should be protected by an access restriction. Or, for example, only the Export Department should have access to sales data. Setting up database security and permissions is important when designing a system.

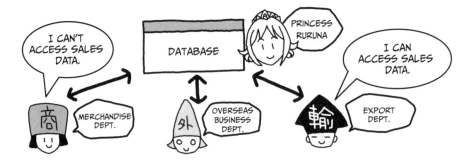

The new system can have other problems, too. The database can be used by many people at one time. Assume that someone in the Overseas Business Department and someone in the Export Department both try to change the name of a fruit at the same time—the former, from *Apple* to *AP*, and the latter, from *Apple* to *APL*. If they do this, what will happen to the product name? For a database that will be used by many people, this kind of problem must be considered.

You also need to be careful not to lose any data. Furthermore, the system may go down or a hard disk could fail, causing data to be corrupted. The database must have mechanisms to recover from these common kinds of failures.

In addition, since the database will hold a large amount of data, you must be able to perform searches at high speeds. The new system must have the power to handle that.

Let's start studying databases together with Princess Ruruna and Cain to learn how to solve these problems. Onward to Chapter 2!

Summary

- File-based management can create conflicting data and data duplication.
- A database allows you to share data easily and prevents conflicting and duplicated data.

USING SOFTWARE TO MANAGE DATABASES

The database we are going to study is managed by software called a database management system (DBMS). A DBMS has many useful functions—it allows you to do things like input data into a database, prevent conflicting data, and retrieve a large amount of data at high speed. Thanks to our DBMS, the database can be used by many people simultaneously. In addition, a DBMS can protect the security of the database—for example, it allows the database to operate properly even if a failure occurs. In addition, the DBMS provides an easy-to-use interface between the database and its users. We'll study databases and the functions of a DBMS in the next chapter.

2
What Is a Relational Database?

DATABASE TERMS

TRAPPED!

GEE, WHO IS SHE?

YOU PROMISED TO GO OUT ON A DATE WITH ME TODAY.

NO...UHM... WELL...

THIS IS FOR YOU.

...

WHAT ABOUT MY FLOWERS?

DRAG, DRAG...

PRINCESS RURUNA, I'LL BE BACK...

PHEW!

HE IS SO ANNOYING.

PLOP!

BUT RAMINESS IS THE PRINCE OF THE NEIGHBORING COUNTRY.

YOU SHOULDN'T TREAT HIM SO LIGHTLY.

DON'T I KNOW IT...

GOOD MORNING!

EACH RECORD CONTAINS FIELDS OF THE SAME TYPE.

RECORD

I SEE.

PRODUCT CODE	PRODUCT NAME	UNIT PRICE	REMARKS
101	MELON	800G	WITH SEEDS
102	STRAWBERRY	150G	
103	APPLE	120G	
104	LEMON	200G	SOUR
201	CHESTNUT	100G	WITH BUR
202	PERSIMMON	160G	
301	PEACH	130G	
302	KIWI	200G	VALUABLE

FIELD

FOR EXAMPLE, *PRODUCT CODE* IS A THREE-DIGIT VALUE...

AND *PRODUCT NAME* IS TEN CHARACTERS OR LESS.

PRODUCT CODE	PRODUCT NAME
101	MELON
102	STRA
103	APPL
104	LEMON
201	CHESTNUT
202	PERSIMMON

THEN, NEXT, LET'S THINK ABOUT THE PRODUCT CODE IN A LITTLE MORE DETAIL.

PRODUCT CODE
101
102
103
104
201
202
301
302

HERE!

HMMM... RECORD... FIELD... MUTTER... MUTTER...

CAIN?

SO WE CAN IDENTIFY DATA WITH ITS PRODUCT CODE, BUT NOT WITH ITS UNIT PRICE.

EXACTLY.

IN THE DATABASE WORLD, SUCH A FIELD...

...IS CALLED *UNIQUE*.

PRODUCT CODE IS UNIQUE

UNIQUE?

OTHER PEOPLE OFTEN SAY THAT ABOUT MY FATHER...

UMMMM...

HA, HA, HA, KING KOD IS UNIQUE. MWAHAHA

IT MEANS THE ONE AND ONLY.

ONE!

ONLY! —

IT HAS A SPECIFIC MEANING, YOU KNOW.

THEN, NEXT, LET'S THINK ABOUT *REMARKS*.

REMARKS?

REMARKS ARE REMARKS, AREN'T THEY?

TAKE A LOOK FROM THE POINT OF VIEW OF A DATABASE.

SOME VALUES UNDER REMARKS HAVE NO ENTRIES, RIGHT?

CHARACTER-ISTICS LIKE THIS...

PERSON	REMARKS
RURUNA	BLONDE ACTIVE
CAIN	BRUNET RELAXED

RELAXED?

I SEE YOUR POINT...

	REMARKS
G	WITH SEEDS
0G	
120G	
200G	SOUR
0G	WITH BUR

BUT, IF YOU CONTINUE USING THE CURRENT INDEPENDENT FILES,

THERE ARE ALL KINDS OF PROBLEMS YOU CAN'T SOLVE.

THAT'S RIGHT.

THAT'S WHY I WANT TO CREATE A DATABASE.

SO, TELL ME, TELL ME NOW.

HOLD ON!

WHEN YOU SAY DATABASE, YOU MUST UNDERSTAND THAT THERE ARE MANY KINDS OF DATABASES.

JUST LIKE FRUIT.

IS THAT SO?

FOR EXAMPLE,

THIS IS A HIERARCHICAL DATA MODEL, IN WHICH

THERE IS A TREE-LIKE RELATIONSHIP BETWEEN DATA.

ACK, SOMETHING APPEARED.

BOINK!

DATA

BOINK!

DATA

DATA

DATA   DATA   DATA   DATA

SHAZAM!

Relational Databases

IN ADDITION, THE RELATIONAL DATA MODEL IS DESIGNED SO THAT YOU CAN PROCESS DATA WITH MATHEMATICAL OPERATIONS.

ER...MATH?

AS I SUSPECTED, THIS IS DIFFICULT...

NOT AT ALL.

HMM...

FOR INSTANCE, LET'S LOOK BACK AT THE PRODUCT TABLE.

PRODUCT CODE	PRODUCT NAME	UNIT PRICE	REMARKS
101	MELON	800G	WITH SEEDS
102	STRAWBERRY	150G	
103	APPLE	120G	
104	LEMON	200G	SOUR
201	CHESTNUT	100G	WITH BUR
202	PERSIMMON	160G	
301	PEACH	130G	
302	KIWI	200G	VALUABLE

PRODUCT NAME
MELON
STRAWBERRY
APPLE
LEMON
CHESTNUT
PERSIMMON
PEACH
KIWI

MAGIC!

YOU CAN EXTRACT THE PRODUCT NAME?

AN OPERATION TO EXTRACT A COLUMN LIKE THIS IS CALLED PROJECTION.

SO EXTRACTING THE PRODUCT NAME IS AN OPERATION?

YES, IT'S SIMPLE.

THERE ARE MANY OTHER OPERATIONS. IN FACT, THERE ARE EIGHT!

SO MANY!

UNION

DIFFERENCE

CARTESIAN PRODUCT

DIVISION

PROJECTION

INTERSECTION

SELECTION

JOIN

ANOTHER MERIT OF THE RELATIONAL DATA MODEL IS THAT YOU CAN PROCESS DATA BY...

COMBINING THESE OPERATIONS.

I SEE.

TYPES OF DATA MODELS

When you use the term *database*, what kind of database do you mean? There are many types available for data management. The data association and operation methods that a database uses is called its *data model*. There are three commonly used data models.

As I described to Ruruna and Cain, the first type is the hierarchical data model. In the *hierarchical data model*, child data has only one piece of parent data. The second type is the network data model. Unlike the hierarchical data model, in the *network data model*, child data can have multiple pieces of parent data.

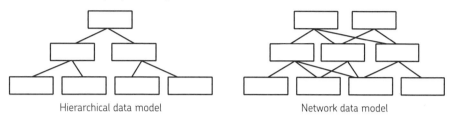

Hierarchical data model   Network data model

To use either of these models, you must manage data by keeping the physical location and the order of data in mind. Therefore, it is difficult to perform a flexible and high-speed search of your data if you use a hierarchical or network data model.

The third type of model is the relational data model. A *relational* database processes data using the easy-to-understand concept of a table. Let's discuss this model in more detail.

Relational data model

DATA EXTRACTION OPERATIONS

How is data extracted in a relational database? You can process and extract data in a relational database by performing stringently defined mathematical operations. There are eight main operations that you can use, and they fall into two categories—set operations and relational operations.

SET OPERATIONS

The union, difference, intersection, and Cartesian product operations are called *set operations*. These operations work upon one or more sets of rows to produce a new set of rows. In short, they determine which rows from the input appear in the output. Let's look at some examples using Product Table 1 and Product Table 2.

Product name	Unit price
Melon	800G
Strawberry	150G
Apple	120G
Lemon	200G

Product name	Unit price
Melon	800G
Strawberry	150G
Chestnut	100G
Persimmon	350G

UNION

Carrying out the *union* operation allows you to extract all products included in Product Table 1 and Product Table 2. The result is below.

Product name	Unit price
Melon	800G
Strawberry	150G
Apple	120G
Lemon	200G
Chestnut	100G
Persimmon	350G

Performing a union operation extracts all rows in the two tables and combines them. The following figure shows what the data from the two tables looks like once a union operation has been performed. All rows in Product Table 1 and Product Table 2 have been extracted.

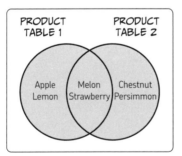

DIFFERENCE

Difference is an operation that extracts rows from just *one* of the tables. For example, a difference operation can extract all of the products from the first table that are not included in the second. The results depend on which table contains rows to extract, and which table has rows to exclude.

Product name	Unit price
Apple	120G
Lemon	200G

Product name	Unit price
Chestnut	100G
Persimmon	350G

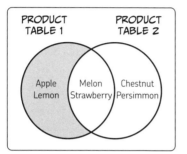

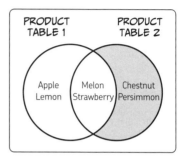

INTERSECTION

You can also extract products that are included in *both* Product Table 1 and Product Table 2. This operation is called an *intersection* operation. Here is the result of the intersection of Product Tables 1 and 2.

Product name	Unit price
Melon	800G
Strawberry	150G

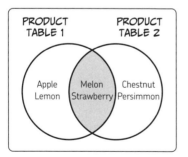

CARTESIAN PRODUCT

The *Cartesian product* operation is a method that combines all rows in the two tables. Let's look at the Product and Export Destination Tables below.

The Cartesian product operation combines all rows in the two tables. In this example, it resulted in 3 × 3 = 9 rows. Notice that the column names (or fields) in these two tables are not the same—unlike our previous examples.

PRODUCT TABLE

Product code	Product name	Unit price
101	Melon	800G
102	Strawberry	150G
103	Apple	120G

EXPORT DESTINATION TABLE

Export dest. code	Export dest. name
12	The Kingdom of Minanmi
23	Alpha Empire
25	The Kingdom of Ritol

3 rows

CARTESIAN PRODUCT

Product code	Product name	Unit price	Export dest. code	Export dest. name
101	Melon	800G	12	The Kingdom of Minanmi
101	Melon	800G	23	Alpha Empire
101	Melon	800G	25	The Kingdom of Ritol
102	Strawberry	150G	12	The Kingdom of Minanmi
102	Strawberry	150G	23	Alpha Empire
102	Strawberry	150G	25	The Kingdom of Ritol
103	Apple	120G	12	The Kingdom of Minanmi
103	Apple	120G	23	Alpha Empire
103	Apple	120G	25	The Kingdom of Ritol

3 x 3 = 9 rows

RELATIONAL OPERATIONS

A relational database is designed so that data can be extracted by set operations and relational operations. Let's look at the other four operations specific to a relational database, called *relational operations*—projection, selection, join, and division.

PROJECTION

Projection is an operation that extracts columns from a table. In the example shown here, this operation is used to extract only product names included in the Product Table.

Product name
Melon
Strawberry
Apple
Lemon

       Think of projection as extracting "vertically," as shown below.

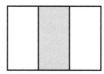

SELECTION

The *selection* operation extracts two rows from a table.

Product name	Unit price
Melon	800G
Strawberry	150G

       Selection is like projection, but it extracts rows instead of columns. Selection extracts data "horizontally."

JOIN

The *join* operation is a very powerful one. This operation literally refers to the work of joining tables. Let's look at the tables below as an example.

PRODUCT TABLE

Product code	Product name	Unit price
101	Melon	800G
102	Strawberry	150G
103	Apple	120G
104	Lemon	200G

SALES TABLE

Date	Product code	Quantity
11/1	102	1,100
11/1	101	300
11/5	103	1,700
11/8	101	500

The Product Code columns in these two tables represent the same information. On November 1st, 1,100 strawberries (product code 102) were sold. The Sales Table does not include the product name, but it does include the product code. In other words, the Sales Table allows you to understand which product was sold by making reference to the product code, which is the *primary key* in the Product Table. The product code in the Sales Table is a *foreign key*. Joining the two tables so that the foreign key refers to the primary key results in the following table.

Date	Product code	Product name	Unit price	Quantity
11/1	102	Strawberry	150G	1,100
11/1	101	Melon	800G	300
11/5	103	Apple	120G	1,700
11/8	101	Melon	800G	500

This creates a new dynamic table of sales data, including date, product code, product name, unit price, and quantity. The figure below shows a join—the shaded area represents a column that appears in both original tables.

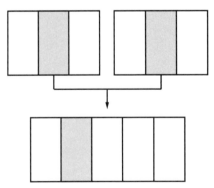

DIVISION

Finally, let's look at division. *Division* is an operation that extracts the rows whose column values match those in the second table, but only returns columns that don't exist in the second table. Let's look at an example.

SALES TABLE

Export dest. code	Export dest. name	Date
12	The Kingdom of Minanmi	3/5
12	The Kingdom of Minanmi	3/10
23	Alpha Empire	3/5
25	The Kingdom of Ritol	3/21
30	The Kingdom of Sazanna	3/25

EXPORT DESTINATION TABLE

Export dest. code	Export dest. name
12	The Kingdom of Minanmi
23	Alpha Empire

Dividing the Sales Table by the Export Destination Table results in the following table. This allows you to find the dates when fruit was exported to both the Alpha Empire and the Kingdom of Minanmi.

Date
3/5

QUESTIONS

Now, let's answer some questions to see how well you understand relational databases. The answers are on page 48.

Q1

What do you call the key referring to a column in a different table in a relational database?

Q2

The following table displays information about books. Which item can you use as a primary key? The ISBN is the International Standard Book Number, a unique identifying number given to every published book. Some books may have the same title.

ISBN	Book name	Author name	Publication date	Price

Q3

What do you call the operation used here to extract data?

Export dest. code	Export dest. name
12	The Kingdom of Minanmi
23	Alpha Empire
25	The Kingdom of Ritol
30	The Kingdom of Sazanna

➡️

Export dest. code	Export dest. name
25	The Kingdom of Ritol

Q4

What do you call the operation used here to extract data?

Export dest. code	Export dest. name
12	The Kingdom of Minanmi
23	Alpha Empire
25	The Kingdom of Ritol
30	The Kingdom of Sazanna

Export dest. code	Export dest. name
15	The Kingdom of Paronu
22	The Kingdom of Tokanta
31	The Kingdom of Taharu
33	The Kingdom of Mariyon

⬇️

Export dest. code	Export dest. name
12	The Kingdom of Minanmi
15	The Kingdom of Paronu
22	The Kingdom of Tokanta
23	Alpha Empire
25	The Kingdom of Ritol
30	The Kingdom of Sazanna
31	The Kingdom of Taharu
33	The Kingdom of Mariyon

Q5

What do you call the operation used here to extract data?

Export dest. code	Export dest. name
12	The Kingdom of Minanmi
23	Alpha Empire
25	The Kingdom of Ritol
30	The Kingdom of Sazanna

Export dest. code	Date
12	3/1
23	3/1
12	3/3
30	3/5
12	3/6
25	3/10

↓

Export dest. code	Date	Export dest. name
12	3/1	The Kingdom of Minanmi
23	3/1	Alpha Empire
12	3/3	The Kingdom of Minanmi
30	3/5	The Kingdom of Sazanna
12	3/6	The Kingdom of Minanmi
25	3/10	The Kingdom of Ritol

ᄃHE RELATIONAL DATABASE PREVAILS!

In a relational database, you can use eight different operations to extract data. The extracted results are tabulated. If you combine the operations explained in this section, you can extract data for any purpose. For example, you can use the name and price of a product to create gross sales aggregate data for it. Relational databases are popular because they're easy to understand and provide flexible data processing.

Summary

- One row of data is called a *record*, and each column is called a *field*.
- A column that can be used to identify data is called a *primary key*.
- In a relational database, you can process data using the concept of a table.
- In a relational database, you can process data based on mathematical operations.

answers

Q1 Foreign key

Q2 ISBN

Q3 Selection

Q4 Union

Q5 Join

3
LET'S DESIGN A DATABASE!

THE E-R MODEL

RUSTLE

RUSTLE

CAIN? WHERE ARE YOU?

...RIGHT, RIGHT.

PSST

PSST

WHAT'S WRONG WITH CAIN?

!!

PSST

HE IS MUMBLING TO HIMSELF....

...DATABASE OR SOMETHING...

SHH!

GOOD MORNING, GIRLS!

OH, CAIN...

PRINCESS RURUNA!

G...G... GOOD MORNING!

...

OH, I'VE GOT IT.

CAIN!!

I SEE.

NORMALIZING A TABLE

IT IS DIFFICULT TO START TO CREATE A DATABASE.

THAT'S RIGHT! THE FIRST THING TO DO IS TO ANALYZE THE ACTUAL CONDITION. THAT IS VERY IMPORTANT.

NOW THAT YOU KNOW ABOUT THE ACTUAL CONDITION OF THE KINGDOM OF KOD...

YE-E-E-S!!

LET'S CONSIDER THE DESIGN OF AN ACTUAL DATABASE.

MR. CAIN?

STARTLED

SHHH!

SHHH!

PRINCESS?

HMM...

I FOUND IT.

DIVING IN!!

SALES REPORT

1101 TO THE KINGDOM OF MINANMI DATE: 3/5

101 MELON @800G×1,100=880,000G
102 STRAW-BERRY @150G× 300= 45,000G

THE KINGDOM OF KOD   TOTAL 925,000G

THIS IS...A SALES REPORT WE CREATE WHEN EXPORTING FRUIT TO A FOREIGN COUNTRY.

THIS REPORT SHOWS THE CURRENT STATUS OF EXPORT MOST CORRECTLY.

FLUTTER

YES, INDEED! SO, WE TAKE ALL THE DATA FROM THE REPORT...

TO CREATE A DATABASE TABLE.

NOT JUST YET. FIRST...

TABULATE IT!!

SWISH

LET'S...

HERE YOU ARE.

REPORT CODE	DATE	EXPORT DEST. CODE	EXPORT DEST. NAME	PRODUCT CODE	PRODUCT NAME	UNIT PRICE	QUANTITY
1101	3/5	12	THE KINGDOM OF MINANMI	101	MELON	800G	1,100
				102	STRAWBERRY	150G	300
1102	3/7	23	ALPHA EMPIRE	103	APPLE	120G	1,700
1103	3/8	25	THE KINGDOM OF RITOL	104	LEMON	200G	500
1104	3/10	12	THE KINGDOM OF MINANMI	101	MELON	800G	2,500
1105	3/12	25	THE KINGDOM OF RITOL	103	APPLE	120G	2,000
				104	LEMON	200G	700

TABLE CREATED FROM SALES REPORT

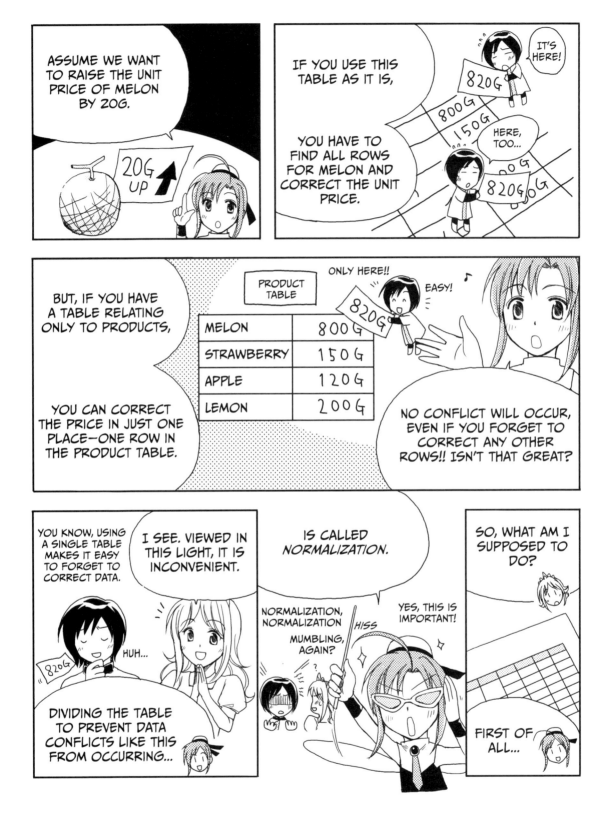

LET'S TRY CHANGING IT SO THAT ONE ROW HAS ONE VALUE.

REPEATED DATA IS A CLUE THAT ROWS HAVE TO BE DIVIDED.

SO, I'LL DIVIDE IT INTO...

ONE TABLE WITH DATE, EXPORT DESTINATION CODE, AND EXPORT DESTINATION NAME...

AND ANOTHER TABLE WITH PRODUCT CODE, PRODUCT NAME, UNIT PRICE, AND QUANTITY.

SALES TABLE (FIRST NORMAL FORM (1))

REPORT CODE	DATE	EXPORT DEST. CODE	EXPORT DEST. NAME
1101	3/5	12	THE KINGDOM OF MINANMI
1102	3/7	23	ALPHA EMPIRE
1103	3/8	25	THE KINGDOM OF RITOL
1104	3/10	12	THE KINGDOM OF MINANMI
1105	3/12	25	THE KINGDOM OF RITOL

SALES TABLE (FIRST NORMAL FORM (2))

REPORT CODE	PRODUCT CODE	PRODUCT NAME	UNIT PRICE	QUANTITY
1101	101	MELON	800G	1,100
1101	102	STRAWBERRY	150G	300
1102	103	APPLE	120G	1,700
1103	104	LEMON	200G	500
1104	101	MELON	800G	2,500
1105	103	APPLE	120G	2,000
1105	104	LEMON	200G	700

BUT THE REPORT CODE IS PROVIDED IN BOTH TABLES, ISN'T IT?

HUH.

YES, THAT WAY YOU CAN IDENTIFY IF THERE IS AN ASSOCIATION BETWEEN THE TWO TABLES.

THE TABLE THAT RESULTS FROM A DIVISION LIKE THIS IS CALLED THE *FIRST NORMAL FORM.*

FIRST NORMAL FORM, FIRST NORMAL FORM

STOP MUMBLING!

THE TABLE THAT HAS ROWS WITH TWO OR MORE VALUES BEFORE IT IS DIVIDED IS CALLED THE *UNNORMALIZED FORM.*

IT MEANS THAT THE FIRST NORMAL FORM IS CREATED BY DIVIDING THE UNNORMALIZED FORM.

DIVIDE

FIRST NORMAL FORM

LET'S SEE...

WAIT A MINUTE.

THESE ARE THE "FIRST NORMAL FORMS." DOES THAT MEAN THERE ARE THE "SECOND" AND "THIRD" NORMAL FORMS, TOO?

BINGO!

THE FIRST NORMAL FORM CANNOT BE USED AS A RELATIONAL DATABASE TABLE AS IT IS.

HANG IN THERE!

AH, I SEE...

COME ON!!

IT'S A LONG WAY!!

FIRST NORMAL FORM

MT. RELATIONAL DATABASE

STUMBLE STUMBLE

YOU CAN'T MANAGE PRODUCTS INDEPENDENTLY USING TABLE (2).

HMM.

TABLE (2)

THAT'S RIGHT!! SO,

DIVIDE TABLE (2)

INTO TWO!!

DUH!

THESE ARE THE TABLES THAT RESULT FROM DIVIDING THE FIRST NORMAL FORM (2) INTO TWO.

PRODUCT TABLE
(SECOND NORMAL FORM (1))

PRODUCT CODE	PRODUCT NAME	UNIT PRICE
101	MELON	800G
102	STRAWBERRY	150G
103	APPLE	120G
104	LEMON	200G

SALES STATEMENT TABLE
(SECOND NORMAL FORM (2))

REPORT CODE	PRODUCT CODE	QUANTITY
1101	101	1,100
1101	102	300
1102	103	1,700
1103	104	500
1104	101	2,500
1105	103	2,000
1105	104	700

TABLE (1) CONTAINS DATA RELATING TO THE PRODUCTS.

IF A VALUE IN THE PRODUCT CODE COLUMN IS DETERMINED, WE CAN FIND THE VALUES IN THE PRODUCT NAME AND UNIT PRICE COLUMNS.

OH, GEE.

SO THAT MEANS THE PRODUCT CODE, AS THE PRIMARY KEY, DETERMINES VALUES IN OTHER COLUMNS.

EXACTLY.

THE TABLE THAT RESULTS FROM DIVISION ACCORDING TO THIS RULE IS CALLED

THE SECOND NORMAL FORM.

WE CAN ADD THE MANDARIN ORANGES WE WERE TALKING ABOUT EARLIER TO THE SECOND NORMAL FORM (1).

WE CAN ALSO ADD KIWIS AND GRAPES,

WHICH HAVE NOT BEEN SOLD YET!

EVEN IF THE PRICE OF MELON CHANGES, WE JUST CORRECT THE DATA ON ONE ROW, RIGHT?

820G

...BY THE WAY, YOU DIVIDED THE FIRST NORMAL FORM (2),

UH?

SO ISN'T IT NECESSARY TO DIVIDE THE FIRST NORMAL FORM SALES TABLE (1)?

OH, YOU ARE WEARING GLASSES NOW.

FLOOMP

CHECK!

GOOD POINT!

SALES TABLE
(FIRST NORMAL FORM (1))

REPORT CODE	DATE	EXPORT DEST. CODE	EXPORT DEST. NAME
1101	3/5	12	THE KINGDOM OF MINANMI
1102	3/7	23	ALPHA EMPIRE
1103	3/8	25	THE KINGDOM OF RITOL
1104	3/10	12	THE KINGDOM OF MINANMI
1105	3/12	25	THE KINGDOM OF RITOL

DETER-MINED

PRIMARY KEY

IF THIS VALUE IS DETER-MINED,

THIS VALUE IS

DETER-MINED.

FOR THIS TABLE, IF ONE VALUE IN REPORT CODE IS DETERMINED, ALL OTHER VALUES IN DATE, EXPORT DESTINATION CODE, AND EXPORT DESTINATION NAME ARE DETERMINED.

YEAH!!

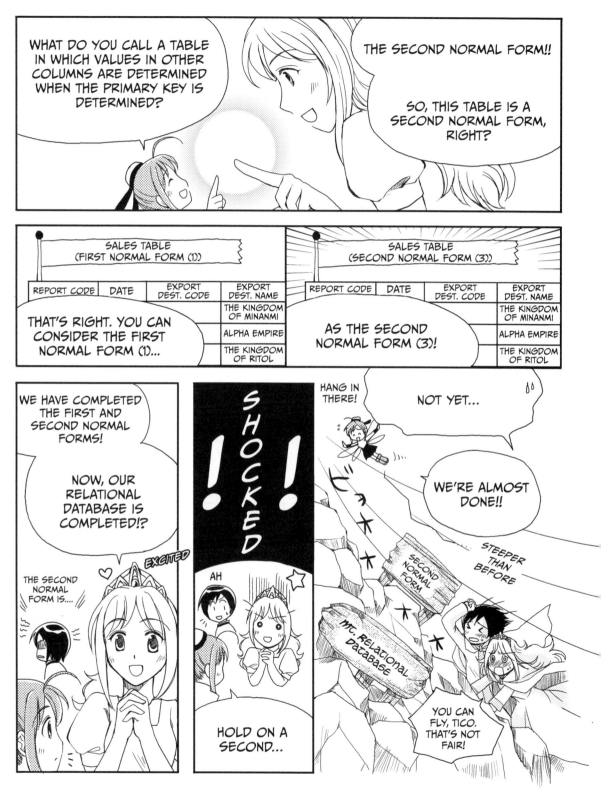

IN THE SECOND NORMAL FORM (3), EXPORT DESTINATION NAME IS DETERMINED ACCORDING TO REPORT CODE.

YES.

BUT IN FACT, DETERMINATION OF REPORT CODE DETERMINES A VALUE IN EXPORT DESTINATION CODE,

THEREBY DETERMINING EXPORT DESTINATION NAME INDIRECTLY.

REPORT CODE

EXPORT DESTINATION CODE

EXPORT DESTINATION NAME

TO DEAL WITH SUCH CONCERNS,

YOU DIVIDE THE TABLE SO THAT NO PART IS DETERMINED INDIRECTLY.

DETER-MINATION

DETER-MINATION

REPORT CODE	DATE	EXPORT DEST. CODE

DETER-MINATION

EXPORT DEST. CODE	EXPORT DEST. NAME

THAT'S RIGHT. A TABLE THAT DOES NOT ALLOW ANY NON-PRIMARY KEY TO DETERMINE VALUES IN OTHER COLUMNS...

IS CALLED THE THIRD NORMAL FORM!!

FINALLY, WE'VE GOTTEN TO THE THIRD NORMAL FORM!!

NOW, YOU CAN MANAGE EVEN THE KINGDOM OF SAZANNA.

BREATHING HARD...

"THIRD" NORMAL FORM

SALES TABLE

REPORT CODE	DATE	EXPORT DEST. CODE
1101	3/5	12
1102	3/7	23
1103	3/8	25
1104	3/10	12
1105	3/12	25

EXPORT DESTINATION TABLE

EXPORT DEST. CODE	EXPORT DESTINATION NAME
12	THE KINGDOM OF MINANMI
23	ALPHA EMPIRE
25	THE KINGDOM OF RITOL

SALES STATEMENT TABLE

REPORT CODE	PRODUCT CODE	QUANTITY
1101	101	1,100
1101	102	300
1102	103	1,700
1103	104	500
1104	101	2,500
1105	103	2,000
1105	104	700

PRODUCT TABLE

PRODUCT CODE	PRODUCT NAME	UNIT PRICE
101	MELON	800G
102	STRAWBERRY	150G
103	APPLE	120G
104	LEMON	200G

THESE ARE THE TABLES THAT RESULT WHEN YOU DIVIDE A TABLE UP TO THE THIRD NORMAL FORM.

A RELATIONAL DATABASE NORMALLY USES TABLES DIVIDED UP TO THE THIRD NORMAL FORM.

NOW, OUR DATABASE TABLE IS COMPLETE!

UP HIGH!

STARTLED

CAIN? ? PRINCESS ?

—ZOWIE!

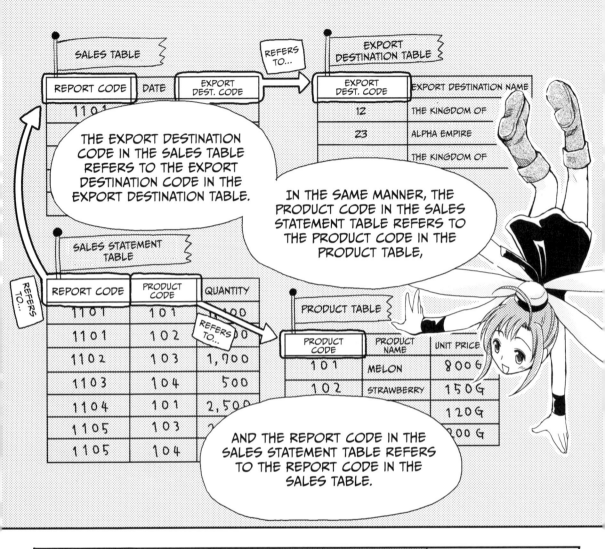

What is the E-R Model?

Princess Ruruna and Cain have figured out the actual condition of the Kingdom of Kod using an E-R (entity-relationship) model. When you try to create a database yourself, the first step is to determine the conditions of the data you are trying to model.

Using the E-R model, try to define an entity in your data. An *entity* is a real-world object or "thing," such as *fruit* or *export destination*.

In addition, an E-R model shows the relationship between entities. Princess Ruruna and Cain performed their analysis on the assumption that there was a relationship called *sales* between fruit and export destination. Fruit is exported to multiple export destinations, while each export destination also imports multiple kinds of fruit. For this reason, an analysis was made for the E-R model assuming that there was a relationship called *many-to-many* between fruit and export destinations. M fruit have a relationship with N export destinations. The number of associations between entities is called *cardinality*.

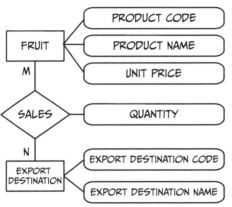

How to Analyze the E-R Model

How would you perform analyses in the cases below? Think about it.

CASE 1: ONE-TO-ONE RELATIONSHIP

One export destination manages one piece of export history information. This kind of relationship is called a *one-to-one* relationship.

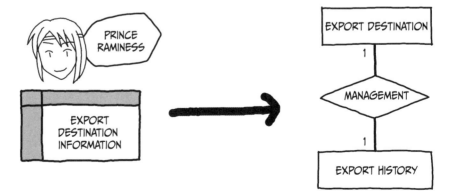

CASE 2: ONE-TO-MANY RELATIONSHIP

Multiple servants serve one princess. The servants do not serve any other princess or even the king.

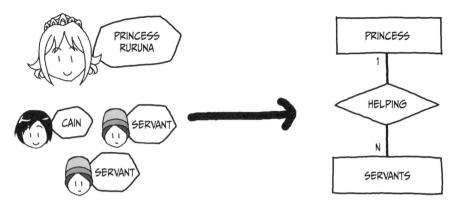

This kind of relationship is called a *one-to-many* relationship.

CASE 3: MANY-TO-MANY RELATIONSHIP

Fruit is exported to multiple export destinations. The export destinations import multiple kinds of fruit.

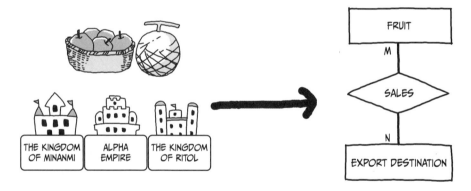

This kind of relationship is called a *many-to-many* relationship.

QUESTIONS

How well do you understand the E-R model? Analyze and draw an E-R model for each of the cases below. The answers are on page 82.

Q1

One staff member manages multiple customers. One customer will never be contacted by more than one staff member.

Q2

One person can check out multiple books. Books can be checked out to multiple students at different times.

Q3

Each student attends multiple lectures. Each lecture is attended by multiple students. One teacher gives multiple lectures. Each lecture is given by one teacher.

Q4

Each customer can open multiple deposit accounts. Each deposit account is opened by one customer. Each bank manages multiple deposit accounts. Each deposit account is managed by one bank.

Keep in mind that E-R model–based analysis does not necessarily produce one "correct" result. There can be many ways to logically organize data to reflect real-world conditions.

NORMALIZING a TABLE

Princess Ruruna and Cain learned about normalization, the process of tabulating data from the real world for a relational database. It is necessary to normalize data in order to properly manage a relational database. Normalization is summarized here (the shaded fields are *primary keys*).

UNNORMALIZED FORM

Report code	Date	Export destination code	Export destination name	Product code	Product name	Unit price	Quantity

FIRST NORMAL FORM

Report code	Date	Export destination code	Export destination name

Report code	Product code	Product name	Unit price	Quantity

SECOND NORMAL FORM

Report code	Date	Export destination code	Export destination name

Report code	Product code	Quantity

Product code	Product name	Unit price

THIRD NORMAL FORM

Report code	Date	Export destination code

Export destination code	Export destination name

Report code	Product code	Quantity

Product code	Product name	Unit price

The *unnormalized form* is a table in which items that appear more than once have not been removed. We've seen that you cannot manage data well using this kind of table for a relational database. Consequently, you need to divide the table.

The *first normal form* refers to a simple, two-dimensional table resulting from division of the original, unnormalized table. You can consider it to be a table with one item in each cell. The table is divided so that no items will appear more than once.

The *second normal form* refers to a table in which a key that can identify data determines values in other columns. Here, it is the *primary key* that determines values in other columns.

In a relational database, a value is called *functionally dependent* if that value determines values in other columns. In the second normal form, the table is divided so that values in other columns are functionally dependent on the primary key.

In the *third normal form*, a table is divided so that a value is not determined by any non-primary key. In a relational database, a value is called *transitively dependent* if that value determines values in other columns indirectly, which is part of functionally dependent operation. In the third normal form, the table is divided so that transitively dependent values are removed.

QUESTIONS

It is important to be able to design a relational database table for various situations, so let's look at some examples of normalizing tables. Determine how the table was normalized in each of the cases below. The answers are on page 82.

Q5

The following table manages book lending like the example in Q2. To what stage is it normalized?

Lending code	Date	Student code	Student name	Student address	Department	Entrance year

ISBN	Book name	Author name	Publication date	Total page count

Lending code	ISBN	Quantity

Q6

The following table also shows a book lending situation. To what stage is it normalized?

Lending code	Date	Student code

Student code	Student name	Student address	Department	Entrance year

ISBN	Book name	Author name	Publication date	Total page count

Lending code	ISBN	Quantity

Q7

The following table shows monthly sales for each staff member. Each department has multiple staff members. A staff member can only be part of one department. Normalize this table to the third normal form.

Staff member code	Staff member name	Month	Member's sales	Department code	Department name

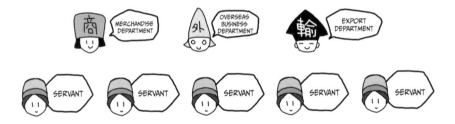

Q8

The following table represents an order-receiving system. Normalize it to the third normal form. However, process one customer per order-taking code. You can process multiple products based on one order-taking code. In addition, one order-taking code should correspond to only one representative.

Order-taking code	Date	Customer code	Customer name	Product code	Product name	Unit price	Representative code	Representative name	Quantity

The following table represents an order-receiving system. Normalize it to the third normal form. Assume that products are classified by product code.

Order-taking code	Date	Customer code	Customer name	Product code	Product name	Unit price	Product classification code	Product classification name	Quantity

STEPS FOR DESIGNING a DaTaBaSE

You have learned how to design a database! However, you have to do more than just that. You need to design a detailed file structure inside the database and devise methods for importing and exporting data. In general, you can divide the whole database design into three parts: conceptual schema, internal schema, and external schema.

The *conceptual schema* refers to a method that models the actual world. Namely, it is a way to determine the logical structure of a database. The conceptual schema is designed taking into consideration an E-R model–based understanding of the actual world and normalization of a table.

The *internal schema* refers to a database viewed from the inside of a computer. Namely, it is a way to determine the physical structure of a database. The internal schema is designed after creating a method to search the database at high speed.

The *external schema* refers to a database as viewed by users or applications. The external schema is designed after creating data required for application programs.

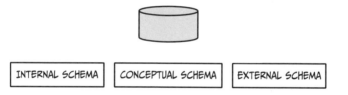

| INTERNAL SCHEMA | CONCEPTUAL SCHEMA | EXTERNAL SCHEMA |

Princess Ruruna and Cain have designed a database with a focus on the conceptual schema in this chapter. They are in the midst of improving the database.

Now that you've completed the basic design of a database, we'll go straight to using the database in the next chapter.

SUMMARY

- An *E-R model* is used to analyze entities and relationships.
- Relationships between entities can be one-to-one, one-to-many, and many-to-many.
- The data in a table must be normalized before you can use it to create a relational database.
- The design of a database can be divided into three types: conceptual schema, internal schema, and external schema.

answers

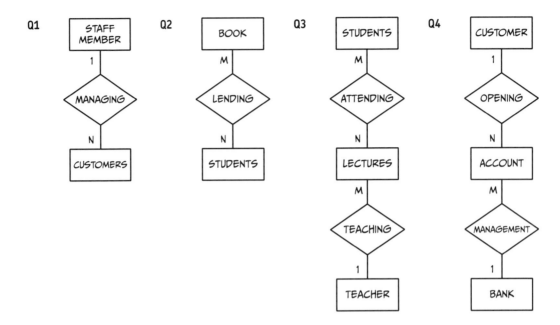

Q1 STAFF MEMBER — 1 — MANAGING — N — CUSTOMERS

Q2 BOOK — M — LENDING — N — STUDENTS

Q3 STUDENTS — M — ATTENDING — N — LECTURES — M — TEACHING — 1 — TEACHER

Q4 CUSTOMER — 1 — OPENING — N — ACCOUNT — M — MANAGEMENT — 1 — BANK

Q5 Second normal form

Q6 Third normal form

Q7

Staff member code	Month	Member's sales

Staff member code	Staff member name	Department code

Department code	Department name

Q8

Order-taking code	Date	Customer code	Representative code

Customer code	Customer name

Order-taking code	Product code	Quantity

Product code	Product name	Unit price

Representative code	Representative name

Q9

Order-taking code	Date	Customer code

Customer code	Customer name

Order-taking code	Product code	Quantity

Product code	Product classification code	Product name	Unit price

Product classification code	Product classification name

DESIGNING A DATABASE

In this chapter, you learned how to design a relational database. However, there are other database design methods. Usability and efficiency of a database depend on an analysis and design method. Therefore, it is important to create an appropriate database in the design stage.

In the database design stage, you need to perform various tasks in addition to table design. For example, you need to consider a datatype to use in the table. You may also need to specify columns indicating numerical values, currencies, and character strings. In addition, you need to devise a search method so you can carry out fast searches. Sometimes, you must create a design while keeping physical file organization in mind. And you have to control which users can access the database to ensure security. There are many factors you need to think about when designing a database. We'll look at some of these factors in the following chapters.

4

LET'S LEARN ABOUT SQL!

RURUNA, YOU HAVE GONE TOO FAR.

ACK!

THWOCK

NO, YOU DON'T UNDERSTAND...!!

IT'S MY FAULT... I CONVINCED PRINCESS RURUNA TO LEAVE THE CASTLE...!!

CAIN...

...

OH, REALLY?

~~~~

LET'S GO HOME, PRINCESS.

CAIN HAS TAKEN CARE OF ME...

SINCE I WAS A CHILD.

WE NEED TO RETRIEVE ONLY PRODUCT NAMES TO CREATE A PRODUCT NAME LIST USING SQL.

HOW DO YOU DO THAT?

JUST ASK THE DATABASE TO RETRIEVE THE PRODUCT NAME COLUMN...

PLEASE,

FROM THE PRODUCT TABLE.

MR. DATABASE...

PLEASE RETRIEVE THE PRODUCT NAME COLUMN...

YOU DON'T NEED TO PRAY! JUST USE SQL...

YOU'D WRITE THIS:

```
SELECT product_name

FROM product;
```

IN SQL, ONE CONVERSATION IS CALLED A STATEMENT.

THIS SQL STATEMENT CONSISTS OF TWO GROUPS OF WORDS: SELECT PRODUCT_NAME AND FROM PRODUCT.

IN THAT CASE, YOU DON'T WANT ALL THE PRODUCT DATA.

YOU ONLY NEED TO RETRIEVE PRODUCTS WHOSE UNIT PRICE IS GREATER THAN OR EQUAL TO 200G.

YES, OF COURSE.

IN SUCH CASES, YOU SPECIFY CONDITIONS WITH THE WHERE PHRASE. FOR EXAMPLE,

WHERE

```
WHERE unit_price>=200
```

YOU WRITE IT LIKE THIS.

I SEE... BUT...

IT IS INCONVENIENT TO SPECIFY A COLUMN NAME EACH TIME, ISN'T IT?

HMM...

IT'S A PAIN!

NO PROBLEM! TO SPECIFY ALL COLUMNS,

YOU CAN USE *! IT CAN BE SUMMARIZED AS FOLLOWS.

BANG!!

```
SELECT *

FROM product

WHERE unit_price>=200
```

SO,

THIS STATEMENT RETRIEVES ALL THE DATA FROM THE PRODUCT TABLE...

HERE YOU ARE!

PRODUCTS THAT COST 200G OR MORE

PRODUCT CODE	PRODUCT NAME	UNIT PRICE
101	MELON	800G
104	LEMON	200G

THAT HAS A UNIT PRICE OF GREATER THAN OR EQUAL TO 200G.

WHAT ABOUT WHEN YOU AREN'T SURE ABOUT THE PRODUCT NAME?

WHAT DO YOU DO IN THAT CASE?

YOU COMBINE THE WORD *LIKE* WITH A SYMBOL.

EXPRESS THE UNKNOWN PART USING %, LIKE THIS...

THIS WILL RETRIEVE PRODUCT NAMES THAT END WITH *N*.

MELON

LEMON

```
SELECT *
FROM product
WHERE product_name LIKE '%n';
```

PRODUCT CODE	PRODUCT NAME	UNIT PRICE
101	MELON	800G
104	LEMON	200G

MELON AND *LEMON* ARE RETRIEVED LIKE THAT!

ISN'T IT?

THAT'S CONVENIENT!

USING AGGREGATE FUNCTIONS

YOU CAN ALSO SORT RETRIEVED RESULTS WITH AN *ORDER BY* PHRASE.

TO SORT PRODUCTS IN ORDER OF ASCENDING PRICE, ADD A STATEMENT LIKE *ORDER BY UNIT PRICE.*

YOU CAN FIND OUT INFORMATION ABOUT PRODUCTS BY DOING THIS.

THAT'S GREAT!!

```
SELECT *
FROM product
WHERE unit_price<200
ORDER BY unit_price;
```

PRODUCT CODE	PRODUCT NAME	UNIT PRICE
103	APPLE	120G
102	STRAWBERRY	150G

I WANT TO KNOW MORE ABOUT SQL, TICO!

OH, REALLY?

I'M GLAD.

HOW ABOUT THIS ONE?

IN THE SELECT PHRASE, USE *AVG (COLUMN NAME)* TO OBTAIN THE AVERAGE OF EACH ROW.

```
SELECT AVG(unit_price)

FROM product;
```

ばん!!

IT'S AMAZING.

ZZOOP!!

AVERAGE UNIT PRICE
317.5

WE NOW HAVE THE AVERAGE UNIT PRICE OF PRODUCTS.

I DIDN'T KNOW THE AVERAGE FRUIT PRICE WAS AT THIS LEVEL...

AVERAGE UNIT PRICE
312.5

EXACTLY.

THERE ARE MANY THINGS I DON'T KNOW ABOUT, EVEN THOUGH THEY ARE HAPPENING IN MY COUNTRY.

SQL ALSO HAS A FUNCTION THAT AGGREGATES THE RETRIEVED DATA VALUES.

ISN'T IT CONVENIENT?

SO YOU CAN GET DATA OTHER THAN THE AVERAGE VALUE?

OF COURSE. FOR EXAMPLE...

THE NUMBER OF ITEMS, SUM, AVERAGE, MAXIMUM VALUE, AND MINIMUM VALUE CAN BE OBTAINED BY SPECIFYING AN AGGREGATE FUNCTION.

AGGREGATE FUNCTIONS IN SQL

Function	Description
COUNT(*)	Obtains the number of rows
COUNT(column_name)	Obtains the number of times the column is not null
COUNT(DISTINCT column_name)	Obtains the number of distinct values in the column
SUM(column_name)	Obtains the sum of the column's values in all rows
AVG(column_name)	Obtains the average of the column's values in all rows
MAX(column_name)	Obtains the maximum value of the column
MIN(column_name)	Obtains the minimum value of the column

LIKE THIS...

WOW!

JOINING TABLES

THIS WAY, YOU CAN RETRIEVE SALES REPORT DATA FROM TABLES, EVEN IF THEY ARE DIVIDED.

REPORT CODE	DATE	EXPORT DEST. CODE	EXPORT DEST. NAME	PRODUCT CODE	PRODUCT NAME	UNIT PRICE	QUANTITY
1101	3/5	12	THE KINGDOM OF MINANMI	101	MELON	800G	1,100
1101	3/5	12	THE KINGDOM OF MINANMI	102	STRAWBERRY	150G	300
1102	3/7	23	ALPHA EMPIRE	103	APPLE	120G	1,700
1103	3/8	25	THE KINGDOM OF RITOL	104	LEMON	200G	500
1104	3/10	12	THE KINGDOM OF MINANMI	101	MELON	800G	2,500
1105	3/12	25	THE KINGDOM OF RITOL	103	APPLE	120G	2,000
1105	3/12	25	THE KINGDOM OF RITOL	104	LEMON	200G	700

THIS IS THE SAME AS THE TABLE WE HAVE BEEN USING. WE RECREATED IT!

YOU CAN RETRIEVE DATA RELATING TO THE SALES REPORT EVEN IF YOU MANAGE PRODUCTS, EXPORT DESTINATIONS, AND SALES INDEPENDENTLY.

THAT'S GREAT!!

WOW!

CREATING A TABLE

NOW I REMEMBER. YOU MADE THIS TABLE USING SQL, RIGHT TICO?

SO YOU HAVE ALREADY INPUT A TABLE AND DATA, RIGHT?

THAT'S RIGHT.

HOW DID YOU MAKE IT?

CREATE TABLE

YOU USE A *CREATE TABLE* STATEMENT TO MAKE A TABLE.

```
CREATE TABLE product
(
product_code int NOT NULL,
product_name varchar(255),
unit_price int,
PRIMARY KEY(product_code)
);
```

PRODUCT CODE	PRODUCT NAME	UNIT PRICE

YOU MUST SPECIFY THE PRIMARY KEY, AS WELL. I USED THE PRODUCT CODE AS A PRIMARY KEY.*

WE'VE ALSO SET THE DATATYPE OF EACH COLUMN. YOU CAN SEE THAT PRODUCT AND UNIT_PRICE ARE INTEGERS (INT). *VARCHAR* MEANS THAT THE DATABASE EXPECTS TEXT, AND *(255)* LIMITS THE PRODUCT_NAME TO 255 CHARACTERS.

LIKE THIS...

THIS PREVENTS YOU FROM ENTERING INCORRECT VALUES.

* SEE PAGE 115 FOR A COMPLETE EXPLANATION OF CREATE TABLE STATEMENTS.

SQL Overview

In this chapter, Princess Ruruna and Cain learned about *SQL*, or *Structured Query Language*, a language used to operate a relational database. SQL's commands can be broken down into three distinct types:

Data Definition Language (DDL)   Creates a table

Data Manipulation Language (DML)   Inputs and retrieves data

Data Control Language (DCL)   Manages user access

SQL has commands that create the framework of a database, and a command that creates a table within a database. You can use this language to change and delete a table as well. The database language that has these functions is called the *Data Definition Language (DDL)*.

SQL also has commands that manipulate data in a database, such as inserting, deleting, and updating data. It also has a command that allows you to search for data. The database language with these functions is called the *Data Manipulation Language (DML)*.

In addition, SQL offers the capability to control a database, so that data conflicts will not occur even if multiple people use the database at the same time. The database language associated with these functions is called the *Data Control Language (DCL)*.

Searching for Data Using a *SELECT* Statement

Princess Ruruna and Cain started learning SQL by using a basic data search function. SQL searches for data when one *statement* (a combination of phrases) is input. To search for a certain product with a unit price of 200G, for example, you would use the following SQL statement.

```
SELECT *
FROM product
WHERE unit_price=200
```

> Create an SQL statement by combining phrases.

A SELECT statement is the most basic SQL statement. It specifies *which column*, *from which table* (FROM), and *matching which conditions* (WHERE). You can combine these phrases to make intuitive, query-type statements in SQL—even a user unfamiliar with databases can use them to search for data.

CReating Conditions

Cain said earlier, "Now we need to learn how to make conditions." Let's look at some ways to create conditions using SQL.

COMPARISON OPERATORS

One way to express conditions is by using *comparison operators* like >= and =. For example, the condition "A is greater than or equal to B" is expressed using >=, and the condition "A is equal to B" is expressed using =. More examples of comparison operators are shown in the table below.

COMPARISON OPERATORS

Comparison operator	Description	Example	Description of example
A = B	A is equal to B.	`unit_price=200`	Unit price is 200G.
A > B	A is greater than B.	`unit_price>200`	Unit price is greater than 200G.
A >= B	A is greater than or equal to B.	`unit_price>=200`	Unit price is greater than or equal to 200G.
A < B	A is less than B.	`unit_price<200`	Unit price is less than 200G.
A <= B	A is less than or equal to B.	`unit_price<=200`	Unit price is less than or equal to 200G.
A <> B	A is not equal to B.	`unit_price<>200`	Unit price is not 200G.

LOGICAL OPERATORS

In some cases, you need to express conditions that are more complex than simple comparisons. You can use *logical operators* (*AND*, *OR*, and *NOT*) to combine operator-based conditions and create more complicated conditions, as shown in the table below.

LOGICAL OPERATORS

Logical operator	Description	Example	Description of example
AND	A and B	Product code >= 200 AND unit price = 100	The product code is greater than or equal to 200 and the unit price is 100G.
OR	A or B	Product code >= 200 OR unit price = 100	The product code is greater than or equal to 200 or the unit price is 100G.
NOT	Not A	NOT unit price = 100	The unit price is not 100G.

PATTERNS

When you don't know exactly what to search for, you can also use pattern matching in conditions by using wildcard characters. When using pattern matching, use characters such as % or _ in a LIKE statement; this will search for a character string that matches the pattern you specify. You can search for a value that corresponds to a partially specified character string using %, which indicates a character string of any length, and _, which specifies only one character.

An example of a query using wild cards is shown below. This example statement searches for a character string that has *n* at the end of the product name.

```
SELECT *
FROM product
WHERE product_name LIKE '%n';
```

This statement matches patterns using a wild card.

Product code	Product name	Unit price
101	Melon	800G
104	Lemon	200G

The wild cards you can use in an SQL statement are explained below.

WILD CARDS

Wild card	Description	Example of pattern	Matching character string
%	Matches any number of characters	%n n%	Lemon Melon Nut Navel orange
_	Matches one character	_t t_	it to

SEARCHES

There are also many other search methods. For example, you can specify BETWEEN *X* AND *Y* for a value range. If you specify a range as shown below, you can extract products with unit prices greater than or equal to 150G or less than 200G.

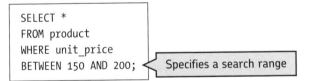

```
SELECT *
FROM product
WHERE unit_price
BETWEEN 150 AND 200;
```
Specifies a search range

In addition, you can specify IS NULL when searching for rows. If you use the search shown below, you can extract products with null unit prices.

```
SELECT *
FROM product
WHERE unit_price is NULL;
```
Searches for a null

QUESTIONS

Now, let's create SQL statements using various kinds of conditions. Let's use the Export Destination Table below (assuming the unit for population is 10,000). Answer the questions below using SQL statements. The answers are on page 119.

EXPORT DESTINATION TABLE

Export destination code	Export destination name	Population
12	The Kingdom of Minanmi	100
23	Alpha Empire	120
25	The Kingdom of Ritol	150
30	The Kingdom of Sazanna	80

Q1

To find countries in which the population is greater than or equal to 1 million, extract the table below.

Export destination code	Export destination name	Population
12	The Kingdom of Minanmi	100
23	Alpha Empire	120
25	The Kingdom of Ritol	150

Q2

To find countries in which the population is less than 1 million, extract the table below.

Export destination code	Export destination name	Population
30	The Kingdom of Sazanna	80

Q3

Find countries in which the export destination code is less than 20 and the population is greater than or equal to 1 million.

Q4

Find countries in which the export destination code is greater than or equal to 30 and the population is greater than 1 million.

Q5

What is the population of the Kingdom of Ritol?

Q6

Find countries whose names contain the letter *n*.

aggregate functions

Princess Ruruna and Cain have learned about various aggregate functions. Aggregate functions are also known as *set functions*. You can use these functions to aggregate information such as maximum and minimum values, number of items, and sum.

If you specify a WHERE phrase along with an aggregate function, you can obtain an aggregated value for just the specified rows. If you specify a phrase like the one shown below, you can figure out the number of products with unit prices greater than or equal to 200G.

```
SELECT COUNT(*)
FROM product
WHERE unit_price>=200;
```

COUNT(*)
2

AGGREGATING DATA BY GROUPING

If you group data, you can obtain aggregated values easily. For example, if you want to obtain the number of products and average unit price based on district, you can use the grouping function.

To group data, combine the aggregate function and the GROUP BY phrase. Let's use the Product Table shown below.

PRODUCT TABLE

Product code	Product name	Unit price	District
101	Melon	800G	South Sea
102	Strawberry	150G	Middle
103	Apple	120G	North Sea
104	Lemon	200G	South Sea
201	Chestnut	100G	North Sea
202	Persimmon	160G	Middle
301	Peach	130G	South Sea
302	Kiwi	200G	South Sea

To obtain the average unit price for each district in the Product Table, specify the District column and the AVG function for the GROUP BY phrase. This will group data based on district and give you the average unit value of the products in each district.

```
SELECT district,AVG(unit_price)
FROM product
GROUP BY district;
```

Enables grouping

District	AVG(unit_price)
South Sea	332.5
North Sea	110
Middle	155

What if you wanted to further restrict your results, based on a particular property of the data? Assume that you want to find products with regional average unit prices greater than or equal to 200G. In this case, do not specify a condition in the WHERE phrase, but use a HAVING phrase instead. This allows you to extract only districts in which the average unit price is greater than or equal to 200G.

```
SELECT district,AVG(unit_price)
FROM product
GROUP BY district;
HAVING AVG(unit_price)>=200;
```

Filters results after being grouped

District	AVG(unit_price)
South Sea	332.5

QUESTIONS

Answer the questions below using this Export Destination Table (assuming the unit for population is 10,000). The answers are on page 120.

EXPORT DESTINATION TABLE

Export destination code	Export destination name	Population	District
12	The Kingdom of Minanmi	100	South Sea
15	The Kingdom of Paronu	200	Middle
22	The Kingdom of Tokanta	160	North Sea
23	Alpha Empire	120	North Sea
25	The Kingdom of Ritol	150	South Sea
30	The Kingdom of Sazanna	80	South Sea
31	The Kingdom of Taharu	240	North Sea
33	The Kingdom of Mariyon	300	Middle

Q7

What is the smallest population?

Q8

What is the largest population?

Q9

What is the total population of all countries included in the Export Destination Table?

Q10

What is the total population of the countries in which the export destination code is greater than 20?

Q11

How many countries are there in which the population is greater than or equal to 1 million?

Q12

How many countries are in the North Sea district?

Q13

Which country in the North Sea district has the largest population?

Q14

What is the total population of every country excluding the Kingdom of Ritol?

Q15

Find the districts in which the average population is greater than or equal to 2 million.

Q16

Find the districts that contain at least three countries.

SEARCHING FOR DATA

There are more complicated query methods available in SQL, in addition to the ones we've already discussed.

USING A SUBQUERY

For example, you can embed one query in another query. This is called a *subquery*. Let's look at the tables below.

PRODUCT TABLE

Product code	Product name	Unit price
101	Melon	800G
102	Strawberry	150G
103	Apple	120G
104	Lemon	200G

SALES STATEMENT TABLE

Report code	Product code	Quantity
1101	101	1,100
1101	102	300
1102	103	1,700
1103	104	500
1104	101	2,500
1105	103	2,000
1105	104	700

You can use these two tables to search for the names of products for which the sales volume is greater than or equal to 1,000. The following SQL statement will conduct that search.

```
SELECT * FROM product
WHERE product_code IN
(SELECT product_code
FROM sales_statement
WHERE quantity>=1000);
```

This statement contains a subquery.

In this SQL statement, the SELECT statement in parentheses is performed first: The product code in the Sales Statement Table is searched for first, and product codes 101 and 103 are found (as these are the only reports with sales volume greater than 1,000). These product codes are used as a part of the condition for the SELECT statement outside the parentheses. For IN, the condition is satisfied when a row matches any value enclosed within parentheses. Thus, products that correspond to the product codes 101 and 103 will be returned.

In other words, in the case of a subquery, the result of the SELECT statement within parentheses will be sent to the other SELECT statement for searching. The following information will be the result of the whole query.

Product code	Product name	Unit price
101	Melon	800G
103	Apple	120G

USING A CORRELATED SUBQUERY

Let's consider a subquery as being *contained inside* another query. Such a subquery may refer to data from the outer query. This is called a *correlated subquery*. In the query below, the `sales_statement` table in the outer query is temporarily given the new name U so the subquery can refer to it unambiguously. The syntax `U.product_code` indicates which `product_code` column is intended, since there are two sources for that column inside the subquery.

Because the subquery refers to data from the outer query, the subquery is not independent of the outer query as in previous examples. This dependency is called a *correlation*.

❶
```
SELECT *
FROM sales_statement U
```
❷
```
WHERE quantity>
```
❸
```
(SELECT AVG(quantity)
FROM sales_statement
WHERE product_code=U.product_code);
```

Report code	Product code	Quantity
1104	101	2,500
1105	103	2,000
1105	104	700

This query extracts statements with sales volume greater than the product's average.

Let's look at how this correlated subquery is processed. In the correlated subquery, the query outside is implemented first.

❶
```
SELECT *
FROM sales_statement U
```

This result is sent to the query inside to be evaluated row by row. Let's explore the evaluation of the first row, product code 101.

❸
```
(SELECT AVG(quantity)
FROM sales_statement
WHERE product_code=101)
```

The product code for the first row is 101, or melons—the average sales quantity of melons is 1,800. This result is then sent as a condition for the query outside.

❷
```
WHERE quantity>(1,800)
```

This process continues for all rows in the sales statement—steps ❷ and ❸ are performed for all possible product codes. In other words, this query extracts reports in which the sales volume of a fruit is greater than that particular fruit's average sales quantity. Consequently, only the fifth, sixth, and seventh rows of ❶ are extracted.

QUESTIONS

Now, answer the following questions based on the Product Table and the Sales Statement Table. The answers are on page 122.

Q17

Find the sales statement for fruit with unit prices greater than or equal to 300G, and extract the table below.

Report code	Product code	Quantity
1101	101	1,100
1104	101	2,500

Q18

Obtain the average sales volume by product, and find items that have sales volumes that are less than the average.

JOINING TABLES

After conducting an SQL-based search, Princess Ruruna and Cain created a sales report by combining tables. Joining tables by combining columns with the same names is called an *equi join*. For an equi join, rows with the same value are designated as join conditions for joining tables. Joining columns with the same name into one is called a *natural join*.

The join method in which only rows having a common value like equi join are selected is called *inner join*.

In contrast, the join method that keeps all rows of one table and specifies a null for rows not included in another table is called an *outer join*. If you place a table created from an outer join on the right or left of an SQL statement, it is called a *left outer join* or a *right outer join*, depending on which rows are kept.

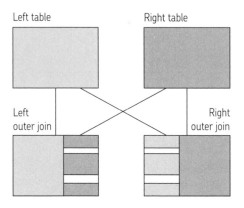

CREATING a TABLE

Finally, Princess Ruruna and Cain learned about the statement syntax that creates a table, CREATE TABLE. The statement syntax inside a CREATE TABLE statement often depends on the particular kind of database you use. An example is shown below.

```
CREATE TABLE product
(
product_code int NOT NULL,
product_name varchar(255),
unit_price int,
PRIMARY KEY(product_code)
);
```

> This statement creates a table.

When you create a table, you must specify its column names. Additionally, you can specify a primary key and a foreign key for each column. In this example, the product code is specified as a PRIMARY KEY and product code is not allowed to be null. When creating a table, you may need to include the following specifications.

Constraint	Description
PRIMARY KEY	Sets a primary key
UNIQUE	Should be unique
NOT NULL	Does not accept a NULL value
CHECK	Checks a range
DEFAULT	Sets a default value
FOREIGN KEY REFERENCES	Sets a foreign key

These specifications are called *constraints*. Giving constraints when creating a table helps to prevent data conflicts later on and allows you to correctly manage the database.

INSERTING, UPDATING, OR DELETING ROWS

You can use the INSERT, UPDATE, and DELETE statements to insert, update, or delete data from a table created by the CREATE TABLE statement. Let's insert, update, and delete some data using SQL.

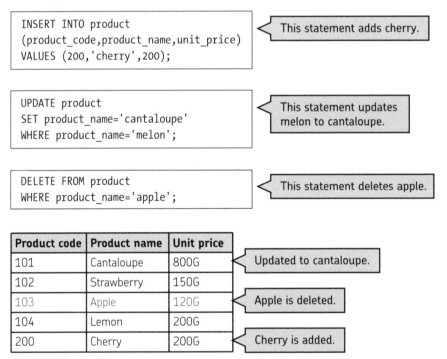

```
INSERT INTO product
(product_code,product_name,unit_price)
VALUES (200,'cherry',200);
```

> This statement adds cherry.

```
UPDATE product
SET product_name='cantaloupe'
WHERE product_name='melon';
```

> This statement updates melon to cantaloupe.

```
DELETE FROM product
WHERE product_name='apple';
```

> This statement deletes apple.

Product code	Product name	Unit price	
101	Cantaloupe	800G	Updated to cantaloupe.
102	Strawberry	150G	
103	Apple	120G	Apple is deleted.
104	Lemon	200G	
200	Cherry	200G	Cherry is added.

When inserting, updating, or deleting a row, you cannot violate the constraints set by the CREATE TABLE statement. If a product with product code 200 already exists, you cannot add cherry, since you cannot add duplicated data as a primary key. When you insert, update, or delete data in a database, you must consider the database's constraints.

CREATING A VIEW

Based on the table you created with the CREATE TABLE statement, you can also create a virtual table that exists only when it is viewed by a user. This is called a *view*. The table from which a view is derived is called a *base table*.

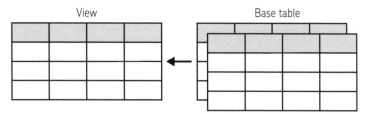

Use the SQL statement shown below to create a view.

```
CREATE VIEW expensive_product
(product_code,product_name,unit_price)
AS SELECT *
FROM product
WHERE unit_price>=200;
```

> This statement creates a view.

The Expensive Product Table is a view based on the Product Table, which is a base table. It was created by extracting data with unit prices greater than or equal to 200G from the Product Table.

EXPENSIVE PRODUCT TABLE

Product code	Product name	Unit price
101	Melon	800G
104	Lemon	200G
202	Persimmon	200G

Once you create the Expensive Product view, you can search for data in it the same way you would search for data in a base table.

```
SELECT *
FROM expensive_product
WHERE unit_price>=500;
```

> Allows the view to be used in the same manner as a base table

It is convenient to create a view when you want to make part of the data in a base table public.

There are also SQL statements for deleting a base table or view. The statement used to delete a base table or view is shown below.

```
DROP VIEW expensive_product;
```

```
DROP TABLE product;
```

QUESTIONS

Create SQL statements for the following questions (assuming the unit for population is 10,000). The answers are on page 123.

Q19

The following Export Destination Table was created using a CREATE TABLE statement. Add the data below.

EXPORT DESTINATION TABLE

Export destination code	Export destination name	Population	District
12	The Kingdom of Minanmi	100	South Sea
15	The Kingdom of Paronu	200	Middle
22	The Kingdom of Tokanta	160	North Sea
23	Alpha Empire	120	North Sea

Q20

From the Export Destination Table in Q19, create a view titled *North Sea Country* that shows countries belonging to the North Sea district.

EXPORT DESTINATION TABLE

Export destination code	Export destination name	Population
22	The Kingdom of Tokanta	160
23	Alpha Empire	120

Q21

Change the population of the Kingdom of Tokanta in the Export Destination Table to 1.5 million.

Q22

In the Export Destination Table, delete all data for the Kingdom of Paronu.

summary

- You can use SQL functions to define, operate, and control data.
- To search for data, use a SELECT statement.
- To specify a condition, use a WHERE phrase.
- To insert, update, and delete data, use INSERT, UPDATE, and DELETE statements.
- To create a table, use a CREATE TABLE statement.

answers

Q1

```
SELECT *
FROM export_destination
WHERE population>=100;
```

Q2

```
SELECT *
FROM export_destination
WHERE population<100;
```

Q3

```
SELECT *
FROM export_destination
WHERE export_destination_code<20
AND population>=100;
```

Export destination code	Export destination name	Population
12	The Kingdom of Minanmi	100

Q4

```
SELECT *
FROM export_destination
WHERE export_destination_code>=30
AND population>100;
```

None of the countries meet this criteria, so this query returns an empty set.

Q5

```
SELECT population
FROM export_destination
WHERE export_destination_name='the Kingdom of Ritol';
```

Population
150

Q6

```
SELECT *
FROM export_destination
WHERE export_destination_name LIKE '%n%';
```

Export destination code	Export destination name	Population
12	The Kingdom of Minanmi	100
25	The Kingdom of Ritol	150
30	The Kingdom of Sazanna	80

Q7

```
SELECT MIN(population)
FROM export_destination;
```

MIN(population)
80

Q8

```
SELECT MAX(population)
FROM export_destination;
```

MAX(population)
300

Q9

```
SELECT SUM(population)
FROM export_destination;
```

SUM(population)
1,350

Q10

```
SELECT SUM(population)
FROM export_destination
WHERE export_destination_code>20;
```

SUM(population)
1,050

Q11

```
SELECT COUNT(*)
FROM export_destination
WHERE population>=100;
```

COUNT(*)
7

Q12

```
SELECT COUNT(*)
FROM export_destination
WHERE district='north sea';
```

COUNT(*)
3

Q13

```
SELECT MAX(population)
FROM export_destination
WHERE district='north sea';
```

MAX(population)
240

Q14

```
SELECT SUM(population)
FROM export_destination
WHERE NOT(export_destination_name='the Kingdom of Ritol');
```

SUM(population)
1,200

Q15

```
SELECT district, AVG(population)
FROM export_destination
GROUP BY district
HAVING AVG(population)>=200;
```

District	AVG(population)
Middle	250

Q16

```
SELECT district, COUNT(*)
FROM export_destination
GROUP BY district
HAVING COUNT(*)>=3;
```

District	COUNT(*)
North Sea	3
South Sea	3

Q17

```
SELECT *
FROM sales_statement
WHERE product_code IN
(SELECT product_code
FROM product
WHERE unit_price>=300);
```

Q18

```
SELECT *
FROM sales_statement U
WHERE quantity<
(SELECT AVG(quantity)
FROM sales_statement
WHERE product_code=U.product_code);
```

Report code	Product code	Quantity
1101	101	1,100
1102	103	1,700
1103	104	500

Q19

```
INSERT INTO export_destination(export_destination_
code,export_destination_name,population,district)
VALUES(12,'the Kingdom of Minanmi',100,'south sea');
INSERT INTO export_destination(export_destination_
code,export_destination_name,population,district)
VALUES(15,'the Kingdom of Paronu',200,'middle');
INSERT INTO export_destination(export_destination_
code,export_destination_name,population,district)
VALUES(22,'the Kingdom of Tokanta',160,'north sea');
INSERT INTO export_destination(export_destination_
code,export_destination_name,population,district)
VALUES(23,'Alpha Empire',120,'north sea');
```

Q20

```
CREATE VIEW north_sea_country(export_destination_
code,export_destination_name,population)
AS SELECT export_destination_code,export_destination_name,population
FROM export_destination_name
WHERE district='north sea';
```

Q21

```
UPDATE export_destination
SET population=150
WHERE export_destination_name='the Kingdom of Tokanta';
```

Q22

```
DELETE FROM export_destination
WHERE export_destination_name='the Kingdom of Paronu';
```

STANDARDIZATION OF SQL

SQL is standardized by the International Organization for Standardization (ISO). In Japan, it is standardized by JIS (Japanese Industrial Standards).

Other SQL standards include SQL92, established in 1992, and SQL99, established in 1999. Relational database products are designed so that queries can be made in accordance with these standards.

Some relational database products have their own specifications. Refer to the operation manual for your database product for further information.

5
LET'S OPERATE A DATABASE!

ACTUALLY, I SHOULD THANK YOU...

BUT WE STILL HAVE SO MUCH TO LEARN.

FOR EXAMPLE, I WONDER WHY A DATABASE CAN STILL OPERATE WHEN SO MANY USERS ARE ACCESSING IT AT THE SAME TIME.

FOR THAT MATTER, THE ISSUE OF SECURITY ALSO CONCERNS ME A BIT.

APPARENTLY, YOU HAVE SOME WORRIES ABOUT YOUR DATABASE.

SORT OF.

WELL, TO BETTER UNDERSTAND THE ISSUES,

AHEM!

I HAVE DONE A LITTLE RESEARCH.

OH, YEAH?

THE TITLE OF MY PRESENTATION IS:

HOW CAN A DATABASE LET A LARGE NUMBER OF USERS ACCESS IT SIMULTANEOUSLY?

FLASH!

I HAVE EVEN PREPARED ILLUSTRATIONS TO HELP YOUR UNDERSTANDING!

OH!

GEE, THAT'S GREAT.

DATABASE THEATER

I LOVE A GOOD SHOW!

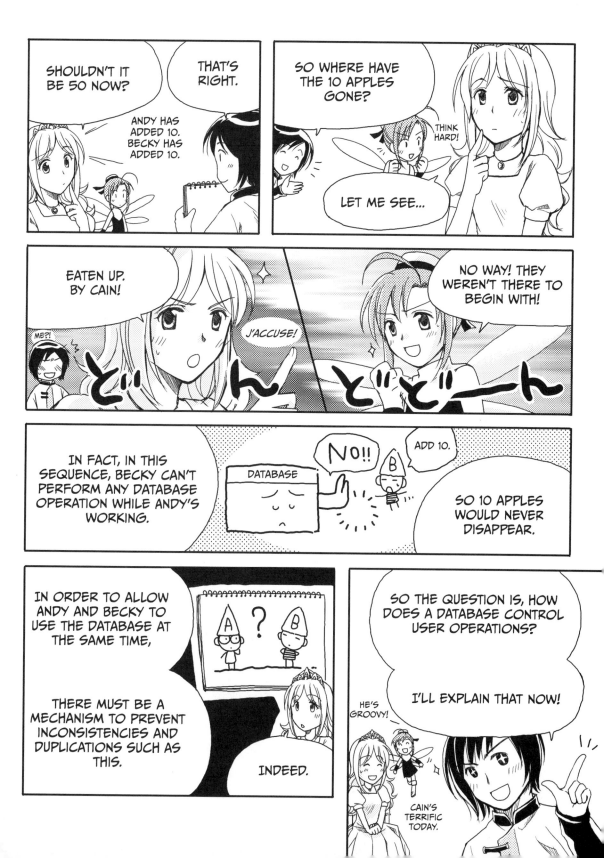

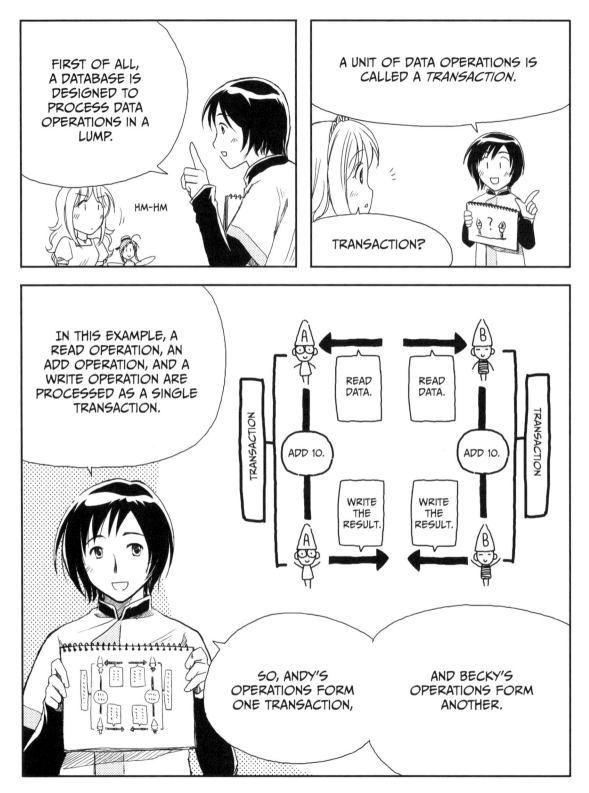

What Is a Lock?

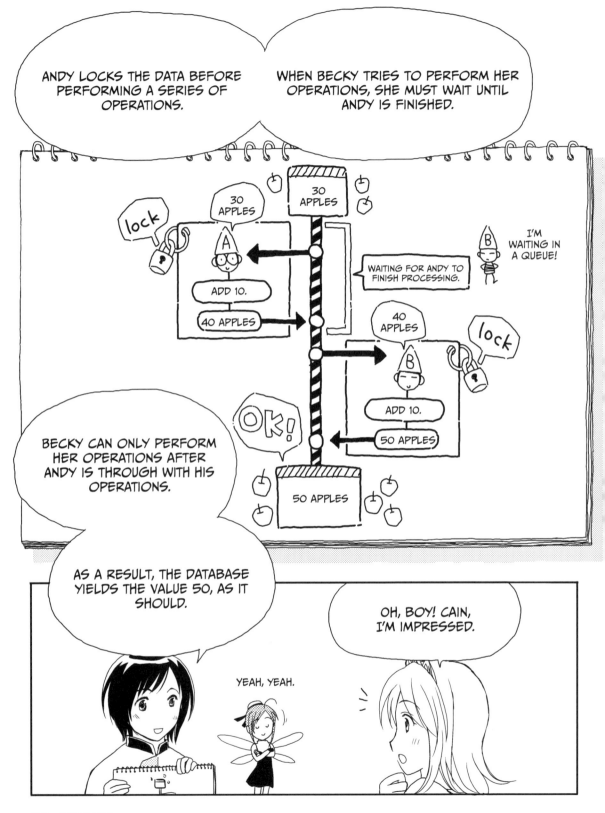

BECAUSE YOUR INVOICES ARE SUCH A MESS, MY COUNTRY, AN IMPORTER, IS EXPERIENCING HAVOC.

A DATABASE IS A NASTY THING.

AS PART OF THE COMPENSATION FOR THIS TROUBLE...

WHY DON'T YOU ACCEPT MY PROPOSAL, PRINCESS RURUNA? COME OVER TO MY COUNTRY AND BE MY BRIDE.

IGNORING

......

SOMEONE WITH MALICIOUS INTENT MIGHT HAVE PERFORMED AN UNAUTHORIZED DATA OVERWRITE.

HOW AWFUL!

YOU ARE BEHAVING AS IF I WERE NOT HERE.

PRINCE RAMINESS,

WE ARE VERY SORRY.

WE PROMISE TO TAKE ACTION FOR DATABASE PROTECTION TO PREVENT THIS KIND OF THING FROM HAPPENING AGAIN.

FORGIVE US FOR THIS, WON'T YOU?

...

YOU SAY YOU'LL FIX IT, BUT...I'M NOT SO SURE.... BE MORE SPECIFIC, WILL YOU?

THE CAUSE OF THIS TROUBLE IS THAT EVERYBODY IN THE KINGDOM OF KOD HAS FREE ACCESS TO THE DATABASE.

FIRST OF ALL, WE WILL HAVE SET UP ACCESS CONTROL TO LIMIT USERS OF THE DATABASE.

WHICH MEANS...?

A GOOD SOLUTION MAY BE TO REQUIRE USERNAMES AND PASSWORDS TO ACCESS THE DATABASE, TO CONFIRM THAT EACH USER IS TRUSTWORTHY ENOUGH TO BE GIVEN ACCESS RIGHTS.

SOUNDS CLEVER!

SECOND, WE WILL CONFIGURE SETTINGS TO GIVE PERMISSION FOR CERTAIN OPERATIONS ONLY TO AUTHORIZED USERS.

· PERMISSION TO SEARCH (SELECT), INSERT, UPDATE, AND DELETE PRODUCT DATA
· PERMISSION TO SEARCH AND INSERT PRODUCT DATA, WITHOUT UPDATE/ DELETE PERMISSION
· MISSION TO SEARCH PRODUCT...

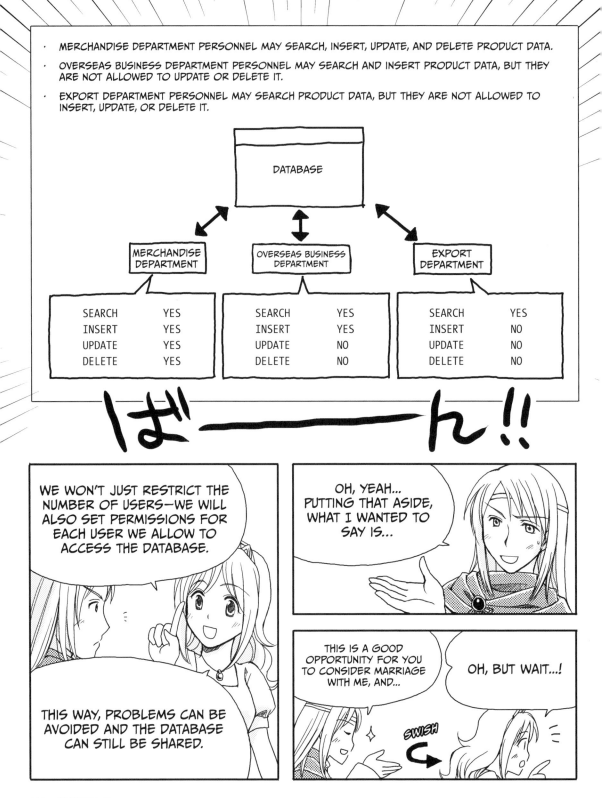

- MERCHANDISE DEPARTMENT PERSONNEL MAY SEARCH, INSERT, UPDATE, AND DELETE PRODUCT DATA.
- OVERSEAS BUSINESS DEPARTMENT PERSONNEL MAY SEARCH AND INSERT PRODUCT DATA, BUT THEY ARE NOT ALLOWED TO UPDATE OR DELETE IT.
- EXPORT DEPARTMENT PERSONNEL MAY SEARCH PRODUCT DATA, BUT THEY ARE NOT ALLOWED TO INSERT, UPDATE, OR DELETE IT.

IF YOU CREATE INDEXES FOR PRODUCT CODES,

YOU CAN INSTANTLY LEARN WHERE PRODUCT DATA IS STORED FOR A PRODUCT ASSIGNED PRODUCT CODE 101.

101 MELON

DATA

IT TELLS YOU WHERE ON THE DISK THAT PRODUCT DATA IS LOCATED.

INDEXING HELPS SPEED UP THE SEARCH.

WELL, IT'S NOT SO EASY FOR ME TO FOLLOW.... ANYWAY...

UH-HUH.

IT IS VERY TIME CONSUMING TO BROWSE ALL ROWS WHEN SEARCHING FOR CERTAIN DATA.

SHALL I REPEAT THE EXPLANATION FROM THE START?

NO, NO...

USING INDEXES, WE CAN REDUCE THE DISK ACCESS COUNT.

REDUCE THE DISK ACCESS COUNT, AND OUR SEARCH WILL BE MUCH FASTER!

WHAT'S THAT?

UH-OH.

?

HEY! WHO ARE YOU TALKING TO?

IS SOMEONE HERE?

PRINCESS, BE CAREFUL!

LET'S OPERATE A DATABASE! 145

WHAT IF THE TRANSACTION HASN'T BEEN COMMITTED YET WHEN THE PROBLEM OCCURS?

DON'T WORRY! IN THAT CASE, A ROLLBACK TAKES PLACE.

IN A *ROLLBACK* OPERATION, THE VALUE BEFORE THE UPDATE IS REFERENCED TO CANCEL THE TRANSACTION.

IN OTHER WORDS, IT RESTORES THE STATE OF THE DATABASE BEFORE THE TRANSACTION WAS STARTED.

DATA A

ROLLBACK

DATA A

INITIAL STATE

THE SYSTEM RECOVERS THE DATA WHILE MAKING SURE IT IS FREE FROM INCONSISTENCIES.

UH-HUH.

I AM NOT FAMILIAR WITH TERMS LIKE *COMMIT* AND *TRANSACTION*.

HMM

STILL, IT SEEMS YOUR DATABASE SECURITY MEASURES ARE ALL RIGHT.

SIGH

NOW DO YOU UNDERSTAND?

YOU SEE, A DATABASE IS ROBUST! EVEN WHEN DISASTER STRIKES!

PROPERTIES OF TRANSACTIONS

Cain's research showed that users of a database can search for, insert, update, and delete data. A set of successful operations performed by a single user is called a *transaction*.

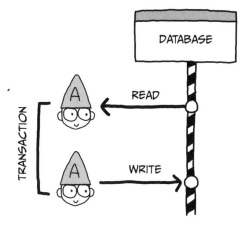

When users share a database, it is important to ensure that multiple transactions can be processed without causing conflicting data. It is also important to protect data from inconsistencies in case a failure occurs while a transaction is being processed. To that end, the following table lists the properties required for a transaction, which memorably spell the word *ACID*.

PROPERTIES REQUIRED FOR A TRANSACTION

Property	Stands for	Description
A	Atomicity	A transaction must either end with a commit or rollback operation.
C	Consistency	Processing a transaction never results in loss of consistency of the database.
I	Isolation	Even when transactions are processed concurrently, the results must be the same as for sequential processing.
D	Durability	The contents of a completed transaction should not be affected by failure.

Let's examine each of these properties in depth.

ATOMICITY

The first property required for a transaction, *atomicity*, means that a transaction must end with either a commit or rollback in order to keep a database free of inconsistencies. In short, either all actions of a transaction are completed or all actions are canceled. A *commit* finalizes the operation in the transaction. A *rollback* cancels the operation in the transaction.

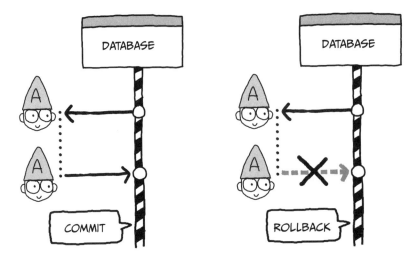

In some cases, a commit or rollback is performed automatically. You can also specify which one should be carried out. For example, you can specify a rollback if an error occurs.

You can use the SQL statements COMMIT and ROLLBACK to perform these operations.

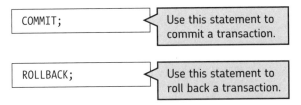

```
COMMIT;
```
Use this statement to commit a transaction.

```
ROLLBACK;
```
Use this statement to roll back a transaction.

QUESTIONS

Answer these questions to see how well you understand atomicity. The answers are on page 167.

Q1
  Write an SQL statement that can be used to finalize a transaction.

Q2
  Write an SQL statement that can be used to cancel a transaction.

CONSISTENCY

A transaction must not create errors. If the database was consistent before a transaction is processed, then the database must also be consistent after that transaction occurs.

Cain gave the example of Andy and Becky each trying to add 10 apples to an original total of 30 apples. Rather than yielding the correct amount of 50 apples, the database shows a total of 40 apples. This type of error is called a *lost update*.

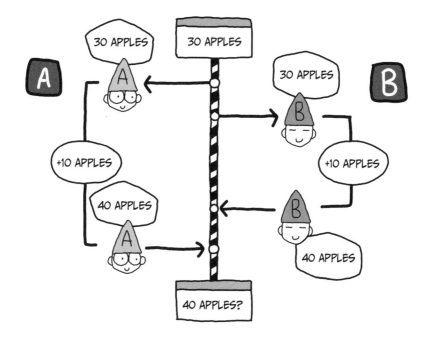

When transactions are processed concurrently, more than one transaction may access the same table or row at the same time, and conflicting data may occur.

Tables and rows subject to operations in a transaction are referred to as *resources*. In a database, transactions should be able to access the same resource concurrently without creating inconsistencies.

ISOLATION

When two or more concurrent transactions yield the same result as if they were performed at separate times, that order of processing is referred to as *serializable*. The *isolation* property requires the schedule to be serializable and protects against errors.

In order to make the order of processing serializable, you need to have control over transactions that are attempted at the same time. The most commonly used method for this purpose is the lock-based control. A *shared lock* is used when reading data, while an *exclusive lock* is used when writing data.

When a shared lock is in use, another user can apply a shared lock to other transactions, but not an exclusive lock. When an exclusive lock is applied, another user cannot apply a shared lock or an exclusive lock to other transactions. The following summarizes the relationship between a shared lock and an exclusive lock.

CO-EXISTENCE RELATIONSHIP BETWEEN LOCK TYPES

	Shared lock	Exclusive lock
Shared lock	YES	NO
Exclusive lock	NO	NO

QUESTIONS

Do you understand locks? Answer these questions and check your answers on page 167.

Q3

When Andy has applied a shared lock, can Becky apply a shared lock?

Q4

When Andy has applied an exclusive lock, can Becky apply a shared lock?

Q5

When Andy has applied a shared lock, can Becky apply an exclusive lock?

Q6

When Andy has applied an exclusive lock, can Becky apply an exclusive lock?

TWO-PHASE LOCKING

In order to make sure a schedule is serializable, we need to obey specific rules for setting and releasing locks. One of these rules is *two-phase locking*—for each transaction, two phases should be used: one for setting locks and the other for releasing them.

For example, suppose there are resources A and B, both subject to locking. Transaction ❶ observes the rule of two-phase locking, while transaction ❷ does not. Serialization can only be achieved when each transaction complies with the rule of two-phase locking.

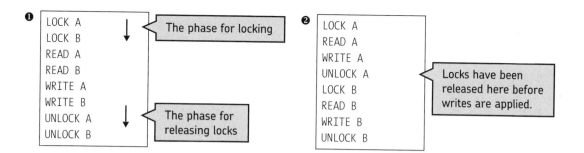

LOCKING GRANULARITY

There are a number of resources that can be locked. For example, you can lock data in units of tables or units of rows. The extent to which resources are locked is referred to as *granularity*. *Coarse granularity* occurs when many resources are locked at once, and *fine granularity* occurs when few resources are locked.

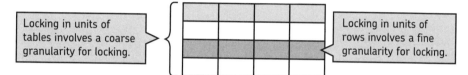

Locking in units of tables involves a coarse granularity for locking.

Locking in units of rows involves a fine granularity for locking.

When granularity is coarse (or high), the number of locks needed per transaction is reduced, making it easier to manage granularity. In turn, this reduces the amount of processing required by the CPU on which the database is operating. On the other hand, as more resources are locked, it tends to take longer to wait for locks used by other transactions to be released. Thus, the number of transactions you can carry out tends to drop when granularity is high.

In contrast, when granularity is fine (or low), a greater number of locks are used in one transaction, resulting in more operations for managing locks. This results in greater processing required by the CPU. However, since fewer resources are locked, you will spend less time waiting for other transactions to release locks. Thus, the number of transactions you can carry out tends to increase.

QUESTIONS

Answer these questions, and check the correct answers on page 168.

Q7

The target resource for locking has been changed from a table to a row. What will happen to the number of transactions you can carry out concurrently?

Q8

The target resource for locking has been changed from a row to a table. What will happen to the number of transactions you can carry out concurrently?

You can use locking to effectively carry out two or more transactions at the same time. However, using locking comes with the burden of lock management, since *deadlocks*—places where user actions conflict—can occur. Simpler methods for concurrency control can be used when you have a small number of transactions or a high number of read operations. In such cases, the following methods may be used:

Timestamp Control

A label containing the time of access, referred to as a *timestamp*, is assigned to data accessed during a transaction. If another transaction with a later timestamp has already updated the data, the operation will be not permitted. When a read or write operation is not permitted, the transaction is rolled back.

Optimistic Control

This method allows a read operation. When a write operation is attempted, the data is checked to see if any other transactions have occurred. If another transaction has already updated the data, the transaction is rolled back.

LEVELS OF ISOLATION

In a real-world database, you can set the level of transactions that can be processed concurrently. This is referred to as the *isolation level*.

In SQL, the SET TRANSACTION statement can be used to specify the isolation levels of the following transactions:

- READ UNCOMMITTED
- READ COMMITTED
- REPEATABLE READ
- SERIALIZABLE

```
SET TRANSACTION ISOLATION LEVEL READ UNCOMMITTED;
```

Depending on the isolation level setting, any of the following actions may occur.

	Dirty read	Non-repeatable read	Phantom read
READ UNCOMMITTED	Possible	Possible	Possible
READ COMMITTED	Will not occur	Possible	Possible
REPEATABLE READ	Will not occur	Will not occur	Possible
SERIALIZABLE	Will not occur	Will not occur	Will not occur

- A *dirty read* occurs when transaction 2 reads a row before transaction 1 is committed.
- A *non-repeatable read* occurs when a transaction reads the same data twice and gets a different value.
- A *phantom read* occurs when a transaction searches for rows matching a certain condition but finds the wrong rows due to another transaction's changes.

DURABILITY

A database manages important data, so ensuring security and durability in the case of failure is critical. Security is also important for preventing unauthorized users from writing data and causing inconsistencies.

In a database, you can set permissions for who can access the database or tables in it. Cain avoids dangers to the Kingdom's database by enhancing the database's security.

In a relational database, the GRANT statement is used to grant read and write permissions to users. You can use GRANT statements to grant permission for other users to process tables you have created. Setting permissions is an important task for database operation.

```
GRANT SELECT, UPDATE ON product TO Overseas_Business_Department;
```
This statement grants permission to process data.

You can assign the following privileges (permissions) with SQL statements.

DATABASE PRIVILEGES

Statement	Result
SELECT	Allows user to search for rows in a table.
INSERT	Allows user to insert rows in a table.
UPDATE	Allows user to update rows in a table.
DELETE	Allows user to delete rows in a table.
ALL	Gives user all privileges.

Granting a privilege with WITH GRANT OPTION enables the user to grant privileges to other users. With the statement shown below, the Overseas Business Department can allow other users to search and update the database.

```
GRANT SELECT, UPDATE ON product TO Overseas_Business_Department
WITH GRANT OPTION;
```
The granted user can grant privileges to other users.

You can also take away a user's privileges. To do this, use the REVOKE statement.

```
REVOKE SELECT, UPDATE ON product FROM
Overseas_Business_Department;
```
This statement revokes the user's privileges.

Some database products can group a number of privileges and grant them to multiple users at once. Grouping makes privilege management easier.

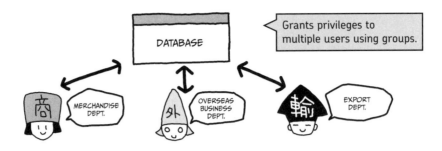

Using views, as described on page 117, enables even more controlled management for enhanced security. First, extract part of a base table to create a view. Setting a privilege for this view means the privilege is also set on the selected portion of data in the view.

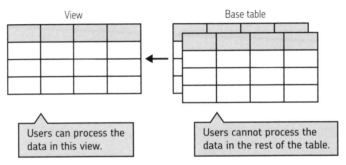

View　　　　　　　　　　　Base table

Users can process the data in this view.

Users cannot process the data in the rest of the table.

QUESTIONS

Try these questions on durability. The answers are on page 168.

Q9

Write an SQL statement that allows the Export Department to search for data in the Product Table.

Q10

Create an SQL statement to revoke the Overseas Business Department's privilege to delete data from the Product Table.

Q11

Privileges were set as follows on a Product Table created by the administrator. Enter a YES or NO in each cell of the table below to indicate the presence or absence of the privilege for each department, respectively.

```
GRANT ALL product TO Overseas_Business_Department;
GRANT INSERT, DELETE ON product TO Merchandise_Department;
GRANT UPDATE, DELETE ON product TO Export_Department;
```

	Search	Insert	Update	Delete
Overseas Business Dept.				
Merchandise Dept.				
Export Dept.				

WHEN DISASTER STRIKES

A database needs to have a mechanism that can protect data in the system in the event of a failure. To ensure durability of transactions, it is mandatory that no failure can create incorrect or faulty data. To protect itself from failure, a database performs various operations, which include creating backup copies and transaction logs.

TYPES OF FAILURES

Database failure can occur under various circumstances. Possible types of failure include the following:

- Transaction failure
- System failure
- Media failure

Transaction failure occurs when a transaction cannot be completed due to an error in the transaction itself. The transaction is rolled back when this failure occurs.

System failure occurs when the system goes down due to a power failure or other such disruption. In the case of a system failure, disaster recovery takes place after you reboot the system. Generally, transactions that have not yet been committed at the time of failure are rolled back, and those that have already been committed when a failure occurs are rolled forward.

Media failure occurs when the hard disk that contains the database is damaged. In the case of a media failure, disaster recovery is carried out using backup files. Transactions committed after the backup files were created are rolled forward.

CHECKPOINTS

In order to improve the efficiency of a write operation in a database, a *buffer* (a segment of memory used to temporarily hold data) is often used to write data in the short term. The contents of the buffer and the database are synchronized, and then a *checkpoint* is written. When the database writes a checkpoint, it doesn't have to perform any failure recovery for transactions that were committed before the checkpoint. Transactions that weren't committed before the checkpoint must be recovered.

Now, suppose the transactions shown below are being performed at the time a system failure occurs. Which transactions should be rolled back? Which ones should be rolled forward?

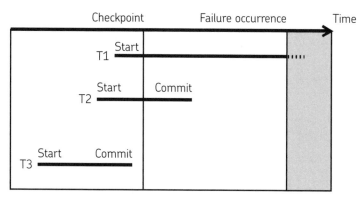

Try these questions based on the table on the previous page. The answers are on page 168.

Q12

How should T1 be processed?

Q13

How should T2 be processed?

Q14

How should T3 be processed?

In case of database failure, the recovery mechanisms described above will protect the database against inconsistency. That is why you can be reassured of database integrity when you use it.

INDEXES

A database manages massive amounts of data, so searching for specific data can be very time consuming. But you can use indexes to speed up searches!

Product code	Product name	Unit price	District
101	Melon	800G	South Sea
102	Strawberry	150G	Middle
103	Apple	120G	North Sea
104	Lemon	200G	South Sea
201	Chestnut	100G	North Sea
202	Persimmon	160G	Middle
301	Peach	130G	South Sea
302	Kiwi	200G	South Sea

It is very time consuming to search for each item row by row.

An *index* is a tool that allows you to speedily access the location of the target data. When looking for some data in a large database, searching with indexes promises fast results.

Product code	Product name	Unit price	District
101	Melon	800G	South Sea
102	Strawberry	150G	Middle
103	Apple	120G	North Sea
104	Lemon	200G	South Sea
201	Chestnut	100G	North Sea
202	Persimmon	160G	Middle
301	Peach	130G	South Sea
302	Kiwi	200G	South Sea

The target data location can be accessed quickly by using its index.

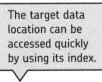

Index

Indexing methods include B-tree and hash methods. A *B-tree index* is composed of parent nodes and child nodes, which can have further child nodes. The nodes are arranged in sorted order. Each parent contains information about the minimum and maximum values contained by all of its children. This allows the database to navigate quickly to the desired location, skipping entire sections of the tree that cannot possibly contain the desired value.

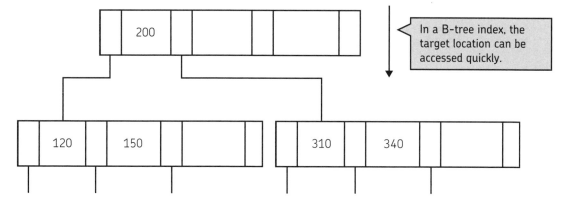

> In a B-tree index, the target location can be accessed quickly.

The *hash* index method finds the location of target data by applying a hash function to the key value of the data. The hash acts as a unique fingerprint for a value. The hash index method can perform specific full-match searches, such as a search for *product code 101*. However, it is not designed to search effectively for comparative conditions like *product codes no less than 101* or for fuzzy references like *products with names ending in* n.

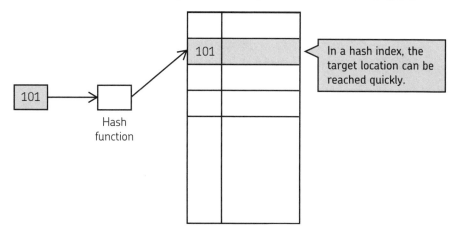

> In a hash index, the target location can be reached quickly.

In some cases, using an index may not speed up the search—using an index doesn't save time unless you are looking for only a small portion of the data. Additionally, there are cases where indexes are recreated every time data is updated, resulting in slower processing of an update operation.

QUESTIONS

Try these questions on indexing. The answers are on page 168.

Q15

Which index would be more powerful in a search with an equal sign, a B-tree or hash index?

Q16

Which index would be more powerful in a search with an inequality sign, a B-tree or hash index?

OPTIMIZING a QUERY

When you query a database, the database analyzes the SQL query and considers whether to use an index so it can process the query more quickly. Let's examine the procedure for processing a query.

The database can decide on an optimal order to process a query. Most queries can be processed in several orders with the same results, but with possibly different speeds. For example, suppose there is a query to extract dates of sale and product names for products with a unit price greater than 200G. This query can be seen as consisting of the following steps.

```
SELECT date, product_name
FROM product, sales
WHERE unit_price>=200
AND product.product_code = sales.product_code;
```

1. Join the Product Table and the Sales Table.

2. Select products whose unit price is greater than 200G.

3. Extract columns of dates and product names.

For example, the figure on the left below shows the query processed in order from 1 to 3. The figure on the right shows the query processed in order from 3 to 1. Either way, the queries are equivalent.

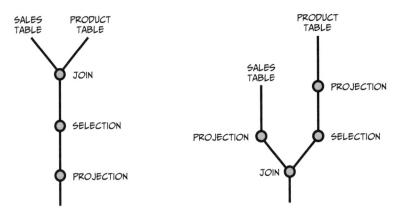

However, when processed from 1 to 3, the same query would generally require a longer processing time, because when the first join is performed, an intermediate table with many rows may be created. On the other hand, the procedure from 3 to 1 requires a shorter processing time, since selection and projection happen first, trimming unwanted data as soon as possible. Thus, the same query may require a different processing time, depending on the order in which projection, selection, and join are performed.

Generally, the database should use the following rules to find the best querying order:

- Execute selection first to reduce the number of rows.
- Execute projection first to reduce the number of columns irrelevant to the result.
- Execute join later.

There are different techniques for executing projection, selection, and join, respectively. For selection, you can use either a full-match search or an index-based search. For join, the following methods are available.

NESTED LOOP

The *nested loop* method compares one row in a table to several rows in another table (see the figure below). For example, one of the values in a row in Table T1 is used to find matching rows in Table T2. If the values are the same, then a joined row is created.

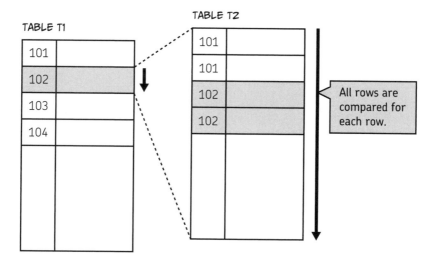

SORT MERGE

The *sort merge* method sorts and then merges rows in multiple tables (see the figure below). First, all or part of Tables T1 and T2 are sorted. Then they are compared starting with the top row, and a joined row is created whenever the same value is found. Since they have already been sorted, processing only needs to be done in one direction, so it will take less time. You should be aware, however, of the time needed for the initial sorting.

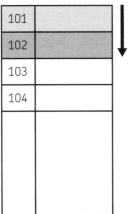

TABLE T1

101	
102	
103	
104	

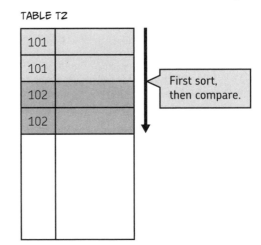

TABLE T2

101	
101	
102	
102	

First sort, then compare.

HASH

A *hash* divides one of the tables using a hash function and then merges it with a row in another table that has the same hash value. This method effectively selects the row to join.

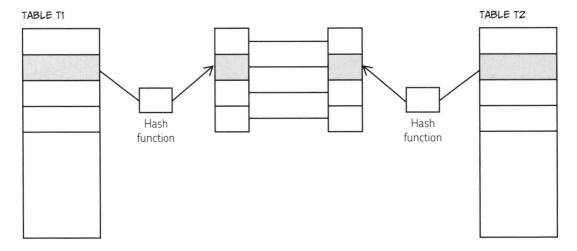

TABLE T1

TABLE T2

Hash function

Hash function

OPTIMIZER

When a query is processed, these different techniques are examined for optimal performance. In a database, the function in charge of optimization of queries is referred to as the *optimizer*. There are two common types.

RULE-BASED PROCESSING

Certain rules are established before any operations are performed. For example, some operations can be combined or reordered in much the same way an algebraic equation can be manipulated and still mean the same thing. The optimizer tries to find the most efficient way to process the query that gives the same results.

COST-BASED PROCESSING

This method tries to estimate the cost of processing the query, based on statistics that the database maintains. Cost-based processing is sometimes more flexible than rule-based processing, but it requires periodical updates of the database's statistics. Managing and analyzing these statistics requires a lot of time.

SUMMARY

- You can set user privileges for a database.
- Locking ensures consistency when a database has multiple users.
- Indexing enables fast searches.
- A database has disaster recovery functions.

ANSWERS

Q1

```
COMMIT;
```

Q2

```
ROLLBACK;
```

Q3 Yes

Q4 No

Q5 No

Q6 No

Q7 Increases

Q8 Decreases

Q9

GRANT SELECT ON product TO Export_Department;

Q10

REVOKE DELETE ON product FROM Overseas_Business_Department;

Q11

	Search	Insert	Update	Delete
Overseas Business Dept.	YES	YES	YES	YES
Merchandise Dept.	NO	YES	NO	YES
Export Dept.	NO	NO	YES	YES

Q12

A rollback is performed since it is not committed at the time of the failure occurrence.

Q13

A roll forward is performed since it has been commited at the time of the failure occurrence.

Q14

No recovery operation is needed since it has been committed at the time of checkpoint.

Q15

Hash

Q16

B-tree

6
Databases are Everywhere!

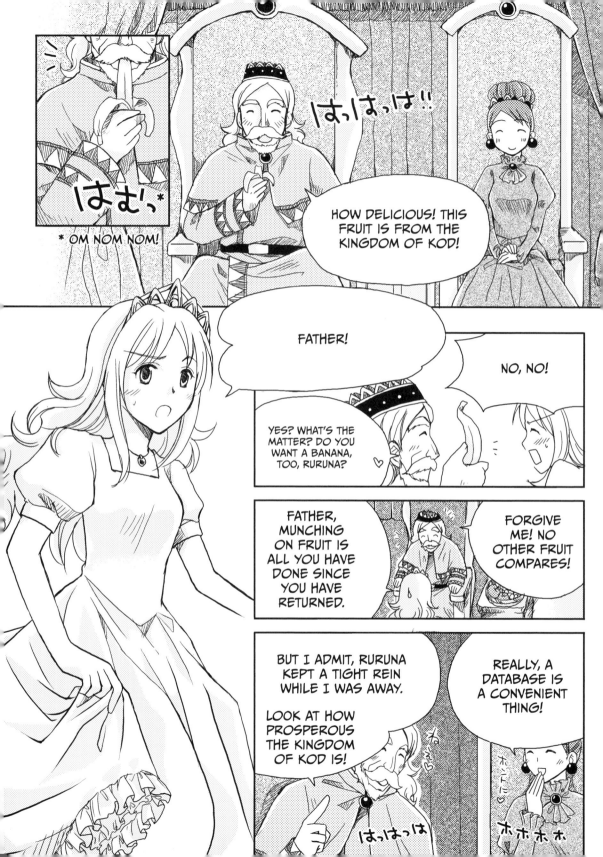

* OM NOM NOM!

HOW DELICIOUS! THIS FRUIT IS FROM THE KINGDOM OF KOD!

FATHER!

YES? WHAT'S THE MATTER? DO YOU WANT A BANANA, TOO, RURUNA?

NO, NO!

FATHER, MUNCHING ON FRUIT IS ALL YOU HAVE DONE SINCE YOU HAVE RETURNED.

FORGIVE ME! NO OTHER FRUIT COMPARES!

BUT I ADMIT, RURUNA KEPT A TIGHT REIN WHILE I WAS AWAY.

LOOK AT HOW PROSPEROUS THE KINGDOM OF KOD IS!

REALLY, A DATABASE IS A CONVENIENT THING!

DaTabases in USE

FOR EXAMPLE, IN SOME COUNTRIES, DATABASES ARE USED AT BANKS TO MANAGE ACCOUNTS!

BANKS WITH DATABASES!

SUPPOSE AN ACCOUNT CAN BE SHARED BY A LOT OF PEOPLE....

WITHDRAWAL

TRANSFER

YOU COULD WITHDRAW FROM YOUR OWN ACCOUNT AS WELL AS TRANSFER MONEY INTO SOMEBODY ELSE'S ACCOUNT.

THAT SOUNDS SO CONVENIENT!

PAYMENTS CAN BE MADE THROUGH A DATABASE!

ALL ABOARD!

TICKET

SOMETIMES TRAIN SEAT RESERVATION SYSTEMS USE DATABASES.

WITH A DATABASE, BOOKING WOULD BE POSSIBLE FROM ANY STATION.

EXACTLY.

REMEMBER THE LESSON ON LOCK-BASED OPERATIONS?

lock

Databases and the Web

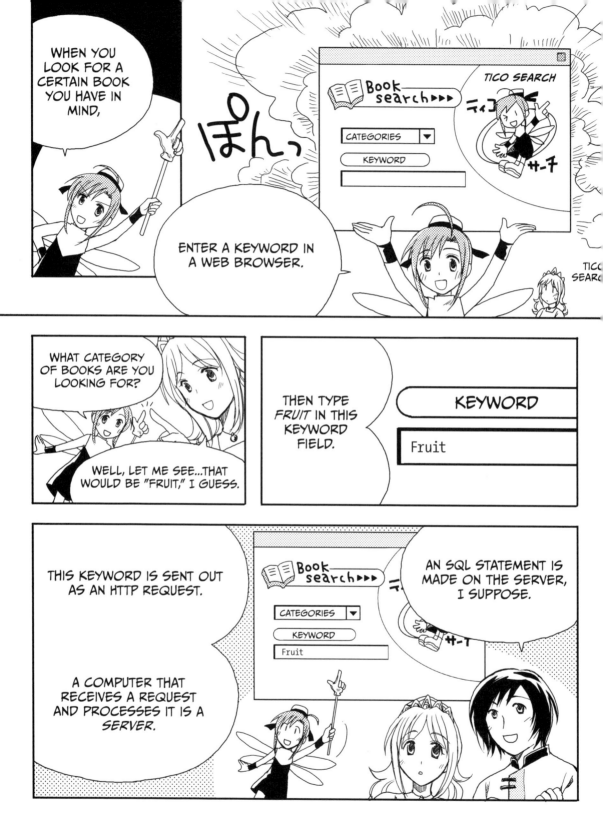

Distributed Databases

CAN THE LOAD BE SHARED AMONG *DATABASE SERVERS?*

YES, AND WHEN THAT HAPPENS, IT IS REFERRED TO AS A *DISTRIBUTED DATABASE.*

IT SOUNDS LIKE A DATABASE MANAGED BY A NUMBER OF SERVERS.

YOU'VE GOT IT.

YOU SHOULD NOTE, HOWEVER, THAT THESE SERVERS CAN ACT AS A SINGLE DATABASE.

DATABASE

SERVER

SERVER

SERVER

IT IS CONVENIENT THAT A NUMBER OF SERVERS CAN ACT AS A SINGLE DATABASE.

THAT MAKES IT POSSIBLE FOR EACH SERVER TO MANAGE ACCORDING TO ITS CAPACITY.

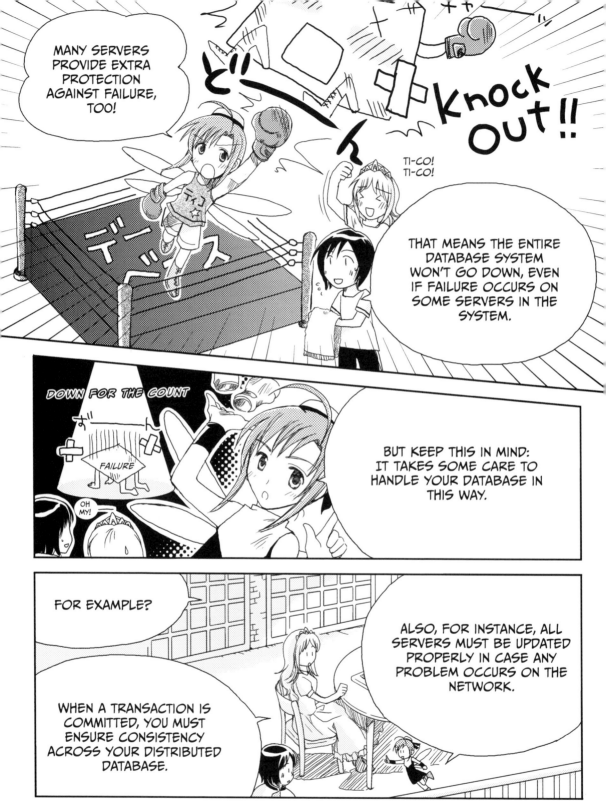

STORED PROCEDURES AND TRIGGERS

A NETWORK IS A MUST IN ANY ENVIRONMENT WHERE A SET OF SERVERS IS USED.

RIGHT! THAT'S WHERE STORED PROCEDURES ARE USEFUL;

THEY ARE SOMETIMES CREATED TO HELP REDUCE THE BURDEN ON THE NETWORK.

STORED...?

AHA!

DOESN'T *STORE* MEAN *PUT INTO MEMORY*, IN OTHER WORDS?

RIGHT!

IN ORDER TO REDUCE THE BURDEN ON THE NETWORK, FREQUENTLY USED OPERATIONS CAN BE STORED IN DATABASES.

FREQUENTLY USED OPERATIONS, YOU SAY...WHAT KIND OF OPERATIONS ARE THEY, I WONDER?

WELL, SINCE WE WERE TALKING ABOUT OPERATIONS FOR BUYING A BOOK, SUBTRACTING FROM THE IN-STOCK COUNT IN THE INVENTORY TABLE AND ADDING DATA TO THE SHIPPING TABLE—

LET'S SEE...

AREN'T THOSE TYPICAL OPERATIONS?

WHEN DATA IS UPDATED, FOR EXAMPLE, A STORED PROCEDURE CAN AUTOMATICALLY START.

IT'S CALLED A *TRIGGER.*

TRIGGER...

OH, YES!

BECAUSE IT DOES WHAT A TRIGGER ON A GUN DOES!

YEE HAW!

PULL THE TRIGGER AND A BULLET IS SHOT. UPDATE DATA AND A STORED PROCEDURE IS ACTIVATED.

IT WOULD BE CONVENIENT, INDEED, IF PLACING AN ORDER AND UPDATING THE DATABASE

WHY AM I ALSO IN THIS OUTFIT?

AUTOMATICALLY LAUNCHED AN OPERATION TO REDUCE THE INVENTORY AND ARRANGE FOR SHIPPING.

JUST BUYING ONE BOOK CREATES A LOT OF WORK BEHIND THE SCENES, DOESN'T IT?

THANK YOU!!

SHE'S GONE.

IT IS PAINFUL FOR ME TO SEE YOU LOOKING SO SAD, PRINCESS.

WE HAVE THE TASK OF IMPLEMENTING THE KNOWLEDGE TICO HAS GIVEN US

INTO A REAL SYSTEM.

OH, YES, YOU'RE RIGHT.

DAYS HAVE GONE BY...

IS EVERYTHING ALL RIGHT WITH YOUR BOOK ON DATABASES, PRINCESS?

YEAH!

I AM MAKING THINGS EASY FOR EVERYBODY TO UNDERSTAND.

DO YOU WANT TO TAKE A LOOK?

SURE!

IT'S A GOOD IDEA TO DO IT IN A COMIC BOOK STYLE.

AND CAIN'S DRAWINGS ARE EXCELLENT.

SO CUTE...

AND LOOK!

HERE! THIS IS THE FRONT COVER.

FABULOUS!

Databases on the Web

Databases are used for many different purposes, such as train seat reservation systems and bank deposit systems. They are indispensable in daily life and in business operations. As I showed Ruruna and Cain, web-based database systems are popular as well. In a web-based system, the communications protocol used is HyperText Transfer Protocol (HTTP). Server software running on a web server waits for a request from a user. When a user request (HTTP request) is sent, the software answers the request and returns a corresponding web page (HTTP response).

A *web page* consists of text files in HTML format. Other files specified by Uniform Resource Locators (URLs) are embedded within a web page to present information such as images.

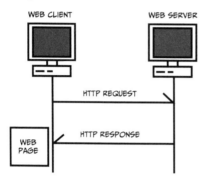

When a database is used with a web page, a database server is added to the system shown above. This system can be configured in three layers and is referred to as a *three-tier client/server system*. A three-tier client/server system consists of a presentation layer, a logic layer, and a data layer.

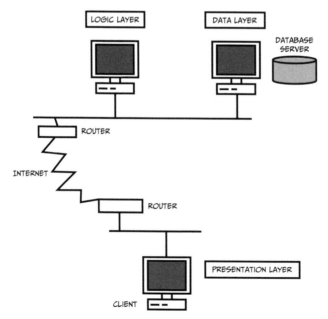

The *presentation layer* receives user input, such as search conditions, that needs to be passed on to the database. The presentation layer also processes query results received from the database so that they can be displayed. A web browser (such as Internet Explorer or Firefox) functions as a presentation tool for the user.

The logic layer performs data processing. This layer is where SQL statements are composed. Processes performed here are written in one or more programming languages. Depending on the contents and load of processes, several servers, such as an application server and a web server, may be used to handle processing.

The data layer processes data on a database server. Search results are returned from the database in response to SQL queries.

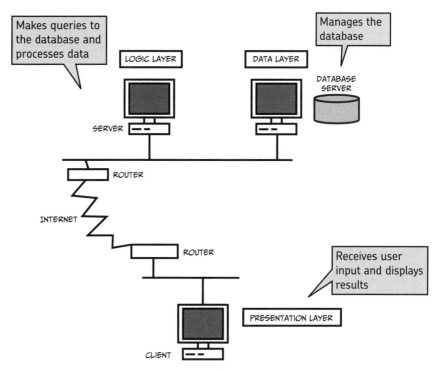

The three-tier client/server configuration is a flexible and simple system. For example, when making additions or modifications to an application, you can separate the portion you want to edit as a logic layer. In the presentation layer, you can use a web browser, eliminating the need for installing a separate software program.

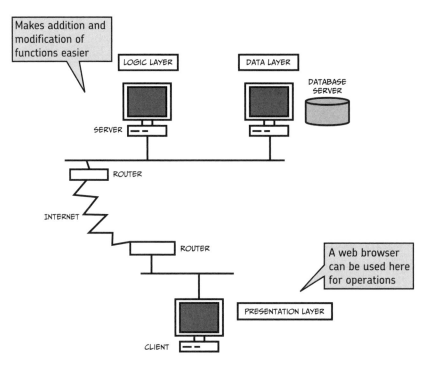

USING STORED PROCEDURES

In a web-based system, too much traffic on the network can be a problem. Fortunately, you can store program logic inside the database server itself as stored procedures.

Storing procedures on the database server helps reduce the load on the network, because it eliminates the need for frequent transfers of SQL queries. In addition, storing procedures also makes it easier to develop applications, since standard processes can be encapsulated into easy-to-use procedures. Actually, stored procedures are just a special kind of a more broad category called *stored programs*. The other two types of stored programs are *stored functions* and *triggers*.

TYPES OF STORED PROGRAMS

Program	Definition
Stored procedure	Program that does not return values from the processing procedure
Stored function	Program that returns values from the processing procedure
Trigger	Program that is launched automatically before and after the database operations

QUESTIONS

Can you answer these questions? The correct answers are on page 205.

Q1

In a three-tier client/server system, on which layer does the database operate?

In a three-tier client/server system, on which layer are user interactions received and results displayed?

What Is a Distributed Database?

In a Web-based system, processing is distributed among a database server, a web server, and a web browser, with different tasks assigned to each. This type of distributed system allows for flexible processing and decreases the processing capacity required by each server.

But a database server itself can be distributed among several servers. Distributed database servers can be in different locations or on the same network. Note, however, that a distributed database may be handled as a single database. If the distributed database appears to be a single server, the user doesn't have to worry about data locations or transfers.

A database can be distributed horizontally or vertically, as you'll see.

HORIZONTAL DISTRIBUTION

Horizontal distribution uses several peer database servers. Each database server can use data from other database servers, and in turn, each one makes itself available to the other database servers. This structure is used for a system of extended databases that operate separately in each department.

A horizontally distributed database is a failure-resistant system by design, since failure on one server will not affect database operation.

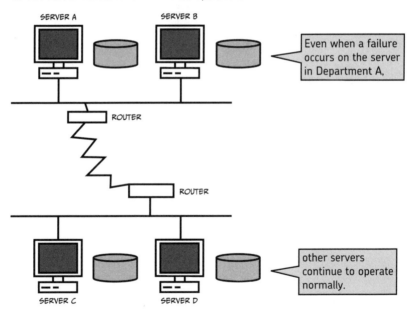

VERTICAL DISTRIBUTION

Vertical distribution assigns different functions to different database servers. One of the servers functions as the main server and performs a key role, while the others are in charge of processing tasks as requested. A vertically distributed database makes it easier to manage the main database server, though this main server will have a heavy load. An example of vertical distribution would include a company-wide main server and individual servers operating in each department.

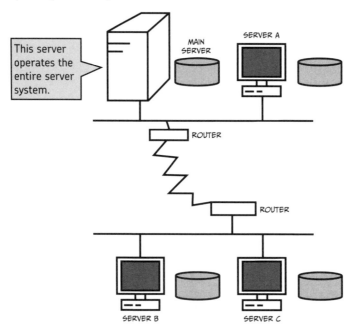

Partitioning Data

In a distributed database, data is spread across servers for storage. You should carefully consider how to divide up the data. Data can be split in the following ways.

HORIZONTAL PARTITIONING

A *horizontal partition* divides data into units of rows. Rows resulting from the split are distributed across servers. This form of partitioning is often used when data can be ordered into groups in such a way that related data, which is often accessed at the same time, is stored on the same server.

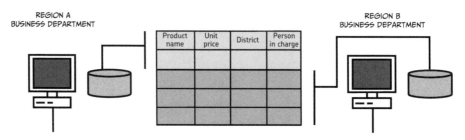

VERTICAL PARTITIONING

A *vertical partition* divides data into units of columns. Columns resulting from the split are distributed across servers. For example, a vertical partition can be used to manage and join independent databases belonging to departments like the Merchandise Department, the Overseas Business Department, and the Export Department.

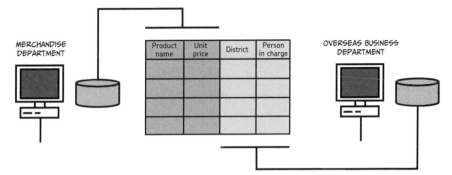

	Product name	Unit price	District	Person in charge
MERCHANDISE DEPARTMENT				

OVERSEAS BUSINESS DEPARTMENT

PREVENTING INCONSISTENCIES WITH A TWO-PHASE COMMIT

Databases on different servers in a distributed database system can be configured to act as a single database in the eyes of users. To achieve this, various steps must be taken to deal with the fact that data is actually distributed across different servers.

First, whenever data is committed, all data on all servers must be updated consistently.

In a distributed database system, the standard commit method may lead to one of the servers being updated while another is not, as shown below. This is a violation of the atomicity property of transactions, as this transaction will not end with either a commit or rollback. This would also cause the database system as a whole to become inconsistent.

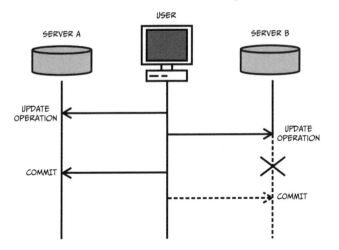

Therefore, a two-phase commit is adopted in a distributed database system. The *two-phase commit* creates one commit operation from both the first and the second commit operations.

A two-phase commit operation involves a coordinator and participants. In the first phase of a two-phase commit operation, the coordinator asks the participants if a commit operation is possible. The participants send an OK reply if it is. This preparatory step is referred to as a *prepare*. In the second phase, the coordinator gives the instructions for a commit, and all participants perform a commit accordingly.

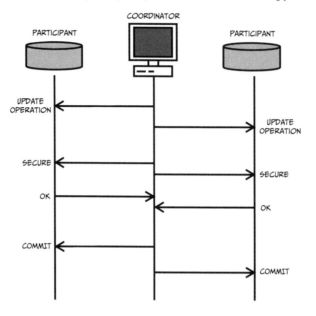

If any one node fails to secure the operation in the two-phase commit, all participants receive a rollback directive. This is how databases on all servers remain consistent with each other.

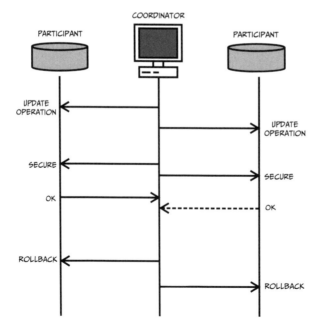

QUESTIONS

Try these questions about two-phase commits. The answers are on page 205.

Q3

In a two-phase commit scheme, what instructions does the coordinator give during the first phase?

Q4

In a two-phase commit scheme, what instructions does the coordinator give during the second phase?

Database Replication

Some distributed databases have a duplicated, or replica, database that reduces the load on the network. This practice is referred to as *replication*. The primary database is referred to as the *master database*, and the copy is called the *replica*. There are several types of replication.

READ-ONLY

A *read-only replica* is created and downloaded from the master database on the main server. To change data, users must connect to the main server.

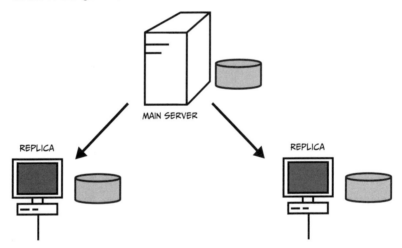

REPLICATION ENABLED FOR ALL SERVERS

In this method, the same master database is shared by all servers. Updates to any of the servers are reflected in all other servers.

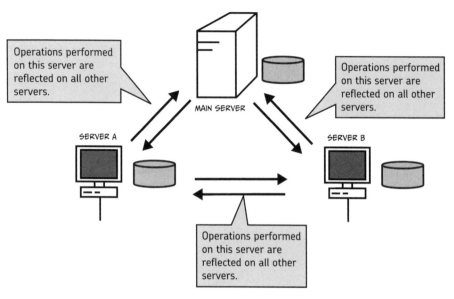

Operations performed on this server are reflected on all other servers.

Operations performed on this server are reflected on all other servers.

MAIN SERVER

SERVER A

SERVER B

Operations performed on this server are reflected on all other servers.

FURTHER APPLICATION OF DATABASES

This final section introduces applied technologies related to databases.

XML

Extensible Markup Language (XML) is becoming increasingly popular as a data storage method. XML represents data by enclosing it in tags. Since these tags can convey information about the data they contain, this language is useful for data storage and retrieval.

XML is useful because its strictly structured grammar makes programmed processes easy. Moreover, XML comes in text files (which are easy to edit) and can communicate with other systems. For these reasons, XML is sometimes used as a data representation method in place of a database.

```
<?xml version="1.0"?>
<products>
  <fruit>
    <product code>101</product code>
    <product name>Melon</product name>
    <unit price>800</unit price>
  </fruit>
  <fruit>
    <product code>102</product code>
    <product name>Strawberry</product name>
    <unit price>150</unit price>
  </fruit>
  <fruit>
    <product code>103</product code>
    <product name>Apple</product name>
    <unit price>120</unit price>
  </fruit>
</products>
```

OBJECT-ORIENTED DATABASES

A relational database stores text data in a table. However, a relational database may be inadequate when handling certain types of data. That's where an object-oriented database (OODB) comes in.

The object-oriented method uses *objects*—sets of data and instructions on how that data should be used. You can hide the data and only expose the operations upon the data in order to handle the object as an independent component. This technique is referred to as *encapsulation*.

In an object-oriented database, each object is represented with an identifier. Sometimes, an object is also called an *instance*.

In an object-oriented database, you can also manage *compound objects*—one object nested within another. This means, for example, that you can store data consisting of an image combined with text as a single object. The object-oriented database allows for flexible management of complex data.

In an object-oriented database, various concepts can ease object-oriented development. The template for objects is referred to as *class*. For example, suppose you have designed an Apple class. Objects (instances) in that class may be Apple A, Apple B, and so on. The Apple class enables the creation of these objects.

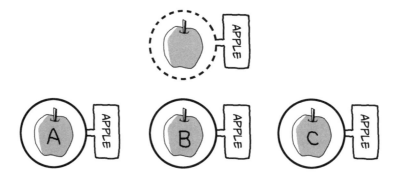

In an object-oriented scheme, a class can also have hierarchical relationships. You can create a child class that has the same data and functions of a parent class. This relationship is referred to as *inheritance*. You can also give unique functions to the child class.

For example, class Apple and class Orange may inherit the data and functions from class Fruit, but they also each have their own unique data and functions. In an object-oriented scheme, you can use hierarchical relationships to allow for efficient development.

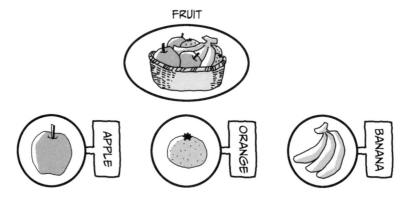

Summary

- The three-tier client/server system is a method of Web-based system configuration.
- A database acts as a data layer.
- A distributed database system handles databases that are dispersed.
- A two-phase commit method is used in a distributed database.

answers

Q1 Data layer

Q2 Presentation layer

Q3 Prepare

Q4 Commit or rollback

CLOSING REMARKS

Have you enjoyed studying databases? You will need to learn even more before you can manage all the aspects of operating a database, but the fundamentals of databases always stay the same. By firmly understanding the basics, you can identify significant data in the real world and design and operate databases. You can acquire advanced database skills by building on your fundamental knowledge. Good luck!

FREQUENTLY USED SQL STATEMENTS

BASIC QUERY

```
SELECT column_name, ...
FROM table_name;
```

CONDITIONAL QUERY

```
SELECT column_name, ...
FROM table_name
WHERE condition;
```

PATTERN MATCHING

```
SELECT column_name, ...
FROM table_name
WHERE column_name LIKE 'pattern';
```

SORTED SEARCH

```
SELECT column_name, ...
FROM table_name
WHERE condition
ORDER BY column_name;
```

AGGREGATING AND GROUPING

```
SELECT column_name, ...
FROM table_name
WHERE condition
GROUP BY column_names_for_grouping
HAVING condition_for_grouped_rows
```

JOINING TABLES

```
SELECT table_name1.column_name, ...
FROM table_name1,table_name2, ...
WHERE table_name1.column_name = table_name2.column_name
```

CREATING A TABLE

```
CREATE TABLE table_name(
column_name1 datatype,
column_name2 datatype,
...
);
```

CREATING A VIEW

```
CREATE VIEW view_name
AS SELECT statement
```

DELETING A REAL TABLE

```
DROP TABLE table_name;
```

DELETING A VIEW

```
DROP VIEW view_name;
```

INSERTING A ROW

```
INSERT INTO table_name(column_name1, ...)
VALUES (value1, ...)
```

UPDATING A ROW

```
UPDATE table_name
SET column_name = value1, ...
WHERE condition;
```

DELETING A ROW

```
DELETE FROM table_name
WHERE condition;
```

REFERENCES

Chen, P.P. 1976. "The Entity-Relationship Model: Toward a Unified View of Data,"
ACM Transactions on Database Systems 1 (1): 9–36.

Codd, E.F. 1970. "A Relational Model of Data for Large Shared Data Banks,"
Communications of the ACM, 13 (6): 377–387.

Date, C.J. and Hugh Darwen. 1997. *A Guide to the SQL Standard*, 4th ed. Reading, MA:
Addison-Wesley.

Masunaga, Yoshifumi. 1990. *Basics of Relational Database*. Tokyo: Ohmsha.

Database Language: SQL, JIS X3005-1-4, 2002.

ISO/IEC 9075, Information Technology—Database Languages—SQL, 1992.

ISO/IEC 9075, Information Technology—Database Languages—SQL, 1995.

ISO/IEC 9075, 1, 2, 3, 4, Information Technology—Database Languages—SQL, 1999.

IT Engineers' Skill Standards—Technical Engineers (Database), Information-Technology
Promotion Agency, Japan.

INDEX

I

inconsistent data, 153, 154, 159, 199–201
independent data management, 19, 72
indexes/indexing, 143–147, 162–164, 167
inner join, 115
inputting data, 21, 90–92, 103–104, 106, 116
INSERT statements, 104, 116, 119, 159
instances, 203
internal schema, 81
International Organization for Standardization (ISO), 124
International Standard Book Number (ISBN), 45
Internet databases. *See* Web-based database systems
intersection operations, 37, 39, 41
ISBN (International Standard Book Number), 45
ISO (International Organization for Standardization), 124
isolation, 153, 155–158
isolation levels, 158

J

Japanese Industrial Standards (JIS), 124
join operations, 37, 43, 44, 48, 165
joining tables, 44, 101–102, 114–115

K

keys
  foreign, 44, 48, 72, 101
  primary, 35, 44, 48, 65, 67, 72, 78–79, 101, 103, 115

L

LIKE statements, 97, 108
locking granularity, 157
locks/lock-based controls, 131–137, 155–157, 167, 175–176, 182
logic layer, 194–196
logical operators, 107
logs, 148–149
lost data, 20, 154

M

many-to-many relationships, 55, 74, 75, 81
master databases, 201–202
mathematical operations. *See* operations

MAX (maximum value) function, 99–100, 110
media failures, 161
memory. *See* stored procedures
MIN (minimum value) function, 99, 110

N

nested loop method, 165
network data model, 33, 39
non-repeatable read, 158
normalization, 60–72, 78–81
normalized tables, 72, 91
null, 30, 108

O

object-oriented databases (OODB), 203–205
one-to-many relationships, 55, 75, 81
one-to-one relationships, 74, 81
OODB (object-oriented databases), 203–205
operations
  Cartesian product, 37, 39, 42
  data extraction, 39–47
  difference, 37, 39, 41
  division, 37, 43, 45
  intersection, 37, 39, 41
  join, 37, 43, 44, 48, 165
  projection, 36, 37, 43, 165
  relational, 43–47
  selection, 37, 39, 43, 47, 48, 165
  set, 39–42
  union, 37, 39, 40, 48
operators, 107
optimistic controls, 158
optimization, query, 164–167
optimizers, 167
ORDER BY statements, 98
outer join, 115

P

partitioning data, 198–199
passwords, 141
pattern matching, 108
permissions, 19, 141–142, 159–160, 167
phantom read, 158
presentation layers, 205
primary keys, 35, 44, 48, 65, 67, 72, 78–79, 79, 101, 103, 115
problems, data management
  conflicting data, 13, 17–18, 21, 60, 71, 116, 153, 158
  corrupted/lost data, 20, 154

database failures, 161
difficulty changing data, 13, 14, 17, 18
duplicated data, 11, 16, 18, 19, 21, 29
inconsistent data, 153, 154, 159, 199–201
shared data, 12, 20, 21, 129, 175
processing data, 35–37, 47–48, 130, 159, 167, 182, 195–198
programming languages, 178, 180, 194, 202
projection operations, 36, 37, 43, 165
protecting data, 19, 127, 138–142, 159–160, 161–164, 167, 176, 182, 184

Q

queries. *See* SQL; SQL statements
query optimization, 164–167

R

READ COMMITTED transactions, 158
read operations, 130, 133, 134, 159
READ UNCOMMITTED transactions, 158
read-only replica, 201
records, 27–28, 34, 48, 148–149
recovery mechanisms, 20, 147–150, 161–164, 167
relational data model, 33–34, 35, 39, 47, 48
relational operations, 43–47
relationships
  concept of, 54, 74
  E-R (entity-relationship) model, 50–55, 74–77, 81
  hierarchical relationships, 32, 33, 39, 204
  many-to-many relationships, 55, 74, 75, 81
  one-to-many relationships, 55, 75, 81
  one-to-one relationships, 74, 81
remarks, 30–31
REPEATABLE READ transactions, 158
replicas, 201–202
resources in transactions, 155
retrieving data, 36–37, 39–47, 90–92, 95–99, 101–102, 106, 180, 202
REVOKE statements, 159, 160, 168
right outer join, 115
ROLLBACK statements, 136–137, 150, 153–154, 205
rolling forward, 149
rows, 34, 84, 116
rule-based processing, 167

ABOUT THE AUTHOR

Mana Takahashi is a graduate of Tokyo University, Faculty of Economics. She is an active technical writer and has published a number of books on topics such as Java, C, XML, Information Engineering, and System Administration.

PROJECT TEAM FOR THE JAPANESE EDITION

Production: TREND-PRO Co., Ltd.

Founded in 1988, TREND-PRO produces newspaper and magazine advertisements incorporating manga for a wide range of clients from government agencies to major corporations and associations. Recently, TREND-PRO is actively participating in advertisement and publishing projects using digital content. Some results of past creations are publicly available at the company's website, *http://www.ad-manga.com/*.

Ikeden Bldg., 3F, 2-12-5 Shinbashi, Minato-ku, Tokyo, Japan
Telephone: 03-3519-6769; Fax: 03-3519-6110

Scenario writer: re_akino

Cartoonist: Shoko Azuma

UPDATES

Visit *http://www.nostarch.com/mg_databases.htm* for updates, errata, and other information.

The Manga Guide to Databases was laid out in Adobe InDesign. The fonts are CCMeanwhile and Chevin. The book was printed and bound at Malloy Incorporated in Ann Arbor, Michigan. The paper is Glatfelter Spring Forge 60# Smooth Eggshell, which is certified by the Sustainable Forestry Initiative (SFI).

MORE MANGA GUIDES

Find more Manga Guides at your favorite bookstore, and learn more about the series at *http://www.edumanga.me/*.

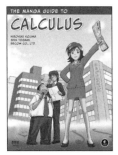
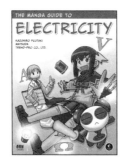

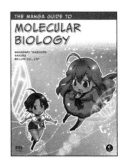

Author and Chapter List

Foreword

The racial and ethnic composition of the United States has changed substantially over the last 25 years and continues to change quickly. Racial and ethnic diversity in the legal profession lags behind the diversity of the nation as a whole as well as the composition of numerous other professions. Throughout the nation, educational programs have been created in the hope of improving educational outcomes for children of color and reducing the disparity between the nation's increasing diversity and the limited racial and ethnic diversity in the legal profession.

Professor Sarah Redfield has been deeply involved in efforts to solve the conundrum of disparate educational outcomes and educational access for children of color, ultimately leading to a lack of racial and ethnic diversity in the legal profession, for two decades. During that time, she has been a consultant on matters related to education reform. She also co-founded a conference focused on education law, co-founded and/or helped to launch pipeline programs and charter schools, co-founded a consortium designed to encourage analysis of education related issues, and wrote numerous articles and books on educational access and diversity. She has also spoken nationally on topics related to diversity and educational access nearly thirty times in seven years. Simply put, she is an expert on these matters. More than that, she is passionate about improving educational outcomes for students of color, increasing diversity in legal education and increasing diversity in the legal profession. Professor Redfield brings to this subject a unique and important combination of academic knowledge, hands on experience and personal commitment.

To date, most of the effort spent on pipeline programs has been spent developing, operating and seeking funding for specific pipeline programs. It appears that less effort has been spent formally analyzing the efficacy of multiple pipeline programs to determine whether the programs produce measurable results. With the publication of her first book, *Diversity Realized: Putting the Walk with the Talk for Diversity in the Pipeline to the Legal Profession,* Professor Redfield brought needed research and analysis to the historical and current issues that the legal profession confronts in trying to improve its diversity. In this book The *Educational Pipeline To The Professions: Programs that Work to Increase Diversity*, Professor Redfield makes another important contribution to the analysis of pipeline programs by offering guidance on pipeline programs with objectively measurable outcomes that others might replicate. Professor Redfield focuses on criteria that help readers analyze the actual impact of individual pipeline programs—the new 3Rs—Rigor, Relevance and Relationship. She has brought together a wide array of authors with real expertise, real experience, and real results. In providing an analysis related to whether a program achieves measurable results and whether it is replicable, this book provides a wonderful tool for persons trying to understand how to improve educational outcomes for students, particularly in a law related context. In this way, the book offers a how-to manual for expansion of strong pipeline programs that can change the face of the profession. We can all benefit from its advice.

Michelle Gallardo
Chairperson, Council on Racial and Ethnic Diversity in the Educational Pipeline
American Bar Association
Detroit, Michigan
September 2011

Preface

This book is the second in a series of books addressing issues along the educational pipeline, from preschool to law school and the legal profession. The first book offered the factual background on educational issues and approaches to increasing the pool of diverse students interested in, and qualified for, law school and the legal profession. Additionally, it provided a narrative description of efforts (successful and otherwise) by the legal community to work along the educational pipeline to grow interest in the legal profession among a more diverse student body. This book brings together some of the heroes of pipeline work, those who have programs working with underrepresented and previously underserved students along the pipeline to support their persistence, access, and success. The authors are an eclectic group, writing about a range of programs, but all are successful in terms of measurable and measured student outcomes. I am enormously grateful to each of these extraordinary colleagues for the work they do and for finding the time to write about it so that others can enjoy similar success without starting from scratch. Helping to publish any one of these accounts would have been enormously gratifying and useful; a whole book of course even more so. Some of the authors are experienced and published. For others, this is their first venture in this arena; all have my enduring respect and gratitude, and I look forward to continuing to work with them. I invite all of you to get to know them as well; inspiration is contagious.

Introduction and Overview

Chapter 1

The Need for Focused Pipeline Programs with Documented Outcomes

*Sarah E. Redfield**

This chapter reviews the findings of the first book in this series, *Diversity Realized: Putting the Walk with the Talk for Diversity in the Legal Profession*,[1] and, by adding to the extant literature an exposition of a series of successful, replicable pipeline programs, this book moves the agenda for increasing diversity in the profession forward.

Diversity Realized outlined the issues facing the legal community as it seeks to increase its diversity in light of the changing demographics of the nation and concluded, starkly, *that the diversity of the bench and bar remains out of sync* with the changing demographics of the country, where the population is projected to be over fifty percent minority by 2050.[2] Indeed, reports since the publication of the first book suggest the overall employment of minority attorneys is deteriorating.[3]

In any case, without a substantial increase in the pool of qualified, underrepresented minorities interested in law school admission, the profession will remain apart from the population it represents.[4] However, research for *Diversity Realized* suggested that the requisite law student admission numbers to approach

> **What is a pipeline program in the context of education and the legal profession?**
>
> Any program operated or supported by an educationally affiliated institution or an educationally or professionally focused group for the purpose of providing information, motivation, relevant educational programming, or activities in the context of successfully moving students forward along the educational continuum, here with an eye to diversity in the professions. The end goal is to promote knowledge of, interest in, and academic capabilities for careers or higher levels of education or professional preparation in law-related pathways in order to increase the number of diverse students interested in and qualified for admission to law school and the professions.

* Sarah Redfield is a member of the Maine Bar and Professor of Law at the University of New Hampshire School of Law. One of her main fields of interest is diversity of the legal profession, including the educational pipeline to the profession. She thanks her students and colleagues at the University of New Hampshire School of Law: Dean John Broderick, Associate Dean Jordan Budd, and Associate Dean for Faculty Research John Orcutt; her research assistants, Alma Alvarado, Jon Jonsson, Kelly Donahue, and Michael McCubbin; and especially Librarians Judy Gire, Cindy Landau, Melanie Cornell, Kathy Fletcher, Tom Hemstock, and Barry Shanks, for their continued support of her research and scholarship. Professor Redfield also thanks her colleague Rick Roe at Georgetown and his students and staff, Julia Pergola and Ryan Macpherson, as well as her friend John Stump, all of whom graciously reviewed the manuscript and thus truly made the publication possible.

3

parity with the population are impossible to reach in the current educational and admissions milieu.[5] The predictable student numbers for the first grade class of 2009, and those that will precede and follow it, do not support anything near a sufficiently broad pool of potential law school candidates to approach parity with the nation's changing demographics. Projecting population changes to 2030, and assuming that lawyers remain the same percentage of the population they were in the last census (0.3%), in 2030, some 100,000 additional Black attorneys, and more than 230,000 additional Hispanic attorneys would need to join the ranks of the profession to approach parity with the general population. In an overall lawyer population estimated at about 1.1 million, these numbers would involve increasing current Black admission rates from about 4,000 to approximately 5,300 annually, and Hispanic admission rates from 4,400 to approximately 12,000 annually. The numbers would need to be even greater if there is not a relative decrease in the current majority groups. By any count, such an increase (or even half or a quarter of such an increase) cannot be gained by continuing to nibble at the edges of the pool or the larger problem that the size of the pool reflects.[6]

If the diversity numbers are indeed as critical as this brief review suggests, the profession needs to set and stay a new course. The first book in this series reviewed in detail the causes of the leaks in the educational pipeline, which result in achievement gaps among students and, ultimately, in the limited pool of diverse applicants interested in and qualified for admission to law school. Conclusions from a historical perspective, and from an overview of the education issues, show that for the profession to help close the leaks in the pipeline, narrow the achievement gap, and change the face of the applicants qualified for and interested in law school and the profession, *a sustained focus on the education pipeline over a long time horizon is needed.*

Of course, the legal profession has not been absent from the pipeline in the past, but it has lacked the sustained and focused attention that is needed. To date, much of the attention of the profession's diversity efforts has been at the point of entry to law school and then the point of entry to, and retention in, the profession. Acknowledgement of the depth and breadth of the issue of diversity along the educational pipeline leading to the law school gates has remained relatively limited and, where addressed, has remained relatively without analysis, system, or coordination.[7] Currently, there are well over 400 pipeline programs (as self-identified and self-described) in the ABA/LSAC Pipeline Directory.[8] Despite the large number, it is hard to see the impact in real numbers of students entering law schools; indeed, for some racial and ethnic groups, the numbers show a decrease.[9] Given this lack of data showing successful outputs (that is, an increased qualified pool of previously underrepresented minorities interested in admission to law school), a different and tighter focus is needed. The seemingly-infinite variety of individual programs now extant, many of which are one-of-a kind, many of which are splash and dash, are not the answer. Success requires a focus on programs that intervene at an earlier point in the pipeline than the law school gates and on programs that offer proven, effective practice and potential.

The short answer is that the current plethora of pipeline programs needs to be honed; the image used by the Marine diversity leaders for their mentoring programs, *Steel on Steel*, seems apt.[10] But, what should the focus be to achieve change? The research here is clear on the value of collaborative partnerships with a shared goal of increasing diversity.[11] So, too, the research suggests a need to offer a laser focus on what the Gates Foundation and other education researchers have labeled the new 3Rs: Rigor, Relevance, and Relationships.[12] Accountability, or Results—a fourth R—is necessary for all.

Significant to this undertaking is the fact that the educational research clearly suggests that the legal profession is particularly well-positioned to support improved delivery of these 3Rs:

Rigor: all students need to be challenged to have an opportunity to rise to high expectations.

The law's curricula and established teaching methodology—its signature pedagogy[13]—by definition promotes rigor and sustains high expectations.

Relevance: all students need engaging materials relevant to their lives.

One look at the newspaper, the Supreme Court's docket, or today's TV listings shows that the law offers engaging relevant subject matter.

Relationships: all students need someone who knows them; one caring adult can make a difference in student success.

The legal community has a great capacity, which it has already shown in some of its programs, to provide intellectual capital and human resources to establish and support relationships with students as mentors, teachers, internship supervisors, and the like.

Results: sometimes listed as a fourth R, suggesting the need to measure, evaluate, and re-inform pipeline work based on the data.

This is an area where the work of the law community (and others) has been limited.[14]

Against this backdrop, the first book highlighted several selected programs that are consistent with the 3Rs criteria, well-suited to partner relationships with the legal community, and have documented results. This book now offers more detail on some of the specific programs previously reviewed, offering thoughtful writing on programs at each level of the pipeline by those closely involved in their startup and continuing results.

Pre-K	Elementary	Middle	High School	College	Law School	Profession

In totality, the chapters of this book span the pipeline, starting with an interesting and unique program at Georgetown University Law Center that partners law students and faculty with preschoolers, moving on through elementary, middle, and high school programs, and then to college and prelaw.[15] These programs vary in length; some run for the summer, others for a term, others significantly longer; all are more than a single day or a few meetings. The programs in the book also vary in delivery method. Some are curriculum-based. Some are high school and college classes; in some cases the classes are taught by law students and/or lawyers. Some programs are surround programs that envelop students in support and skill-building as they progress through their own programs at various schools; and some are their own schools. There is also variety in cocurricular activities such as moot court, youth court, and internships, but again, all are intense and extend over time.

In each chapter, the authors lay out their beginnings, together with their location and demographics, and they explain their current programs through a general narrative and specific details on their approach, their students, and their outcomes. Each program involves a partnership for two or more levels of the pipeline, and these critical relationships are explained. Each chapter also addresses issues of budget and administrative structure. Each author considers the program's results, and many describe their programmatic approach to professional development as it informs and re-informs their work. Many chapters also include a more individual touch, describing the hardest issue the authors and their programs faced or are facing. The programs that are discussed in the book have both a record of general success and a lot of "poster" children. Many chapters include a story or two from among their populations to indicate individual potential and success. Such individual stories are anecdotal and inspiring, but they are only an illustration of the results from programs, which show intensity and consistency over time. All chapters offer key advice for others who may want to replicate their efforts, and all authors are available for further conversation.

A Note on How Chapters Were Selected

As discussed previously, the legal profession has not been absent from the pipeline. Despite the hundreds of "pipeline programs," the flat trends in diversity admissions, and in the profession, evince that current programs, whatever their number, have not been sufficient to change the face of the legal academy or practice. Honing these programs and placing resources within a selected group of documented initiatives that incorporate the known essential elements is needed.

This second book was guided by some basic principles and definitions that set a context for the individual chapters that follow. While there are differences in approach, the commonalities are more striking. Selection for inclusion required a sustained focus on the new 3Rs of rigor, relevance, and relationship. Also requisite was a partnership of at least two parts of the pipeline and often more. For example, Legacy Charter Academy is a partnership between an elementary school and a law firm; the Texas Institutes are partnerships between the colleges and law schools. So too, the selection was guided by a program's ability to show success, not just in anecdotal terms, but in measurable outcomes. For example, the Saturday Academy of Law, which set out to increase positive interest in legal careers and raise students' skills, *did both* as demonstrated by qualitative and quantitative data. This focus on results and accountability now is crucial if successful outcomes are to be more than the *talk*.

Successful Programs: Essential Elements

- Recognize the education reality and the depth of the issues dividing underderrepresented minorities (Black, Hispanic, American Indian Alaskan Native) from their White and Asian peers.

- Have clear diversity goals.

- Focus on the significance of high expectations, aspirations, and incorporate the new 3Rs.

- Involve students in intense, iterative, or extended work, including an intensive relationship with a student over time.

- Involve more than one segment of the pipeline.

- Emphasize and value partnerships and mutual visioning among partners—a precept more easily stated in the negative, that is, it is not the law community approaching a school with "do we have a deal for you," but, rather, a mutual statement of capacities and needs.

- Use common course development, research/evaluation design, professional development, networking, and grant-writing support to increase effectiveness.

- Support rigorous, themed curricula, career pathways and academies, which present opportunities to bring together professional resources and educational resources in meaningful engagement.

- Track participants and their results, using their data to form and re-inform the projects.

- Connect to the pipeline for the long haul.

The chapters in this book show programs that embody these factors; each is consonant with the ideas of pipeline and partnership. In addition, they are all programs that understand and acknowledge the deficits in the current educational system; they are all programs involved with underrepresented minorities and the profession; they are all results-oriented programs, committed to documentation; and they are all programs whose founders and leaders are, themselves, open to partnering with others and sharing lessons learned.

There are other pipeline programs consonant with these principles not included in the book.[16] Some were "discovered" after the length of the book was determined. Others were known to me, but their organizers could not secure the time to write a chapter, which is hardly surprising. In many cases, pipeline programs are run with intense involvement from their organizers or founders, and the time to write about the work just does not materialize. Programs that I hope to include in the *next* book include the ENLACE family programs, the elementary school work of the State Bar of Texas, Len Bayne's college-level work, the Cleveland Bar's extraordinary initiative in Cleveland high schools, and the various pipeline initiatives of the Bar Association of San Francisco.[17] I hope to know of many more by then as well!

A Note on Partnerships and Wingspread

Much of my work in this book, and its predecessor, was inspired by the work of Dean Parker at Pacific McGeorge and the other early adopters of pipeline programs, particularly those who attended what have come to be called the Wingspread meetings.

In June 2004, a group of law-school-led teams (forty participants in all) met at the Johnson Foundation's Wingspread Conference facilities in Racine, Wisconsin to discuss how law schools, and their colleagues, could work effectively in teams along the educational pipeline to repair leaks and widen that pipeline so that more diverse students could successfully traverse the pathway from preschool to the profession.

Since that meeting, the concepts of collaboration and pipeline have taken hold as more leaders and educators recognize that a meaningful response to the achievement gap, and resultant issues confronting the workforce of the future, lie in a longer time horizon and systemic approach. So too, the concepts of evaluation and documentation have grown in stature. Today, hardly a pipeline discussion or meeting occurs without reference to these concepts. Should Wingspread have accomplished nothing else, this would be sufficient. But, Wingspread has accomplished more. As an intellectually and conceptually driven partnership, it has provided a forum for work outside of silos toward a common diversity goal.

After its first meeting, Wingspread issued a Call to Action. Many responded, formally and informally. Meanwhile, Wingspread took on the task of conceptualizing the core points of pipeline work and bringing colleagues together in an ongoing series of formal and informal meetings across the country. At these meetings, attendees shared their successes and failures; outside of these meetings networks were created and thrived. Word spread easily from Cleveland to Los Angeles about lawyer mentoring, easily from Utah to Sacramento about law school mentoring, from the District of Columbia to Virginia and California about law-themed high schools, from Nova Scotia to New Hampshire, about inclusion, and on and on throughout the United States and some Canadian provinces. New programs were modeled after old, first adopters were consulted by others, and initiatives grew.

Overall, Wingspread focused on the following matters, which are critical to further pipeline and collaboration efforts for the profession:

1) Framing the issues around diversity and the law community and the need for systemic and systematic change—

- Issued a Call to Action to work collaboratively to maximize educational aspirations and opportunities for diverse students, who are disproportionately under-represented in colleges, universities, and professional schools, particularly law schools.

- Called attention to the critical data illustrating the state and national crisis in diversity, in the workforce for the legal profession and for our national leadership, and to the significance of the educational data as to leaks and narrowing along the educational pipeline from preschool to the profession.

- Highlighted the commonality among the professions in regard to under-represented minorities and the pipeline.

- Focused particularly on breaking down education silos, especially in regard to collaborative inclusion of the professional schools, and their relationships with the bench and the bar.

- Recognized and publicized the significance of law-themed education and pedagogy to the new 3Rs (rigor, relevance, relationship).

2) Emphasizing and creating *teams* to work along the educational pipeline in site-specific projects—

- Developed the now-replicated, and replicable, team model, using a "visioning session" as the starting point for work along the pipeline to form local goals and projects that are not top-down, but collaborative. The work with Los Angeles law school deans, the Los Angeles County Bar Association, and the formation of a Hawaiian team through the University of Hawaii Law School.

- Inspired, reached out to, and supported collaborative pipeline initiatives of state, local, and national bar associations.

- Highlighted the importance of community colleges, a group often ignored previously, though noteworthy as a source of future law students, as potential participants.

- Recognized, supported, and brought together varied and diverse pipeline teams. Three, of many, examples include Tech Law School, Estacado High School, & Texas Tech Medical School; Georgetown University Law Center, Georgetown University, Thurgood Marshall Academy, and the Citizens Commission on Civil Rights; and Cleveland Marshall School of Law, Cleveland Bar, Cleveland Metropolitan School District High Schools, Cleveland School of Education, and Cleveland State College of Urban Affairs.

- Inspired and supported newer, and stronger, pipeline initiatives. Northeastern, Texas Wesleyan, Thomas Jefferson, Hamline, Texas Tech, and the California law schools working with LAUSD and its law magnets, for example.

- Inspired and supported the Cleveland Bar's 3Rs program, involving teams of over 700 lawyers in all Cleveland Metropolitan School District high schools, to teach social studies and constitutional law once a month and played a key role in dispersing information about this program.

3) Assuring that lessons learned are lessons shared: evaluation and replication of successful ideas and projects—

- Raised the bar for programmatic development and evaluation.

- Organized almost a dozen Wingspread meetings, with increasing interest and participation, and encouraged a program where teams visited specific sites as models for replication, including an entire group visit to the ENLACE Latino pipeline program of law and medicine at the University of New Mexico, as well as smaller groups visits, like to the Brigham Young mentoring program and the LAUSD magnets.

- Held historic meetings among law, dental, and medical professional schools.

- Offered conceptual support to emerging pipeline initiatives.

- Succeeded in seeing these highlighted models adopted and adapted elsewhere. For example, the influence of ENLACE on other pipeline programs' attention to family has been virtually uniform, and the Brigham Young University mentoring model has provided a reference point for similar ventures in other venues.

- Succeeded in highlighting the importance of tracking and evaluation, leading to an increase in the existing work in this area. For example, in Cleveland, they are tracking the results of the Cleveland Bar Association's intensive tutoring program for all 10th graders in the Cleveland Metropolitan School District on the social studies portion of the Ohio Graduation Tests.

- Showcased other existing law-related programs to inspire their adoption in new venues; for example, Street Law, highlighted by the University of San Francisco, and others, was adopted in Sacramento directly because of Wingspread; Marshall Brennan Fellowships, highlighted at Wingspread VIII, are now being promoted by the California Bar's Council on Access and Fairness and adopted, or considered for adoption, in several west coast schools.

4) Enhancing the intellectual presence of the community of law schools and their sister professional schools in the field of pipeline issues—

- Developed conceptual analysis of law pedagogy as it relates to the new 3Rs, educational rigor, relationships, and relevance.

- Spoke and wrote widely on pipeline concerns of the profession and encouraged replication of documented successful initiatives, through public appearances, as well as significant, individual conversations.

- Working on the conceptual and practical relationships between Law Related Education (LRE), and diversity.

Pre-Kindergarten and Elementary School Programs

Chapter 2

Pre-K Reading and Literacy

The Emerging Voices Project of the Latin American Montessori Bilingual Public Charter School (LAMB) and the Georgetown Street Law Clinic

Georgetown University Law Center
Washington, D.C.

Richard Roe*

Pre-K	Elementary	Middle	High School	College	Law School	Profession

This chapter discusses a pipeline program at preschool, a partnership between the faculty and students at Georgetown University Law Center and the District of Columbia's Latin American Montessori Bilingual Public Charter School. While the research is clear that differences among students start as early as preschool in terms of letter-recognition, reading, and vocabulary, few pipeline programs are willing to reach this far along. Professor Roe aptly illustrates the value of developing children's cognitive and expressive skills from early ages as a foundation for more complex thinking and expression that is essential for later academic success and the practice of law. While we have no way of knowing that these young children might become interested in the legal profession or might consider applying to law school, we can predict that their literacy skills will be stronger than they might otherwise have been and that their opportunity to gain entrance to law school will have been increased. It is also likely that their perceptions of the law students and law professors who teach them will leave them with a positive attitude toward the profession. President Kennedy's sentiment that a rising tide raises all boats[1] is surely relevant here where early involvement with young people works to increase their literacy and their potential as citizens of the democracy.

---

* Professor of Law and Director, D.C. Street Law Clinic since 1984. Professor Roe has also taught the seminar, Literacy and Law, since 1999. Professor Roe would like to thank his research assistants Ryan Macpherson and Julia Pergola for their help researching and preparing this chapter.

Lawyers and Literacy

Should lawyers and legal educators be interested in developing the literacy skills of preschool and early elementary students? If so, are they competent to do so? What are the connections between early literacy and later "legal thinking"? This chapter seeks to demonstrate that the legal profession should promote high quality early literacy development because the work of lawyers and the qualifications to enter upon legal training require strong abilities in language, literacy, expression, critical thinking, and organization. Both research and experience show these skills have their foundations in early childhood learning.[2] Secondly, strong literacy and critical thinking skills are essential for democratic participation under the rule of law.

For these reasons, lawyers should be actively interested in promoting quality early childhood education. Moreover, lawyers are highly capable of working with young children to develop their literacy skill due to their own strengths in language and expression. To do so effectively, however, legal professionals must conduct their classroom activities at the language and experience levels of the children they are working with.

This chapter describes the benefits of and methodology for lawyers to help to improve children's literacy in elementary schools. First, it will describe an elementary school's collaboration with a legal educator, in the Emerging Voices Project (Voices). Second, an effective "law focused" or civics lesson for young children will be described and its methodological principles discussed. In connection with this lesson, a framework of law focused or civic goals for children will be set out. Third, these lessons and objectives will be connected to best practices and principles of elementary education.

The LAMB Charter School and Its Demographics

Latin American Montessori Bilingual Public Charter School (LAMB) serves students in Washington, DC from age three through fifth grade. It is a public charter school and is free for all students. Because it is a charter school it does not have specific neighborhood boundaries and LAMB's students live throughout the District. In 2011, LAMB has a total of 172 students, 37 of whom are identified as Black, 99 as Hispanic and 36 as White.[3] Of the 172 students at LAMB 27% are eligible for free and reduced price lunch.[4] During the Voices project, the population was similar.

LAMB was founded by the Latin American Youth Center[5] "with the simple premise that all children can learn and deserve a school that supports nurtures and transforms their natural curiosity and eagerness into knowledge."[6] The school's charter was approved by the Public Charter School Board in 2001 and it opened its doors to its first students in 2003.[7] The school's mission is to: "foster bilingualism in a self-directed learning environment in which children build a foundation of knowledge essential for a lifetime of learning."[8] To accomplish this mission, LAMB provides a dual language Spanish/English immersion program in a Montessori setting.[9] The premises of a Montessori approach to teaching and learning include the following:

  • That children are capable of self-directed learning.

- That it is critically important for the teacher to be an "observer" of the child in-stead of a lecturer. This observation of the child interacting with his or her envi-ronment is the basis for the continuing presentation of new material and av-enues of learning. Presentation of subsequent exercises for skill development and information accumulation are based on the teacher's observation that the child has mastered the current exercise(s).

- That children are masters of their school room environment, which has been specifically prepared for them to be academic, comfortable, and to encourage independence by giving them the tools and responsibility to manage its upkeep.

- That children learn through discovery, so didactic materials with a control for error are used. Through the use of these materials, which are specific to Montessori schools (sets of letters, blocks and science experiments) children learn to correct their own mistakes instead of relying on a teacher to give them the correct answer.

- That children most often learn alone during periods of intense concentration. During these self-chosen and spontaneous periods, the child is not to be inter-rupted by the teacher.

- That the hand is intimately connected to the developing brain in children. Children must actually touch the shapes, letters, temperatures, etc. that they are learning about—not just watch a teacher or TV screen tell them about these discoveries.[10]

These principles and premises, we believe, are not only foundations for quality learn-ing and literacy development, but also of democratic civic capacity. Different from tradi-tional classrooms, Montessori classrooms are grouped by age clusters, for example preschool through kindergarten, rather than having a single grade in each classroom.[11] This way younger children learn academic and social skills from older students, and older students learn leadership, patience, and tolerance through interactions with younger students.[12] Additionally, students choose their own work throughout the day from a variety of self-correcting materials. This allows children to hone concentration skills and to gain inde-pendence, self-reliance, and self-confidence.[13] In the early grades students are taught primarily in Spanish, and as they get older, instruction is split equally between English and Spanish.

The Emerging Voices Project in Practice

The goal of the Voices Project was to advance the literacy development of LAMB students. The project used a multi-tiered approach, helping parents and children to engage in the full range of literacy experiences: family discussion and discourse, fam-ily reading, and story creation (including drawing and use of pictures), verbal expres-sion, and writing. The focal point of the project was the creation of family "books," age-appropriate histories and descriptions of family stories, events, or activities. These books range from very simple drawings and recounted stories by Pre-Kindergarten aged children of family events, to more sophisticated and elaborate depictions and stories by children in the third and fourth grades. The approach, methodology, and staffing of this program were provided by Professors Richard Roe and Charisma Howell and the staff of the D.C. Street Law Clinic of Georgetown University Law Center.[14]

The first stage of Voices consisted of workshops for teachers and parents on reading children's books relating to families in various topic areas and discussing family stories, histories and activities. Strategies were developed for engaging children in family stories; books about family stories, either bilingual or in Spanish, were distributed to participants as models and for family reading development and practice. In the fall of 2008, Street Law clinic faculty and staff conducted several workshops for parents and teachers, both immediately after school and later in the evening, to reach parents at their available times. The workshops were continued in the spring semester.

In the second stage of the project, in an effort to reach parents and children together, meeting times were changed from evenings to directly after school. Instructors met with parents and their children in the library to directly facilitate the parent-child interactions and the development of the books. LAMB designated a staff person to coordinate these sessions, which resulted in strong participation among a number of families.

In the third stage of the project, the instructors worked directly with the children in each of the six classes in the school to help produce the books. In the PreK-K grades, we met for an hour with each class; in grades 1–3 and 1–4, we met for 90 minutes. With each group, we discussed the assignment to make "books" of a family event, suggesting a family vacation to the child's country of origin but leaving the topic to the children's own choice. We also conducted critical thinking activities based on lessons from *Educating for Citizenship*, a collection of interactive lessons for Kindergarten through fourth grade, explained in more detail in the Education for Citizenship Section, below.

To illustrate the accomplishments of the children, and their literacy development, we will present discussions of examples of books, two from Pre-Kindergarten, one from K–2nd, and two from the 3rd–4th grade stages of literacy at LAMB. Using the examples as a backdrop we will examine how the children's literacy abilities develop in a trajectory of increasingly higher levels of thinking and expression. We will then connect this cognition and expression to the kind of legal thinking required to attend and to succeed in law school and to conduct the practice of law.

The first of the Pre-Kindergarten books for discussion was done by Marco (all student names have been changed to respect their privacy). A three-year-old, Marco drew what appear at first glance to be very simple pictures, without writing. On Marco's single page, he initially chose not to depict a story of his biological family but rather of something else. The drawing consists of three groups of circles, one blue, one red, and one green. The meaning of the pictures was not apparent, however, until Marco was asked to describe his book. When Professor Roe asked Marco to tell him about his book, Marco said and Professor Roe wrote: "Thomas is a train in a movie. A movie about Thomas. James has six wheels and a whistle (indicating four smaller circles and a vertical mark on the drawing). Percy is an engine. He sometimes teases Thomas." His circles were engines from Shining Time Station, a popular children's TV show featuring Thomas the Tank Engine. His mother affirmed that Thomas is a common theme in Marco's conversation. It is a topic evidently important to him. Marco drew Thomas (blue), James (red) and Percy (green). These colors correspond to the actual colors of the engine characters in the TV show.

The sophistication of Marco's work takes on new dimensions after he was given the opportunity to describe it in his age-appropriate verbal language. Marco demonstrates significant perception, insight, and descriptive detail. His abstract renditions of the engines are colored to correspond to their actual colors and he adds detail (wheels and a whistle). Interestingly, he states that James has six wheels but depicts only four; rather than being considered inaccurate, it is possible that Marco is depicting James from a side view, where only four wheels would be visible, or showing the wheels symbolically.[15] His attention to detail is accurate and can be thought of as a foundational skill that will allow him to examine details of texts and events in his academic and professional life. Perhaps more strikingly, he describes the relationship among the engines. With his statement about Thomas as "an engine in a movie, a movie about Thomas," he identifies Thomas as the main character. This is a highly significant intellectual attainment. What Marco has shown he can do is identify the main idea of a text or event, an act that he will be called upon to accomplish many times in his future academic life, from summarizing the main idea from reading passages in his school work and other reading to answering questions on standardized tests. Marco has also demonstrated the foundational capacity to identify the main idea of a legal case, as in determining a holding of a case, or the summary of an argument or position. Lastly, Marco shows awareness of important interpersonal relationships as he elaborates on Percy's treatment of "teasing" Thomas. We can imagine Marco's awareness of personal dynamics and power increasing with his maturity.

There are several key ingredients that contribute to the effectiveness of the methodology involved in Marco's book. The first is that the goal is for the student to depict a story that is important to him. The open-ended topic of a family vacation was suggested, but for purposes of giving Marco the opportunity to depict something important to him, any subject he chooses is acceptable. The second is giving Marco the opportunity to describe his "book," since he is too young to write his description. The third is writing down what the child says. This begins to establish the connection to and importance of writing as a way of recording language. It also shows the child that you are taking his words seriously

The second of the Pre-Kindergarten level books was done by Juan, a four-year-old. On a single page, he drew a sun (yellow), a tree (green), a car with lights on (green), a wavy line of water (red), a line of sand (brown), a path from the sand to a house, and a house with stairs, a door, and windows (multiple colors). Professor Roe asked him to name his objects and labeled them accordingly, in English and Spanish. This was done not only to learn their meaning from Juan but also to provide a connection between pictures and written language. Professor Roe then asked him about his story and wrote his response: "I like when my brother plays with me. I like when my uncle told me I put sand on [his] stomach and body, then he laughs." This is a typical literacy activity for a three- to five-year-old.[16] The various elements can be integrated to tell a story over time, establish the location, and give substantial supporting detail of a beach vacation. Colors may not be accurate in a physical sense, but are appealing and symbolic. At this phase, children seem to pick colors because they like them, not for similitude. Juan's verbal account goes beyond his depicted items to describe his positive feelings about family interactions during the beach vacation. The stray picture of a door appears to be an initial attempt at the house, which he subsequently relocated on the page to where there was more room and in geographic relation to the beach, in a more sensible orientation. Revision is an ingredient of quality writing. His "book" clearly tells a story and makes sense of his world. He seems well on the way to making meaning through symbols, and through words, when given the opportunity. The role of the teacher or parent is to encourage the story, imagination, detail, and verbalization of images, keeping in mind that it is the child's, not the adult's story. The use of diverse components in his picture that can be integrated into a whole story shows Juan's emerging capacity to make sense of disparate elements, a skill that will benefit him both in his later schooling and in his professional life. Developing an opening statement or a theory of a case are examples of how this talent would find use in the legal profession.

The books of the older children, in K–1st grade and 3rd–4th grade show a rapidly advancing trajectory of literacy, language, cognition, and expression. The first grader, Alicia, shows significantly advancing literacy. She is able to write her own story in her own words, using invented spelling when necessary. Half of the words are spelled accurately; the others show phonological consistency (e.g., "anthan" for "and then" and "far-e" for "ferry") Research indicates "evidence that supporting children to write with invented or estimated spelling generates phonological awareness as effectively as explicit curricula."[17] In later pages, she tackles more complex words: "famale" for "family" and "bathensoos" for "bathing suits." She clearly has mastered the "th" diphthong. Alicia also shows emerging differentiation between upper and lower case. Moreover, Alicia has observed and integrated the concept of hyphens (e.g., "far-e"). Her graphics and language depict the chronological events of the trip as well as her happy engagement with her family (she says "wahoo" in the car and later on a bicycle with her mom). In discussing her book with Professors Roe and Howell, Alicia described her father on the sofa watching a soccer game on TV. Her story is detailed, rich, and humorous and reflects an enjoyable family vacation. She demonstrates emerging ability in language—is clearly engaged in the process of synthesizing rules of language, syntax, spelling, and grammar—and is a confident risk taker. With the positive support of her mother and teachers, she is willing to expand her boundaries, make new connections, and bring her world increasingly under her maturing control. One can easily imagine her organizing a litigation strategy, preparing for trial, synthesizing cases, or trying out new legal theories.

In a more advanced third–fourth grade book, Marta's emerging mastery of literacy is evident. Marta writes about a trip she wants to take to Florida, to be her first. Marta's title page shows a snapshot of the beach with the sun setting over the sand, water, and crab. Her title: "My first trip to Florida." She identifies herself as "Author and Illustrator." On the back page, she adds her bio: "About the author," drawing herself as a photograph, and a telling a brief personal history. Clearly, she is familiar with and observant about books. One major advancement from the previously described "books" is that she primarily uses text, rather than images, to convey her ideas. The text of the book is spread across two facing pages, with supporting drawings, and elaborates where she wants to go, how, where she will stay, what she will do, who she will go with, and what her goals are (e.g., "I would love to see new animals in Florida.") She clearly has prior knowledge of Florida and has considered this trip. Her writing is clear, correct, grammatical, logical, thorough, and fluid. She states her theme and elaborates it thoroughly and thoughtfully. Marta can clearly state a theme and elaborate it with supporting detail in a rich and powerful way. It isn't difficult to see the foundations of legal writing, for instance writing a legal brief, in her work.

In the second of the third–fourth grade books, Felicia wrote a book for her grandfather's birthday. The book was developed in cooperation with her parents. Felicia and her grandfather are Hispanic; the text is appropriately in English and Spanish. It is illustrated with thoughtfully selected photographs of her and her grandfather engaged in various activities together, her grandfather as a younger man with Felicia's mother as a child, and other photos appropriately aligned with the text (e.g., photo with Felicia with her arms wide open, with text: "I really missed you when I didn't see you. I love you so much that I could hug you as hard as I could hug you.") Accompanying a photo of the extended family, she writes "You are the best grandpa, father, uncle, husband in the whole world!," reflecting her knowledge of the complex family structure. This book clearly depicts the value of the family both to Felicia herself and in her culture. In her work, she demonstrates the capacity to tell a rich story, complex, multidimensional, and nuanced.

The selected early elementary student works show early and emerging traces of complex thinking and expression that can develop into the level of high cognitive and expressive ability necessary for academic success in high school, university, and law school. Indeed, the development from Pre-K to fourth grade suggests a trajectory of learning that, with the proper educational opportunities and experiences in later grades, will lead to successful college, graduate and professional school, and professional life.

Very young children possess the intellectual and academic abilities that, when properly developed, can mature into the high cognitive and expressive capabilities required by legal study and practice. The act of children depicting important stories by creating written and pictorial accounts, the "books," demonstrates the power of age-appropriate, learner-centered education and the importance of developing students' voices through drawing, writing, and storytelling. In contrast to much of conventional schooling, where children are treated as recipients of meaning, in these examples the students themselves are the meaning makers. Simply put, we want our lawyers and citizens also to be meaning makers, not simply meaning reciters or repeaters.

Lawyers can work at two levels to advance this type of learning. First, they can volunteer in their community schools to read with children in learner centered and developmentally appropriate ways. Second, they can advocate for increased employment of interactive, learner-centered educational methodology in schools in order to achieve the development of highly qualified and capable learners and effective citizens desired in the legal profession and society.

"Educating for Citizenship" Law Focused Lessons

There are many "law focused" lessons designed specifically for elementary school students. These lessons typically do not address specific legal issues as they do in the high school years, but rather have to do with aspects of "legal" concepts that appear in the children's everyday life. These lessons tend to draw upon children's own lives and are geared toward children's language, ability, and experience levels, using media typical of elementary school classrooms For instance, they might feature coloring, drawing, simple role plays, children's books, hypothetical situations using children or animals, or storytelling. As in quality law-related educational lessons generally, these lessons develop not only some important content, but also age appropriate and foundational skills.

"Mess is Not Best" is a lesson that aspires to help children to learn to treat their community and their world in a respectful, environmentally sound, and systemic way. As it synthesizes the children's own sense of their own community, it differs strikingly from a more prescriptive "don't litter" type of lesson. The goal of the lesson is for students to identify good and bad aspects of their neighborhood and reflect on how to maintain or improve them.

The instructor begins by drawing on the board a house and, some distance away, a school, and then a road connecting them. The children can be provided a page with a similar graphic. There are three phases of the lesson. In the first, the instructor asks the children to think of "good things" they might see on the way to school from home, and in pairs to make a list of these "good things." Pairs are used to make the lesson fun, to generate ideas, and to engage students in collaborative practices. The pairs can make their list orally or on the paper using words or pictures. The instructor might ask for a volunteer to give an example before the groups begin. After the groups work on this for a minute or two, the instructor then asks the children to report their ideas to the whole class and writes the responses on the board as a list. One class's results included the following:

    People
    Family
    Cats and dogs
    Birds
    Friends
    Motorcycles
    Gum
    Medicine
    Nature
    Water fountain
    Food
    Fruit

In a parallel way, the instructor then asks the children to identify some "bad things" they might see. The same class's results included:

    Weapons
    Littering
    Cutting trees
    Poor people
    Ticks
    Drinking and smoking
    Weeds
    Hitting
    Screaming
    Kicking

In the second phase of the lesson, the instructor takes the children a step higher cognitively, moving from listing and classifying[18] to analyzing and reflection on their work. The instructor asks the children, "What makes the good things good?" either in the pairs or a whole class, depending on how best to have the children process the question, and writes the responses in a column next to the "good" list. Typical responses include: happy, safe, fun, feel good, beautiful, and nice. The instructor may choose to focus on particular words to bring out a specific quality, e.g., "medicine" may evoke "health." In a parallel way, the instructor then asks, "What makes the bad things bad?" Typical responses include: harmful, hurtful, unhappy, sad, angry, and ugly. Once the categories and their criteria are established, the instructor can move to deeper processing by examining terms that could possibly be in either category. For instance, "policeman" and "school" have sometimes appeared in the "bad" category. In a clear distinction from prescriptive education, where the categories and their content are specified and told to the children, here the instructor probes the reasons for why the item might be placed in one category or the other, e.g., "Why did you say "school" should be in the "bad" category? What are some things about school that might put it in the "good" list?"

In the third phase, the instructor moves from concepts into action, and from analysis to synthesis, by asking the children in larger groups of four to consider, "How do we keep the good things good?" The children take this opportunity seriously and generate numerous responses, which they report to the class as a whole. Responses might include: water the trees and plants, take care of them, be nice to people, talk with friends and do things with them, and hire people to help. The final question is, "How do we make the bad things good?" In their responses it is possible to see the seeds or the elements of the important dimensions of criminal and civil law, in ways that may be punitive, regulatory, and collaborative: take away the weapons, punish bad things, teach people to be good, pick up trash, put garbage cans around, be nice, help people or don't sell bad things.

This lesson demonstrates important dimensions of a learner-centered curriculum: students engage in a thoughtful and well-structured framework that engages the students in high levels of expression and cognition toward important learning goals. Students draw upon their own knowledge and experience and are guided to process these ideas at higher cognitive levels, based on important values, reasoning, and democratic principles. In this lesson, students not only observe and think deeply about the world around them, but also examine ways that they can positively impact on their world. The suggested actions that the students come up with in the third phase have real meaning to the students not only because the proposals are theirs, but also because throughout the lesson the students actually experience the affirmation of their own voices in the classroom. Moreover, the lesson begins to develop the concept of systemic thinking, in which forces and actions are seen as part of larger systems with complex causes and effects, not as individual or isolated events.

The overarching curricular objectives for *Educating for Citizenship* and the collection of lessons from which this portion of "Mess is Not Best" is derived, is to show the educational value and scope of this type of learning. The 15 competencies developed for children at levels of Kindergarten through fourth grade, roughly ages 4–9, could also readily serve as a blueprint for civics throughout one's education and life. The competencies and lessons of a child who is educated for democracy are highlighted in the follow chart:

1. Develops personal sense of helping, cooperating, and participating.
2. Actively listens to what another person thinks, feels and intends.
3. Recognizes there is more than one point of view than his/her own.

4. Communicates own viewpoints to another person in a group context.

5. Develops competencies in leadership roles among peers; increasingly knowledgeable and able to use democratic processes, i.e., open group discussion, due process, decision-making strategies, voting, compromising.

6. Collects accurate information, begins to organize it systematically

7. Develops an increasing degree of personal freedom and self-discipline based on a reasoned approach to making choices, determining personal values, learning limits set by supportive authority.

8. Begins to understand the need for rules, laws, and the processes for democratically making and changing rules/laws in the group life of the classroom, local settings.

9. Is increasingly knowledgeable about citizen-oriented subject matter; for example, poverty, racism, environmental protection, scarcity of resources, conflict, global interdependence.

10. Clarifies misconceptions through questioning, observing, comparing with accurate information.

11. Demonstrates a reasoned approach to conflict situations and can apply due process and advocacy techniques for constructive change.

12. Is able to assume a viewpoint other than his/her own and views self from that vantage point; "putting himself in someone else's shoes," gaining a sense of mutuality of roles.

13. Is able to alter behavior to achieve and promote more effective personal relationships.

14. Recognizes reciprocal influences people have on each other's thoughts, feelings, and behavior.

15. Distinguishes the political and governmental world from other areas of life and has knowledge of the general purpose and functions of government.

These objectives and others like them, such as the ABA's "Essentials for Law Related Education," align nicely with the overarching principles for high quality education in elementary school set out in the next section.

General Principles for Teaching, Learning, and Literacy Link to Democratic Education

This chapter began by asking whether lawyers and legal educators could be competent and effective in the role of teachers in an elementary school classroom. The answer is a resounding "yes"—when the lawyer understands his/her role is in a sense like the role of a lawyer in a direct examination. The student, like the witness, is the star. While the lessons should be carefully conceived and prepared, the goal is for the children to do the intellectual and expressive work, the thinking, and the talking. This is because the goals and methods of civic education, where the principles of due process, respect for the human personality in all its variation and diversity, and fundamental democratic values such as fairness and justice are not just talked about but put into practice in the classroom and larger school environment.

The principles of a democratic, due process model of instruction correspond closely with the principles and best practices of quality education and literacy development generally. The core, driving concept of learner centered or student centered learning has to do with the "nature of the learning process[:] The learning of complex subject matter is most effective when it is an intentional process of constructing meaning from experience."[19] The learner creates his/her own "cognitive structures," the learner's way of organizing his/her knowledge and experience in a conceptual framework. Learning is best understood not simply as putting facts and ideas into one's cognitive structure, but more significantly as shaping and building one's cognitive structure as learning progresses. Learning, then, is a process, not just a product. Put another way, the process *is* the product. Teachers and schools can greatly influence this process, but ultimately one's cognitive structure is one's own creation. This view is both derived from and supported by educational research where "one of the primary characteristics of the new science of learning [is] its focus on the process of knowing."[20] This principle is echoed in recommendations for teaching and teachers. For example, the framework of "what should be taught ... (knowledge-centeredness) and "who learns, how and why (learner-centeredness)" was adopted in a leading book on teacher education.[21] It is also central to policy recommendations and books on children's literacy. For example, the National Association for the Education of Young Children observes that "[y]oung children especially need to be engaged in experiences that make academic content meaningful and build on prior learning ... Such access is even more critical for children with limited home experiences in literacy."[22] The examples in this chapter of Marco's "book" and those of the other children at LAMB reflect this principle.

While a number of other important learning principles, such as the significance of motivation, social contexts, and individual differences and diversity are worth noting for their mutual interconnectedness between civics and best educational practices generally, a second major concept stands out: the primacy of "learning how to learn" or metacognition. The National Research Council includes as the third of its three key findings: "A 'metacognitive' approach to instruction can help students learn to take control of their own learning by defining learning goals and monitoring their progress in achieving them."[23] Reflecting and thinking about learning in both strategic and larger conceptual senses is as important to learning as thinking about governance is to civics, or reflecting about justice is to lawyering. At the end of a lesson, students should consider not only what was learned, but also why it was learned, how it was learned, and how it fits into the larger picture of the way the world works or should work.

In conclusion, this chapter sets out two levels of potential involvement lawyers and other legal professionals could bring to elementary education: literacy development and law focused, developmentally appropriate teaching. They can do this either in the classroom directly or as advocates of education generally. These approaches correspond well with the theory and practice of quality teaching and learning. Through learner-centered methodology along with this due process, democratic model, classrooms and schools can be transformed into places where every child can develop toward his/her full potential as a learner. This holds the promise of leading to fuller civic participation in society, greater academic success throughout schooling, and greater representation of the full diversity of our nation's population in the legal profession.

Chapter 3

Law Firm-Sponsored Elementary School

Legacy Charter School
Chicago, Illinois

Errol Stone*

Pre-K	Elementary	Middle	High School	College	Law School	Profession

The Legacy Charter School is a unique partnership between SNR Denton (formerly Sonnenschein, Nath & Rosenthal LLP) and an African-American inner-city neighborhood. In 2005, SNR started a charter elementary school in Chicago. The charter started with just over 100 students in pre-kindergarten–second grade and has added two to four classrooms, and one grade, per year, to a point where Legacy's enrollment is now approaching 500 students and is still growing. Legacy's philosophy and approach is in every way consistent with current research and effective practices for 21st-century learning; it has meaningful and engaged partners, it has only high expectations, it offers a carefully crafted, rigorous, and relevant curriculum, and it provides engaging supplemental educational opportunities. While they may not call it this, the leadership and staff are also committed to providing day-to-day due process to students, giving them notice and opportunity to be heard and, thus, modeling and teaching communication skills and values. The accomplishments of the Legacy Scholars, as the students are called, and their school, show these commitments. Legacy is indeed what Errol Stone calls a Bold Vision, a large-scale commitment to a partnership that offers a premier model for those willing and able to make a sustained and long-term commitment of a wide variety of resources.

A Bold Vision

After more than a century as a leading Chicago-based—and then national—law firm, Sonnenschein Nath & Rosenthal, now SNR Denton ("SNR"), made a mark, be-

---

* Partner, SNR Denton US LLP and Chairman of the Board, Legacy Charter School. As of September 30, 2010, Sonnenschein Nath & Rosenthal LLP combined with Denton Wilde Sapte LLP and became SNR Denton. © 2010 Errol Stone.

yond the world of law, that could be as important as any groundbreaking legal case the Firm ever handled. With the approach of SNR's 2006 centennial, the Firm's leaders were casting about for ways to mark the event in a manner that conveyed the depth of their appreciation for the city where SNR had first opened its doors. Recognizing the centrality of education, the Firm established programs to support education in all of the cities where it was located, in Chicago and nationally. The boldest of these was Legacy Charter School. What better way, they reasoned, to mark the Firm's century of growth and achievement, than to establish an outstanding inner-city elementary school. With that inspiration as a guide, the Firm established Legacy in Chicago in 2005. Legacy started with just over 100 students, in pre-K through second grade. With about 450 "scholars," as students are known, set to enroll at Legacy in fall 2010 in pre-K through seventh grade, the school is on track to enroll some 500 scholars in pre-K through eighth grade in the 2011–12 school year.

Mission and Guiding Principles

Legacy Charter School's mission is to create an outstanding center for teaching and learning for children and their families that recognizes and nurtures the full potential of every child, provides a foundation for a college education, and educates students to be creative and critical thinkers, and responsible citizens in school, at home, and in the community.

Legacy believes that education should embrace the ability and potential of each child and should emphasize both social-emotional growth and academic achievement. Legacy also maintains that high-quality elementary education must prepare students to be lifelong learners and independent thinkers who can apply knowledge from many disciplines to solve problems. In the 21st century, people with a college education will continue to have far more choices and opportunities. Therefore, Legacy believes elementary education should motivate and begin to prepare students for success in college, and it must teach the foundations of a just society, along with ethics and values that prepare and encourage students to participate in the global community with wisdom, understanding, and honesty. To emphasize these aspirations and assumptions, Legacy students are referred to, by the Legacy community and by themselves, as "scholars," as a means to elevate academic expectations and instill a sense of self-respect. Since a high-quality education can have its greatest impact if it begins at an early age, Legacy starts at pre-K. The school is open to all Chicago children, charges no tuition, and has no entrance exams.

Community and Demographics

Legacy is located on the west side of Chicago in the overwhelmingly African-American, inner-city neighborhood of North Lawndale. The median income of a North Lawndale resident, according to 2000 U.S. Census figures, is approximately $18,000, less than half the city-wide median income of approximately $39,000. Nearly 70% of men in

North Lawndale between the ages of 18 and 45 have an involvement with the criminal justice system (i.e., prison, probation, or parole). Ninety-nine percent of Legacy's scholars are African American and about 95% are eligible for free or reduced-cost lunches.

Size and Growth Strategy

Legacy opened its doors in August 2005 to 102 scholars in pre-K through second grade, with one classroom per grade and two teachers per classroom. From the outset, a low student/teacher ratio permitted a large amount of personalized attention. In Legacy's first year, the student/teacher ratio was 10:1, with 24 scholars in each classroom except for pre-K, which had 20. Having two teachers per classroom allowed Legacy to develop teachers trained in the Legacy approach in the first year so that it could double the classrooms per grade in the second year. In the 2006–07 school year, Legacy doubled in size, expanding to two classrooms in pre-K through second grade and adding a third grade classroom. Every year since, Legacy has added at least two new classrooms, and a new grade level. In the 2010–11 school year, classroom size has increased to 26 scholars in each classroom, from kindergarten to fifth grade, and the student/teacher ratio will be about 14:1. Legacy also decided to significantly expand its sixth grade in the 2009–10 school year. In that school year, departing from its previous practice of having a single class in the highest grade, the school added two sixth grade classrooms, thereby, achieving more critical mass in middle school, and facilitating subject area specialization by teachers.

Administration

The SNR Role

In starting the school, SNR pledged $1 million over five years to fund the planning and creation of Legacy, and an additional $3 million toward the design and construction of a new school building. Legacy is believed to be the first charter school to be sponsored and so extensively supported by a law firm. In addition to providing funding and in-kind contributions, such as technology and furniture, SNR, and its personnel, offers extensive operational and management support. The Firm handles accounting, budgeting, payroll, and check-writing; technology management; human resources and marketing services; and, of course, legal representation. The Firm's personnel also volunteer as weekly tutors, teach in various programs, clean and paint classrooms, contribute to holiday gifts, share hobbies such as chess, quilting and guitar, and act as judges at school events.

SNR provides substantial management support, largely (but certainly not exclusively) through my involvement. For the past seven years, with the Firm's support and encouragement, I have spent virtually all of my working time on Legacy. Although my title is Board Chair, that title does not really describe what I do. I believe that SNR and I have a unique engagement with Legacy. I am deeply involved in management of the school. Although it may not be the first thing that one thinks of, starting and operating a school involves lots of business expertise, which I bring to the school. The extremely close working relationship that I have with Lisa Kenner, Legacy's principal, provides an excellent foundation of both academic and business expertise for building the school.

In addition to traditional Board Chair roles, such as fundraising, I have a major involvement in managing the financial side of the school and supervising, or jointly supervising (with Ms. Kenner), key personnel involved in that area. Ms. Kenner and I confer multiple times a day about virtually any significant issue affecting the school, including our search for a permanent facility (which I head up), and financial, personnel, student discipline, facilities, and technology questions. I defer to Ms. Kenner on academic issues and she to me on financial issues, but we both ask questions about, and discuss, everything. Our intense collaboration results in a far better school.

Ms. Kenner and I meet with every teacher and staff member for an annual review. Ms. Kenner focuses on performance evaluation, and I on compensation issues. I also typically attend teacher/staff meetings and frequently make presentations on major issues, such as our budget.

I believe that I cannot effectively manage or even govern the school without firsthand knowledge and experiential understanding of what goes on there. Therefore, I visit classrooms and go to various special programs, like Legacy Circle and the Science Fair. I also tutor reading and math once a week and teach a law-related program to fifth graders.

Other SNR lawyers teach at Legacy, via the Junior Achievement and Lawyers in the Classroom programs. The Junior Achievement program is a business and economics curriculum for students in kindergarten through eighth grade. There is a different curriculum for each grade, covering such subjects as our families, our community, our city, our region, and our nation. The curriculum is "hands-on" and provides an excellent opportunity for SNR lawyers to share their experience and knowledge with the scholars. The Lawyers in the Classroom program is coordinated by the Constitutional Rights Foundation Chicago and helps students understand the U.S. Constitution and legal system. This program culminates in a moot court presentation by the students at our offices and in a visit to an actual court room. These are enriching experiences for the Legacy scholars and their SNR teachers.

Legacy scholars feel "at home" at SNR's office in the Willis (formerly Sears) Tower. One day, I received a call from a third grade teacher asking if the class could come visit. Thinking that this was planning for a future field trip, I said "Of course." The teacher said, "Great, we're in the lobby, we'll be right up." Legacy scholars get exposure to the corporate world that most children in North Lawndale never get. This experience broadens their horizons and gives them confidence in their abilities.

Staff

The Legacy staff consists of a principal, assistant principal/dean of academics, social worker, dean of scholars, 35 teachers, and other staff, all supplemented by SNR and other volunteers. In addition to classroom teachers, the school has intervention teachers, who work with scholars in small groups to provide additional instruction. We also have two special education teachers, a music teacher, a visual arts teacher, an oratory teacher, and a physical education teacher. More than 90% of Legacy's staff has returned for the past three school years. Such stability is rare and is very important to Legacy's success.

Legacy's talented and hardworking teachers have won numerous awards, including the Kohl McCormick Early Childhood Teaching Award. Another teacher was a quarter-finalist in the statewide Golden Apple Award. Legacy's teachers have also consistently received grants to conduct professional development study groups, which have been very successful. Two teachers are National Board Certified, which means they have met rigorous standards through intensive study, expert evaluation, self-assessment, and peer review.

Legacy's exceptional Principal is a graduate of the innovative and much-lauded New Leaders for New Schools program, and its Dean of Academics was a primary consultant and developer of the STEP assessment and devotes much of her time to professional development and meeting regularly with teachers to discuss strategies that focus on the process of learning, as well as on the outcome. Part of the school's success stems from having a highly dedicated and extremely qualified staff.

Budget

Legacy's funding originated with SNR, but now includes a variety of sources. The largest source of funding that Legacy receives is public funding. Most funding is on a per student basis and is not sufficient to cover all of Legacy's operating costs. This was especially true during the early startup years. During the startup period, a school needs to cover more of the fixed costs (such as the principal and other key staff members) with lower revenues because of the per capita funding, which obviously produces less revenue when there are fewer students. In addition, a lot of furniture and equipment, as well as educational supplies, especially books, need to be purchased as each grade starts. The $1 million contribution from SNR was essential to covering these startup expenses, but would not have been sufficient by itself. We also received additional governmental funding for startup costs, as well as significant grants from foundations and individuals for startup costs. In addition, we fundraise for annual operations and receive support from various foundations and individuals for this. Most of our focus in fundraising so far has been to build up funds to pay for a new facility. We have received support from a variety of individuals and foundations for this and have accumulated pledges of about $8,500,000 to date.

Curriculum and Approach

Curriculum

Legacy's curriculum serves the interests of the whole child. With emphasis on both academic achievement and social-emotional growth, Legacy is helping scholars learn to draw conclusions and make good decisions, to interpret meaning, and to be of service to others. The rigorous academic curriculum is standards-based, presented through differentiated instruction guided by regularly scheduled assessment, with an emphasis on critical thinking and intellectual acceleration.

Legacy has an extended school year and a regular weekly schedule that is approximately 25 percent longer than that of most Chicago Public Schools (CPS) district schools. Teachers have more time to offer varied instructional approaches that are geared toward the "whole" child, building self-awareness and social awareness, healthy relationships, responsible decision making, and self-management skills. Scholars have longer periods of engagement in diverse disciplines. Music, graphic, oratory and performing arts, physical education, frequent study trips, and special programs (including Junior Achievement and Lawyers in the Classroom, mentioned previously) are all integral parts of the curriculum. Scholars learn by making and experiencing visual arts and by understanding and appreciating music and physical education. These experiences allow scholars to build skills with new materials, explore different ways of expressing ideas, and deepen their critical thinking.

In addition to the regular curriculum, Legacy offers All Community Explorations (ACE). ACE classes are small, multi-age groups of scholars that meet on Friday afternoons for seven weeks during the fourth quarter of the school year. Topics include music recording, improv, theater, gardening, jewelry making, cooking, poetry, recycling, and cheerleading. Offerings at the school also include a computer lab, daytime and after-school tutoring, and after-school activities such as knitting, chess, and yoga.

The culmination of all of these activities is the Legacy Circle, which enhances and reinforces the academic program. The weekly school-wide gathering celebrates scholar participation and achievement. An important part of the school's culture, Legacy Circle involves impromptu public speaking by scholars and sharing of their work and ideas. This school-wide recognition of individual scholar achievement provides strong, positive reinforcement for the scholar's best efforts. Legacy Circle also provides an opportunity for scholars to recognize other scholars who have demonstrated good citizenship and academic achievement, to show respect for the accomplishments of others, and to learn to receive compliments and praise.

Educational Projects

Many additional projects offered throughout the school illustrate the learning that goes on at Legacy. A number of classes have emphasized learning about history, especially the cause and effect of events over time. Following are some examples:

- Legacy kindergarteners spent weeks developing their own timeline of President Barack Obama's life and path to the White House. The timeline is approximately 4 feet high and 14 feet long and covers the wall outside the kindergarten rooms. The timeline is written in the scholars' own words and contains clippings selected by them and drawings made by them, recording President Obama's early childhood, his education, and his books. The timeline was a hands-on learning experience that personalized our President and showed the connection between his childhood and education and his success. This message is obviously one that Legacy wants to communicate. In addition, a group of scholars assisted the art teacher in planning, installing, and acting as docents for an art exhibit of scholar artwork; all of this builds a wonderful learning community in which everyone—of all ages—participates as a learner and a teacher. Also highlighting Legacy's responsible citizenship theme, scholars voted for President, but only if they had properly registered to vote.

- The second graders constructed personal timelines of their lives, based on family interviews, using a computer-generated template. A number of them are quite moving, reflecting the challenges and victories of our scholars' families. This is a wonderful integration of technology into social studies. Scholars in the second grade also learn about the Underground Railroad and how ordinary people faced injustices. Each year, they study a new original play (written by their teachers) and perform it for the entire school. One year, the play was based on the life and times of Henry, a slave who used his ingenuity and determination to escape to freedom, as retold in the book, Henry and the Freedom Box. In another year, the class produced an original film based on Harriet Tubman's life.

- After a presentation by two practicing journalists, scholars in the fourth grade worked on a newspaper project and produced their own newspaper. The class focused on understanding why writers write and what is newsworthy. The fourth grade scholars culminated their study of the American civil rights unit by writing, producing, and performing for the entire school, a play illustrating the profound inequities of segregation and explaining the collective actions that led to increased access to education and other opportunities for African Americans. The audience was deeply moved and affected by the performance. Recognizing the play's richness as a teaching tool, a local high school invited the fourth graders to perform the play there. This type of teaching, which results in authentic demonstrations of learning, allows the audience (parents, scholars, faculty, and staff) to be educated, moved, and inspired along with the actors and writers. The scholars' confidence and learning was exhilarating to behold.

- The sixth grade science class did a unit on the oil spill in the Gulf of Mexico. They worked in teams to design ways to cap the gushing well and then tested their designs by lowering their devices into a long cylinder. Video cameras at the bottom of the cylinders simulated the effect of remote underwater control and allowed them to see the effectiveness of their designs. The sixth graders competed and were judged in a Science Fair, which allowed them to demonstrate their knowledge of the scientific method. The entire school community visited the Science Fair, which served as a springboard to the world of scientific exploration at all grade levels. The rest of the school had the opportunity to demonstrate knowledge and understanding of science in Legacy's school-wide Science Exploration Day. Although the program was not "judged," it provided an opportunity for scholars to demonstrate and explain increasingly sophisticated science concepts. Over the course of a day, scholars visited all the exhibits and asked questions, with first graders explaining to sixth graders what their experiments were about, and sixth graders doing the same in return. It was thrilling to see this interaction.

- Legacy holds a Book Fair twice a year. As a reward for completing the Illinois Standards Achievement Test (ISAT), scholars were entitled to select a book at the fair. The excitement about reading was so intense that scholars were bumping into each other because they had their noses in their books while walking the hallways. They even brought their books to breakfast and lunch to read and compare.

- Legacy also holds an annual Spelling Bee, inspired by the scholars reading Akeelah and the Bee. SNR client, Allstate Insurance, sends personnel to tutor students and run a mock bee on the Saturday before the actual event. Allstate employees serve as judges and a cheering section. The preparation helps advance the scholars' learning and makes the bee far more productive. Finalists receive dictionaries or thesauruses from Allstate. The scholars do extremely well, not simply in spelling some very difficult words, but in displaying composure and acceptance of the outcomes. One of the most gratifying aspects of the Spelling Bee is how well the scholars support and encourage one another.

Leadership and Problem Solving (Discipline)

Legacy's high expectations for its scholars are reflected in its approach to discipline. When a fifth grade scholar stole a laptop, he was required to attend an "honor board" (in addition to receiving a one-week suspension). Accompanied by his mother and older sister, the scholar attended the honor board and discussed what had happened with the Principal, a special education teacher, a Legacy father (who is a retired Chicago police officer), and me. The scholar participated fully in this open and candid discussion, acknowledged that he had breached the trust of the school and of his family, and understood why this was a serious matter. By the end of the discussion, everyone was close to tears. I subsequently received a sincere and moving "thank you" note, in which, the scholar wrote, "I promise to take the words that we discussed and apply it to my life." Legacy's approach in such circumstances is unusual. In most schools, the student would have been disciplined and simply written off. Legacy instead turned the incident into an opportunity for learning and change, with a lasting impact. The approach requires a huge investment of time, but is well worth it.

Another example: When three fourth graders had a loud, emotional argument that was the culmination of an ongoing conflict, Ms. Kenner asked two fifth grade scholars to help resolve it. The five scholars went to the Principal's office alone. When she returned to her office a half hour later, Ms. Kenner found a note signed by all five scholars that read, "We solved the problem. Thank you for letting us use your office." The issue has never resurfaced. In most schools, adults would take charge of a situation like this and determine the consequences. Legacy scholars are authorized and empowered, and are expected to make good choices and to fix a problem arising from a failure to make good choices. High expectations, trust, and independence can and does lead to meaningful results.

Legacy scholars are taught that their voice is important and that they should participate as responsible citizens in the school community. They also learn "stage presence" and self-confidence at the weekly Legacy Circle, in oratory class (in which they practice oral presentation and speech writing), and other speaking opportunities. A recent example of how this translates into action: Part of the charter renewal process was a public hearing in the very imposing CPS board room in downtown Chicago. A fifth grade scholar, J'Khai, accompanied his mother, who came to speak at the hearing and didn't have childcare for him. When J'Khai arrived at the hearing he asked if he could speak. The official summary of the hearing stated: "The student likes the curriculum. Discipline is handled in a spirit of cooperation and not harsh. The teachers talk to him. He is changing his past and improving his future. Teachers help him if he is failing. He was below in reading and they took him out [of class for individual work] to help him understand how to do it. They are trying to prepare him for college." This says it all about Legacy. J'Khai has learned that his voice matters, and he feels empowered to express himself, even in a potentially intimidating atmosphere. He knows he is "changing his past and improving his future." What more can anyone ask of the scholars or of ourselves?

Parental and Community Engagement

Legacy encourages a high level of parental involvement, through parent support of school-wide events and parent collaboration with teachers to set individual learning goals. At Legacy Circle, parents are often invited to share their hopes and aspirations for their children. These parent testimonials are moving and inspirational. Legacy has also made a particular effort to engage fathers. One father has thrilled the community at Legacy Circle on two occasions, sharing his original rap about global diversity and the responsibilities of ordinary people. Another father, who is also a spoken word artist, performed with his fourth grade daughter a poem/song that debunks negative stereotypes of poverty and people of color titled "Good in the Hood." The performance brought down the house. Curriculum nights, numerous events and celebrations, and goal-setting conferences also are well attended by families. Semiannual goal-setting conferences involve the scholar, family, and teacher. A specific social-emotional and academic goal for each scholar is determined in these conferences. In many classrooms, these goals hang on the wall. Our Parent Leaders have organized a successful fundraiser, popular skating event, movie nights, and family education programs, and they direct traffic outside the school every day. Parent and family engagement and involvement are critical to our scholars' success.

On the second to last day of school, Legacy holds awards ceremonies—one for each grade level grouping. Each classroom comes onto the stage separately, and each scholar is presented with an award certificate. Upon leaving the stage, each scholar shakes my hand. The certificates, presented by the teachers, are highly personalized and describe each scholar's strengths. Ms. Kenner instructs all scholars in advance on how to receive a certificate and shake hands, explicitly as preparation for receiving their diplomas in at least three graduations—eighth grade at Legacy, high school, and college. Then, Ms. Kenner asks family members who are present to come up and face the scholars and speak about their hopes and aspirations for their scholars. They speak about the importance of education, hard work, goal setting, and college. Most often, they profusely thank the teachers, the Principal, and Legacy. There are a substantial number of family members, including fathers and grandfathers present, even though this occurs during the workday. Much of what is said to the scholars is extremely moving and demonstrates that these families clearly understand the importance of the education that their children are receiving at Legacy.

Legacy also stresses community engagement and service. Since Legacy's start, SNR personnel have donated money to purchase holiday gifts for Legacy scholars and Levy Home Entertainment has donated books. Although Legacy scholars joyfully receive these gifts, the school teaches the importance of giving as well. Scholars have held a food drive and mitten tree for local families in need. One December, a busload of fourth and fifth graders went to a nursing home and brought books to read to the seniors. The scholars connected with aged, ailing seniors on an intensive-needs floor in such a profound way that the nursing home staff spread the word, and people kept coming in to witness this. The experience was marvelous for scholars and faculty, supporting empathy, social justice, the power of literacy, and communication among generations.

This is just one example of scholar engagement in the community. Scholars also initiated fund raising efforts for Hurricane Katrina and Haitian earthquake victims, as well as food drives for the local community and a read-a-thon for a community charity.

The Results

Scholar Achievement

Legacy has strong student participation and persistence. About 90% of scholars have returned for the past 3 school years, an exceptionally high rate. Legacy's scores on the ISAT, for the 2009–10 school year, reflect consistent academic improvement at the school. The school's composite score was 79.6% meeting or exceeding grade level. This result is up from 73.4% the prior year, which was itself a 16.3 percentage point increase over school year 2007–08. The scores by subject matter were 72.8% meeting or exceeding grade level in reading, 84.9% meeting or exceeding in math, and 85.4% meeting or exceeding in science. By way of comparison, CPS's composite meet-or-exceed score was 69.5%, and its scores by subject matter were 65.3% in reading, 75.1% in math, and 65.3% in science. These CPS scores are for all of CPS, which includes selective enrollment schools and other schools with very different demographics from Legacy. Notwithstanding that difference, Legacy exceeded all of these scores. Legacy's performance far exceeds the average that the CPS calculates for the district schools that Legacy's scholars would most likely have attended if they were not with us. According to CPS' 2008–09 Performance Report (the most recent one we have), the average composite score for those schools was 56.6%.

To assess reading in pre-K through second grade, Legacy uses the Strategic Teaching and Evaluation of Progress (STEP) assessment. STEP is a developmental literacy assessment, tightly aligned with scientifically established milestones in reading development, which includes a set of tools to follow the students' progress. This assessment, developed at the University of Chicago, sets a much higher bar than the ISAT for grade level achievement. In fact, when Legacy has tested the same scholars using STEP and the ISAT, being at grade level on STEP roughly corresponded to "exceeding grade level" on ISAT. The percentage of Legacy scholars who ended school year 2009–10 at STEP grade level was 93% in pre-K, 75% in kindergarten, 58% in first grade, and 51% in second grade. These remarkable scores highlight Legacy's long-term potential. As these scholars advance up the grades, these tests suggest that their performance will be outstanding and their academic opportunities will be substantial as they move on to high school and college. Because of this achievement level in the 2009–10 school year, Legacy had to significantly revamp its first grade curriculum since the former kindergarten scholars were entering first grade so well prepared.

More significant in many ways than test scores are the assessments that Legacy receives from educators who visit the school. These educators have had high praise for the school, describing it as remarkable, praising the scholars' engagement and focus on learning, the high expectations of all, and the use of best practices.

Legacy scholars have also been noticed outside of the school. For example, a fourth grade teacher and one parent chaperone took 24 fourth grade scholars on a research study trip to the city's Harold Washington Library, where the scholars received nearly a dozen compliments from library staff. The staff member who gave a presentation about the basics of research was impressed with their knowledge of various books and authors. She also complimented their behavior and their ability to express themselves. Because the group was so large, they were escorted from one area to the next by a security guard who said, "I was not looking forward to another school group, they are always loud, out of control, and don't listen; I don't know why teachers even bring them. But this group has proved me wrong." The librarian said the scholars' natural love of books and knowledge made her want to cry and that she was amazed how well they worked together and how quiet they were during a library scavenger hunt. She also said she saw some future librarians among them. As they left the library, another security guard on a different floor commented that a "buzz" had made its way around the library about how well the children behaved. She quipped, "What school is this? I need to sign my grandchildren up."

Awards and Recognition

Every five years, a Chicago charter school must renew its charter. Legacy went through the renewal process in the 2009–10 school year, which resulted in the Chicago Board of Education voting to renew Legacy's charter for another five-year term. A key part of the renewal process is a two-day renewal site visit (RSV) by a team of reviewers from SchoolWorks and Chicago Public Schools (CPS). The educational consultants from SchoolWorks have evaluated roughly two-thirds of CPS charter schools, as well as many other schools in the U.S. and around the world. During the two-day (almost 20 hours) visit in November, the team observed classes, conducted numerous focus groups with school leaders, teachers, staff, board members, parents and scholars, and reviewed voluminous materials, including Legacy's charter renewal application.

At the conclusion of the two-day visit, the team reported that best practices permeated and directed all that Legacy does and that, unlike many other schools, Legacy actually lives its mission. One consultant said that Legacy was her "dream" as an educational reformer—a school that she knew was possible, but had not seen. The other consultant repeatedly called Legacy "thrilling" and "stunning." They described Ms. Kenner, as "visionary" and the rest of the leadership as outstanding. Delia Rico, the Assistant Principal/Dean of Academics, "knocked their socks off." The team commented that teachers said they had "blossomed" at Legacy and that, although the work was hard and stressful, they wouldn't want to be anywhere else.

The review team used a rubric to determine to what extent instruction promotes higher order thinking. The rubric typically results in scores in the 15–20 percent range; at a "good" school, the average is about 40%. At Legacy, the review team judged the result to be 85%, with 96% of the instruction at a nationally appropriate grade level.

In a parent focus group, according to the consultants, parents teared up talking about how important Legacy was to their children. In the scholar focus group, scholars said "everyone" at Legacy was responsible for their education. The team repeatedly said that it was a "privilege" to have been at Legacy. They noted that there is lots of love at Legacy and called Legacy a "Chicago treasure" that other educators should see.

In April, Legacy received the RSV Report, which was detailed, specific, and enormously affirming of the school. The Report said the two-day RSV "revealed an unwavering commitment to the school's mission, focus on teaching and learning, and an extraordinary place for all to get better at what they do." Ms. Kenner was described as someone who "effectively empowers all staff to participate in continuous refinement of the school." Classroom instruction was described as "rigorous and meaningful to scholars," and school leaders and teachers were said to "display a deep knowledge of scholars' academic and social progress." Legacy was described as "an authentic learning community" and "an outstanding school" with a "uniquely supportive climate and culture, exceptional leadership and commitment among stakeholders, and an unyielding belief in each scholar's potential." The Report noted that "governance provides competent stewardship and oversight of the school, has intimate knowledge of scholars, staff and school programs, and demonstrates an acute awareness of the challenges that lie ahead. The exceedingly effective school/business partnership is instrumental to school development and operations and can serve as a model for other school business partnerships." Overall, the Report is a remarkable affirmation of what Legacy has accomplished and what it has contributed to education.

Legacy was one of 30 schools in Illinois, and one of nine in Chicago, to receive both the 2009 Academic Improvement Award and to be recognized as a 2009 Illinois Spotlight School by the Illinois Honor Roll. Developed by Northern Illinois University and the Illinois State Board of Education in 2003, the Illinois Honor Roll each year celebrates the accomplishments of exemplary Illinois public schools. The Academic Improvement Award goes to schools that have made substantial gains in performance over the past three years and demonstrate that exemplary progress is possible at every level and can be sustained. Illinois Spotlight Schools are high-poverty schools, where high academic performance is closing the "achievement gap." These schools are honored for exhibiting achievements that are contrary to the conventional wisdom that test scores will reflect demographics, despite local efforts.

Parent–Scholar Testimonials

At the end of each school year, CPS conducts a parent survey called "My Voice, My School." The results from school year 2008–09 showed that more than twice as many Legacy parents, compared with the CPS average, described their level of satisfaction with the quality of the academics and the environment at the school as "excellent." Legacy also conducts its own survey of family satisfaction and had similar highly positive responses, with parents stressing excellent communication with teachers and the school, and praising the school's support for academic progress and social-emotional growth. In school year 2009–10, Legacy surveyed its third through sixth grade scholars to learn their opinions about the school. The scholars were overwhelmingly happy at Legacy and said they feel challenged by the work. Following are some scholars' comments on what they most enjoy about Legacy: "We get to do awesome things" (third grade); "Teachers really support us and explain things in a better way" (fourth grade); "Teachers push my thinking" (fourth grade); "[I am] supported to do things independently" (fifth grade); and "[I'm] learning a lot" (sixth grade). This high level of parental and scholar satisfaction, combined with outstanding teaching, is what makes Legacy so special.

Thoughts on Replicability

I was asked to comment on the "replicability" of Legacy, i.e., the creation of additional schools or campuses based on the original model. Replication, at least directly, is not an option for Legacy. The original 15 charters, granted within the City of Chicago, allowed the addition of multiple campuses under the original charter. Subsequent charters permit only one campus. Since Legacy is not among the original 15 charter holders, it is not able to replicate and we have operated on the assumption that we would have only one campus. Replication, like the expansion of any business, can bring great benefits or significant problems. If we were able to replicate, I believe it would be a very difficult question for us.

Some replication efforts have been highly successful, others have not been. I would think that it is very important to have your core school solidly and reliably performing before one even considers replication. In addition, a management structure needs to be built to manage a multi-campus operation, which would be different from the structure needed to manage a single school. I am keenly aware of how much time and effort it takes to build a single high-quality school and that the work at Legacy is by no means done at this point, although we have been at it for about seven years. Although creating additional campuses based on an existing model is undoubtedly easier than starting from scratch, there would still be a huge amount to do. In particular, hiring the right teachers and staff is enormously time intensive, regardless of whether you are following an existing model. Replication does offer the opportunity to increase the impact of a successful school and to realize economies of scale. Replication also produces "scalability," which has become very important to many philanthropists and, thus, it can be easier to raise money for a replicating school than a single campus one, such as Legacy.

Legacy's goal is for its educational model, and its education-business partnership, to have an impact beyond Legacy. Indeed, as indicated above, our recent renewal site visit report commented that Legacy should be a model for others. Currently, we are committed to building Legacy into as fine a school as possible. This is more than a full time job. We hope to have broader influence by having others observe Legacy and adopt some of its best practices.

Conclusion

Potentially, Legacy is a pipeline to many careers, including law, and to a life of learning and responsible citizenship. At a recent discussion of high school readiness, Legacy scholars spoke about their career ambitions. Along with becoming a lawyer, they listed doctor, physicist, and teacher. The education they are receiving at Legacy will pave the way for many opportunities. Legacy believes that lives are being changed and saved.

Chapter 4

Law School-Sponsored Mentoring

Brigham Young University
Provo, Utah

Brett G. Scharffs*, Jana B. Eliason†, Rachel A. Miller‡

Pre-K	Elementary	Middle	High School	College	Law School	Profession

The Brigham Young mentoring program is the "grandparent" of law school pipeline mentoring programs, serving as the model for the McGeorge program and many others. Focused on sixth grade, it has a remarkable record and is beloved within the law school community and the community at large. It is an excellent example of a low-cost program that offers partnerships between law students and younger students, giving all of them a stronger understanding of the value of education and giving the younger students a chance to develop an interest in the legal profession.

* Professor Scharffs is the Francis R. Kirkham Professor of Law, J. Reuben Clark Law School, Brigham Young University. B.S.B.A., M.A., Georgetown University; B.Phil Oxford University; J.D. Yale Law School. Professor Scharffs thanks the successive generations of BYU Law student volunteers who have participated in this program, the capable and responsible second and third year students who have managed it, and the teachers and students at Sunset Elementary School and Wasatch Elementary School who have participated. He also thanks Cora Barrett from the Provo School District for her unflinching support, and Rachel Miller and Jana Eliason for their exceptional stewardship of the program over the past two years, and for their work on the survey and this chapter. Professor Scharffs particularly thanks Professor Sarah Redfield for her visionary thinking and leadership with the Wingspread initiative, which has brought to light the failings of the legal academy and the legal profession with respect to pipeline and diversity issues and, more importantly, is focusing attention on the many good programs that have been designed and implemented to help address this problem.

† J.D. Candidate, J. Reuben Clark Law School, Brigham Young University (2011). Jana Eliason would like to thank the faculty at BYU, particularly Professor Scharffs, who promote service and the spirit of mentoring. Special thanks to all of the law student volunteers, the fifth graders, the wonderful teachers, and Cora Berrett for all of their work and support.

‡ J.D. Candidate, J. Reuben Clark Law School, Brigham Young University (2011). Rachel Miller would like to thank the numerous teachers, professors, friends, and co-workers who have been her mentors. Their generous gifts of time, a listening ear, and thoughtful advice have set an example as she continues forward. Also, special thanks to Cynthia and Samantha, Wasatch Elementary School fifth graders, who, during her 1L year, made Tuesdays at noon one of the best hours of each law school week.

Abstract

Over the past thirteen years, the Brigham Young University Law School Mentoring Program has provided more than 20,000 hours of one-on-one mentoring to more than 1,000 elementary school students by law school student volunteers. Each year, nearly one hundred fifth or sixth graders come to the law school each Tuesday from noon to one o'clock, for ten weeks in the fall and ten weeks in the spring. Each child works with the same law student mentor for the entire school year, receiving academic support and, more importantly, coming to view themselves not as visitors but as belonging in a university environment. The total cost to the Law School has been about $1,500.00— not per year, but over the entire thirteen years the program has been operating. This translates to a cost of about thirteen cents per volunteer hour—and almost all of this has been spent on pizza! The key to the program's success is its simplicity. It provides a model that can easily be adapted to a variety of contexts. This chapter updates an article written a decade ago that provided a blueprint for starting such a program,[1] describes a number of refinements and lessons learned, and includes data from a recent survey of participants—mentors, teachers, school district administrators, and fifth graders—designed to assess the impact of the program.

Introduction

"Who will get us started with the facts of the case?" the law professor asks his class of thirty students. Twenty-five eager hands shoot into the air and the professor is pressed to involve as many of his charges as possible. Fiction? No. Once a year three lucky law professors at BYU have an opportunity to teach a well-prepared, excited, and insightful class of ... fifth graders. The BYU Law School Youth Mentoring Program is in its thirteenth year of hosting fifth or sixth grade students from a nearby school and providing one-on-one weekly mentoring sessions with first year law students volunteering as mentors. No, volunteer first-year law students is not fiction either.

The BYU Law School Youth Mentoring Program is based upon a big-picture view of the value of mentoring. The program's slogan is, "Everyone needs a mentor." Since the program is run entirely by law student volunteers, the corollary slogan could be, "Everyone can be a mentor."

Each year, nearly a hundred busy first-year law students, about two-thirds of the class, sign up to mentor a fifth grader on a weekly basis. Each Tuesday, at the J. Reuben Clark Law School, fifth graders and law students alike look forward to their weekly mentoring sessions, where fifth graders feel "cool" to be hanging out at the law school and really getting to know their way around it (Emma W.), and law students find that "it is good to get away from the books and give back to their community" (Josh H.). The elementary school children come to the law school, a concession to the law students' busy schedules, but also a deliberate effort to help the children come to feel a level of comfort and belonging in an environment that can initially seem quite alien and intimidating. The program is designed to provide meaningful one-on-one learning for fifth graders and to encourage law students to develop habits of pro bono service at a time when they do not yet have any meaningful legal skills to offer.

Background

The BYU mentoring program began in 1998 when Brett Scharffs, in his first year of teaching at BYU Law School, decided to replicate a law school mentoring program he learned was in the works at the Georgetown Law Center. The Georgetown program bussed in elementary-aged students from inner-city schools directly to the law school, and law students were paired up one-on-one as mentors for the young students. The idea was to focus on each child in the class, not just the students needing particular academic or behavioral assistance. The young students interacted with the law students in the college setting, allowing many of the elementary students to feel comfortable at a place of higher education.

Initially, Scharffs wondered whether such a program would be needed in a place like Provo, Utah, which is a homogeneous college town, dominated by two local universities. He questioned if Provo schools would need a mentoring program since most students seemed college-bound. But this perception turned out to be mistaken. Many children in Provo, especially those on the west side of Interstate 15, which divides the city like a knife, are from socio-economic communities that statistically do not have a high likelihood of college attendance. Sunset Elementary, located on the west side, was the first school to participate with the BYU Law mentoring program, and the elementary school students were bussed directly to the law school each Tuesday afternoon for a fifty minute mentoring session. The program began with one class of sixth grade students and was quickly enlarged to encompass the two other sixth grade classes at Sunset. At first, the sixth graders were expected to identify areas where they needed help. Not surprisingly, many of those with the greatest academic needs proved most adept at convincing their mentors that their work was all done and that what they needed was time at the foosball table, or throwing a Frisbee on the lawn. It didn't take long for the teachers and mentors to figure out that the law student resource could be much more effectively utilized if the sixth graders came with specific assignments. Law students are good at research and writing, and soon the teachers became adept at developing assignments that would utilize these skills.

The most significant cost was bussing the kids to BYU each week. For several years, the Provo School District covered this cost (about a hundred dollars per week, or $2,000 per academic year), but due to the school district's budgetary priorities, Sunset Elementary was unable to continue the weekly bus trips to the law school. The Law School and District coordinator then looked for another school, closer to the law school, where bussing the students would not be necessary. As it happens, the Law School is located across the street from Wasatch Elementary School, which is blessed with a visionary principal, and imaginative teacher, who jumped at the opportunity to team up with the Law School. With the transition from Sunset to Wasatch, the program began working with fifth graders, rather than sixth graders.

The fifth-grade curriculum focuses on American history, which has been a good fit for the mentoring program, since law students have an interesting perspective on the political and legal institutions within the United States government and judiciary. The transition to focusing on nearby students, rather than based upon demographics, was relatively seamless, especially given the program's guiding principle that "everyone needs a mentor." Although some of the fifth graders come from middle-income families, many come from families whose parents are still students themselves, and a number of the children struggle with various family or personal issues, or learning disabilities. And all elementary-school-age children benefit from positive role models. As Cora Berrett, the Provo School District liaison for the program put it, "Every child, no matter what family they come from, can always use another positive adult role model in their lives."

BYU Law School has proven to be a natural home for the mentoring program. BYU students are encouraged from all levels of faculty and administration at the university to focus their lives and professions on service. BYU Law students, in particular, are encouraged to give back to their communities when they enter law practice. The mentoring program reinforces these ideals. Many BYU law students are multi-lingual, since many law students traveled abroad as LDS missionaries. Law students with language skills are often paired with fifth graders with the same language background who are learning English as a second language.

The mentoring program has also produced some unexpected benefits for the law student mentors. There is probably no more self-centered enterprise than the first year of graduate school, when everything is new and uncertainty of how one will measure up against one's peers is high. Law students report benefitting socially, mentally, and emotionally when they take time to focus on the needs of their fifth grade mentees. Law school is rigorous and competitive. In our survey, many law students reported that mentoring allows time for the brain to relax and engage in creative learning and play with the fifth graders.

Furthermore, one of the program's objectives is to help law students learn the value of mentoring, which reinforces the law profession's focus on mentoring between seasoned and new lawyers. Hopefully, law students will seek out good mentors and will become effective mentors as they enter and move through law practice. Lawyers are also encouraged, and in some states required, to provide pro bono services on a regular basis. The elementary school students are not as far along the road of life as law students, and the law students are sometimes surprised to find they are already in a position to be of service to others.

A number of key players at the law school encourage and foster the collaborative nature of this mentoring program. The law school administration encourages and assists the program. The law school deans have been supportive of the program, providing financial assistance. Perhaps most importantly, since the first year of the program, the law school has not scheduled any first-year classes on Tuesdays from noon to one o'clock, when the mentoring program takes place. This enables law students to schedule mentoring as a natural part of their first-year plan. Law professors have provided support by allowing students to make announcements in their classes and by encouraging first-year students to get involved.

The elementary school teachers and the school district collaborate to make this program happen. The teachers select the curriculum or select a project for the students to work on together with their mentors. The teachers and the law students collaborate in coordinating a "mock" law school class and a "mock trial" for the elementary school students. The teachers willingly bring their students across the street to the law school each week, taking precious class time during each week to participate because they have seen the long-term benefits. "We love this program," commented Ms. Davis in a recent survey questionnaire. The program "is a good example of higher education [and provides] an additional caring adult in [the students'] lives." The teachers all described how much their students look forward to coming each Tuesday. Ms. Hatch added, "The BYU students are happy, willing, and helpful. They really invest a lot in the time they're given with our students." Ms. Matthews, another fifth grade teacher, noted that one of her students particularly benefited from the mentoring program. Luis, a native Spanish speaker, found learning in English in the classroom to be very difficult. Because Luis's mentor also speaks Spanish he has been better able to help Luis make the transition to an English language classroom and as a result Luis has particularly enjoyed learning about the American government. Cora Berrett, program director for the Provo School District, agreed that the mentoring program is great exposure for the young students to a college setting. Berrett works with the student-directors to coordinate the mentoring partnerships and activities. She explained that it is the "collaboration between the [law student directors and the district] that makes this program work; the program could not work without both."

Along with the first-year student mentors, the fifth grade teachers, students, and district coordinator, a second and third year student serve as student-directors of the program. They recruit first year law students at the beginning of the school year and make sure mentors are aware of any special needs. They regularly confer with the fifth grade teachers to make sure the program runs smoothly.

Structure of the Program

Before the first mentoring session, mentors and mentees fill out an interests and background survey. The district coordinator oversees a background check, trains the mentors, carefully reads over the information provided on the background sheet, and pairs mentors with mentees. Law students are paired with a fifth graders with whom they share similar interests, or with a fifth grader who has a specific need that the law student has the skills to address. This allows a tailored approach and many students are surprised at how much they have in common with each other. Lisa, a current fifth grader in the program, recently wrote that what she likes about the program is that "my mentor [is] almost the same as me."

One-on-one pairing is the program's ideal and, therefore, the law student coordinators work diligently to recruit enough volunteers to ensure each elementary student has his or her own mentor. When there are not enough law student mentors, two fifth graders are assigned to one law student. This can create difficulties, if for example, the students do not read at the same level and mentors have to be creative in their approach to mentoring two students at a time. These threesomes, however, have seen success as they learn to work together as a team.

Since the fifth graders come to the law school during at a time when no first-year classes are scheduled, the mentoring program is custom-made to provide a service opportunity for busy law students who would be unlikely to take the initiative or make the necessary time commitment to seek out a mentoring opportunity on their own. This enables the students to begin to cultivate the habit of providing service, even at a time when they feel besieged by work and stress. When asked why they signed up as volunteer mentors, many law students cited the ease and convenience of the opportunity. The mentoring program brings the service opportunities to the law students, accounting for much of the program's success.

The BYU Law School Mentoring Program combines tutoring services with easy free time that allows both law students and fifth graders a chance to build friendships. The fifth graders are able to get one-on-one help with school subjects, and often beleaguered or anxious law students are happy to confirm to themselves that they are knowledgeable in basic fifth grade civic. One law student said, "My fifth grader bragged to others about my knowledge. It made me feel appreciated and seemed to inspire her." Another first-year law student said, "It's nice having someone look up to you!"

Academic Focus

The BYU Law School Mentoring Program maintains an academic focus. The law students and fifth graders work on specific assignments from the teachers that typically require thirty to forty minutes to complete each week. Over the last few years, the fifth grade teachers have used the mentoring program as an opportunity to teach American history and government to their students, subjects that often receive less attention than math and science which are heavily tested on state standardized tests. One fifth grade teacher, Mrs. Davis, explained that the mentoring program provides a "chance to cover social studies curriculum."

On a typical Tuesday, the fifth graders are given pre-assigned chapters from their social studies books, and after initially meeting up with each other in the Moot Court Room the mentors and mentees are free to leave and to spread out over the law school campus and library to study the chapters together. Law students are encouraged to ask their mentees' questions or give examples to ensure mastery. Occasionally, the teachers request that everyone stay in the Moot Court Room for a few minutes at the beginning of the hour so the teacher can explain the day's assignment, such as a writing or research project. Teachers have also occasionally assigned math homework, and it can be quite entertaining to see law students pulling out their cell phones as calculators or to hear fifth graders explain to a group of law students how to divide fractions. When asked what they liked best about the law school mentoring program, or how they have most benefited, many fifth grade students wrote that their reading and comprehension skills have improved. They report learning to appreciate the social studies curriculum more and like it when law students explain concepts or answer their questions. One student said "I feel bad for kids who do not do it [participate in the mentoring program]." In describing a notable experience, Nathan W., a law student explained, "I taught a kid with ADD to sit still and finish his work before we played. That was pretty cool."

Ten to Twenty Minutes of Free Time

We feel that the ten to twenty minutes of free time is an integral part to building the mentoring relationship and is beneficial to both the law student and the fifth grader. The mentor and mentee are able to build a friendly and trusting relationship as they play tag, football, foosball, ping-pong, Uno, or just talk and hangout. Tutoring and school work go more smoothly when the fifth graders learn that their mentors are normal people who have fun and actually care about how their mentees are doing or what their interests are. It is not uncommon for a law student mentor to read a book that is of interest to his or her student. Fifth grader, Emma W., explained that her favorite part about mentoring is "exploring the law school building." Free time allows Emma to explore with her personal guide, which helps her feel comfortable in a higher education setting.

Unique Campus Location and Field Trips

Our unique university campus location allows us to create some special experiences for the mentors and mentees. We plan one to two "field trips" on campus every semester where the law students and fifth graders get to tour a museum, attend a matinee choir performance, or complete a scavenger hunt that highlights some of the interesting displays on campus. Last semester, the group went to a natural history museum, where the students were also able to see a live reptile show. The law students were impressed with the overall reptilian knowledge of the fifth graders, which often surpassed their own. While budget cuts have forced many elementary schools to eliminate field trips due to the cost of bussing, students at Wasatch Elementary have an opportunity to experience a broader university life, with one-on-one attention from a knowledgeable adult.

Highlights: Mock Law Class and Mock Trial

Each semester is cap-stoned with a special law-related event—the mock law class or the mock trial. At the end of the first semester, volunteer law school professors teach a mock law class to the fifth graders. Typically, we try to provide one professor for each class of fifth graders. Together, the week before the class, the mentors and mentees study the cases that the law professors will cover in the mock class. We have found three cases that work well. We use a pair of banana peel slip-and-fall cases (one in which the railroad where the accident happened is held liable and one where it is not). We also use *Talmage v. Smith*, which involves a property owner who throws a stick at one trespassing boy and, accidentally, puts out the eye of an altogether different boy. These cases are easily understood and embraced by the fifth graders and their mentors, who are learning these cases in their first-year torts class. The professor draws out basic law principles from the cases using the Socratic method. The fifth graders typically set examples of preparedness and enthusiastic volunteerism that often put the first-year law students to shame; these law students often do not realize how jaded they have already become.

The single most memorable event of the mentoring program is the mock trial that takes place during the Winter semester each year. The law school student-coordinators write or condense a typical moot court/trial advocacy problem down to a two or three page summary. A week or two before the mock trial, the fifth grade students are assigned roles as lawyers, judges, bailiffs, witnesses, jury-members, and court reporters. Members of the law school trial court teams give a short object lesson about the ambiguity of evidence or the way in which eyewitnesses can understand an event differently. Then the children spend the remainder of that mentoring session consulting with their mentors about the case and receiving training so they will be adequately prepared for the trial the following week. Where it would take hours upon hours for one teacher to coach each individual child through his or her part, it only takes a couple of mentoring sessions for the fifth graders to prepare their parts with their mentors. The mock trial provides an educational, hands-on activity for the students without adding an extra load upon the teachers.

Many students show up for the mock trial dressed in suits and formal clothing, and it is not uncommon for parents to attend their child's day in court. One boy even shaved the top of his head, replicating male-pattern baldness. With encouragement from their mentors, the fifth graders give opening and closing statements, direct and cross examine student-witnesses, and conduct the court proceedings. There have been a few tense moments when the audience has wondered whether the child-attorney would be able to deliver his speech or remain completely frozen. However, each time, with the encouragement and thumbs-up of a mentor, the beleaguered student has been able to overcome his or her initial stage fright and give a wonderful performance. In the past, the law school coordinators have provided black graduation robes and gavels for the judges and plastic police-chief badges for the bailiffs, to add an air of authenticity.

After the trial is over, it is fun to watch the young teams of attorneys pacing back and forth, commiserating while anxiously awaiting the verdict. Likewise, the teachers have expressed their amusement with the conflicting verdicts returned by different class juries for the same factual scenario. One year, one class returned a verdict of "guilty," the next class returned a verdict of "not guilty," and the third class resulted in a hung jury, in which a couple of the members of the jury almost came to blows. On another occasion, to the delight of everyone in the courtroom, the fifth grade student who served as the judge for a class that returned a "not guilty" verdict sentenced the prosecutors to 500 hours of extra homework for bringing a frivolous claim.

Program Costs

By pairing with an elementary school that is located across the street from the law school, eliminating the need for bussing, the costs of running the program are minimal. The primary, and sometime sole, costs are photocopying various materials and the pizza party at the end of each semester. The school district and the law school split these costs, with the school district providing the paper products and drinks and the law school supplying the pizza.

Benefits to the Law School Community

By all accounts, the Mentoring Program has had a softening and beneficial effect upon the law school community. In the stressful and competitive law school atmosphere, students and faculty alike have commented on the refreshing quality of the mentoring program. A recent survey asked BYU law student mentors whether they considered mentoring a valuable service activity—74% selected 4 or 5 (on a scale from 1 to 5). Some of the benefits in mentoring include infusing diversity into the law school routine, providing a community service opportunity, providing a balanced perspective, and learning to be sensitive to diverse backgrounds.

Law school, particularly during the first year, is an extremely stressful environment that usually dominates the first-year student's entire life, thinking, focus, and perspective. Despite incredibly successful former academic or professional careers, it is not uncommon for students to start to identify and group themselves according to class rank or success in law school. The opportunity to serve a fifth grader one hour each week provides a reality check for law students who sometimes imagine themselves to be beleaguered and besieged. Several features are worth noting.

First, participating in the mentoring program gives students a nice, regular break from the daily grind of casework, memos, and the Socratic method. First-year student, Josh H., wrote about the mentoring program, "It is good to get away from the books and spend time with energetic kids that love being here." Heath W. added, "Mentoring definitely broke up that monotony, helped keep me sane." While time is precious to first-year law students, most students would agree that mentoring did not hurt their grades, but provided a much-needed break that allowed them to focus better on their schoolwork. Justin C. wrote, "My kid teaches me how to be excited about learning again."

Next, as previously noted, law school is a self-absorbing endeavor that consumes a student's life and dominates her thinking. Mentoring helps provide balance and is a good reminder that there is life outside of law school and there are more important things than grades. Cory C. wrote, "The program has added a level of meaningfulness to my experience, which would not have been possible if I didn't participate in the program at the same time of a tumultuous first semester of law school." Many students have found that the mentoring program has been an antidote to the stress they are feeling in their lives. Sondra K. explained, "I have learned to laugh more and often as I've interacted with my mentee despite the stresses I would be facing." Others wrote about how the fifth graders helped them to have fun. Finally, Stephanie F. wrote, "Mentoring really has helped me focus on what is important. In the grand scheme of things, grades won't matter, but these kids' self-esteem will."

The mentoring program is designed with the law student's convenience and capacities in mind. It provides an extremely convenient opportunity to serve, hopefully instilling early in students' careers a desire to give back to their community, or participate in pro bono activity. In our survey, over half of the law students selected four or five when asked if mentoring has increased their commitment to serve others. Michael H. noted, "I've learned I really DO have time to serve" and Mark E. added, "I've learned not to be too attached to my own time." Many students enter law school with unselfish motives to serve and help people, but as the competition escalates, it is easy to forget original desires and start playing the all-consuming grade game. However, Justin C.

commented, "Mentoring has helped me remember why I came to law school: to help children and protect them according to the law," and Natalie T. explained that mentoring has "reminded me of the people who helped me throughout my education."

As law students develop a desire to serve others, the mentoring program gives them hands-on experience in mentoring and connecting with people—something important not only to law students, but to lawyers in their professional lives. Cory C. explained that she "liked the challenge of engaging a young developing mind and attempting to help the analytical processes." Micah M. noticed the valuable connection between tutoring and free time with his mentee: "I love playing football with my mentee and motivating him with analogies between school and sports."

Finally, while many law schools may be culturally or racially diverse, they are still filled with type-A overachievers, individuals who often have similar intellectual abilities, talents, tendencies, and fears. Infusing the law school with a stream of fifth graders for one hour each week adds elements that likely do not exist at many law schools. The fifth graders have unique perspectives, and some of them are dealing with learning disabilities or trouble at home. Law students are able to develop compassion and empathy with people who are different from themselves and different from the academically successful people that fill law schools. Joseph B. noted, "I have been reminded about what it is like to be a youth." The fifth-grade mentoring program often enables BYU students to use their diverse bilingual skills; wrote Glen W., "It has been a good experience helping my mentee learn because he is still learning English ... I feel like my time with him helps him understand material he might not otherwise understand." Finally, Nate W. simply observed, "I like getting to hang around someone who isn't a law student."

Benefits for the Fifth Graders

The objectives for the elementary school students are focused on enhancing the learning process, helping the children come to feel like they belong in a higher education setting, and providing positive adult role models.

Many of the fifth graders stated that mentoring had helped their learning; 73% said that mentoring helped motivate them in their schoolwork, and 61% said that their grades had improved since starting the law school mentoring program. "It has motivated me to do better in school," said Ryan, a fifth grader. Several other students explained that they enjoyed the mentoring program because their grades had improved. The students enjoy a new learning environment with the law students, who are adults the fifth graders admire. Individual attention is the key to helping the fifth graders excel in academics. When asked to describe a noteworthy experience in mentoring, Beau T. wrote: "I remember when my mentor would quiz me and if I didn't get the question then he would give me some help." Similarly, other students expressed how grateful they were to have mentors that helped them understand. Leah L. liked how her mentor "would explain things to me." Many other fifth graders expressed that they had learned how to like history, reading, or social studies because their mentors had explained the concepts to them and coached them through difficult sections.

Just as the fifth graders' academic engagement in their classrooms has improved through the mentoring program, they have also developed confidence in their ability to read and understand things they are learning. Many of the fifth graders in the mentoring program lack confidence in reading and comprehending their assignments, often feeling the assignment is too difficult for them. The mentors sit side-by-side with the fifth graders coaching them as they read the assignments aloud. The mentors foster the fifth graders' confidence in their reading, comprehension, and analytical skills. This one-on-one format helps facilitate individual feedback, which is so crucial for elementary age students. Kennedy W. mentioned that mentoring has helped him read faster, and Kimball C. explained that mentoring has been helpful because "it makes me more comfortable reading." Toni A. explained that she has learned "how to say the words and tell what it means." This type of learning is invaluable to the students' long-term development in education. One mentor can make a big difference in a student's life if that student changes his or her attitude about learning and realizes that he or she can succeed at something that may have been difficult at first.

The law students also help create a "work before play" ethic for the fifth graders. When the fifth graders first arrive at mentoring session, they are usually eager to play games, go outside and play sports, or engage with their mentors in something "fun." However, mentoring creates a weekly routine where students are expected to do their work before they play, and the fifth graders have learned to appreciate this pattern. "I like that we can learn with someone and I like the sports when we're done," commented Asa J. "We have lots of fun playing after we do our work," Brooke T. emphasized. Not only do students enjoy playing after they work, but many students find that work itself can be fun. As Brooke explained, the mentoring program has benefited her because "it helps me have fun while I work."

The mentors not only help the students with their fifth-grade course work, but the law students introduce the fifth graders to the legal world. The mock trial and mock law school class provide students with the opportunity to explore the law and its practice. The fifth graders' favorite activity has always been the mock trial, put on each Spring. The fifth graders feel they are really a part of the law program with the rest of the law students. Even if informally, the fifth graders count these experiences as their own legal education. Emma W. expressed that the thing that was most helpful about mentoring was "learning about the law and how it works." Several other students agreed. One student shared a personal reason why he felt that having a law student mentor was so important: "Well, my sister always wanted to be a lawyer and my mentor teaches me so I can help her." The law school setting and law student mentors give the fifth graders a unique experience in learning about the world and the law, and unique opportunities to learn in a hands-on way.

One of the objectives of the mentoring program is that students gain confidence in their own learning and then make goals for further education. Placing the students in the law school setting is an ideal way to help elementary age students feel comfortable in a college context and help them gain a college focus. One of the students, Emma F., commented, "I have benefited by consider[ing] law as a future career. I really feel comfortable at the law school.... I think [mentoring] has raised my excitement about attending college;" 81% of the fifth graders said that the law school program has helped them think positively about attending college; and 95% of the fifth graders said that they felt comfortable in the law school. To our minds, these are two of the most encouraging findings from our survey.

Additionally, the positive interaction with college-age students helps the fifth graders learn social skills and gain confidence in relationships. The program makes an effort to match the fifth graders with mentors that have similar interests based on the preliminary survey taken at the beginning of the year. This has a positive effect on the mentoring relationships. Even if the students do not share all of the same interests, the law students and fifth graders learn how to appreciate each other's differences; 88% answered 4 or 5 when asked if they have developed a meaningful relationship with their law school mentor, and 94% answered 4 or 5 when asked if they look forward to meeting with their mentors each week. Joelle S., a fifth grader, said that the most helpful thing about mentoring is "getting to learn how to talk to adults and new people." These social skills will benefit the fifth graders' relationships and interactions just as the academic skills they acquire can benefit their grades. Besides the social skills, the students gain confidence in themselves. The fifth graders expressed that mentoring was meaningful to them because they were able to make new friends. "I have more friends," mentioned Eve T. "I am not as shy," is how Elisabeth F., another fifth grader, summed up how the mentoring program's benefits. These responses show that the mentoring program not only helps mentees with their homework, but also helps them develop social skills.

Conclusion

The BYU Law School Mentoring Program is very simple to organize and manage. It is extremely inexpensive. It generates a large number of one-on-one mentoring hours between individual fifth grade students and law student mentors. It provides opportunities for law students not only think about public service, but also to practice it at a time when many cannot imagine having the time or inclination to do so. For the fifth graders, the academic benefits are palpable, and teachers report the program has a positive impact on the academic climate in their classrooms. For Professor Scharffs, the most remarkable and, for him, unexpected dividend the program pays is in the attitudes the students develop about higher education. For many of the fifth graders, college is an extremely distant dream, and, for some, it is not even a dream at all. However, over the course of the year, because they come to the law school regularly, and because they interact in a positive way with a law student who cares about them, the children stop feeling like visitors on campus and start feeling like this is their law school. They are no longer outsiders. They belong. Whether or for how many this translates into a long-term commitment to pursuing higher education, we do not know for sure. The neighborhood schools that the program works with are extremely transient, and we have yet to find an effective way to track the students' progress when they leave the program. So to some extent, the program is an act of faith—a belief that by helping individual kids, we will light a few sparks of curiosity and purpose to pursue education that will, taken together, ignite a blaze.

Middle and High School Programs

Chapter 5

Peer Court

Smythe Academy of Arts and Sciences Middle School
Sacramento, California

*Gavin E. Mody**

| Pre-K | Elementary | Middle | High School | College | Law School | Profession |

Peer courts are common in many schools and other settings. As the description of the Excel High School program in Chapter 6 indicates, they are a particularly apt addition to other parts of a law-themed approach. They readily take advantage of the legal system and of various possible partners in that system such as area law students, attorneys, or judges. These types of courts have a strong record of success in improving school discipline and climate. They also inherently offer students a glimpse of both the legal profession and the concepts of due process. There are a very large number of programs of this type throughout the country, and they have been fairly well documented. This chapter offers a glimpse into one small program started in Sacramento by the author while he was an Education Law Fellow at Pacific McGeorge School of Law. It's an easy model to replicate, and can be counted on to produce meaningful results for the students and their community.

Peer Courts: An Introduction

Peer courts—variously termed youth courts, student courts, teen courts—are programs staffed and often administered by youths, designed to impose sentences, and sometimes determine guilt or innocence, of youths exhibiting some form of problem behavior. Peer courts vary widely in structure, purpose, setting, and types of issues addressed. Some programs, for example, are administered by community-based organizations (e.g., Boys and Girls Clubs, YMCA), others by the local justice system or by schools, and still others through cooperative relationships between two or more of these entities. Some programs use youths only as juries; in others, youths function as attor-

---

* Gavin Mody earned his J.D. from Boston University. While at the University of the Pacific McGeorge School of Law, he served as a 2007–08 Downey Brand Education Law Fellow and developed and implemented a model youth court program.

neys and judges as well. Peer courts can also be distinguished by the problem behavior addressed. With some exceptions, programs address either chargeable offenses normally handled by the justice system (e.g., referrals from juvenile court, law enforcement) or school-based disciplinary infractions (e.g., truancy, defiance) that a school's discipline office otherwise would address.

The literature on peer courts, including some research-based studies, identifies myriad purposes for and benefits of these programs, no matter the program's particular design, both for those youths staffing and sentenced/tried by the courts and for the wider community (if the program is school-based, the relevant community is that school; if community-based, it is the community at-large). These numerous benefits can be summarized as follows:

- Peer court programs promote accountability and pro-social attitudes (e.g., increased self-esteem, more positive attitude toward authority, youth empowerment). As a result, recidivism may be reduced.

- Peer court programs develop life skills (e.g., communication skills, decision making skills, conflict resolution skills) and knowledge of good citizenship.

- Peer court programs educate youths about the purposes and operation of the legal system.

Smythe Academy and Its Students

Smythe Academy of Arts and Sciences Middle School, a charter school, is located within the Twin Rivers Unified School District, which in 2008–2009 served approximately 31,000 students in 59 schools in California's northern Sacramento County.[1] In 2008–2009, Smythe's diverse enrollment—approximately 407 students in grades 7 and 8—was 57.2% Hispanic or Latino, 18.4% African American, 16.5% White (non-Hispanic), 6.4% Asian/Pacific Islander/Filipino, and 0.74% American Indian/Alaska Native.[2] 88% of students participated in the free or reduced-price lunch program in 2008–2009.[3] Finally, of the 84% of Smythe students who responded in 2008–2009, 37% indicated at least one parent's education level as "some college," "college graduate," or "graduate school," 24% indicated parent education level as "not a high school graduate."[4]

In 2008–2009, 28.3% of Smythe's students qualify as English Language Learners.[5] In that same year, 40.2% of students scored "At or Above Proficient" in English-Language Arts, and 42.7% in Mathematics under NCLB-based standards.[6] Under California's STAR standards, 55% of Smythe students grades 7–8 scored at or below "Basic" on the California Standards Test in English-Language Arts; 58% scored at or below "Basic" in Mathematics/General Mathematics.

Smythe Academy Peer Court

Program Origins

The peer court at Smythe Academy of Arts and Sciences grew out of a partnership between Smythe and the University of the Pacific McGeorge School of Law. Pacific McGeorge

Law School, through its Pipeline Program, partners with several Sacramento-area K–12 schools, including Smythe.[7] Through these relationships, the law school seeks to develop, particularly among groups underrepresented in the legal profession, interest in careers in the legal field, and the skills necessary to succeed in law school.

Within its LL.M. program, Pacific McGeorge offers the Downey Brand Education Law Fellowship. Those graduate law students holding this fellowship manage and expand the law school's Pipeline Program. The idea for a peer court program at Smythe emerged from research by these students on law-related outreach programs and conversations in late 2007, between these law students and Smythe's administration. The Law School and the Academy both recognized that such a program would further many elements of Smythe's mission:

> The mission of Smythe Academy is to provide an enriched educational environment for an ethnically and socio-economically diverse student population that emphasizes the arts, technology, and community service and applies a holistic approach to education by involving the parent community, and the teacher in assessment coupled with project-based instruction and authentic assessment.[8]

Specifically, a peer court enriches a school's education environment by promoting a sense of community and good citizenship, providing opportunities for community service and increasing parent involvement, and offering an authentic instructional approach to familiarize students with the U.S. legal system.

Beyond the benefits of peer court programs generally, and those benefits that correlate with Smythe's mission statement specifically, school-based peer courts administered solely within the school and adjudicating school-based disciplinary infractions, offer additional advantages:

- Such programs are likely to be less costly and complex—and therefore more easily and quickly established and implemented—than those with multiple stakeholders.
- These programs expand the type—and therefore the appropriateness and educational value—of consequences available for disciplinary infractions. Schools no longer need to be limited to one-size-fits-all responses, like detention and suspension.
- Peer court programs reduce the sometimes-overwhelming burden and volume of cases carried by school discipline personnel, freeing time to address more serious disciplinary issues.
- By allowing for consequences beyond those that remove the sentenced child from the classroom, peer court programs may enhance schools' ability to meet increasingly stringent state requirements (e.g., graduation rates, standardized test passage rates).
- Because all program activity occurs within the school—all roles are filled by the school's students and staff, all sentenced students matriculate at that school, and sentences more likely address the school community's concerns—the school alone reaps the numerous benefits peer court programs provide. That is, school-based programs adjudicating solely disciplinary infractions offer more "bang for the buck."

For these reasons, in the spring of 2008, Smythe's administration and the McGeorge law students elected to establish a peer court based within and administered solely by the school, adjudicating disciplinary infractions only.[9]

Program Description

Because of its design, Smythe's peer court began as a fairly developed program, based on a manual developed by McGeorge students. Nonetheless, based on experience, school staff and students have modified the program to meet Smythe's needs since its inception in early 2008. The following description reflects that modified design.

Participants

School-based youth courts are implemented generally either out of an existing class, course, or as an extracurricular activity. Smythe elected the class-based model, staffing its program with students enrolled in its highly selective elective course, Leadership Class. Officially, students are tasked with all significant elements of the court's operation; other than through her standard duties (e.g., course grading, classroom management), the Leadership Class teacher's official role is largely to support court operations. Student-staff not only manage day-to-day operations but also influence program design as well. Specifically, each year the Leadership Class's teacher assembles the staff to identify modifications to be made in program design and operation for the ensuing year.

Consistent with initial intent, the peer court's design and operation remain largely contained within the Leadership Class. Other school staff, except the vice-principal, who selects those cases to be heard by peer court—participates by providing written disciplinary referrals and supporting information. Depending on the imposed sentence, staff members also participate in monitoring sentence-completion, as described in the Design and Operation section. Students not in the Leadership Class participate as the matter warrants, that is, as victims providing the court information or as offending students to appear before the court for sentencing. Occasionally other classes attend a hearing for educational purposes.

The program is self-contained within Smythe Academy functioning free from outside authority over decision making. As originally designed, McGeorge and other entities serve only as consultants on program design and operation. Outside parties, such as parents or school personnel, however, do participate in some consequences the court imposes. Parents also play a role in court operation. Occasionally, parents will attend hearings to support their children through the process. Further, parents must grant permission for their child's matter to be heard at peer court.

Design and Operation

As indicated, Smythe staffs its peer court with students enrolled in the Leadership Class. Students submit applications for this elective and Smythe's principal selects participants based on grades and citizenship.

Smythe's peer court begins each year by conducting a school-wide election to select those Leadership Class students to serve as judges. Students fill the following roles:

- Judges (3, including a Chief Judge)
- Prosecuting Attorneys (2)
- Defense Attorneys (1 or 2)
- Jury (remainder of Leadership Class + prior offending students)
- Bailiff/Court Clerk
- Student Mentor (serves also as jury-member)

After selection, training for these roles occurs in several ways. First, the Program Manual developed by McGeorge students serves as a guide before and during the program. Second, for two weeks prior to staffing their first hearing, students participate in several mock trials. After receiving its first referral, but prior to hearing the matter, the student-staff conduct a mock trial based on the offense to be tried. Third, Leadership Class students come from both seventh and eighth grade; those seventh graders remaining in the class into eighth grade serve as unofficial mentors for eighth graders newly admitted into Leadership Class. Fourth, occasionally law students from area law schools and local judges meet with the students. Fifth, but not directly in preparation for their peer court roles, these students gain a general understanding of the court system through United States history classes.

Cases are referred to the peer court by the vice-principal who obtains teachers' written disciplinary referrals. As with most peer courts, Smythe's court assumes offending students' guilt; its role is only to impose appropriate sentences. The court assumes the truth of teachers' statements in written referrals. Teachers often submit supplementary statements to the court, detailing the child's behavior in class generally. The court hears about one case per week, during Leadership Class's scheduled period.

The day prior to a hearing, the offending student meets with court staff to prepare. At the hearing, the court hears the offending student's testimony and arguments on sentencing from prosecution and defense. (If the case involves a victim, court staff will interview the victim outside of the hearing.) The jury retreats to an adjoining room to deliberate and rejoins the court to announce its recommendation. In recognition of its important place in the school's culture as an elected body, the judges may modify the sentence to be imposed. School-based peer courts provide schools the ability to impose consequences to promote outcomes or values the school administration and/or community deem important. At Smythe, sentences generally are designed to serve two purposes: first, to educate students and second, to reinforce positive behaviors. Sample consequences include:

- Creating posters
- Conducting interviews: e.g., police, firefighters, school dropouts, ex-gang members
- Cleaning tasks
- Assisting teachers
- Producing and performing a skit
- Writing essays on various topics: e.g., college research, respect, friendship
- Offering written and verbal apologies
- Visiting effective classrooms to observe positive behavior
- Lunching with a teacher

- Volunteering at community organizations
- Writing a "behavior journal"

If a student fails to complete their sentence within the allotted time, that student is called before the court again to account for this failure and, depending on the explanation, the court may modify the sentence. Like probation officers, student mentors are tasked with monitoring students through the process. Sentences requiring work product (e.g., essays, posters, journals) are evaluated by the student mentors and the judges for effort. If the work product demonstrates little effort, the student is provided time to modify and re-submit. Accepted submissions are displayed around the school. After a student completes her sentence, that student, along with the Leadership Class students, serves on the jury for the next matter to be heard.

Student-staff are charged with most of the administrative tasks before and after the hearing. Specifically, the bailiff/court clerk maintains a record during proceedings, and most importantly of the sentences and deadlines imposed. Student mentors monitor adjudicated students' completion of sentences. Peer court staff members are evaluated as part of standard course grading. That is, the teacher utilizes a rubric identifying performance criteria, and includes the results within course grades.

Because the court operates as part of an already-established course during normal school hours, its operation requires no specific budget outlays by the school for material, personnel, etc. The McGeorge law students' contributions to the program's design and operation came through those students' fellowship duties; indirectly, therefore, these services to Smythe were funded through the fellowship. The fellowship also provided the time for program manual development, which is necessary to establish an appropriate program. Once initiated and the students trained, as designed, the program operates largely free of outside interference, except occasional communications and visits by the law students to observe and discuss court operations.

Program Results

Smythe Academy Middle School has existed in its current form for three years; its peer court began operations two years ago. No formal program evaluation has been conducted, and it may be too soon to draw meaningful conclusions from the court's operations. However, its brief history offers some evidence of effectiveness as judged by the rate-of-recidivism. To wit, in its first period of operation (January to June 2008) the majority of the school's discipline infractions were referred to the court. In that period, the court heard 33 cases; three students were called before the court for subsequent infractions—a nine percent recidivism rate in the court's first year.[10] The program's start in a start-up school environment, however, appears promising.

Whatever numbers may indicate, "the word" among students is that being hauled before the court is "the worst thing they can get … all the kids dread it." Some beg their parents to deny permission for referral to court. Some parents too have opined that suspension would have been an easier consequence to fulfill. Most parents react positively, hopeful that these targeted consequences are more likely to alter their children's problem behavior.[11]

Smythe Peer Court: Design and Operation

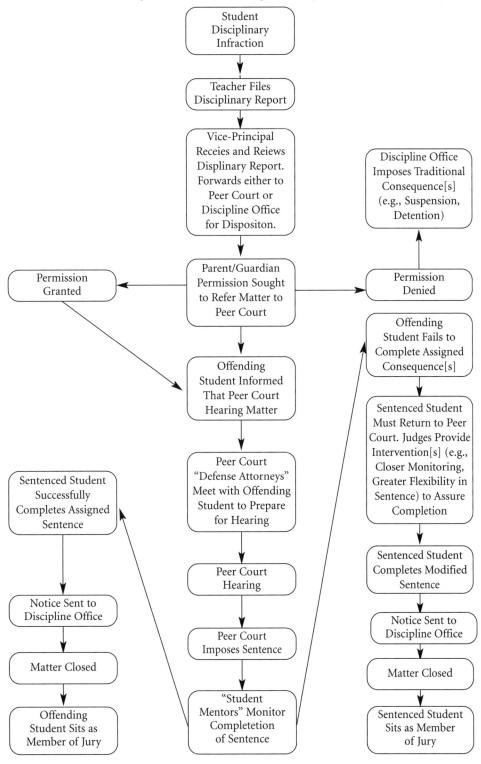

Recommendations and Thoughts on Replication

The peer court model offers many design options. An organization's purpose and circumstances in establishing such a program influence design selection. For example, in designing Smythe's program, the McGeorge law students considered that Smythe was a small charter school in its first years of operation, with a challenging and diverse student population. The program's design reflected a perceived need to optimize the investment-to-outcome ratio, (i.e., to provide more "bang for the buck,") and to allow for flexibility for experimentation and modification, so the program might grow and develop suitably with the school. These considerations lead, for instance, to the design's simplicity and limited number of stakeholders.

Because peer court program design should be tailored to the host's circumstances and goals, general guidance for those seeking to establish such programs is of limited value. Nonetheless, some recommendations applicable across design types may be offered:

- A school or organization's local legal community likely offers vast resources, and its members often demonstrate great interest in assisting in the design and operation of such programs. Such involvement therefore should be sought.

- Training increases program effectiveness. Mock hearings can be particularly helpful in increasing court staff understanding of court operations and their roles within the program.

- The program should be designed to continue despite staff changes. A detailed manual, updated as necessary, allows a program to function no matter personnel disruptions.

- Regular reconsideration and modification of program design and operation, with input of student-staff, can improve program effectiveness and efficiency.

- Consequences imposed for various offenses must receive careful consideration, both initially when designing a peer court program and throughout implementation, and should be consistently applied. Program staff should monitor for possible bias—by race, gender, etc.—in sentencing.

- Organization staff commitment to the program is critical for effectiveness. In the school context, inviting staff to observe hearings and publicizing the program and its benefits for the school at-large can increase buy-in.

- Rigorous evaluation will enhance program effectiveness and relevance to the wider community and staff, and community commitment to the program.

The design and execution of a youth court the program will ultimately fall on the creators of a given youth court program. But as we have seen at Smythe such a program can be successful even in circumstances that would traditionally be considered difficult.

Chapter 6

Law-Themed High Schools

EXCEL High School Law Academy
West Oakland, California

Ina Bendich, JD*

Pre-K	Elementary	Middle	High School	College	Law School	Profession

While pipeline programs exist in all shapes and sizes, the most effective are those that are intense and extend over time. These typically involve a series of opportunities, curricular and co-curricular, including opportunities to work with partners in the profession. The epitome here is a law-themed school. Most often a high school, these programs involve students from their first year forward in a rigorous law-themed curriculum, together with opportunities for project-based learning and for work experience. Law-themed schools occur in a variety of configurations, including both regular and charter public schools. They may well be small learning communities or schools within schools. The two described here, in this chapter and the next, are both regular public schools, the first, a school within a school on the east coast, the second, a California Partnership Academy. As these chapters illustrate, these schools and others like them have remarkable records of success generally — in comparison to their wider communities — and specifically for individual students.

Our Origins and Participants

The Law Academy at EXCEL High School in West Oakland, CA, was established as part of the California Partnership Academy (CPA) model. Operating under specific legislative authority, the California Department of Education developed CPAs to address the staggering increase across the state in dropout rates among urban and rural high school students. The California Partnership Academies operate as "small learning communities" composed of a cohort of students, teachers, and business partners focused on a particular career area. Academy courses are scheduled as "electives" and take place during the regular school day. Initially, 250 academies operated in large, comprehensive high schools across the state, emphasizing a wide variety of career paths. These programs have

---

* Ina Bendich is the Law Academy Director, EXCEL High School, Oakland, CA.

proved to be so successful[1] that the state legislature has provided funding to nearly double the number of academies.[2] Currently, more than 350 academies operate in California.

EXCEL High School, founded in 2005, is one of two small schools housed at the McClymonds Educational Complex in West Oakland, CA. The conversion to a small school model was developed in conjunction with the Bay Area Coalition for Equitable Schools (BayCES) and the Bill & Melinda Gates Foundation. Based on accepted educational research, the small school model was viewed as a viable strategy to address issues experienced by students, parents, and teachers working and learning within an urban school context. This model requires a limited enrollment of 400 students, with the expectation that teachers and students are able, based on this small size, to develop more meaningful relationships and benefit from individualized support to foster greater learning outcomes for students.[3]

Within this context, EXCEL High School serves approximately 265 predominately at-risk students. The student populations include African Americans (82.9%) Latinos (7.2%) and Asian/Pacific Islanders (3.1%). Approximately 71% percent of West Oakland residents earn annual incomes below $20,000 and 45% of residents ages 25 years or older do not possess a high school diploma.[4]

Given the high cost of living in the Bay Area, most students and their families live at or below the poverty line. Many reside in group homes, foster care, or kinship care with a relative. These kinship care arrangements are often constructed outside of the formal foster care process. Thus, many students and their families are excluded from the additional financial assistance available to legally established foster care. Within this community, students' daily interactions include exposure to gang activities, crime, and substance dependency. Within a three-month period (May 2010–August 2010), 767 crimes were reported in West Oakland, including 155 crimes involving narcotics, 217 assaults, 176 theft cases, and six homicides.[5] EXCEL students are adversely impacted further by substantial environmental risks and poor health conditions. Malnutrition and diseases related to air pollution, often coupled with chronic fatigue and stress, are factors which are typically overlooked, but which substantially impact student learning. According to the most recent Oakland/Berkeley Asthma Coalition statistics, 20% of youth and 37% of adults in West Oakland suffer from chronic asthma.[6]

The challenges that the West Oakland community faces are immense. Based on administrative decisions, resources have been funneled towards staff professional development, counseling, and intervention models to address these challenges. Many of the student gains are directly attributable to intensive staff development, integration of test preparation courses, and concentrated focus on math and English skill development.

Program Description

Using the academy goals and requirements, my objective as Academy Director is to engage students who fit the profile of the "urban disengaged student" in a variety of academically rigorous hands-on projects that are related to their everyday experience. These students are overwhelmingly African American, low-income, and most perceive themselves as disconnected from the institutions of government. We have learned during my ten years with the academy, that students learn best when they are actively engaged in solving "real world" problems. Achieving an optimal learning environment requires both a steady involvement of many caring adults and a well-crafted, high-expectation curriculum, with appropriate co-curricular and skill-building activities, typically project-based. These attributes are discussed further in this section.

Academy Structure and Curriculum

Students enter the academy during their tenth grade year and begin a three-year progressive course of study. The first year curriculum introduces students to the various areas of law and the multitude of employment opportunities that the legal field provides. During the 2009–2010 school year, the Law Academy was one of five sites chosen to pilot a "Foundations in Law" course made possible by the generous support of the Irvine Foundation. This curriculum will be made available to high schools throughout the State of California and supports the study of legal and public safety career options.

The second year curriculum introduces students to civic engagement by focusing on projects that have a stated purpose and prospect for a positive outcome. The overarching goal during this year is to empower students to become informed, engaged leaders who actively participate as competent civic citizens. To achieve this, the Law Academy's curricular goals are to:

- Support students in their own exploration of their community environment.
- Provide historical content lessons that include critical analysis of power structures, including issues of race, class, and inequality.
- Design a project that engages students in environmental justice work that will have a positive impact on their community.
- Engage students through the development of research, writing, and presentation skills that they will use to support their project.
- Teach students how to affect policy change on issues of concern in their community.

In this context, students have worked on a particular environmental project in their community. They explore the relationship between environmental justice and public policy, and they consider the impact of race and economic status on communities whose residents were primarily people of color. They grapple with issues of equity and develop strategies to meet the needs of those community members who were disproportionately marginalized in the decision making process. Finally, they apply the knowledge and skills developed through their study of environmental justice and the political process. Through written testimony, formal report presentations, and public speaking opportunities, students engage as confident civic actors. Further study is needed to determine whether or not they will apply these skills and mature into competent and active citizens.

In addition to the second year curriculum goals, the objectives of this particular environmental project are to maximize student engagement with environmental issues of particular relevance to them, which form the basis of their investigation, and to provide opportunities for students to enhance their reading, writing, research, and oral presentation skills. To this end, we set out to:

- Design a series of workshops to expose students to the area of environmental law and justice, and to the recourse available when environmental laws are not observed by businesses in local communities.

- Engage students in the examination of their own experiences and those of others in their community.

- Assist students in the selection of a business or entity that could warrant a potential action, map out the parameters of the project, determine the appropriate monitoring process, and design a campaign that engages agencies and other interested parties with the ultimate goal of devising a solution to the problem.

- Include experts who will provide the relevant background information and historical content through research and critical analysis focusing on issues concerning race and class.

Working in partnership with the UC Hastings School of Law and the Marshall Brennan Constitutional Law Project, the third year curriculum provides twelfth grade students with the opportunity to analyze, debate, and critique U.S. Supreme Court cases that deal specifically with the rights and limitations of high school students' activities on campus. This project has been extremely successful in developing students' reading, writing, and analysis skills as they study materials on students' rights and the limits on those rights within a school setting. Ultimately, students earn the opportunity to prepare for and participate in a moot court competition between a group of participating schools.

Youth Court[7]

Beginning in 2006, a "youth court" was developed as a prophylactic alternative to the traditional discipline system to effectively reduce suspensions for classroom related misbehavior. Since its inception, Youth Court has processed hundreds of "cases" that are referred by teachers and administrators before review by the court. Court proceedings are held during the school day as part of an elective course, allowing student participants to engage in the process while receiving academic credit for the court's operation. Each participating student is responsible for every aspect of the process. Students interview teachers, defendants, victims, and witnesses, determine the appropriate consequence for each referral, and follow-up on each case to ensure that the accused complete their assignment. Youth Court students also determine recommendations for those who do not comply. In 2009, the court incorporated a "restorative justice" component that has proved particularly successful when dealing with conflicts (both physical and emotional) between students.

Student Advisory

The members of the EXCEL teaching staff function as student advisors responsible for approximately twenty students. The advisory curriculum is structured to address the needs of each grade level with a primary focus on the acquisition of job readiness skills, and information regarding the college admissions process. Students take numerous field trips to various college campuses and participate in career fairs as part of their advisory. Outside speakers regularly visit classrooms and are encouraged to engage in more concentrated interactions with students, including job shadowing, internship opportunities, or mentoring.

After School

Recognizing the difficult circumstances that result from neighborhoods coping with crime and poverty, a wide variety of after-school programs are available to students to strengthen both their academic skills and emotional competency. An on-site Student Success Team coordinator assists teachers and administration with the development of a workable plan to support both students and families when serious academic concerns arise. Counseling services are available through an on-site, full service health center to assist students with emotional health. The administration and staff also contribute countless hours outside of the classroom to assist students with academic and personal issues when needs arise.

Parental Involvement

Robust parent and teacher communication is critical to the success of our students. To that end, the staff has worked to develop systems that include parents, but also take into consideration their limited time and sometimes inadequate resources. The ability to reach parents on a consistent basis has been strengthened with the acquisition of "Tele-parent" an automated phone system that allows teachers to communicate a variety of concerns about students via a phone message. This system has received rave reviews from parents as a useful resource. Our parent attendance at back-to-school and report card nights have improved with each passing school year.

Budget

Each California Partnership Academy is allocated state funding based on a variety of criteria, including student attendance, at-risk criteria (irregular attendance, under achieving, low motivation, economically disadvantaged, GPA below 2.2). Currently, each academy receives $800 per student for up to 90 students or a total of $81,000 annually. This ongoing funding stream allows academies to integrate fully into the fabric of the broader high school program and ensures sustainability of the particular career focus.

Each academy is also required to develop a cohort of teachers in core subjects (math, English, science, and social studies) and to develop meaningful relationships among students and staff. Academy funding is available to supplement teachers for prep-time before, during, and after school, thus recognizing the additional hours of planning time required to operate a successful, fully integrated academy program. The annual fund allocation may be used to purchase classroom equipment and supplies to support the overall academy goals. For example, the Law Academy provides state of the art computer equipment as well as a variety of field trip options, such as the annual Yosemite Institute outdoor education program.

Federal funds are also available through the school district's Perkins Regional Occupation Program to support the salary for the lead teacher in academy lab courses as well as general academy expenses that may not be covered by the California Partnership.

Partnerships

Partnerships with outside supporters, particularly those in the legal community, have been critical in providing students with "real world" opportunities to practice the skills learned in the classroom. The combination of partners and activities is critical to the success of academy programs. Partnerships offer opportunities to practice the skills learned in the classroom in engaging and meaningful situations. Students develop relationships as they interact with professionals associated with various career paths. These connections often result in internship and mentorship opportunities that students from less privileged backgrounds may not otherwise encounter. Students consistently report high satisfaction with their interactions, both with partners and with the activities that they experience. For students interested in pursuing either a career path or college, the partner connections that are established during high school provide many with the incentive necessary to graduate. The engagement with various enrichment activities allows students to practice research, writing, and presentation skills that are developed in the classroom. The successful collaboration between academies and partners ensures that students are prepared for both college and career.

The following relationships have been developed over the years and continue to support the work of the Law Academy:

Center for Youth Development through Law

The Center for Youth Development through Law promotes educational achievement, legal knowledge, and the pursuit of legal careers among young people from disadvantaged and underrepresented groups. Each summer, the program provides local disadvantaged high school students with instruction in law on the Boalt Hall campus, life skills workshops, and law related internships. During the school year, the youth are provided with follow-up mentoring.[8]

Each summer, EXCEL students are referred to this nine-week intensive program. For those interested in legal careers CYDL provides practical experience in this field as well as long-term mentors that maintain contact with participating students beyond high school.

Alameda County Mock Trial[9]

The Alameda County Mock Trial Competition is a county-wide high school criminal trial competition designed to demystify and increase understanding of our judicial system, and the processes necessary as we strive to create a just society. Teams of ten to twenty students study a hypothetical case, conduct legal research, and receive individual coaching by volunteer attorneys in trial preparation, courtroom protocol, courtroom procedure, analytical skills, and communication skills. Preparation begins in the fall and culminates in grueling elimination-rounds over four weeks of competition in February. The winning team represents Alameda County at the state competition in March.[10]

Students participating in the Alameda County Mock Trial Competition gain a number of invaluable skills including preparation and presentation of a large body of material, argument and debate, memorization and retention of complex issues, and critical thinking. Students are coached by practicing attorneys and grapple with complex legal material over the course of four months. They develop lasting relationships with both the attorneys and team members.

Urban Debate

The National Association of Urban Debate Leagues (NAUDL) serves urban public school systems within the United States. Urban Debate Leagues currently operate in school systems with approximately 87% people of color and 78% low-income student populations. The primary goal is to increase the number of active debaters. The secondary goal is to maintain and improve the educational quality of the debating experience and promote the sustainability of local Urban Debate Leagues.[11]

Oakland Unified School District's commitment to this program allows each participating school to engage with both seasoned debaters and college students who are actively participating in debate after school, two times each week. In Urban Debate, high school students develop arguments, explore the fundamentals of debate and argument, and perform in bi-weekly competitions with local high schools. Students gain skills similar to those acquired through participation in mock trial programs.

Rose Foundation for Communities and the Environment

EXCEL is engaged with the Rose Foundation in the *New Voices Are Rising* Project. *New Voices Are Rising* strives to develop young leaders in low-income communities and communities of color in Alameda and Contra Costa Counties by helping young people gain the skills and experience in civic engagement required to tackle the many problems—especially environmental health problems—that disproportionately impact their communities. In so doing, the project seeks to reduce pollution, especially diesel air pollution and associated particulates, which severely impact both human health and the health of the San Francisco Bay.[12]

For the past four years students have engaged in leadership opportunities based on environmental justice principles. Students have developed and delivered presentations for various government agencies including the State Air Resources Board, Bay Area Air Quality Management District, and local City Council Representatives. Leadership skills are a high priority, and, to this end, students have researched their local community to identify possible polluters, presented information gathered to the press, and are in the process of developing a documentary on their work.[13]

Yosemite Institute

Yosemite Institute connects youth to nature and inspires the next generation of environmental stewards. Since 1971, their residential field science and environmental education programs have introduced almost one million students to the wonder of our National Parks and inspired them to engage in conservation and service.[14]

In partnership with the Rose Foundation, each winter, 35–40 students attend the week-long field science and environmental education program offered by the Institute. Many students have not experienced an intensive outdoor program or been challenged to push their limits. Most return with stories about their experiences that they will recall throughout their lives and reflect positively on their adventures. Ultimately, the goal is to expose students to nature so they understand the importance of conservation and access to clean air and water for everyone.

Results

EXCEL High School has made significant gains towards closing the achievement gap and preparing students for postsecondary education. When EXCEL formed in 2005, McClymonds' API score was 486. EXCEL's most recent API score of 552 reflects significant increases since the conversion.

Although the academic performance on the CST continues to be a challenge, efforts to establish a college-going culture at EXCEL High School have been successful. In 2005–2006, EXCEL High School had the highest percentage of students (59%) who completed the A-G course sequence in the Oakland Unified School District. The 2008 senior class achieved the highest California High School Exit Exam pass rate in Oakland Unified School District with 95% passing both sections. Over 80% have applied and received acceptance letters to four-year colleges. EXCEL college matriculation rates demonstrate that the students are not only gaining admittance to college, but are obtaining the necessary academic skills to successfully complete a course of study.

Student Successes

These are a few of the many examples of students that found their voice through experiences provided through their participation in the Law Academy.

Pamela came to EXCEL and the Law Academy as a transfer student during her tenth grade year. Her early education was in Mexico where she developed her literacy skills in Spanish. At age twelve, she moved to California and was "immersed" in an English only classroom with little transitional support. Despite minimal intervention, Pamela became proficient in English. At EXCEL, her keen comprehension skills became evident, and she was encouraged to participate in the Environmental Justice project. Pamela accepted the challenge by conducting research on air pollution sources and developing testimony based on her research and personal experience with asthma. She has presented her findings at a federal EPA hearing as well as to the California Air Resources Board on numerous occasions. Pamela is developing her journalism skills by becoming a contributing writer for the "Oaktown Teen Times," a school district-wide newspaper. Evidencing further linkages with community partners, last summer Pamela participated in the Center for Youth Development through Law. Although a tenth grader at the time, we encouraged the summer program director to accept her to ensure her continued participation. Past experience with immigrant students indicated that there was a chance that Pamela would not return to EXCEL for her eleventh grade year. Pamela continues to grow and mature as an exceptional student and advocate for her community. Her long-term goal is to become an immigration attorney.

Arthur described himself as, "a knucklehead with a lot of potential," when he entered as a freshman at McClymonds High School. He joined the Law Academy during his tenth grade year, and quickly "found" himself as both a scholar and advocate. Perhaps the competition that developed between Arthur and his peers was the greatest motivating factor. He graduated as valedictorian and successfully completed his degree at UC Berkeley. After a year stint as a CORO fellow at UCLA he returned to EXCEL as director of the College and Career Center. He plans to continue in this role for a second year before pursing either a Masters in Public Policy or Law degree. Arthur believes that he has much to contribute to current students, and works diligently to assist them on their path towards college and career.

Patricia is of Tongan descent and is fiercely proud of her heritage. She joined the Law Academy during her tenth grade year after experiencing incredible success during ninth grade as a member of the Mock Trial Team. Her talent as an attorney earned her accolades and prompted her to continue on the team for her four years of high school. Patricia's determination to succeed was rewarded when she was one of the first students in the high school's history to be accepted into the freshman class at UCLA. She is currently a senior, and after spending a semester in New Zealand, she looks forward to graduation and pursuing a career in law where she will use her skills to advocate for international women's rights.

Terranisha entered the Law Academy during her ninth grade year as part of a pre-law introductory course. She quickly established herself as a leader by immersing herself in the class environmental justice project. Terranisha eagerly conducted research and fearlessly made presentations before local, state, and federal agencies responsible for air quality issues. During her tenth grade year, she lost her mother to colon cancer, and although she had been raised by her grandmother, the loss affected her ability to control her emotions and she was suspended numerous times for conflicts with both teachers and students. Law Academy teachers committed extra time and resources to assist Terranisha with this difficult period, and when she returned to begin her eleventh grade year, she applied for and won the Princeton Prize in Race Relations based on the air quality work she continued to do despite her setback. She looks forward to entering her twelfth grade year with lucrative connections, a positive mind frame, and real hope for a successful future.

Replicability

According to a recent study by ConnectED, replication varies depending on the location of a particular program. In California, the first two academies were funded in 1981 by a non-profit organization. The state quickly followed in 1985 by making the program available to high schools located in qualified school districts around the state. The National Academy Foundation began supporting academies in various states beginning in 1982, and currently supports programs in 40 states. An equal number of academies operate with outside funding sources, including the federal government. The success of these programs has been thoroughly documented and resources to replicate are readily available.[15] Perhaps the most important consideration while exploring replication is to require open communication and attentive listening to those who will be served in order to ensure that their needs will be addressed through the program's implementation.

Appendix

California Partnership Academies[16]

§ 54692. (Second of two: Operative July 1, 2011) Funding eligibility

In order to be eligible to receive funding pursuant to this article, a school district shall provide all of the following:

(a) An amount equal to a 100 percent match of all funds received pursuant to this article in the form of direct and in-kind support provided by the district.

(b) An amount equal to a 100 percent match of all funds received pursuant to this article in the form of direct and in-kind support provided by participating companies or other private sector organizations.

(c) An assurance that state funds provided by the partnership academies program shall be used only for the development, operation, and support of partnership academies.

(d) An assurance that each academy will be established as a "school within a school." Academy teachers shall work as a team in planning, teaching, and troubleshooting program activities. Classes in the academy program shall be limited to academy pupils as specified in subdivision (e). Each participating school district shall establish an advisory committee consisting of individuals involved in academy operations, including school district and school administrators, lead teachers, and representatives of the private sector.

(e) Assurance that each academy pupil will be provided with the following:

(1) Instruction in at least three academic subjects each regular school term that prepares the pupil for a regular high school diploma, and, where possible and appropriate, to meet the subject requirements for admission to the California State University and the University of California. These subjects should contribute to an understanding of the occupational field of the academy.

(2) Career technical education courses offered at each grade level at the academy that are part of an occupational course sequence that targets comprehensive skills and that does the following:

(A) Provides career technical education in high skill occupations of regional and local economic need.

(B) Focuses on occupations requiring comprehensive skills leading to higher than entry-level wages, or the possibility of significant wage increases after a few years on the job, or both.

(C) Provides a sequence of courses that build upon each other in knowledge, skill development, and experience, and ends in a capstone course that includes an internship component.

(D) Prepares pupils for employment and postsecondary education. Sequenced courses shall be linked to certificate and degree programs in the region, where possible.

(E) Whenever possible, prepares pupils for industry-recognized certifications.

(F) Whenever possible and appropriate, offers career technical education courses that also meet the subject requirements for admission to the California State University and the University of California.

(3) A class schedule that limits the attendance to the classes required in paragraphs (1) and (2) to pupils of the academy. Whenever possible, these classes should be block scheduled in a cluster to provide flexibility to academy teachers. During the 12th grade the number of academic classes may vary.

(4) A mentor from the business community during the pupil's 11th grade year.

(5) An employer-based internship or work experience that occurs in the summer following the 11th grade or during 12th grade year.

(6) Additional motivational activities with private sector involvement to encourage academic and occupational preparation.

(f) Assurance that academy teachers have a common planning period to interchange pupil and educational information. A second planning period should be provided for the lead teacher in addition to the normal planning period for full-time teachers and be supported as a part of the school district's matching funds, whenever practical.

Chapter 7

Law-Themed High Schools

First Colonial High School Legal Studies Academy Virginia Beach, Virginia

Paige Scherr, JD*

Pre-K	Elementary	Middle	High School	College	Law School	Profession

Background

On February 19, 2002, the Virginia Beach City Public Schools (VBCPS), School Board approved the proposal for the Legal Studies Academy at First Colonial High School. Currently, there are five themed academies and two advanced academic programs, including an International Baccalaureate Program and a mathematics and science program within VBCPS at the high school level. In part due to research indicating that students enrolled in career oriented and/or magnet programs had higher attendance rates and lower dropout rates, as well as improved behavior and greater satisfaction with school, the academies were established to provide a broad array of choice for students. In establishing the academies format as schools-within-schools, division leaders also relied on extensive research demonstrating that some students learn better in a smaller school setting.[1]

VBCPS is the largest school division in Hampton Roads—southeastern Virginia— serving approximately 69,000 students in grades K–12. Currently, the school system includes 56 elementary schools, 14 middle schools, and 11 high schools. In addition to the academy programs, the division also includes elementary and middle school

---

* Paige Scherr is the Coordinator of the Legal Studies Academy at First Colonial High School in Virginia Beach, Virginia. Mrs. Scherr holds a Bachelor's Degree in Political Science with an Education Endorsement in Secondary Social Studies from Texas A&M University. She also holds a law degree from The University of Oklahoma and an Ed.S. in Supervision and Instruction from The George Washington University. Mrs. Scherr is licensed to teach in Virginia and Texas and is a member of the Texas Bar.

gifted centers, a career and technical education campus, Advanced Technology Center, and the Renaissance Academy, which provides a variety of alternative education programs.

On October 21, 2008, Virginia Beach City Public Schools adopted a new strategic plan. *Compass to 2015* has been designed to equip students with the skills they need to succeed as 21st century learners, workers, and citizens. All VBCPS students will be:

- Academically proficient;

- Effective communicators and collaborators;

- Globally aware, independent, responsible learners and citizens; and

- Critical and creative thinkers, innovators, and problem solvers.

Therefore, academy instruction and assessment practices are designed to foster the development of these attributes.[2]

Program Description

The Legal Studies Academy (LSA), which was created to provide students with a challenging curriculum infused with law, functions as a school-within-a-school. The Academy offers students the opportunity to embrace an academic curriculum that will prepare them for a post-secondary education. Students are also afforded the opportunity to explore career options in the legal field. Courses of study are extended through law-related seminars and field trips. Students have many hands-on experiences including: criminal investigations, internships, and mock trials in the Academy's courtroom/classroom.

The Legal Studies Academy was created to provide students who have an interest in law, law-related fields, and legal and ethical issues the opportunity to extend their knowledge beyond what a typical high-school program would provide. As stated in the program proposal: "The program helps students develop the skills needed to acquire information about the role of law in constitutional democracies and other societies and how it is connected to their lives."[3] Academy students are full-time students enrolled at First Colonial High School and enjoy access to all high school programs and activities, including those sponsored by the Virginia High School League. Although the focus is on law related studies, the curriculum provides students access to high quality curriculum in all disciplines.

Academy students take their required law, social studies, science, and English classes as a cohort. In order to promote active learning and the importance of community involvement, all LSA students are required to participate in job shadowing, legal internships, and community service. All non-law classes such as health/physical education, mathematics, foreign language, and other general electives are taken with the rest of the First Colonial student body. Academy students are strongly encouraged to pursue an Advanced Studies Diploma.

The academy has two major components: Law and Administration of Justice. The Law Component is designed to allow students to explore careers open to lawyers, paralegals, court reporters, and judges. The Administration of Justice component introduces students to career possibilities such as police officer, criminal psychologist, forensic scientist, criminal investigator, and other law enforcement related options.

Academy Curriculum

The first year in the academy provides the foundation for the entire four year curriculum. Students take Introduction to Law (based on the *Street Law* curriculum), LSA World History I, LSA Honors English, and LSA Earth Science or LSA Biology as a cohort. Students also take a math, foreign language, and health/physical education to complete their ninth grade year, however, these courses are taken with the First Colonial student body.

During the first year, students participate in a cross-curricular project known as "World Simulation." The majority of the work is completed in the World History class, however, students also work on related components of the project in their other LSA courses. The project requires students (working in groups of four) to develop a country, which includes the constitution and culture of their country. The project builds to the day long World Simulation. All student countries are set up in the school gymnasium and the entire day is spent in a mock world simulation in which countries use the resources they are given to survive. World disasters are presented to the student groups to test their survival skills. Countries overtake each other throughout the day. A mock or Model United Nations is also an important part of the project where each country selects a student to represent them in the Model United Nations. The entire project is a true testament of 21st century skills, allowing students to use critical and analytical skills, as well as presentation and negotiation techniques.

During the second year, LSA students are introduced to the Administration of Justice component through the Introduction to Criminal Justice course. The class is a year-long survey course that covers all aspects of the criminal justice system. Other academy courses taken as a cohort include Academy Honors English, Academy Government, and LSA Biology or Chemistry. Upon completion of the second year, students are introduced to their first work skills based component during the summer job shadowing.

Third year LSA students take two law classes, Legal Oratory & Debate and Ethics & Law, each of which are semester long classes. Additional courses taken as a cohort are Academy Honors English and Academy US/VA History. New to the third year curriculum for the 2011–2012 school year will be a cross-curricular project centered around *The Innocent Man*, by John Grisham. Students will analyze the legal and ethical issues presented in this novel within their English, Law, and Forensic Science course. During the spring semester of the third year, students also begin taking after school seminars in preparation for their summer internship.

During the final year, students also take Academy Honors English and Academy World History II as a cohort. The curriculum consists of Legal Research & Writing and Senior Project, which are semester courses. Legal Research and Writing builds upon the legal analysis skills students have gained throughout their previous law courses. Utilizing both LEXIS/NEXIS and Westlaw databases, students refine their ability to brief cases, utilize traditional legal analysis paradigms, and construct a closed legal memorandum. Senior Project is a learner-centered course in which students have the ability to propose a project, write a legal based research paper, document their findings, and present their project to a panel of community professionals. This capstone project requires a significant effort in legal research, planning, and implementation of 21st century skills. It allows the students an opportunity to integrate skills they have acquired throughout their four years in the program. All students are required to successfully complete the Senior Project class as a graduation requirement for the academy. The overall goal of the course is to provide a strong foundation for the learner upon graduation.

It should be noted that students have the opportunity to substitute an Advanced Placement course for the Academy class, if one exists. In these instances, academy students still stay in cohorts to the greatest extent possible.

In addition to the above mentioned required courses, academy students also have the exclusive opportunity to take the following elective courses:

- Introduction to Criminology (semester course; Prerequisite: Introduction to Criminal Law and Introduction to Criminal Justice)

- Criminal Psychology (semester course; Prerequisite: Introduction to Criminal Law and Introduction to Criminal Justice)

- Forensic Science (year long course; Prerequisite: Chemistry)

- Mock Trials/Moot Court (year long course; Prerequisite: Introduction to Law)

- Criminal Evidence and Procedures I (semester course; Dual Enrollment course with Tidewater Community College)

- Criminal Evidence and Procedures II (semester course; Dual Enrollment course with Tidewater Community College)

- Introduction to Juvenile Justice (semester course; Dual Enrollment course with Tidewater Community College)

Academy Co-Curricular Requirements

Skills based learning opportunities are an important component to the Academy student's experience. Three of these experiences have been integrated into the required curriculum and will be discussed below.

Community Service

All academy students are required to complete a minimum of 200 hours of community service prior to graduation. Students arrange their service on an individual basis, although the academy office does make regular announcements of various opportunities. The service does not have to be legal in nature, and in fact, students are encouraged to participate in a wide variety of opportunities. Some examples of service activities are assisting local elementary schools with tutoring programs, working with various homeless shelters and food banks, assisting city recreation centers with after school programs, and working with the many local charitable organizations such as Operation Smile, American Red Cross, and Dolphin Watch.

Although the minimum of 200 hours is required, many students far exceed that number. The Class of 2010 (78 members) logged 24,318 hours, which averages to over 300 hours per student. In a longitudinal study of academy graduates, 96% of 2010 graduates indicated that the service requirement was very or somewhat useful.[4]

Job Shadowing

Following the completion of their 10th grade year, all students are required to complete an eight hour job shadowing requirement. Students work with a legal professional to obtain a working knowledge of the chosen career. Students complete the requirement in a variety of legal settings, law firms, police departments and other local government agencies. Students often use the job shadowing requirement as an introduction to their legal internship. In some instances, students who entered the academy focused on a particular career have changed their mind as a result of their job shadowing experience. Reaching this conclusion prior to the internship still leaves them an opportunity to get a hands-on experience in another legal field. More than 94% of 2010 academy graduates rated the job shadowing component as very or somewhat useful.[5]

Internship

Students begin preparing for the internship requirement during the spring semester of their junior year. A parent/student meeting is held in which the requirements of the program are explained. Informational packets are distributed which contain medical and legal liability forms, explanations of seminar topics and dates, and rubrics for how students will be graded in the course.

Seminars, totaling 20 hours, are held after school during the spring semester. During the first seminar, students complete a survey in which they are permitted to request their choice of placement. Six more seminars are held throughout the semester and focus on such topics as building a professional resume, ethics and confidentiality, professional dress and business etiquette, interview techniques, and stress/time management. Placements and work schedules are provided during the final seminar. Some of the internship mentors choose to attend this seminar to meet with their assigned students. Others hold an orientation at the work site.

Students are closely supervised by an internship instructor and must complete a minimum of 50 hours on site. The instructor closely monitors the student's progress throughout the summer through site visits, email, and phone contact with internship mentors. Seminars are held during the summer with the students and instructors to give students an opportunity to share their experiences with their peers. In accordance with VBCPS's Strategic Plan, the 2011–2012 interns will begin documenting their journey through the summer internship via on-line blogging. Students will have the ability to network remotely with mentors, faculty members, and peers. The internship program has been very successful and is a cornerstone of the academy curriculum. Students have turned internships into full time employment positions and contacts made have proven to be valuable in the college application and scholarship process. Longitudinal studies have confirmed this, with over 98% of 2010 academy graduates rating it as a somewhat useful or very useful experience.[6]

Academy Demographics

Academy students are admitted as a result of a rigorous selection process. The application is open to all students within the VBCPS attendance zones. Students complete one application for all division academies and advanced academic programs at the high school level. Each academy is permitted to have unique components for their applicants. Legal Studies Academy applicants are required to submit an interest essay, as part of the general application.

Applications are reviewed by a 12- to 15-member selection committee made up of teachers, administrators, guidance counselors, and central office administrators. Each application is reviewed and scored by a minimum of three members. After all applications have been scored, the academy coordinator determines how many seats will be offered for each grade level. Applicants are assigned a status of accept, wait, or reject, based on the application score. All applicants are notified, regardless of status.

Academy students come from all areas of Virginia Beach. This allows for a diverse academy student body, and it also contributes to the diversity of First Colonial High School. Minority students account for 32% of the academy student body. The academy demographics are depicted in the table below:[7]

Grade	Male/ Female	African American	Asian	Caucasian	Hispanic	NATV/ Pacific Islander	Unspecified
9	34 Males; 64 Females	12	3	71	7	1	4
10	32 Males; 53 Females	24	2	53	5	1	0
11	39 Males; 54 Females	17	5	64	6	1	
12	29 Males; 43 Females	15	2	46	8	0	1
Total	348	68	12	234	26	3	5

Partners in Education

A major part of the academy's success is due to work with the community. Leaders in the various legal professions served on the committee to establish the academy, and have retained close ties with the program. VBCPS has a formal partnership program, known as "Partners in Education." The academy has formal partnerships with the following organizations: Virginia Beach Police Department (VBCPS Model Partnership, 2008); Bullock & Cooper, Attorneys at Law (VBCPS Model Partnership, 2007); NASA Langley (VBCPS Model Partnership 2007); Wahab Law Library (VBCPS Model Partnership, 2006); Virginia Beach Sheriff's Department; United States Naval Legal Services Division-Mid- Atlantic; The Law Offices of Kathleen Cipriano; Marcari, Russotto, Spencer, & Balaban; Cox & Cox Attorneys;;Virginia Beach Bar Association; and the Federal Bureau of Investigations/Norfolk Division.

The work with the community partners is crucial to the program's success. Partners provide students with internship and job shadowing opportunities. They also serve as guest speakers for classrooms, and curriculum consultants for teachers. In addition to service from partner personnel, the academy has received grants, scholarships, and other financial assistance to supplement its annual budget.

The academy also works with the law schools of The College of William & Mary and Regent University. These academic institutions have organized mock law school days for academy students. Students and teachers have been invited to special classes and seminars sponsored by the schools. Students have also served as witnesses for collegiate and law school mock trial competitions hosted by Regent Law School. Professors from Regent Law have served as consultants for academy teachers in writing curriculum.

Administrative Structure

The Academy Coordinator is the academy's key administrator. In overseeing day-to-day operations of the academy, the coordinator reports to the building principal. Because the academy programs are budgeted through the Department of Curriculum & Instruction, the coordinator also reports to the Director of Secondary Instructional Services and Academy Programs, in central administration.

The duties for the coordinator can be divided into the following categories:

- Marketing: Marketing the academy to prospective students and parents, as well as community partners, the local business community, and other stakeholders.

- Application and Selection: Manages the student application and selection process, which includes course registration.

- Curriculum and Staff Development: Oversees the entire curriculum development process and ensures that staff development opportunities are available.

- Data Collection and Budget Management: Maintains data for the Department of Educational Leadership and Assessment and manages all academy budget receipts and expenditures.

- Teacher Hiring, Retention, and Evaluation: Manages the hiring and evaluation process as well as the master schedule component for all academy staff.

- Student Discipline and Grade Monitoring: Manages all aspects of student academic progress, including disciplinary issues.

Professional Development

Academy teachers are afforded the same professional development opportunities as other VBCPS teachers. Participation in the division's Professional Development Program (PDP), is a contractual requirement for all instructional staff. All ten month instructional staff members are required to earn 22 PDP hours per year. Sixteen of the hours are site based and are earned by participating in the teacher's respective building. The remaining six hours can be earned in variety of ways, including taking graduate level courses or taking PDP courses sponsored by the division.[8]

Academy teachers have many opportunities for professional development, including courses offered by VBCPS that are tailored to academies. For instance, each academy can also develop opportunities at the site level that are specific to the academy theme. This can include bringing in consultants from law-related education organizations, local lawyers and law enforcement officers, as well as law professors to work with teachers on a specific topic.

Academy teachers also have opportunities to attend local, state, and national conferences. Each year, a group of teachers attends the summer conference sponsored by the Association for Supervision and Curriculum Development (ASCD). This conference provides teachers with the opportunity to attend various sessions, some which are subject specific, and many of which focus on curriculum development and instruction. Teachers also have the opportunity to attend conferences that are specific to their subject area. For example, the academy forensic science teachers have attended a week long institute sponsored by the National Academy of Forensic Science and several teachers have attended and presented at the National Law Related Education Conference, a bi-annual conference sponsored by the American Bar Association.

Teachers in the Legal Studies Academy also have a common planning period. This time has proven particularly valuable as it can be used for whole group meetings, formal professional development offerings, or a time for grade level or content area teachers to plan together. This time also allows for teachers to work on cross-curricular projects, as well as receive peer feedback on curriculum design. A priority is given to provide teachers with professional development days during the school year to work as a team.

Results to Date

As with any new program, the first years are a learning process. The structure of the curriculum, as it currently exists, is a product of refinement based upon student, parent, and community partner feedback after a rigorous evaluation process. Recent longitudinal studies confirm that the changes have been met with positive results. For example, in response to the question "Did the academy experience prepare you to be successful in college?", only 79% of students in the first cohort agreed, when responding to a survey one year after high school, as compared to 100% of students in the second cohort.

Longitudinal studies have also compared academy students and non-academy students on a variety of factors. When comparisons are made, the studies have created comparison groups by choosing non-academy students who are similar in standing to academy students. Even so, larger percentages of academy students agree that they were academically challenged (91% compared to 68%), that their educational program helped them make choices about future education and/or employment (90% compared to 69%), and that they were prepared for college (over 90% compared to 74%).[9]

The exclusive components of the academy curriculum (courses, work experience, community service, and Senior Project) serve to provide a unique experience for academy students. This allows academy students to "stand out" in the college and scholarship application process. This is demonstrated through the tremendous success academy students have had in scholarship offers. First Colonial's 2008 and 2009 graduating classes received an average of 4.8 million dollars in scholarship offers. Academy students, although accounting for less than 20% of these graduating classes, were offered almost 50% of the scholarship dollars.[10]

Student Success Stories

Evan came to LSA from a small religious private school with only seven students in his eighth grade class. He had a difficult time transitioning to a large public high school, but found that the Legal Studies Academy, LSA, was the environment he needed to thrive. The small community found within LSA enabled Evan to acclimate to public school while having a support network generally found in a smaller school. This enabled him to explore career interests throughout high school. While he was first interested in becoming a prosecutor, this exploration led him to work for four years with the Virginia Beach Police Department and develop a strong interest in public service. Evan is now a junior at the University of Virginia, where he majors in Political Science. He has continued his interest in public service and is now completing his third year as a volunteer Firefighter/EMT with the Charlottesville Fire Department. Recently, he combined his interest in government and the emergency services through an internship with the International Association of Fire Chiefs in their Government Relations Department. Evan is considering attending law school and pursuing of a career in emergency preparedness and homeland security policy. He credits LSA with providing an atmosphere to encourage hands-on learning, academic and professional preparation, and exploration of career opportunities.

Shavarae ("Sha") applied to the academy during the summer after her sophomore year. She had recently moved into the Virginia Beach City Public School attendance zone after a tumultuous year at a school that has a history of discipline problems. Most students begin the Legal Studies Academy as ninth graders. In order for Sha to successfully complete the program, she was starting at a big disadvantage. She would have to take her required ninth and tenth grade classes, along with her junior and senior classes in two years. Sha says that "having to take these classes, on top of a regular course schedule, was extremely hard but it was also the best decision of my life." Sha is currently a junior at Clark Atlanta. She is planning a career in the fashion industry. Sha is a true success story and her story is best told by her

> The pressure of the classes was very stressful and demanding, but they prepared me for college. Having to take classes such as Legal Oratory and Debate prepared me for giving college speeches. I always feel prepared, especially when my college peers are experiencing nervousness at giving speeches, normal feel-

ings that I learned to deal with in high school. The LSA has taught me so many things to use in and out the classroom. I began high school with a 1.0 GPA but due to the rigorous course work and relationships I established with faculty and peers, I graduated with an Advanced Diploma, being accepted to eight out of ten colleges.

Replicability

Organizationally, the academy can be easily replicated, but a firm budgetary commitment to the program is required. A school-within-a-school focused on the concept of law and law-related fields does not require large capital outlay in the form of buildings, or additional staff allocations. The biggest additional expenditure is related to student transportation, which is crucial to the success of the program. Because the VBCPS School Board made a commitment to the academy programs overall, the financial support was put in place. The Board is frequently apprised of the success of the programs through evaluations and longitudinal studies. The biggest challenge, as with any unique program, has been to work through the need for change. When the academy was established, there were few similar programs in existence nationwide, and none in Virginia. After the program was established, it was evident that modifications were necessary. It is the intention of the academy faculty and staff to continuously revise our curriculum and assessment practices to meet the needs of our 21st century learners.

Chapter 8

Multi-Faceted Outreach: High School and Beyond[1]

Legal Outreach
New York, New York

James O'Neal, Esq.[*]

Pre-K	Elementary	Middle	High School	College	Law School	Profession

The best pipeline programs are the ones that start reasonably early and stay with the students; they are rigorous, intense, and relevant. In addition to high-expectation curricula and cocurricular offerings (including the scaffolding and skill support needed) successful programs provide students with important mentoring and other relationships. In some cases, such programs are their own schools. In others, they are what I like to call surround programs, that is, they are built around a student's regular school life—after school, weekends, summers. Legal Outreach is such a surround program: a prize-winning pipeline program with a remarkable record of success in New York City. The Legal Outreach model is also used in Cleveland, and Legal Outreach is engaged in expansion to other locations.

Origins and Background

In 1982, I came from Harvard Law School to New York City as Harvard's first Public Interest Law Fellowship recipient. My mission was simply to create opportunities for students from urban communities to experience the law from a more positive and balanced perspective, and to inspire some to pursue careers within the profession. My desire was to serve students on whom many had given up. My initial destination and placement was Boys and Girls High School in Brooklyn. Fortunately, the school, as part

---

* James O'Neal is the Co-Founder/Executive Director of Legal Outreach. In 1982, Mr. O'Neal received the Harvard Fellowship in Public Interest Law and co-founded Legal Outreach in 1983. He became a Columbia University Charles Revson Fellow in 1990. Mr. O'Neal attended Oxford College of Emory University, A.A., 1977; Emory College, Emory University, B.A., 1979, Political Science; and Harvard Law School, J.D., 1982.

of its regular offerings, had a law elective course, which they allowed me to teach on a daily basis. The course was open to seniors and a smattering of juniors. Excited but nervous, my journey, which was meant to last only a year, began.

Though I envisioned myself as a teacher, in actuality I became a student because there were so many lessons that I was learning through my day-to-day classroom interactions. One of the most important lessons was the following: our education system was failing our children. It only took a day to learn that the educational deficits in the lives of my students were pronounced and inexcusable. The literacy skills of the great majority were so low it was hard to imagine how they had made it this far. Even more difficult to imagine was how they could ever be admitted to college. I had met social promotion face to face. Yet, even in the midst of the despair, there were rays of hope. Although the reading and writing abilities of my students were below par, many of these same students were impressive thinkers. Their ability to analyze situations and come to reasoned conclusions often surprised and even astounded me. Our discussions of legal issues were fascinating. If one could overlook grammar and syntax and focus purely on the substance of a student's comments, it was easy to see that many of these students were extremely smart and some even brilliant. Their insights became the impetus that pushed me to continue this work rather than give up on them like so many others had.

The second lesson I learned was that it was entirely possible to inspire students to seek careers within the legal profession. My very first day of teaching, I innocently asked the question "How many of you want to become lawyers?" Not a single individual raised his or her hand. I was shocked. Yet, by the end of the semester, a number of students had approached me individually (never in a group) to pose the same basic question. "So, Mr. O'Neal what does it take to become a lawyer?" Students who had never thought of becoming lawyers now saw it as an option for their lives. Sadly, those dreams were not likely to be realized, through no fault of their own. That conclusion led me to the third and perhaps most important lesson. Helping students to realize their dreams of becoming legal professions could only be achieved by closing the educational deficits in their lives. Failure to tackle this problem would guarantee that the dreams of the great majority of these students would forever be imaginary. Thus, my journey to equalize opportunity and to diversify the legal profession began.

The Early Years: 1982–89

After completing my first semester of education at Boys and Girls High School, I decided to follow-up on the lessons learned. Rather than teaching high school students, I chose to work with middle-schoolers, specifically eighth graders. Again, I was fortunate to have the opportunity to teach a law elective class at a school in East Harlem. At Boys and Girls, I introduced students to the Bill of Rights and Constitutional Law. In doing so, I noticed that the amendment that generated the most discussion was, of course, the fourth amendment and search and seizure. I also noticed that when students would stay after-class to talk with me or to ask law-related questions, it was seldom about constitutional issues. More often than not, it was about community and personal issues. Concluding that these issues were not only relevant to the lives of the students asking the questions, but also to those living in like circumstances, I developed a new curriculum, called "Law and the Community." This curriculum has since been broken up into three different curricula: "Law and Social Problems"; "Law, the Legal System, and Dispute Resolution"; and "Criminal Justice: Theory and Practice. "Focusing on issues that permeate the lives of residents in urban areas, I discovered that I could ignite the spark for learning in almost every child, because the issues were pertinent to their lives. Most students had either experienced the problem, knew folks who had, or, at the very least, knew that the problem existed and was prevalent. Lively discussions raged over topics like child abuse and neglect, domestic violence, and police use of force. With their interest piqued and sustained, I also discovered that I could use the law to help students develop skills critical to their educational advancement—ranging from comprehension, to decision making, reasoning, critical thinking, advocacy, and writing. The success of the program led me to codify the information in lesson plan form and to share it with social studies and English language teachers interested in replicating the program in their schools.

In 1984, Legal Outreach began the process of expanding the pilot law program that I had created by providing professional development workshops to interested schools and teachers. We also developed relationships with law-related organizations—Bar Associations, Prosecutor Offices, Legal Aid Offices, courts, and law schools—to supplement the teaching, we organized mock exercises that would allow students to experience the power and operations of the law. Within two years, a model law program was developed within Harlem, which was followed by an expansion to other school districts and neighborhoods within New York City. The results were encouraging. Students who, in taking a pre-course survey, never listed law as a potential career option now had it listed as one of their top two choices. Students also expressed a more positive outlook towards the legal system and more confidence in their ability to advocate for themselves when situations arouse. Those who participated in the mock trial felt challenged by the exercise, felt pride in their accomplishments, and felt more ready for the transition to high school. The multi-faceted, one year law program was working. Surely these students, motivated by their experiences, were well on their way to one day diversifying the legal profession. Or so we thought.

Independent assessments of the work that we were doing were extremely positive. We received lots of encouragement and feedback. Yet, as we continued to implement this multi-layered law program for eighth graders throughout the 1980s, we started to see a trend. When we encountered former students now in their sophomore, junior, or senior year of high school, we noticed that many of our bright and talented performers had lost their resolve and seemed to be less committed to pursuing their goals. Questioning the students revealed that many were attending large high schools where they were just a number. Many were not receiving encouragement, most were not developing the necessary skills needed for success, and some were succumbing to the negative pressures that often plague young people in urban communities.

Decision time was again upon us. Were we content to continue implementing a great one-year program with a proven success record or would we challenge ourselves to take the next step to develop a program that would keep our bright and talented youth on track through the high school years? We chose the latter route and the results of doing so speak for themselves.

The College-Bound Program

In 1989, the Legal Outreach Board of Directors made a decision that has been life changing for many students from poor communities in New York City. In addition to continuing to implement our much heralded middle school law program, we would also start a follow-up program, which quickly became known as "College Bound." Over the next four years, College Bound evolved into a comprehensive, four-year skill development program designed to equip students from underserved communities who had experienced the power of the law with the opportunities and tools they would need to achieve their dreams. It took us seven years, from 1982 to 1989, to learn a key lesson. Superior, well-implemented law programs can be the catalyst to a dream for urban students but structured skill building support programs are essential to propel them to the goal. Over the course of four years, from 1989 to 1993, Legal Outreach built a comprehensive program designed to close the achievement gap and keep students on the road to higher education and the legitimate pursuit of their dreams. The program is multi-faceted, operates after school, on Saturdays, and during the summers over the four years of high school, and literally consumes 2,400 hours of our students' lives, over and beyond what their high schools require.

College-Bound Program Components

The College Bound Program (CB) consists of the following components:

After School Study and Tutorial Center (All Years)

CB students with averages below 85 are required to attend the study center two hours a day, four days a week, after school to improve their academic performance in school.

Writing Classes (9–12th Grades)

CB students attend Saturday classes to master the elements of grammar, essay writing, persuasive writing, and research. The four-year Saturday Writing Program plays an integral role in preparing CB students with the skills to succeed in the nation's top colleges and universities. Often cited by alumni as one of the programs that conferred the most practical and essential skills for academic and professional success, the Saturday Writing Program employs professional writers from all walks of life, including lawyers, journalists, academics, and novelists. Under their instruction, students work from 10 a.m. to 2 p.m. on two to three Saturdays per month to develop fundamental writing skills, focusing on grammar their freshman year, essay writing sophomore year, persuasive writing junior year, and research writing senior year.

Mentoring Program (10th–12th Grades)[2]

During their sophomore year, CB students are assigned individual mentors from the legal profession who provide one-on-one support and assistance through their mentees' senior year. Over 130 attorneys and judges from New York's best firms, public interest organizations, and business institutions serve as mentors to our students. The mentor/mentee relationship, which ideally continues until the student graduates high school and often into adulthood, provides students with an advisor, role model, and friend during a critical time in their lives and academic development. Mentors participate in debate preparation, social/cultural events, and general support as advisor and role model.

Mentors are required to have a law degree, and the mentoring time commitment is approximately five hours of face-to-face contact per month, excluding occasional correspondence by email and phone. Most of this contact occurs at debates and social/cultural events. Debates, for which experienced attorneys can earn up to 3 CLE credits per year, take place on three Friday evenings and one Saturday morning per year. Social/cultural events, of which there are three or four per year, are usually scheduled for Saturday or Sunday afternoons on months that no debate is scheduled. We accept mentor applications throughout the year and make mentor/mentee assignments in September. Legal Outreach is available to give a presentation about the mentoring program at area law firms or organizations.

Constitutional Law Debates (10th–12th grades)

CB students participate in bi-monthly debates, modeled after law school moot court programs to enhance their reasoning, articulation, and advocacy skills. Beginning in their sophomore year, students participate in four debates per year that are designed to hone students' analytic and public speaking skills. Each debate focuses on a different constitutional law topic such as the Establishment Clause, Equal Protection Clause, Due Process, Freedom of Speech, and Miranda Rights. Law students and attorneys are invited to guest judge at our debates and to help draft debate fact patterns.

With the assistance of law-student debate coaches and attorney mentors, students learn the substantive law at issue in a given debate, read and analyze legal cases, outline their argument with supporting and distinguishing facts, statistics and law, and ultimately deliver an oral argument to a panel of judges who also ask the students questions that force them to think on their feet. The winners of each debate are awarded trophies and become eligible to compete in our annual Debater-of-the-Year Competition for college scholarships.

Academic and Life Skills Workshops (9th Grade)

During their freshman year, CB students participate in after-school workshops to sharpen their academic and life skills, and to enhance their preparation and planning for the future. The purpose of the Life Skills Workshops is to give College Bound freshmen the skills and resources necessary for academic success and to empower young people to make healthy, informed decisions. The series is divided into four distinct but mutually reinforcing curricular units:

1. **Colleges and Careers.** The Colleges and Careers unit is designed to help students plan for their futures by considering what they must do now in order to attain the goals they have set for themselves. Topics include the connection between educational attainment and careers and salaries, avenues for getting on the right track to a top college or university, the link between high school performance and college prospects, and the SAT.

2. **Study Skills.** After motivating young people by exploring their future prospects, we supply them with the skills they must employ to get there. Topics in the Study Skills unit include time management, how to read a textbook, and what it means to study effectively.

3. **Adolescence and Sexuality.** The Adolescence and Sexuality unit is designed to empower young people to effectively deal with the social and emotional issues of adolescence by empowering them to make healthy and informed decisions. Topics include exploring adolescence, the link between sexual decision making and values, sexual education, physical and emotional consequences of being sexually active, and sexual diversity.

4. **Conflict Resolution.** The Conflict Resolution unit addresses how to effectively deal with personal and interpersonal conflicts in the lives of young people. An emphasis is placed on providing students with practical tools for devising creative resolutions to arising conflicts. Topics include looking at conflict as a natural part of life, how to respond to conflict, defusing situations without losing control, and handling conflict with parents and teachers.3

Social and Cultural Events (10th–12th grades)

CB students participate in bi-monthly outings to expand their understanding and appreciation of cultures and activities outside their everyday experiences.

Summer Law Internships (Rising 10th Graders)

CB students are provided with opportunities to act as lawyers at some of New York's top law firms, public interest organizations, financial institution, and courts (working directly with judges) for up to five weeks during the summer before their sophomore year of high school. Students gain valuable work experience and a unique exposure to the practice of law.

Participating law firms and organizations have the flexibility to structure their four-day internships however they choose. Some arrange for students to draft briefs, deliver oral arguments, and participate in mock negotiations. All expose students to the practice of law and to lawyers who inspire and motivate them to work hard and pursue professional careers.

SAT Preparation (Rising 11th Graders)

SAT Prep is a five-week, full-time summer program for rising juniors in the College Bound program. To prepare for the SAT—a standardized test that is required for admission to most colleges and universities—students receive intensive instruction from Kaplan, a professional test preparation company. These courses are also supplemented with smaller sections led by Legal Outreach tutors. With hard work and dedication, students have typically increased their scores by an average of 300 points over a five-week period.

College Selection and Preparation (Rising 12th Graders)

CB rising seniors participate in an intensive college-level course taught by a college professor, which is designed to simulate the rigors of the college environment. Students are provided with individualized assistance in choosing colleges, writing personal essays, and completing admissions and financial aid applications. The purpose of the College Preparation Session is to prepare rising seniors for the transition into college by exposing them to college-level instruction, and by starting the college application process at an early stage. The course consists of three separate components plus a mandatory study hall.

1. **Philosophy 101: Ethical Dilemmas.** Ethical Dilemmas is a college-level philosophy class taught by a college professor. Students are assigned one final paper, and are required to take a midterm and cumulative final exam.

2. **Study Skills for College Success.** Study Skills for College Success focuses on developing necessary study skills. It utilizes readings from the philosophy course as case studies to teach effective tools for optimal reading comprehension, outlining, note taking, analysis, and much more.

3. **College Application Process.** The College Application Process is a series of workshops where students begin writing their personal statements and essays for college applications, learn about financial aid, scholarships, and begin developing the list of schools to which they will apply.

Results to Date

Since accepting its first six students from Harlem in 1989, Legal Outreach CB has grown slowly but surely, and is now serving 244 students from underserved communities in Manhattan, Brooklyn, Queens, and the Bronx. Since the graduation of our first class in 1993, 336 students, approximately 70% of those who started the program, have completed the four-year program, and 99.3 percent have attended college! In fact, approximately two-thirds of the program's graduates have matriculated to top-ranked colleges and universities including: Harvard, Yale, MIT, Columbia, Dartmouth, Brown, Cornell, Swarthmore, Amherst, NYU, Duke, Emory, University of Virginia, Wellesley, Pomona, Bryn Mawr, Middlebury, Wesleyan, Mt. Holyoke, Smith, and many more. In 2010, the college matriculation list of the Legal Outreach's 33 seniors included Princeton, University of Pennsylvania, Williams, Pomona, and Wellesley. Several seniors also earned competitive city-wide and national academic scholarships including the Gates Millennium Scholarship (University of Pennsylvania), one of the nation's most competitive scholarship prizes, the Seinfeld Scholarship (Wellesley), and six Posse Scholarships (Trinity College, Franklin & Marshall College, Wheaton College and Babson College). Our seniors' acceptance list is even more impressive considering that most will be the first in their families to attend college. From their home communities of Harlem, Washington Heights, Bedford Stuyvesant, and Crown Heights, they are on their way to the nation's finest institutions.

Each year Legal Outreach sees its CB students improve in many ways, but of the most visible ways for comparative purposes is through their success on the SAT. In 2009, Legal Outreach's rising juniors, taking their first diagnostic test, began with an average score of 1421, but through their participation in our five-week summer SAT course in conjunction with Stanley Kaplan, raised their average to 1646 on the actual test. This is compared to an average score of 1509 for all students and 1581 for White students. This type of success has led to the following other successes:

- 100% of College Bound participants graduate high school in four years, as compared to 52.1% of New York City high school students and 77.8% of high school students nationally.

- 99.3% of College Bound participants have matriculated to four-year colleges, while 47% of New York City public high school seniors plan to matriculate to a four-year college (New York City Department of Education, Annual School Reports (2004–2005).

- 68% of College Bound participants matriculate to the "Most" competitive or "Highly" competitive colleges (Barron's two top selectivity categories).

- Based on a 2006 survey (with an 80% response rate), 85% of College Bound participants graduate college in four years as compared to 54.3% of students nationally that graduate college in five years, and 36.4% of African Americans nationally that graduate college in five years.

- 34.7% of Legal Outreach college graduates are pursuing or have obtained a graduate degree of any kind.

- 14.4% of Legal Outreach college graduates are pursuing or have obtained a JD.

In terms of qualitative results, Legal Outreach students report the following:

2010 Students' Perceptions of the Usefulness of the Program: Scale of 1 to 10, with 10 as the Highest		
Importance of program in accomplishing goals by length of time in program	< 2.6 years	> = 2.6 years
Keeping on track to college	9.0	8.9
Preparing to compete at college level	9.1	8.7
Learning new skills	8.1	8.0
Doing well in school	8.3	7.8
Deciding what want to do with life	8.6	7.6

Current Program Demographics and Structure

The students currently participating in Legal Outreach's programs are diverse. Approximately 60% are female, and 40% are male, 33% are African American, 22% multi-ethnic, 21% Latino, 9% Asian, and 15% other. Forty-three percent come from single parent households and 56% qualify for free or reduce-priced lunch.

Legal Outreach's program structure is built upon three key pillars: vision, skill-development, and support. We use the law as a mechanism to inspire students, to envision themselves as legal professionals, and to introduce them to higher level academic skills. This portion of our mission is accomplished by inviting eighth grade students, from underserved communities, to apply to one of five Summer Law Institutes implemented in partnership with five law schools—Columbia, Brooklyn, St. John's, Fordham, and NYU. Up to 32 students are accepted into each Institute, each year. Once accepted, over the course of the five week program, which operates from Monday–Friday, from 9:00 to 3:00 or 4:00 pm, students are immersed in a series of activities designed to inspire, challenge, and push them to achieve their potential. The activities include the following:

- Legal Analysis and Advocacy: Using Legal Outreach's "Criminal Justice: Theory and Practice" curriculum, students develop analytical, critical-thinking, and oral advocacy skills.

- Guest Speakers: By interacting with a wide range of legal professionals, students gain exposure to the legal profession and the myriad of opportunities available to them.

- Field Trips: By visiting a variety of legal institutions including courts, law firms, and governmental agencies, students have the opportunity to observe the legal system in action, in non-confrontational situations.

- Litigation Exercise: Studying from a "Trial Process and Procedure" curriculum, students learn trial practice skills, culminating in a criminal mock trial competition coached and judged by actual attorneys and judges.

By immersing themselves in these law-related activities over the course of the five-week Summer Law Institute, students begin to see new possibilities for their lives. They are prompted to commit themselves to the work necessary to achieve the goal. Once the Summer Law Institute ends, students are invited to apply for admission to the four-year College Bound Program where the focus is developing skills, including the following:

- Discipline, Time Management, Study & Test Taking Techniques—After-School Study Program

- Decision Making, Self-Reflection & Analysis, Planning—Life Skills Program

- Grammar, Vocabulary, Analysis, Argument, Persuasion & Research—Writing Program

- Reading Comprehension, Critical-Thinking, Analysis, Articulation, Advocacy—Constitutional Law Debate Program

- Discipline, Test Taking—SAT Program

- Professionalism, Problem-Solving, Advocacy, Articulation, Etiquette, Networking—Summer Internship Program

- Reading Comprehension, Test-taking, Note-Taking, Analysis, Advocacy—College Class

Currently, 60 to 70 Summer Law Institute participants are accepted each year into the CB program. Our plans, however, call for up to 100 to be admitted in the years to come. Because the transition is not easy, Legal Outreach provides those selected with multiple forms of support, in the form of staff (both full and part-time), law students, and lawyers/mentors who encourage, prod, and push students to stay on track. Classes are kept small so that no one gets lost or overlooked. The importance of support cannot be overestimated. Years ago when Legal Outreach put together a strategic plan for growth, the alumni of the program were surveyed. A key question asked students what compelled them to stay committed to the program for four years. A number one answer was "bonding with staff." When students know that someone cares, they are willing to go the extra mile.

Partners

To accomplish its mission over the past 21 years, Legal Outreach, has relied heavily on the strength of commitments from several New York institutions and individuals to help inspire and prepare students to pursue higher education and law-related careers. Legal Outreach's partners include five law schools, 36 law firms, three financial institutions, three government agencies, three public interest organizations, 16 judges, and 179 attorney/mentors, and 120 law student volunteers. Mentors and law students from Columbia, Brooklyn, St. John's, and NYU, help prepare students for the Constitutional Law Debates. Partnerships with Columbia, NYU, Brooklyn, St. John's, and Fordham Law Schools have led to the establishment of the Summer Law Institutes. Law firms, agencies, departments, and courts have provided summer internships. Each partnership is essential to the success of the organization and the implementation of its programs.

Administrative Structure and Budget

Legal Outreach operates as a 501(c)(3) under the direction of an eight-member board of directors and a 22-member advisory board. It has a core staff of eleven full-time employees including the managing directors, program directors, coordinators and support staff, and 56 part-time staff including tutors, writing and SAT instructors, and program coordinators. Its annual budget is approximately $1.7 million, serving 384 students in 2010 via the Summer Law Institutes and the College Bound Program. Those interested in replicating the program should estimate a per student cost of $4,500 per year.[4]

The work and impact of Legal Outreach's programs are best represented through the life of its current Deputy and Managing Director, Sandy Santana. Sandy, a first generation Dominican-American, grew up and attended school in Harlem. His parents, like many immigrants, came to the United States in search of a better life for their children. They enrolled their children in the local elementary and middle schools even as they took working class jobs to support the family. It was during Sandy's eighth grade year that we at Legal Outreach first encountered him. He was chosen, along with seven other students, to represent his school in Legal Outreach's Annual Mock Trial Competition. Over the course of the twelve-week program, Sandy stood out as being bright but also quiet, shy, and reserved. As a member of the team, he settled for the backseat and never sought the limelight. Recognizing his potential, however, the coaches of his team assigned him to deliver the closing argument, knowing that it would pressure him to speak more assertively and confidently. But most importantly, they saw the role as an opportunity to bring him out of his shell. Their strategy worked, and Sandy did not disappoint. He accepted the challenge, improved week by week, and during the actual competition, performed far beyond his teachers' and even his teammates' expectations as his team took second place. The experience was such a powerful event in his life that to this day, 21 years later, he still remembers key lines from his closing argument.

At the conclusion of the mock trial tournament, Sandy was one of six students selected in 1989 to become a part of Legal Outreach's very first College Bound class. That summer, he, along with the other students, interned at a government agency. The following summer, he interned at a major law firm in New York City, where he had a chance to work directly with associates and partners on various assignments. These experiences filled him with confidence and provided him with vision. Motivated by his mock trial and internship experiences, Sandy poured himself into both his school work and his Legal Outreach activities. Through the Legal Outreach four-year Writing Program and three-year Constitutional Law Debate Program, his skills grew and his confidence soared. Both were reflected in his academic work at school, where he became an "A" student, excelling in almost every subject. His confidence in his oral skills led him to join the school's debate team where he won first place in the state in the novice division. The only hurdle left was the dreaded SAT. Upon taking his first diagnostic test, he scored close to the national average but was sorely disappointed. During the summer preceding his senior year, he took full advantage of Legal Outreach's five-week SAT prep program and saw his scores increase over 250 points, based upon the old 1600 scale. His scores, combined with his grades, and his extra-curricular activities in school and in Legal Outreach, placed him in a position to apply to our nation's top colleges.

With strong recommendations from his teachers, combined with a comprehensive recommendation from Legal Outreach detailing his growth and achievements over four years, Sandy was accepted to Harvard. While there, he performed admirably against the nation's best and brightest and during his senior year was accepted to Columbia Law School. Rather than attending immediately upon graduation, he deferred for a year and decided to come back to Legal Outreach to work as a program coordinator even though he had multiple offers from investment banks in New York City.

In law school, Sandy again proved that a kid from Harlem could compete against those from more privileged backgrounds. He was recognized as a Harlan Stone Fiske Scholar for "superior academic achievement." Even as he achieved academically, Sandy continued to retain his ties to Legal Outreach by serving as a mentor to a College Bound student, and a coach for Legal Outreach's Constitutional Law Debate Program. During his third year, he received multiple offers from law firms, and cast his lot with Cleary, Gottlieb, Steen and Hamilton, LLP where he joined their Corporate

Finance and Securities Group with a focus on Latin American transactions. Again, Sandy maintained his ties to the organization by serving as a coordinator of the Legal Outreach Summer Internship Program at Cleary and by joining Legal Outreach's Board of Directors.

After spending three years at Cleary, Sandy married his college sweetheart and moved to Boston where he joined the law firm, Goodwin Procter, LLP. In 2005, Sandy and his wife made the decision to move back to New York. Though he could have chosen to continue on the path to partnership at a law firm, he chose instead to return once again to Legal Outreach as the organization's Deputy Director. In that position, he has focused his attention on the organization's expansion efforts, and the acquisition of a new 24,000 square foot space that now houses our programs for students from the five boroughs of New York. In addition to his duties as Deputy Director, he is the Managing Director of Programs, and is the heir apparent to succeed the Executive Director.

Sandy is the quintessential role model for our students. He stands as a shining example of the values the organization seeks to instill in each person who steps through the doors, and makes a commitment to the platform of the organization. Each day our students come to the program, they see in Sandy the visible representation of what they can achieve if they simply apply themselves to the tasks before them on a day-to-day basis.

Appendix

College-Bound Mentoring Program FAQs

How can I become a mentor?

> Any attorney who is interested in becoming a mentor may complete an online application. Please contact us for more information or fill out our online Mentor Application.

Do I have to be an attorney to mentor a student in the College Bound Program?

> Yes, one of the benefits of becoming a sophomore in the College Bound Program is receiving an attorney mentor who will be able to assist the student in preparing for the Constitutional Law debates.

Do mentors have to work at a law firm?

> No, mentors are not required to work at a law firm. In fact, mentors don't even have to be practicing attorneys. What matters is that the mentor has gone to law school and understands how to make legal arguments.

How much time would I have to commit to participate in the Mentoring Program?

> The mentoring time commitment is approximately five hours of face-to-face contact per month, excluding occasional correspondence by email and phone. Most of this contact occurs at debates and social/cultural events. Debates, for which experienced attorneys can earn up to 3 CLE credits per year, take place on three Friday evenings, and one Saturday morning per year. Social/cultural events, of which there are three or four per year, are usually scheduled for Saturday or Sunday afternoons on months that no debates are scheduled.

> Mentors remain with their mentees for three years until the student graduates from high school. If, for any reason, a mentor cannot remain in the program for three years, we will assign a new mentor to the student. Mentors are asked to attend one event per month that is planned by Legal Outreach—either a debate or social/cultural event. Each lasts three hours. In the months that students have debates, mentors generally spend an additional hour helping their mentees prepare for debates. Mentors are encouraged to make additional contact with their mentees in person, over the phone, or via email.

What if I can't attend all of the planned events for the year?

> Although mentors should try to attend every event, we understand that occasionally, mentors go out of town or have obligations at work during the weekend. In those instances, we ask that mentors contact their mentee and the Program Coordinator and try to send someone in their place.

Can my mentee and I go out alone?

> Yes, the most successful relationships are the ones that are developed outside of our planned events. However, mentors must also develop a relationship with the mentee's parents and inform parents whenever they plan to meet with mentees.

As a mentor, would I be required to do any research for the debates?

> No, all of the materials that students need and are allowed to use have already been prepared.

Can my friends participate in the Mentoring Program?

> We strongly encourage mentors to refer their friends and colleagues to the program. In fact, if a number of co-workers are interested in participating, the Program Coordinator can arrange to make a presentation on the Mentoring Program at their place of employment.

What are the responsibilities of a mentor?

> Mentors participate in Legal Outreach's debate and social/cultural programs, and serve as a role model, friend, and advisor to their mentee. Regarding the debate program, mentors help their mentee prepare for each debate and serve as a judge at each debate (debates are 4 times a year, every other month, and students meet with their mentor to prepare at least once before each debate). Social/cultural events are activities that Legal Outreach plans for mentors and mentees, such as attendance at dance performances, Broadway shows, and walking tours (social/cultural events are every other month, alternating with debates; mentors must pay for their own ticket to these events, which is usually under $25).

Will I be able to help my mentee prepare for his/her debate if I didn't debate in high school and I'm not a litigator?

> Yes. Our debates are really just moot court arguments. If you went to law school, you'll have no problem helping your mentee prepare for the debate.

Will my mentee's debate preparation fall squarely on my shoulders?

> No. Your mentee will work closely with Legal Outreach as well as a law student debate coach to prepare his or her oral argument. Your mentee will rely on you primarily to practice his or her oral argument and to clarify questions.

Is there anything else I should know about being a mentor?

> If you're assigned a mentee, you will attend a mentor training and learn everything you need to know about mentoring.

Chapter 9

Ninth-Grade Law Classes: High School and Beyond

Saturday Academy of Law
University of California, Irvine, California

Karina Hamilton*, Sarah E. Redfield† #

Pre-K	Elementary	Middle	High School	College		Law School	Profession

This chapter describes a relatively new pipeline program in California. Modeled after a Saturday science academy in Los Angeles, it has shown remarkable success by any measure — student outcomes, involvement of several layers of the pipeline, and community support. The detail in this chapter offers a blueprint for replicability.

Introduction

This chapter describes the launch, operation, and results of the Saturday Academy of Law (SAL) developed and implemented by the Center for Educational Partnerships (CFEP) at the University of California, Irvine (UCI)[1] and offers guidance for others who might want to replicate the effort.

---

* Karina Hamilton is the founding co-director of the Saturday Academy of Law at UC Irvine. She graduated from Stanford University in 1982 and received her law degree from Boalt Hall School of Law in 1986. After practicing law for ten years, Karina shifted her career towards education. She has worked on a variety of educational initiatives including the startup of a charter school and two independent schools in California. For the past 11 years, Karina has worked at UC Irvine. She founded the UCI SAGE Scholars Program that provides training, internships, mentoring and financial support to motivated undergraduates from economically disadvantaged backgrounds so they can become leaders in their careers and in their communities. Karina currently serves on various nonprofit boards including the Tiger Woods Learning Center in Anaheim, California that provides after-school programming for talented, low-income students.

† Sarah Redfield is a Professor of Law at the University of New Hampshire School of Law. Both authors have extensive experience with diversity issues and pipeline programs and welcome readers to communicate with them further on these topics.

Both authors acknowledge with respect and gratitude the work of Co-director Roslyn Soto.

It is axiomatic that you will not go to law school if you do not graduate from high school. So too, it is unlikely you will gain admission to law school if you do not have critical thinking skills, including proficiency in reading[2] and writing.[3] As one leading educator has described it:

> Diversifying the face of any profession requires a fundamental restructuring of the pipeline and the implementation of strategies capable of catalyzing larger scale change:
>
> **First** more students have to graduate from high school college-ready;
>
> **Then** more students have to transfer from community colleges and complete college.
>
> **When** the BA is within reach more students must be informed and empowered to compete for slots in graduate and professional schools.
>
> Without progress on this scale, an elite group of "heroic persisters" will simply migrate from one profession to another in a zero-sum game where the inequalities that we have declared war on will continue to almost effortlessly replicate themselves within every level of the educational pipeline.[4]

Background: Initial Approach and the Santa Ana Context

The Saturday Academy of Law was initially launched with a grant from CaliforniaALL.[5] The CaliforniaALL request for proposals had used as its reference point a similar successful Saturday Science Academy in Los Angeles.[6] While the Science Academy started with first grade, the UCI program as proposed and as implemented began with rising ninth graders. The initial funding from CaliforniaALL was $200,000, followed by a second year grant for $100,000, plus an additional grant from the University of Phoenix for $50,000 to host a professional development session to share results.

Located within ten miles of the UCI campus is the City of Santa Ana. Santa Ana is one of the most densely populated cities in the United States. Santa Ana Unified School District (SAUSD) is the fifth largest school district in California and enrolls over 58,000 students; 95% are Latino; 60% are English learners, and nearly 80% qualify for free or reduced lunch. In SAL-UCI, 96% of the participants were self-identified as Latino/Mexican-American; about 3% were African American; and 2% were Caucasian/Other. About 65% of the SAL-UCI students in spring 2010 were qualified for as free or reduced lunch; almost one-third (29%) of the students were classified as English Learners; and less than one-tenth had family members who had attended some college.[7]

In 1983, UC Irvine founded the Santa Ana Partnership with faculty, administrative, and community partners from UCI, SAUSD, Santa Ana College, and California State University, Fullerton. The Partnership's goal was to improve academic achievement and college access regionally among low-income and first-generation college students. Now in its third decade, the Partnership has expanded the scope of its initiatives and is recognized as one of California's most enduring student-centered partnerships.

Building off of the success of the Santa Ana Partnership, in 1996, UC Irvine became the first UC campus to establish a Center for Educational Partnerships to pursue a sustained commitment to the quality of public education. Through CFEP, UCI has worked in collaboration with K–20 partners to improve low-income, minority, and disadvantaged student academic achievement and college preparation. Given this experience UC Irvine was able to make the case to grantors that it was uniquely situated to establish a comprehensive pipeline for talented students interested in pursuing careers in law. Its likelihood of success was grounded in the dozens of community partnerships formed by CFEP and UC Irvine's new law school that opened in fall 2009. Indeed, Erwin Chemerinsky, one of the leading constitutional scholars in the United States, was appointed as founding dean of the UCI School of Law and has been a vocal advocate for SAL-UCI in the legal community.

SAL-UCI Goals and Approaches

The two primary goals of the Saturday Academy of Law are to:

1   develop the critical reading/writing and speaking skills that will prepare high school students for higher education and professional success; and

2   create excitement and knowledge about the field of law through purposeful activities and interactions with faculty, undergraduates, law students, and legal professionals.

To achieve these goals, SAL-UCI operated within the CFEP structure under the co-direction of Karina Hamilton and Roslyn Soto. From the outset, SAL-UCI was committed to an approach that would maintain a focus on rigor, relevance, and relationships[8] as well as results.

In fall 2008, program staff systematically addressed the implementation of its approach as it—

- developed all of the program materials (including letters to students and parents in both English and Spanish, application forms, waivers, promotional materials, etc.);

- launched a website;[9]

- recruited teachers, teaching assistants, and students;

- developed learning outcomes and a detailed curriculum (based on best practices in pipeline programs);

- created research and evaluation tools to measure student achievement and program effectiveness;

- conducted student and parent orientations (in English and Spanish); and

- worked closely with high school counselors to identify and recruit motivated students.

At the institutional level, SAL-UCI set up two oversight committees, one to oversee the overall program and one to design the curriculum.[10] The Curriculum Committee decided that the focus of the program should be the First Amendment and designed relevant learning outcomes:

- Increased awareness about the legal profession.

- Increased capacity to frame an argument.

- Increased knowledge about landmark U.S. Supreme Court cases.

- Improved academic English skills, particularly in writing.[11]

Starting in January 2009, SAL-UCI has conducted three separate sessions of the Saturday Academy of Law, serving over 130 ninth graders in SAUSD. The sessions were free of charge to qualified students. SAL has measurably improved the reading, writing, and critical thinking skills of these motivated students. Furthermore, in partnership with local attorneys and judges, SAL has also developed and implemented a robust mentoring program to support the SAL participants until they graduate from high school. The program has received statewide and national recognition. Program staff have presented at various legal conferences including the ABA Education Law Conference, the Wingspread Conference, and the Education Law Association Annual Conference.

Program Components

To launch and maintain a successful pipeline program demands attention to a myriad of issues, some at a policy level (*e.g.,* who to admit, how to publicize the program, how to make the program self-sustaining), and some at the very detailed level (*e.g.,* what records to keep, how to organize snacks, how to manage logistics for field trips). This part of the chapter discusses SAL-UCI's thinking and action on several key points.

Overview

The Saturday Academy of Law is a six-week program conducted on consecutive Saturday mornings for ninth grade students enrolled in SAUSD. Each class has 25 students, led by a credentialed high school teacher and supported by five undergraduate teaching assistants. SAL-UCI was held at the Delhi Center[12] in Santa Ana during January/February 2009 and at Santa Ana College[13] (a local community college) during April May 2009. The following year, one session was conducted at the Delhi Center.[14]

During each Saturday session, teachers lead the students through a combination of mini-lectures, interactive exercises, and writing activities. The students study the U.S. Constitution with a focus on the First Amendment and free speech rights. Students read and brief cases including *Tinker*. There is a strong focus on persuasive writing, critical thinking, and oral expression. The curriculum is designed to align with the California content standards for ninth grade in language arts. The curriculum guide contains detailed lesson plans, lists of required materials, and interactive exercises that encourage active student engagement as described further in the Curriculum section. During each class, the students break into groups of five to work with the UCI undergraduate teaching assistants on particular exercises or discussions. Each student receives individual attention, feedback, and encouragement.

In addition to the academic content, the students hear from various guest speakers about the legal profession. Past guest speakers have included a judge, prosecutor, police officer, and several private practice attorneys. Most of the guest speakers grew up in Santa Ana or South Central Los Angeles and faced significant obstacles in pursuing their dreams of joining the legal profession. These speakers have been inspiring, engaging, and informative.

The students have increased their legal skill set by learning to read legal cases, write briefs, and engage in respectful debate. As will be described in more detail in the Evaluation section, the students also learned about the justice system through assigned reading, class discussion, and guest speakers. Furthermore, they learned about the process of becoming a lawyer—graduation from high school and four-year college then law school and then taking and passing the State Bar examination.

The students who graduate from the Saturday Academy of Law are then eligible to receive a mentor and to participate in other CFEP-sponsored academic enrichment and college preparation programs. SAL-UCI students are matched with a UCI undergraduate mentor; the mentors are trained and supervised by SAL-UCI staff. As discussed in more detail below in the Pipeline section, in addition to the direct program delivery to the ninth graders in SAUSD, SAL-UCI intentionally engages undergraduate students from underrepresented communities as teaching assistants and mentors, and provides them with information, encouragement and support to pursue a career in the legal profession. Furthermore, UCI launched the first new public law school in 40 years in fall 2009; the faculty and staff from the UCI School of Law have been integrally involved with the design and implementation of the Saturday Academy of Law. Starting this spring, law students will be matched with our SAL undergraduate mentors to provide advice, counsel, and support. Members of the legal profession have also become actively engaged in the mentoring program.

Student Selection

Students are recruited at all seven comprehensive public high schools in SAUSD in collaboration with CFEP staff familiar with the schools and with the higher education coordinators (college counselors) at each high school. Most recruitment is through flyers and classroom announcements by teachers and/or by SAL-UCI program staff. The staff also worked hard to publicize the program in the legal community in order to create awareness and opportunities for the program.

In order to be eligible for the SAL-UCI program, a student must be enrolled in ninth grade in SAUSD, have a minimum 2.5 GPA and be enrolled in Algebra or Geometry (or higher). Students are required to complete an application, which includes an essay about why s/he is interested in learning about the law and legal careers. An additional and critical requirement is that a parent or guardian attends an orientation session (held in Spanish and English at Santa Ana College in the early evening) for a student to participate in the program. Parent involvement has remained a strong component of the program.[15]

The number of applications has far exceeded the number of participants that the program can accept in all rounds of the program offered to date. The SAL-UCI program goal was not and is not to seek out those students already academically successful, but rather to be as open to all comers as possible.[16] Among students actually participating, the average entering GPA was 2.78, meaning some students were below 2.78 at the end of eighth grade. Similarly, the program's goal was and is to focus on previously under-represented and underserved students representing a variety of diverse backgrounds.[17]

During the spring 2010 session, the students who participated in the Saturday Academy were 94% Latino or Mexican-American; 64% were on free or reduced lunch, and only 11% had a parent who attended college.

Teachers/Teaching Assistants

An experienced and credentialed teacher already working in the district leads each class.[18] Teachers are recruited through email announcements to teachers participating in professional development programs hosted by CFEP and through word of mouth. Teachers are interviewed by the program co-directors, who then make the hiring decisions. The teachers receive a stipend for each six-week session taught (including two to three required meetings with the program's curriculum writer and program evaluator).

Five undergraduate teaching assistants (TAs) from UC Irvine support each teacher. The TAs are selected through a competitive process (and the competition was strong) including an application and interview. The publication of the TA position included these qualifications:[19]

- Enrolled full-time at UCI as a third or fourth year undergraduate.
- Cumulative GPA of 3.0 or above.
- Very strong written and verbal skills.
- Leadership abilities/experience.
- Enthusiasm for working with high school students.
- Experience with underrepresented students is a plus.
- Access to reliable transportation.
- Willingness to work on Saturdays (7:30 a.m.–1 p.m.) and two or three evenings during the quarter.

TAs are recruited through the SAL website, emails to professors teaching under-graduate law classes and emails to campus clubs devoted to the law (Women's Law Association, Latino Law Association, etc.). TAs must be fingerprinted and go through a background check before they are officially hired because they are working with students under the age of 18. TAs are paid an hourly wage. Where possible, bilingual TAs are selected, as are many who have transferred to UCI from community colleges (thus showing participants different possible pathways to professional school). Nearly all the TAs have expressed an interest in pursuing a career in law.[20]

Curriculum

As noted above, the SAL-UCI Curriculum Committee decided to focus on the First Amendment and leadership[21] with the goal of creating a high level of engagement,[22] self-confidence, and competence.[23] The committee decided it was critical to align the curriculum with the California content standards for ninth grade language arts to ensure consistency with work the students are doing concurrently in their ninth grade classes. (This was very important in securing the support of the local high school principals and teachers).

The curriculum was written by one of the committee members with an expertise in high school curriculum for underserved students.[24] The curriculum guide contains detailed lesson plans, lists of required materials, and highly interactive exercises designed to encourage student engagement.[25]

Sample Class Synopsis

On the first day of class, all students are required to take three timed pre-tests: (i) a reading comprehension test (multiple choice); (ii) an essay writing exam;[26] and (iii) a survey of knowledge about areas of the law and attitudes toward the law.[27] Students take these same tests on the final day of class.[28]

Students actively participate throughout the six sessions. During each class, the ninth graders engage in dialogue, discussion, and writing. There is a major focus on building skills in persuasive writing, critical reading, and analytical ability. During each class, the students break into small groups to work with the UCI TAs on particular exercises or discussions. Students do specific self-evaluations of their writing and also receive constructive feedback and encouragement from teachers and TAs. (By design, the students are not assigned much homework since they are carrying full ninth grade courseloads.)

During four of the six sessions, guest speakers visit the classrooms to share their backgrounds, their paths to the legal profession, and their work experience. Speakers include private practice attorneys, judges, federal prosecutors, and law enforcement officers from the community. Most of the speakers are from underserved communities in Orange County or South Los Angeles.[29]

Final SAL-UCI Class/Campus Tour/Parent Involvement/ Recognition Ceremony

During the final classroom session, all students and their families (up to 3 family members per student) are invited to attend a tour of the UCI campus and a celebratory luncheon at the UCI University Club. The students and their family members gather at Santa Ana College and are transported to UCI by bus. The students attend their final class session in a university classroom; the parents attend an information session led by CFEP staff in English and Spanish about the pathway to college, financing a college education, and supporting their students through high school. The parents also receive information from the Padres Promotores (a group of local Spanish-speaking parents who have received formal training in providing college information in the community) and tour the UCI campus along with the students. Nearly 200 students, parents, and invited guests attended the recognition luncheon. Attendees included the students, parents and siblings, UCI faculty and staff (including faculty from the UCI School of Law), SAUSD faculty and principals, local politicians, attorneys and members of the OC Bar Association and Orange County Bar Foundation.

After the Saturdays: Mentoring

On the last day of the SAL class, the SAL students fill out mentee questionnaires to facilitate matching them with the mentors. The mentors are selected through an application and interview process. Like the TAs, mentors are undergraduates recruited by SAL-UCI. Here the job qualifications are similar and include access to reliable transportation; and willingness to mentor tenth or eleventh grade students at their high schools (located in Santa Ana) after school and to attend occasional field trips. Experience working with underrepresented students is a plus factor. Each mentor is required to participate in a mentor orientation; each mentor is provided with a detailed handbook and a mentor coordinator helps support the mentoring activities. Like TAs, mentors must be fingerprinted and receive background checks before they are permitted to work directly with students.

Each mentor has three to four mentees at a single high school (same gender). This structure provides a strong group dynamic and the ability for peer support at each school as well. The higher education counselors at each high school are very supportive of the mentoring program and, in fact, provide space in their counseling areas so that the mentors can visit with their students on the high school campus after school or at lunch. Each mentor is required to contact his/her mentees every week either in person or via email; each mentor is also required to meet in person with his/her mentees at least twice per month.

Much of the mentoring is conducted through these activities, but SAL-UCI staff also arrange for one law-related experience per month. For example, during 2010, mentees and mentors attended lunches hosted by a dozen different law firms in Orange County (six to seven students and two to three mentors went to a particular firm): Allen Matkins, Crowell & Moring, Gibson Dunn & Crutcher, Irell & Manella, Knobbe Maartens, O'Melveny & Myers, Rutan & Tucker, Paul Hastings, Sheppard Mullin, and Stradling Yocca. SAL-UCI coordinated the activity by providing buses and staff to accompany the students from their high schools. The students also attended a screening of a documentary about California Supreme Court Justice Cruz Reynoso, the first Latino appointed to the Court. Justice Reynoso attended the screening and answered questions from the SAL students. The students will be visiting a courthouse this year and will participate in community service activities and workshops on résumé-writing, personal statements, goal-setting, and financial aid. The mentoring will continue throughout high school graduation.

Reaching All Segments of the Diversity Pipeline

SAL-UCI provides direct programming to ninth graders but was intentionally designed to reach other key segments of the diversity pipeline:

- 9th grade students actively participate in the Saturday program.
- 10th grade students who successfully complete SAL-UCI are eligible to receive a mentor and are incorporated into the Early Academic Outreach Program sponsored by the University of California; they are eligible to participate in college-

going workshops and will receive extensive information and support in pursuing higher education.

- 11th and 12th grade students receive mentoring and guidance; UCI is able to track the students through a data sharing agreement with SAUSD.

- UCI undergraduates (sophomores through seniors) actively participate in SAL-UCI as teaching assistants. This year, UCI added nearly 20 undergraduates as mentors to the tenth and eleventh graders. Along with the program participants, the TAs and mentors benefit from guest speakers and field trips related to the law. UCI School of Law is providing the undergraduates with information about applying to law school, securing strong letters of recommendation, and preparing for the LSAT.

- Community College Transfer Students. UCI purposefully selected many teaching assistants who were transfer students from community colleges so that UCI could both help support these transfer students and show the ninth graders that there are many pathways to law school.

- Law students will be incorporated into the program as mentors and guest speakers (the UCI School of Law was launched in August 2009 with a highly diverse faculty and student body).

- Parents play an integral role in the pipeline. UCI actively engages parents during the program and will continue to engage them in student events as their students' progress through high school.

- The teachers have expressed that this has been a very positive professional development experience for each of them. The teachers have told us that they now feel better equipped to talk to all of their students about opportunities in the legal profession.

- UCI has engaged numerous attorneys and judges to serve as guest speakers for SAL-UCI. These volunteers are drawn from underrepresented communities and have provided inspiration and support for the SAL-UCI students. The guest speakers have really enjoyed their experiences in the classroom and all have offered to speak again in the future. They have also provided strong support for the mentoring program through law firm visits. They feel a real connection with the students. As noted above, several law firms have hosted the SAL graduates at their law firms for tours and lunches. Practicing attorneys and judges who have participated in SAL believe that it provides a simple and impactful way for legal professionals to connect with the law pipeline and that this experience will encourage more engagement in and support for pipeline programs.

- SAL-UCI has partnered with the Orange County Diversity Task Force (OCDTF), a consortium of prominent law firms in Orange County committed to diversity, in order to publicize SAL and to create opportunities for lawyers and law firms to interact with the students. The consortium includes firms such as Allen Matkins, Crowell & Moring, Gibson, Dunn & Crutcher, Knobbe Martens Olson & Bear, Latham & Watkins, Irell & Manella, O'Melveny & Myers, Orrick Herrington & Sutcliffe, Paul Hastings, and Sheppard Mullin Richter & Hampton. This year, SAL-UCI received funding from the OCDTF as well as the Orange County Bar Association-Charitable Fund to support program activities. Dozens of attorneys attended the SAL Symposium in February 2010 to learn about SAL and other legal diversity initiatives; the SAL students also participated in the Symposium.

Evaluation Protocol and Results

SAL-UCI has proven itself successful in attracting underrepresented diverse students[30] into the program, which is designed to increase their critical skills and interest them in potential careers in the law. SAL-UCI has demonstrated successful student outcomes for participants in SAUSD including:

- Improved student attitudes towards the justice and legal system.

- Improved persistence and enrollment and success in rigorous academic coursework in high school.

- Improved student interest, attitudes, and behaviors related to attending college and pursuing a career in law.

- Improved reading, writing, and critical thinking skills of participants.

- Increased self-efficacy for writing skills and writing ability.

- As measured against the California standards, a 31% increase in scores from eighth grade to ninth grade on the California English CST.[31]

There were also additional unanticipated benefits including:

- Very strong parent involvement.

- Ongoing mentoring relationships with students well after the sessions ended.

- Professional development of the teaching assistants (sophomores through seniors who themselves were largely drawn from minority student populations).

- Extended support for college students interested in applying to law school.[32]

- Professional growth of teachers, which they can take back to their regular classrooms (including an improved knowledge of information about legal careers).

- Connection of volunteers and guest speakers with students.[33]

The initial evaluation of the first two years of the SAL-UCI program shows success at virtually every level. Students indeed positively discovered law; they interacted with people from similar backgrounds (in some cases, from the same high school) who were successfully engaged in law-related careers. They also showed measurable improvement in the skills which SAL-UCI set out to teach. They came back after their SAL-UCI first year ready to be assigned to mentors and continue along the pipeline; often their parents came with them and expressed their support for both the program and students. As SAL-UCI continues to work with these young people and to track their progress, much remains to be learned, but much has been achieved for the short time investment thus far.

Conclusion: Conditions for Replicability

As the key components of the SAL program suggest, core elements and conditions are prerequisites to a successful SAL initiative. In general, these include commitment to the new 3Rs—rigor, relevance, and relationships. More specifically, these include the following key components:

- a commitment to diversity;
- an understanding of the significance of rigor and high expectations;
- an established and strong partnership structure;
- a commitment to ongoing documentation and improvement; and
- the demonstrated capacity to assure that the entry made through the SAL is followed by additional pipeline interventions.

SAL-UCI is committed to replicating the Saturday Academy of Law in California and beyond. SAL-UCI has reached out to other diversity pipeline programs to learn and share best practices for working with specific populations. Program staff have participated in several conferences to share experiences and have been documenting all aspects of the design and implementation for the Saturday Academy of Law so that it can be successfully replicated. From the outset, the Oversight Committee members agreed that detailed documentation is critical to successful replication of the program. For example, the Co-Directors developed and implemented an internal project management website on Google that facilitates program coordination. All team members and community partners can access the site. The website has copies of all relevant program documents including a detailed curriculum, student recruitment and application materials, student forms (waivers, media releases, parent permissions slips, etc.), letters to parents (in Spanish and English), handbooks for the teachers and teaching assistants, evaluation materials, contact information, checklists, event planning guides, etc. The site has a task management list and calendar that provide a blueprint for implementation.

In addition, through a grant from the University of Phoenix Foundation, SAL-UCI co-hosted (with CaliforniaALL) a symposium at UCI in February 2010 to address diversity pipeline issues and to create specific plans for replicating the Saturday Academy of Law. Teams of educators and attorneys were invited to a day and a half long symposium that provided hands-on workshops and proven strategies for implementing a pipeline program such as the Saturday Academy of Law. Each team was required to bring a high school administrator/teacher, a higher education administrator/outreach coordinator, an attorney from their community (ideally representing a local bar association), and a representative from a law school. Participants included high school administrators, legal nonprofits, law school representatives, attorneys, and high school, college, and law school educators. The Symposium drew participants from Sacramento, Davis, San Francisco, Oakland, Berkeley, Los Angeles, Anaheim, Santa Ana, and San Diego. The Symposium was capped by a keynote speech by Erwin Chemerinsky, Founding Dean of the UCI School of Law. He spoke about the urgent need for increased diversity in the legal profession and issued a call to action to attorneys and educators to address this issue immediately.

The importance of collaboration cannot be overemphasized. The program and curriculum were developed in close collaboration with faculty, staff, and community partners from UCI, SAUSD, Santa Ana College, Delhi Community Center, Padres Promotores, the Orange County Hispanic Bar Association, the Orange County Bar Association, the Orange County Diversity Task Force, and various private law firms including Allen Matkins, Latham & Watkins, O'Melveny & Myers, and Sheppard Mullin. These community partnerships and the collaboration and engagement among each of the diversity pipeline segments — students, parents, teachers, university/community college students, law students, attorneys, and judges — are essential to the eventual success of the Saturday Academy of Law.

Appendix A

SAL Survey (for Pre- and Post-assessment)

The first part of this survey asks questions about how confident you feel about your writing. The second part of this survey asks about your interest in various legal careers. There are no right or wrong answers and your answers will be kept confidential.

Part 1. Background

Please check (√) the response that best describes your feelings. **Only check one box per statement.**

	Strongly Agree	Agree	Slightly Agree	Slightly Disagree	Disagree	Strongly Disagree
I make excellent grades in English.						
I do well on writing assignments.						
Even when I try hard, I do poorly on writing assignments.						
My teachers have told me that I am a good writer.						
I have been praised for my ability in writing.						
I start to feel stressed out as soon as I begin a writing assignment.						
My mind goes blank and I am unable to think clearly when working on a writing assignment.						
I can revise a first draft of any paper so that it is shorter and better organized.						
I can develop main ideas within the body of an essay through supporting evidence.						
When I read an article, I can identify complexities and discrepancies in the information.						
I am able to synthesize information from multiple sources and identify the different perspectives found in each source.						

	Strongly Agree	Agree	Slightly Agree	Slightly Disagree	Disagree	Strongly Disagree
I am able to develop a clear and coherent thesis statement that conveys my perspective on a given topic.						
I can adjust my style of writing to appeal to any audience by using rhetorical devices such as appeal through logic, emotion, or personal anecdote.						
I can come up with memorable examples and evidence to illustrate an important point.						
When I write a paper, I am able to anticipate and address the reader's argument against my position.						

Part 2. Careers in Law

Do you have an interest in pursuing a career in any of the following legal fields? If so, please read each of the following areas of law then select the categories that match your interests. **If you have more than one interest, please check all that apply to you.**

Private Practice Law

Description: involves working alone or with partners in a law firm to provide legal services to clients (individuals or corporations); some lawyers specialize in specific areas while others engage in general practice. The following are categories of Private Practice of Law; please check the category that interests you (check all that apply):

___ Real Estate/Construction
___ Business/Finance
___ Employment/Labor
___ Entertainment
___ Litigation
___ International business
___ Automobile accidents
___ Family Law (divorce, child custody, etc.)
___ Intellectual Property/Copyright (Software)
___ Criminal Defense (defend criminals)
___ Estates and Trusts (prepare wills and trusts)
___ Sports (clients are athletes; many sports agents are lawyers)
___ General (handles a variety of cases)

Public Interest Law

Description: serves low-income individuals, groups without legal rights and social causes; some lawyers work at nonprofit organizations or legal aid clinics. The following are categories of Public Interest Law; please check the category that interests you (check all that apply):

___ Environmental (example: Sierra Club)
___ Immigration

___ Human rights (examples: Amnesty International, United Nations)
___ Civil liberties (example: ACLU)
___ Homeless
___ Legal Aid (provide free legal counsel to low-income individuals/families

Government

Description: defend, prosecute or judge those accused of crimes; work for the government to resolve legal issues such as labor disputes, traffic issues, building permits, etc. The following are categories of Government Law; please check the category that interests you (check all that apply):

___ Public Defender
___ Prosecutor
___ Judge
___ Government lawyer not in criminal area (labor, traffic, buildings, military, etc.)

Non-Lawyer Careers Related to the Law

Description: there are a variety of jobs related to the law that do not require you to be a lawyer. The following are categories of Non-lawyer careers, please check the category that interests you (check all that apply):

___ Paralegal/Legal Assistant (assists lawyers)
___ Mediator (helps resolve disputes without going to court)
___ Court Reporter (records all proceedings in a court case or deposition)
___ Court Clerk (assists judges in doing their duties in the courtroom)
___ Legal Secretary (assists lawyers and paralegals)
___ Police Officer/Law Enforcement (example: FBI, Secret Service)
___ Probation Officer

Appendix B

Sample of Curriculum

Sample Day One General Overview

1. Registration and Welcome

Students must register at the front door, get name badges and receive program binders. Introduce teachers and teaching assistants.

2. Mini-lecture

1. Introduction to the Seminar Model

Students will learn and practice the Seminar Model of class discussion that will be used throughout the Academy.

2. Introduction to Evaluation/Rubric

Show students the rubric that they can use to evaluate their own participation in class. Introduce the idea of "Outstanding Lawyers of the Day," after each weekly session. Teachers, in consultation with the TAs, should pick 1–3 students from each classroom that demonstrated outstanding lawyerly skills such as thoughtful analysis, sharing opinions with the group, playing devil's advocate, facilitating the discussion, taking the unpopular viewpoint, etc. The selected students are then called to the front of the classroom and presented with a small gift (a lapel pin, pen, or the like).

  • Handout II.A: Seminar Rubric for Self-Evaluation—one for each student

3. Pre-test

The topics in the seminar model practice session will be used as a pretest to evaluate each student's writing skills and knowledge/attitude about the law.

  • Handout III.A: Pre-test—one for each student

Break

After pre-test, students should take a short break; fun icebreaker activity.

4. Leadership Qualities/Lawyer Skills discussion

Gear students up for the session by discussing what makes a leader effective. Compare this to skills lawyers must have to be effective advocates.

5. Breakout Group Activity: No Vehicles in the Park

This activity compares the intent of the law to what the law actually says, and the ambiguity surrounding what seems like a simple city ordinance. This introduces kids to the idea that often the law is not black and white, and that there is a lot of room for interpretation.

- Handout V.A: No Vehicles in the Park—one for each student
- Handout V.B: Who Can Go to the Park?—one for each student

6. Homework and Wrap-up: Public Survey of Student Free Speech Rights

- Handout VI.A: First Amendment Public Survey—one for each student

Materials Needed

- Binder, notebook, pen and highlighter for each student
- Name badges for each student, teacher and teaching assistant (TA)
- White board and/or poster easel pads (with sticky) and easel for each classroom
- Dry-erase markers for white boards and regular markers for posters
- 5–6 envelopes per classroom
- 6 to 7 dictionaries (Longman's)
- Cookies and bottled water

Prep

- Make copies of class handouts
- Make copies of pre-test [it will be emailed this week]
- Create student sign-in sheet
- Determine icebreaker activity for the students

3. Specific Materials and Approaches

I. Registration and Welcome

- Welcome the students.
- Introduce teachers and teaching assistants.
- Introduce guests (if any).
- Give a quick overview of the program binder.
- Tell students that they must wear their name badges at all times and return the badge at the end of the day.
- Tell students that we will collect the program binders at the end of each session so they don't have to carry it back and forth each week.
- Tell them that they will learn about the legal profession and learn to be stronger writers.
- Explain that to become lawyers they must complete high school, graduate from college (which usually takes 4 years), and then go to law school for 3 years.
- Talk about the importance of lawyers in our society; for this first session, it might be timely to mention how President Obama is a lawyer.
- Tell them that during the Academy they will hear from guest speakers such as judges, public defenders, and other lawyers.
- Tell them it will be a fun six weeks!!!

II. Mini-Lecture

A. Introduction to the Seminar Model

Objectives

1. Post objectives and a copy of the seminar self-evaluation rubric (Handout II.A) so students are reminded of the goal of the discussion. The idea is to keep the room a SAFE place for students to express themselves.

2. Students will learn the guidelines and procedures for a seminar model of class discussion that will be used throughout the Saturday Academy.

3. Students will participate in group meetings; display appropriate turn-taking behaviors; actively solicit comments or opinions of others; offer own opinions without dominating; respond appropriately to comments and questions; clarify, illustrate or expand on a response when asked to do so.

Teacher Approach

Explain how the seminar model is used in some college classrooms and discuss the importance of having an orderly discussion and exchange of ideas.

Remind students that in the Saturday Academy of Law they will be discussing ideas that some students will have very strong opinions about. One person's idea of what is right may be very offensive to another student. We don't need to agree with each other, but we do need to respect everyone's right to express their opinion.

B. Review of Rubric and Sample Discussion

1. Pass out and discuss rubric, explain "Outstanding Lawyer of the Day" award.

2. Pose the following question: "If everyone in the U.S. owned a gun (over the age of 14, including you) would you feel safer?

3. Ask students to write down 5 reasons for their answer before beginning the discussion.

4. Discuss.

5. After the discussion, have the students look at the rubric and do a self-evaluation.

6. Introduce a new topic: "Students with chores or jobs outside the home should be excused from doing homework (parents would have to verify the hours spent doing chores)." Again, have students write down 5 reasons that support their answer before beginning the discussion.

7. If students are shy or need more practice, have a student generate another controversial proposition to debate.

III. Pre-Test

Objectives

1. Measure students' attitude about the law profession.

2 Gauge students' knowledge of their Constitutional rights.

3 Evaluate students' writing ability in a timed setting.

Teacher Remarks

Remind students that the pre-test is to gauge their knowledge and attitude about the law and to get a writing sample that will be used to measure their progress in the course. Tell them to take the test seriously but not to become stressed if they don't know the answers to the questions; explain that we are just trying to determine their level of knowledge so that we can help them improve their skills and knowledge. The purpose is not to "grade" them on the test.

- Hand out pre-tests
- Remind them of any rules
- Give them periodic reminders of how much time is remaining
- If a student finishes early, have one of the TA's guide the student out of the room and keep him/her engaged until the rest of the students are finished.
- Collect the tests
- The tests must be returned to the Program Coordinator for analysis.

Break

- Cookies and bottled water
- Fun icebreaker for the kids to get to know each other

IV. Leadership Discussion

Discuss with students qualities of a leader. Have students reflect on their own qualities and set personal goals to become better leaders. Compare to the skills necessary for a lawyer to be an effective advocate. Show how law is one pathway to leadership. 100% of U.S. judges are lawyers, 58% of U.S. Senators, 37% of U.S. Reps, 20% of state legislators and 11% of major CEOs are lawyers.

V. Breakout Group Activity: No Vehicles in the Park

Objectives

1. Explain the purpose of a law.
2. Explain the intent of those who created the law.
3. State problems in the application of the law.
4. Generate alternatives.
5. Communicate effectively with others.
6. Choose solutions based on reason.

Activity

1. Pass out "No Vehicles in the Park" (Handout V.A) and read it aloud.
2. Discuss:
   - What does the law say?
   - Why did the city council pass the law?
   - What is it designed to do?
   - What is the intent? What do they want to accomplish with this law?
   - Will everyone understand it? Is it clear?

3.   Break up into small groups (5 to 6 students), with TA's leading.

4.   Read "Who Can Go into the Park" (Handout V.B). For each situation, decide:

- Will you allow the vehicle into the park?

- Why or why not?

- What alternate solution can you suggest?

5.   Reconvene whole group, report back, record answers on a grid on the board (if you want)

- Is the law clear as it is written?

- Does it need to be rewritten?

- What needs to be changed?

- How should "emergency" situations be provided for in the law?

- Who should determine what constitutes an emergency?

- What is the appropriate penalty for violating this law?

- Should the penalty be written into the law?

- How would you rewrite the law?

VI. Homework and Wrap-up

Before Students Leave

- Hand out the Public Survey of Student Rights and the First Amendment (Handout VII.A) to all students

- Encourage them to fill it out and bring it back to class next week

- Thank the students for being active participants

- Name the Outstanding Lawyers of the Day and give out prizes

- Remind them to turn in their name badges and binders to the TAs

- Remind them to come to class on time next Saturday at 7:45 a.m.

- Dismiss students at noon.

Also

- TAs need to collect all name badges and binders from students

- TAs must accompany students to parking lot and make sure that all of the students are picked up by their parents.

- TAs meet with teachers until 1 p.m. to debrief about the day's lesson and prepare for next week's lesson.

VII. Handout: Seminar Rubric for Self Evaluation

Student:	
Seminar Topic:	
Evaluation of Performance:	
o	I spoke clearly and supported my opinion
o	I made interesting and insightful points.
o	I asked peers helpful questions.
o	I offered suggestions to organize discussion.
o	I helped peers get into the discussion.
o	Disruptive—I was involved in side conversations.
o	Not participating—I was doing other things.
o	Disrespectful to classmates.
o	I interrupted when peers were talking.
o	I need to participate more in the seminar.
o	I gave opinions but did not explain reasoning.

VIII.A. Handout — No Vehicles in the Park

Irvine has a lovely, quiet park right in the center of the city. The city council wants to make sure that the park stays safe and unpolluted. The members do not want the park disturbed by city noise. In the park, you can find grass, trees, flowers, playgrounds, and picnic areas. To make sure that the park stays this way, the city council passes a law.

At all entrances to the park the following sign is posted:

No Vehicles in the Park

VIII.B Handout — Who Can Go in the Park?

1. Antonio Vegas lives on one side of town and works on another. He will save 10 minutes if he drives through the park.

2. There are many trash barrels in the park. People put trash in them to help keep the park clean. The sanitation department wants to go in to collect the trash.

3. An ambulance with a seriously injured victim of a car accident needs to get to the hospital quickly. The shortest route is through the park. The victim may die if they don't take the shortcut.

4. Two police cars are chasing a suspected bank robber. If one officer cuts through the park, she can trap the suspect's car between the patrol cars.

5. Some of the children who visit the park want to ride their bicycles there.

6. Mr. Thomas wants to take his baby to the park in a baby stroller.

7. The government donates a military tank to the city. It is to be placed in the park as a monument to the town's veterans who died in a war.

8. Sarah likes to go to the park with her friends. Sarah uses a wheelchair that has a motor.

Appendix C

Sample of Evaluation Protocol[34]

1. Did the SAL program increase student interest and attitudes related to justice and legal system, attending college, and pursuing a career in law?

2. Attitudes towards the Justice and Legal System

3. Increases in Self-efficacy for Writing Skills and Writing Ability

4. Preferences for Legal Careers

5. Did the SAL program increase student enrollment and success in rigorous academic coursework in high school?

6. Increases in Standards-based Writing Skills

7. Cumulative GPA

8. Did the SAL program serve the intended target population?

9. Participant Population

10. Sample Population

11. Evaluation Design

12. The following measures were collected and used in the evaluation of the SAL program in Year 1:

13. Program Attendance

14. Pre and Post Attitude Surveys

15. Pre and Post Writing Ability Tests

16. Law Career Presentation Surveys

17. School Achievement Data

The effectiveness of the SAL program in improving the School Achievement Data Outcomes will be estimated using a matched comparison group sampled from all enrolled ninth graders in the Santa Ana Unified School District. Criteria for selection will include:

   a. Demographic characteristics, including gender, ethnicity/race, family background (education and SES)

   b. Language proficiency (English learner)

   c. Academic history

      i. CumulativeGPA in middle school

      ii. 2008 California Content Standards Test for English/Language Arts scaled score and proficiencylevel

Appendix D

Results SAL-UCI

Attitudes towards the justice and legal system

A measure of perceived competence of the laws and punishment and fairness of laws and judges was piloted to gauge the impact of exposure to the program's legal curriculum.

- The results showed a significant increase in perceived fairness of laws and judges.

- No change was observed for perceived competence of the laws and punishment.

Career interest

- The majority of SAL students are presently leaning towards public interest law careers, such as immigration (72%), human rights (64%), and legal aid (56%).

- Police officer/law enforcement is the second most desired career among the SAL students (65%).

- The most popular private practice careers are in the areas of family law (63%) and entertainment (56%).

- For government careers, public defender is the most popular career among the SAL students (57%).

- Preferences for some careers increased somewhat during the program, sports in private practice careers (+16%), prosecutor in government careers (+18%), and police officer in non-lawyer careers (+11%).

Writing and ELA results

- SAL students increased their self-efficacy for demonstrating skills specific to advanced writing strategies ($p < .05$), such as the ability to revise a draft to make it better organized, adjust their style of writing to suit the needs of any audience, and develop a clear and coherent thesis statement.

- They also reported receiving more praise for their writing ($p < .01$).

- An objective test modeled on the California Content Standards Test for English/Language Arts was administered and scored. The test scores on the objective test correlated positively with incoming eighth grade ELA CST scores (pretest: r=.29, sig < .05; posttest: r=.44, sig < .001).[35]

Cumulative GPA

- The mean cumulative GPA for SAL students at the end of ninth grade was 3.09. About three-quarters of SAL students ended the year with a cumulative GPA of 2.78 or higher.

Chapter 10

Law Summer Program: High School and Beyond

Center for Youth Development through Law
Berkeley, California

Nancy Schiff[*]

Pre-K	Elementary	Middle	High School	College	Law School	Profession

The Center for Youth Development through Law is in many ways the perfect example of a pipeline program. It acknowledges the achievement gap and the deficits in the education system. It works to bring about change at several levels of the pipeline. It takes advantage of the strengths of the law as engaging and rigorous. It takes advantage of the mentoring and relationship potential of the legal community. And it measures its work and finds success. For replication, this is a natural for those connected to law schools, high schools, and the profession.

Introduction

The Center for Youth Development through Law (CYDL) fosters high aspirations and achievement among disadvantaged high school students in the East Bay area of California through a two-month, full-time summer program, and follow-up mentoring. Our summer program provides youth with paid law and government-related internships. It also offers an interactive curriculum integrating legal education with academic and life skills development, career development and college preparatory activities, emotional health curriculum, and conflict resolution training. Many of the activities take place on a university campus and are provided in the context of a small community of supportive peers. We follow the summer program with one year of

---

[*] Nancy Schiff has been the Executive Director of the Center for Youth Development through Law since 1999, and was one of the founders of the Center's Summer Legal Fellowship Program in 1995. She developed some of the curriculum used in the Center's program, including a mock trial curriculum, *Justice in Action*, which was published by McGraw-Hill in 2001. She received her JD from UC Hastings College of the Law and her B.A. from Brown University.

follow-up mentoring by law students and others and educational and career support by staff that continues indefinitely.

Our program provides the young people with an understanding of law and government from several perspectives: as important societal institutions, as practical tools, as avenues for improving the world, and as potential career paths. Most importantly, we help the young people increase their capacity to do well in high school, pursue higher education, and achieve productive and fulfilling careers in law or any field.

Our program has provided a transformative experience to youth who otherwise would have little academic or career support, but the program also benefits youth as one stage in a continuum of pipeline services (e.g., a relevant summer experience for a student in a high school law academy, a follow-up to a Street Law class). Our model could also be adapted to career fields other than law.

Our Origins

The Center for Youth Development through Law, a 501(c)(3) nonprofit organization, was founded in 1999 to administer the Summer Legal Fellowship Program, which had been created in 1995 under the auspices of the Street Law Project at University of San Francisco School of Law. In their Street Law courses, the inner-city high school students were excited to learn about law, but they also asked for help getting jobs, and they were curious about law careers. We decided to help them not only find summer jobs, but to create a program that would increase their capacity to succeed in the long-term in college and careers by offering academic enrichment, meaningful experiences in the professional work world, supportive relationships, and the opportunity to build skills.

Our Participants

We focus on low income, public high school students from Oakland and Richmond because they face some of the most challenging circumstances in the Bay Area. Half of the young people in these school districts do not graduate from high school. In West Oakland and East Oakland, two districts from which almost all of our Oakland students come, more than 50% of households have total incomes below $30,000 annually (in a very high cost of living region). In 2006, there were 36 murders for every 100,000 people, more than five times the national average. At Richmond High School, where our Richmond students go to school, 74% of the students receive free or reduced lunches. In the 2007–2008 school year at Richmond High, there were 2000 suspensions among a student body of 1750 students. In that same year, only 75% of seniors graduated in June.

All of our participants are from low income households. Some of our participants have incarcerated relatives, are in foster care, or have been victims of abuse or other violent crimes. Some have had to take on a parental role for themselves and/or for their siblings. Some have been in trouble with the law, or have been gang-affiliated. Others have parents who speak little English and who are not able to provide guidance on navigating the academic or employment world. These parents may well be skeptical and possibly even disapproving of higher education. Approximately 55% of CYDL participants are African American, 35% are Latino, and 10% Asian American, Pacific Islander American, or Middle-Eastern American.

So why do the young people get involved with our program, when it is not required for school, takes up their entire summer, and is located (in most cases) far from their homes? Some get involved because they want to learn more about law, in some cases because they have been affected by the legal system, for example through government benefits, the criminal justice system, child protective services and/or immigration agencies. Some of our participants are interested in pursuing some type of law career. Some are thinking about pursuing higher education, but want help getting there. Some of the youth have not thought much about what they will do after high school, and see this program as giving them some guidance about the real world and gaining independence. Others simply need a summer job. For all of the students, the stipends we pay (approximately $1400 for the summer) are an important motivator, as they need to earn money over the summer. We have also worked with some of the local school districts so that we can offer some of our participants high school credit.

The young people bring with them many assets, including curiosity about law and motivation to overcome obstacles. Each summer, 25–30 disadvantaged youth participate, after their sophomore, junior or senior year in high school. We recruit young people through teachers and other professionals who work with youth. Our participants have had varying levels of academic success. But we encourage youth to get involved as long as they have the motivation and maturity level to benefit from the program, which we assess through personal interviews and discussions with adults who know them.

Our Approach

To keep all of the young people involved and benefiting given the challenges they face, and their diverse ages and skill levels, we create an environment where they will all feel comfortable participating actively, trying new things that feel strange or intimidating, and confiding in and accepting guidance from staff.

Our approach includes:

- Holding the young people to high standards of responsibility, participation, and respectful behavior.
- Making the program fun.
- Communicating that we understand their world.
- Recognizing and building on the assets the young people already possess.
- Working with ethnically diverse staff that can relate well to disadvantaged youth.
- Offering small classes, varied teaching strategies, and individualized attention.
- Valuing individual growth and improvement rather than level of achievement.
- Giving participants roles of responsibility within the program.
- Building a community among the youth and staff where each young person feels a sense of belonging and safety.

- Fostering mutually supportive bonds among the students that last beyond the summer.
- Providing substantive interactions with professionals who have similar backgrounds to the youth.
- Holding classroom activities on a college campus so they can see college as more accessible.

Program Structure

The program begins in late June, with ten full days of classroom activities on the UC Berkeley School of Law campus. During this time, the staff gets to know each of the participants, and match each with an appropriate internship based on their interests, skills, and goals. In July and August, the young people work in their internships for four full days per week and continue their classroom activities on the campus one full day per week. During the subsequent school year, a mentor works with each young person on his or her educational and career goals. During that year and beyond, our staff continues to stay in contact with them and offers follow-up services.

Classroom Activities

Law and Government

The young people learn about law through a curriculum that employs varied teaching strategies, including traditional reading and writing as well as discussions, debates, and mock Supreme Court hearings. They improve their academic, communication, and advocacy skills, while learning about the role of law and government, learning how to handle legal issues in their own lives, and exploring whether they might want to pursue a law career.

Our constitutional law segment examines how the Supreme Court has handled issues of race and education throughout history. These are issues close to the students' lives and experiences. The students analyze excerpts from cases including *Plessy v. Ferguson, Koramatsu v. U.S., Brown v. Board of Education, San Antonio v. Rodríguez,* and *Regents of U.C. v. Bakke,* and discuss how the historical circumstances and legal principles in those cases are relevant to today's world. Students learn to think critically and examine issues from diverse viewpoints. In other curriculum segments, students learn about rights and responsibilities on the street and in the workplace. They also learn about various cooperative problem-solving strategies used in legal contexts, such as negotiation and mediation, providing a link to the Conflict Mediation program component.

Our participants appreciate making connections to issues faced by their own communities today, and come to understand both the benefits and limitations of the law's protections. Youth in this age group are often beginning to think about issues of justice, and their role in the greater society and this curriculum provides an opportunity for them to voice their opinions and learn ways they can make change.

Career Development

Through readings, role plays, discussions, and individual exercises, the young people learn about: appropriate workplace attire, habits and etiquette, networking, resumes, job interviews, communication skills for the workplace, and different types of law, government, and social justice careers, and the corresponding educational pathways.

Before students' internships begin, we focus on preparing the youth for doing well in their internships. After the internships begin, we facilitate discussion of the different internship activities so that students can learn from each other's experiences. Guided by staff, the young people help each other resolve problems that arise, which develops their problem-solving abilities and confidence.

We help each student discover which types of careers relate to their talents and interests as well as which would be personally fulfilling for them. Each student prepares a professional resume, and goes through a videotaped mock employment interview in which they are interviewed by a realistic mock employer and receive feedback from staff.

College Readiness

Through interactive lessons, students learn how academic skills, a high school degree, and education beyond high school are related to work success. We discuss the full spectrum of post-high school education options; how to prepare for higher education; how to access and pay for college; and how to access resources while in college. Students meet a college admissions counselor, people representing various career paths, and past program graduates who have gone to college. In addition, we provide practical information on college access and financial management, and we help each participant develop individual educational, career and personal goals, and a plan to achieve those goals.

Emotional and Social Development Curriculum

Because healthy emotional development and social competence are as important for well-being and career success as academic and employment skills, this curriculum, led by a psychotherapist who has experience working in the local public schools, fosters the young people's emotional and social development.[1]

All youth in our society face the challenging task of developing self-esteem and healthy identity in a complex, media-saturated, and competitive world. Beyond that, many of our participants have experienced traumatic circumstances such as emotional, physical, or sexual abuse; family instability or abandonment; witnessing violence; or losing family or friends to violence. Most have not received sufficient counseling or help with learning how to cope with the emotional consequences of these experiences in constructive ways. Without attention to these issues, the young people are in danger of acting destructively or being unable to manage life as an adult.

In our curriculum, the young people first explore how all people are affected psychologically and emotionally by past experiences, socialization, and their own racial, cultural, gender, and other identities. Gradually, they begin to explore how their own identities and past events have affected their feelings, motivations, accomplishments, and challenges. They come to know who they are more deeply, apart from external influences. As the young people gradually delve into more personal and sensitive topics, they have a chance to get support for traumatic issues they have faced. We help them discover the strengths they have developed, and find constructive ways to cope with difficult circumstances. Sometimes class discussions lead to one-on-one discussions with the instructor or referrals to other counseling resources.

In a second component, students are asked to experience the different perspectives of others and to appreciate how all individuals have unique perspectives that may conflict with each other. This generates empathy toward people with different viewpoints and circumstances. We also address the stigma most of our participants feel as people of color, immigrants, or children of immigrants, and/or as children from low income households. By understanding the societal and psychological processes involved in stereotyping and racism, the young people are better able to cope with them and avoid participating in them. Students gain an appreciation for their own background, and the value of diversity in general, and see how they can personally promote inclusiveness.

Through these interactive sessions, the young people develop close bonds with each other. The increased self-management abilities, self-knowledge, and peer support they develop help to fortify them for challenges they will face in the future—for example, financial or academic setbacks, conflicts with family members, or peers encouraging destructive behavior. Their increased pride in their own unique characteristics and purpose in life, and greater capacity to connect with other people, help them to be productive as well as fulfilled in their lives.

Conflict Management

Using the psychological understanding and emotional intelligence they have acquired as a foundation, students learn ways to relate and communicate with others in challenging interactions, whether with a parent, peers, employer, or others, in a way that leads to greater understanding and cooperation, and potentially enhanced relationships. The participants examine emotional triggers and unrecognized emotional needs at the root of conflicts. They learn techniques for resolving their own conflicts peacefully, and for helping others resolve their conflicts either informally or through formal tools such as conflict mediation. Most of the sessions in this part of the curriculum involve the youth practicing the techniques with peer and staff feedback. The skills the youth learn are useful in careers in law and many other fields as well as in life in general. The attention to mediation also serves as a link to the program's legal curriculum on mediation.

Our Emotional Health and Conflict Management curriculums, together, enable the youth to cultivate greater emotional stability and peace in their own lives as well as to help foster a more compassionate, responsible, and peaceful society.

Internships

After preparatory activities in the career development curriculum, each student works for seven weeks, four full-time days per week, in a law firm, nonprofit organization, or government department. Internship agencies have included: East Bay Community Mediation, La Raza Centro Legal, California Attorney General, Congresswoman

Barbara Lee's Office, police departments, city councilmembers' offices, U.S. District Court, and the American Civil Liberties Union.

At these placements, interns are able to observe the workings of law and government firsthand and become more comfortable in a professional environment. They have the opportunity to develop relationships with coworkers and supervisors who often become mentors and contacts for future employment. By learning about the requirements and tasks involved in different positions in their agencies, the youth are able to appreciate the connection between school success and the work world. The internships generally entail clerical tasks, such as data entry and filing, combined with substantive projects such as observing court proceedings, conducting research, participating in community mediation trainings, summarizing depositions, maintaining constituent services for elected officials, attending city council meetings, helping conduct "know your rights" presentations, and planning events.

At their internships, the young people also develop capacities that will help them succeed in the work world: computer skills, maintaining a professional demeanor, time management, communication skills, problem-solving skills, and the ability to work with people of different ages and backgrounds. In addition, acquiring a sense of mastery leads to self-confidence and higher aspirations.

We communicate regularly with internship supervisors and visit the work sites to help the interns recognize their strengths, provide positive reinforcement, and help them improve where needed. We also help the young people see how they can maintain their unique personal and cultural identity and still be successful in the professional world, and to appreciate that they can offer many assets as a member of an underrepresented group.

Other Activities

Mock Trials

After learning trial procedures and skills during the classroom component of the program, participants work in teams to conduct two mock trials. One is a criminal trial dealing with a death caused by drunk driving and the other is a civil trial about HIV transmission between teenagers in a sexual relationship. Each student plays the role of attorney, witness, or bailiff in one trial and juror in the other. Real judges preside over the trials, and families and mentors are invited to observe. The young people gain analytical, teamwork, and communication skills, as well as meaningfully experiencing what lawyers do in their jobs.

Courthouse Field Trip

As a group, participants visit a local courthouse to observe proceedings and talk in-depth with judges.

Graduation Ceremony

We conclude the summer program with a graduation ceremony on the campus in which students make presentations, receive certificates, and hear a keynote speech by a legal luminary. We invite program supporters and participants' families, mentors, and internship supervisors. For the participants' families, this is an opportunity not only to celebrate, but to better understand the young person's hard work and accomplishments, to appreciate the value of education, to motivate younger siblings in a positive direction, and to see that there is a community of caring people who are willing to help the young person.

Mentors

Toward the end of the summer, participants are matched with mentors who provide educational and career guidance to the young people for at least one year after the summer ends. Some mentors are law students, some are lawyers, and some are contacts the young people have met in their internships. Typical mentor-mentee activities include academic tutoring, attending a job or college fair, or working on college applications.

Follow-up Career and Educational Support

In addition to the year of support by a mentor, our staff stays in contact with the participants on an ongoing basis to offer guidance, assist them with college applications, networking, employment contacts, and referral to community resources. We also produce a quarterly newsletter with articles on various educational and career topics as well as updates on graduates' accomplishments.

We help students maintain the supportive bonds they formed with our staff and each other through a program yearbook, annual reunion parties, educational events, and a Facebook group.

Program graduates also give back to the program while furthering their own development by participating as guest speakers, administrative assistants, mentors, and board members. Two of our graduates even worked as program instructors while in law school.

Our Funding and Community Partners

Our funding comes from private foundations, law firms, bar associations, individuals, and city governments. The UC Berkeley School of Law provides us with rent-free office space along with the use of classroom and auditorium facilities. In addition to the benefits of bringing young people to the campus, being located on campus facilitates the recruitment of law students as teachers and mentors, and inspires financial support and other involvement by Law School alumni.

Public high school personnel and other professionals working with youth refer young people to us. The summer youth employment programs in local city governments also refer youth to us, and in some cases, pay partial stipends for those youth. Other significant partners are the firms, government offices, and nonprofit organizations that host interns in their offices. Law firms and other for-profit entities are asked to cover the cost of the young person's stipend, while government offices and nonprofit organizations receive their intern for no cost.

Our Results

Our staff consistently observes improvement in the participants' skills, attitudes, and self-confidence during the course of each summer. These observations are backed up by a variety of qualitative and quantitative evaluations we conduct at the end of each summer. A few representative results from our most recent program (which are consistent with previous years' results) are shown in the following table of anonymous surveys asking the students to indicate how the program affected them in specific competencies and attitudes. For each competency, they were asked to indicate "much better," "somewhat better," "the same," or "I don't know" according to how they felt the program affected them.

Competency	Percentage of youth indicating "much better" or "somewhat better" as a result of the program
Understanding of how the law works	100%
Skills for succeeding in the workplace	100%
Ability to communicate	100%
Likelihood of succeeding in school	100%
Commitment to pursuing higher education	94%
Ability to network	94%
Self-confidence	88%
Ability to work with others	82%
Academic skills	76%
Ability to handle conflicts with others	83%
Ability to understand and express my emotions	76%
Percentage of students that felt they improved in at least eight (67%) of the 12 competencies	100%

We also conducted qualitative evaluations in which participants answered open-ended questions either in anonymous questionnaires or in private interviews with trained volunteers (not program staff). All of the participants stated that the program had influenced them in a positive way. Here are some of the specifics:

Question: "What do you plan to do after you graduate from high school?"

Responses: All but one student expressed a clear intention to attend higher education. The one student who did not mention higher education nevertheless stated that he plans to become a veterinarian.

* * *

Question: "What are some things you learned or achieved in the program this summer?"

Responses: The most common response was different variations on "I learned how to be responsible." Almost all of the students mentioned more than one thing they had learned, and their responses varied. 90% of the responses not relating to learning how to be responsible fell into four general categories:

1. How to be successful at work (e.g., being professional, getting along with people in the workplace, specific job skills),
2. Skills for obtaining employment (e.g., how to network, "how to get a job"),
3. Knowledge about the legal system (e.g., Due Process, the Constitution, mediation), and
4. Interpersonal effectiveness (e.g., how to communicate, how to present my opinions, how to get along with people, how to resolve conflicts).

* * *

Question: "Can you describe any ways that you have changed over the course of the summer?"

Responses: 100% of the students stated one or more positive ways they had changed. More than half stated they felt more confident in themselves. Additional responses included feeling more responsible, smarter, and " … more able to speak my mind and share my ideas."

Over the years, many youth have expressed how their overall outlook has been transformed. Here are just a few examples:

• "Because of this program, I realize that I am someone."
• "The program changed my life!"
• "The program opened up a whole new world for me. It teaches you how to survive, and how to be a good person."
• "This program showed me how, if I put my mind, body, and soul into something, I can get anything accomplished."
• "I learned how to believe in myself."

Tracking of Participants' Educational and Career Progress

Between 1995 and 2010, 374 youth have graduated from the program, and we have remained in contact with approximately 75% of them. None of these youth have dropped out of high school, and of the graduates who have completed high school, approximately 90% have enrolled in higher education. Eight have attended law school, and three that we know of have pursued other types of graduate degrees. One received her Masters of Social Work and is currently working for a foster care organization. Of the eight who have attended law school, three are currently still attending and five have earned law degrees. Three of the law graduates are members of the California Bar; one recently passed the bar exam, and the other two have practiced law in California since 2008.

Stories

A few individual stories will help to illustrate the transformations that can occur as a result of our program:

J.

J. heard about our program when he was a student at Castlemont High School in Oakland. He had previously been involved with a gang, but was working hard to leave that life behind. He had not even thought about college or life after high school. One of his teachers and our staff encouraged him to participate in our 2004 program. We arranged an internship for him at an office in the Oakland City Hall, and he did so well that they hired him to continue working part-time after the summer ended. He still works there today while attending a local community college part-time, and plans to become a juvenile probation officer. In 2008, he sent us the following message:

> This program was the first step towards a new life for me.... Before, college was far from my mind. After completing the program I made an emphasis to go. I'm still working at the location I was placed in as an intern.... Without the program I wouldn't be here and I probably wouldn't be going to school.... I can really say that the program was a life altering experience.

R.

R. attended our program when she was 16. She had lived in and out of foster care since the age of 11, and was a student at an alternative public high school in West Oakland. In our program, she quickly displayed her sharp mind and interest in social justice. We placed her in an internship with the National Lawyers Guild, where she learned about political activism. Looking back on the program a few years later, she said: "I feel that this program really changed my life. It made me see that even though I came from a poor background, I could still have a good future.... The program showed me that there are ways to get people to listen to you, and to change things."

After high school, she attended Mills College in Oakland, where she graduated in 2006. She now works at a social service agency in Oakland, where she helps children who are facing similar challenges like those she faced growing up.

Dorian Peters

Dorian Peters participated in our program in 2000, and is now a practicing attorney in California. He wrote this letter recently about his experiences:

> When I was in high school, I had very little academic focus and motivation. My mother was going through tough times, forcing me to worry about basics, such as having shelter and food. I had no plans to attend college. I learned about the Center for Youth Development through Law program from a Street Law student teacher. At the time, I was particularly interested in the prospect of having a paid summer job. Little did I know, the program was much more than a summer job.
>
> I remember a work skills class where I learned practical skills, such as creating a strong resume and interviewing. I also remember a legal class where I learned the significance of landmark legal decisions, such as *Brown v. Board of Education*.
>
> I was also placed in a summer internship at the U.S. District Court of the Northern District of California, in San Francisco. My experience was amazing. Being able to have access to real court proceedings, and seeing real people perform their legal jobs motivated me to seek a career in law. Since doing the program, I attended Diablo Valley College. I transferred to UC Berkeley and graduated in 2005. I subsequently attended Vanderbilt University Law School and I passed the California bar exam in 2008, and since then I have worked as a Deputy District Attorney.
>
> I can say that I would not be where I am today had I not had the benefit of the Center for Youth Development through Law program and the staff's continued support.

Dorian enjoys his work at the District Attorney's Office, and he often visits our program to volunteer and inspire current participants.

Guidance for Those Who Want to Replicate Our Program

We are happy to provide information and assistance to anyone wishing to replicate our entire program or parts of it, or to adapt our program to a different career field. More than particular knowledge, what will make the biggest difference in the young people's lives are the skills, attitudes, and relationships they acquire. With that in mind, we have learned the following lessons that might be useful for those who wish to implement similar programs:

Staff and Volunteer Qualities

Minimal legal background is needed for teaching the legal curriculum topics. Most importantly, all of the staff should be competent in working with disadvantaged high school students, as well as in community building and youth development principles. Similarly, meeting high-profile legal professionals is not as meaningful to the students as is interacting with college students, law students, or legal professionals with backgrounds similar to theirs and/or with an ability to relate to their interests and concerns.

Community Building

The young people will gain more from the program if they feel part of a supportive community, and maintain relationships with some of the adults and peers from the program after the program ends. It is well worth time and energy to engage in community building activities and pay close attention to group dynamics.

What Makes an Effective Internship

We've learned that for an internship to be successful for both the intern and the agency, the intern must be able to:

- Provide useful assistance to the office
- Understand how their assignments are related to the goals of the organization
- Have a reasonable level of variety in assignments
- Interact with people in a variety of professional roles
- Receive appropriate training and supervision
- Develop transferable skills
- Feel welcome and included socially
- Feel valued as an important contributor to the organization's goals

In setting up internships, it is important to have a good understanding of each organization's office environment, to make sure the agency understands the program's goals for the internship, and to ask the agency to specify how the internship will work in terms of tasks, training, and supervision.

Although students are often excited by the idea of working in a law firm, the reality usually does not live up to their expectations. The large size and hierarchical nature of law firms means that a high school intern will not have meaningful contact with attorneys unless the firm makes a concerted effort to make that happen. In addition, there is a danger that the intern will spend all of the time doing repetitive clerical work, and not see the connection to the work that lawyers do. We work with a few law firms that provide great experiences, but most of our effective internships are with small law offices, nonprofit organizations, and the offices of elected officials.

Before matching students with particular internships, it's important to understand each student's interests, goals, personality, and skills. Some students will thrive in a fast-paced environment where they will be given substantive projects, such as in an elected official's office, while other students might find that overwhelming, and may benefit from a quiet environment where they can learn basic computer tasks.

Lastly, program staff should establish frequent and candid communication with agency supervisors, and encourage supervisors to provide ongoing, specific feedback to interns. A common issue is supervisors' hesitation about "complaining" to staff or criticizing interns, which perpetuates the problem and deprives the interns of the opportunity to learn. Make sure the supervisors understand that the staff wants to know as soon as possible about any problems. In some cases, the staff might need to suggest constructive ways for supervisors to handle problems, and provide backup.

Age Range

Our summer program includes students who have completed their sophomore, junior, and senior years in high school. Although this works well for us, in replicating a program like this, one might choose instead to work with students who are all at the same grade level. This would facilitate the college counseling and follow-up services because the young people will all be dealing with similar issues at roughly the same time.

Required Resources

We employ one full-time executive director who is also the program director, four part-time summer instructors, a year-round part-time (.2 FTE) program assistant, and clerical assistants during the spring and summer who work only a few hours per month. Our organizational budget is approximately $170,000. We have no facility-related expenses since we receive donated office and classroom space from the law school. If a program like ours were part of a much larger organization, it would be able to take advantage of economies of scale and thus might require fewer financial resources.

Conclusion

Although our program graduates pursue diverse paths, we hope that we have helped them become more educated, more self-sufficient, more engaged with their community as citizens and leaders, and better able to fulfill their own goals and ideals and to be the individuals they were meant to be.[2]

Chapter 11

Law School–High School

Street Law Clinics at Georgetown University Law Center Washington, D.C., and Others

*Richard Roe**

Pre-K	Elementary	Middle	High School	College	Law School	Profession

Street Law is one of the best known of the legal pipeline programs. Street Law exists across the country and internationally in a very wide variety of iterations. The Street Law Clinic at Georgetown University Law Center described here was the first of the Street Law law school clinics and remains one of the strongest. In addition to its law-focused, activity-based curriculum, which includes classroom instruction on a wide range of legal topics and an annual mock trial competition typically on a controversial topic of interest to students, the Georgetown Street Law program incorporates mentor aspects involving local law firms. Street Law is highly consonant with the identified values for pipeline success—rigor, relevance, and relationship—and shows remarkable success with both its high school students and its law school teachers. This chapter offers not only how-to materials but also the rationale for its learner-centered methodology, analysis of the clinic setting and examples of the positive value and impact on both law students and high school students.

Introduction to Street Law

The idea of using law students to teach in high schools about the law affecting people's everyday lives was born in 1972, when Street Law was taught in two District of Columbia senior public high schools by four students from Georgetown University Law Center (GULC). The Street Law Clinic provides law-focused education to laypersons while contributing to the professional development of the law students.[1] As in law school clinical courses generally, law students engage in learning by doing by providing legal services to the public. What distinguishes the Street Law Clinic from other law school

* Richard L. Roe is Professor of Law and Clinic Director of the Street Law Clinic at Georgetown University Law Center. The Clinic web site is www.law.georgetown.edu/clinics/dcstreet. Professor Roe's e-Email is roe@law.georgetown.edu. Professor Roe would like to thank his research assistants Ryan Macpherson and Julia Pergola for their help researching for and editing this chapter.

clinics is that law students in Street Law do not represent clients. Instead, law students teach classes about the law, the legal process, and the knowledge and skills that laypersons can use to recognize, prevent, and in some cases resolve legal problems. Since its founding, the Street Law clinic has provided law-related educational services in high schools and community settings in the District of Columbia and has served as a model for Street Law programs nationally and internationally.

What began as a course of study in "practical law" soon evolved into a dual focus: 1) a course characterized by rich legal content, examining practical law, the legal process, the Constitution, legal policy, and the fundamental principles and values upon which law is based, expanded to not only what the law *is* but what students think that the law *should be*, and 2) a course that uses students' inherent interest in the law and the quality of discourse generated by examination of and inquiry into the law to develop students' literacy, their academic skills, their high level cognitive and expressive skills, critical thinking, problem solving, motivation, self-esteem, organization, and other important personal and interpersonal skills useful in academic, social and economic success.

The hallmark Street Law methodology of highly participatory, interactive, and engaging activity-based instruction, where the learning is accomplished largely through the cognitive, expressive, and reflective work of the learners themselves in substantively rich, thoughtfully structured lessons, draws from both the hands-on model of clinical legal education as well as the best practices for effective teaching and learning generally. This student-centered approach to teaching and learning is well suited both for the law students and for the learners they teach, from high school students to adults.

The rationale for Street Law's increasingly greater emphasis on an interactive teaching process in furtherance of students' substantive understandings can be attributed to several factors. First is the dialectic nature of the law and advocacy. Since the law is dynamic, not static, and involves interpreting and making meaning of law, not simply knowing the law, instruction in the law for both law students and laypersons should include high-level thinking, analysis, and expression about values, policies, and alternatives. Second, as a matter of democratic civic participation, layperson involvement with the law is not simply a matter of following or abiding by the law but also, and more importantly, a matter of appreciating that laws involve value choices and having a voice in shaping the law. This means Street Law should encompass not only what law, legal processes, and legal rights are, but also what they should be. As a corollary to this, law must be taught not in absolute terms but in a context of values and diversity. As in a diverse, pluralistic, democratic society, it should be open to multiple points of view. Third, from an educational perspective, learners need high-level literacy, cognition, expression, and critical thinking in order to realize deeper understanding of the law and to have a voice in it.[2]

The Work of the Street Law Clinic

Overview

The Street Law Clinic quickly expanded from its initial two schools to nearly all D.C. public high schools and correctional facilities, and was subdivided into two separate clinics, Street Law: High Schools and Street Law: Corrections, where law students taught in the various D.C. prisons.[3] In 2011, twenty-five law students participated in Street Law: High Schools and four enrolled in the summer course, Street Law in the Community, a reincarnated modification of Street Law: Corrections now taught in a prison and rehabilitation centers. A full-time Professor of Law serves as the Clinic Director along with a Clinical Fellow who is appointed for a two-year position supervise the law students.

The Street Law curriculum and approach are designed both to provide the high cognitive and expressive quality of learning required to develop lay facility with the law as well as to meet the needs of the widely diverse learners in these settings. Street Law operates effectively in the full academic range of high schools in DC.[4] The learner-centered, due process model of learning and teaching embodied in Street Law allows both the highest functioning high school students to excel and nurtures and develops students with lower levels of academic skill. Street Law is characterized not only by relevant and highly engaging subject matter but also by highly participatory, interactive, and responsive methodology. The students are motivated to put forth the required effort because classroom activities are at the same time doable, challenging, meaningful, and creative on a variety of substantive, cognitive, and expressive planes. Street Law puts into practice the precepts and values of responsible, participatory, democratic citizenship, which makes the Street Law classroom an exercise of genuine citizenship.

Moreover, this approach is consistent with the high cognitive and expressive dimensions of legal education generally. The application of quality instruction in complex, demanding, challenging, and diverse "law-related" interactions hones the legal understanding, critical thinking, decision-making, problem solving, and self-reliance abilities of the law student instructors. In a real sense, Street Law becomes a forum for law students to develop their advocacy—not through direct advocacy on behalf of others (although many opportunities for informal advocacy on behalf of the high school students arise), but rather by instilling others with the skills and confidence to be their own advocates. By engaging in and reflecting on teaching and learning as a forum for advocacy, law students advance their own awareness and skills as advocates.[5]

Value to High School Students

In the District of Columbia, Street Law is implemented in year-long Street Law courses in D.C. public senior high schools. High school students take Street Law as an elective. Legal topics include small claims court, criminal, tort, family and individual rights law, and the corresponding constitutional foundation and principles. The course culminates in an extensive mock trial competition. High school students learn: (1) the basic structure of the legal system, including the relationship among legislatures, courts, and agencies, and how citizens relate to the lawmaking processes of each branch of government; (2) the fundamental constitutional rights, laws and processes involved in the criminal and juvenile justice systems, and pertaining to consumer, family, housing, and individual rights areas; and (3) the function and operation of trials and other legal proceedings.

In the GULC Street Law courses, besides learning what the law is, students also learn to examine underlying policies and values to assess what the law should be. The students are encouraged to draw on their own knowledge and experience to assess laws and their underlying policies, rationales, and values. For instance, when students examine a specific problem, they are asked to think about it first in their own terms and then from other points of view. They determine and apply the appropriate law, determine available legal remedies, and discuss the often-competing policy concerns, societal interests and the underlying values on which these policies are based. Along with studying specific constitutional rights, students inquire as to whether such goals as fairness, due process, and justice are attained. Students also study how our legal system balances competing values that come into conflict. For instance, students examine how the First Amendment "freedom of speech" may be balanced against society's interest in protecting itself from injurious, obscene, or dangerous words. The Street Law courses accomplish these objectives by using a variety of learner-centered methods, including role plays, simulations, large and small group discussions, lectures, case studies, news articles, video clips, guest participants, field trips, and simulations of legal proceedings.

The centerpiece of the program is the annual citywide mock trial competition. High school students play the roles of lawyers and witnesses in a hypothetical case brought before actual judges at the District of Columbia Superior Court. Each Street Law class fields at least one team, and sometimes as many as three teams, to present the case in the two rounds of the tournament. Typically, over two dozen teams participate in simultaneous trials in each of two nights of competition. More than seventy judges, lawyers, and former Street Law instructors help in judging the trials and scoring the participants. The mock trial is a strong example of involvement of the broader legal community in the work of the students.

In addition to learning communications and preparation skills, trial procedures, and teamwork, students practice the spectrum of cognitive skills as they comprehend a complicated fact pattern, apply the facts to the law, analyze, and evaluate factual and legal issues, and synthesize the many components into a unified presentation. The mock trials are designed to appeal to young persons by being topical and controversial. In 2009 and 2010, the trials raised the issues of date rape and cyber-bullying, respectively. Raising important issues in the mock trial context allows the high school students to explore these issues in depth in an authentic way. The mock trial competition provides the academic structure for the students to develop and display high-level abilities.

Street Law for Law Students

The instructors in the Street Law courses are Georgetown Law Center students. Each year, we select around twenty-two law students for participation in the Street Law Clinic, where they serve as the instructors for the Street Law courses. The law students receive three credits per semester for teaching in the year-long Street Law Clinic. Some high schools conduct the Street Law class in the spring semester only; law students are also recruited for that period. The law students, in their second or third year of study, are selected, trained, supervised, and evaluated by the Street Law Clinic Director and the Street Law Clinic Fellow at Georgetown. Clinic faculty works with the principal and social studies departments of participating high schools to coordinate the scheduling and administration of the courses taught by the law students.[6]

Law student instructors typically are assigned to regular classrooms for the length of a semester or school year, coordinate their teaching with a "cooperating teacher" or teacher of record, and teach upwards of three hours per week (but not more than three class periods) for twenty-four weeks. Class schedules vary widely from school to school. Classes range from two to five times per week, and for forty-five minutes to over two hours in length. Occasionally, law students are paired in teams to cover five-day-per-week classes. Law student instructors have the primary responsibility for the instruction and grading of their students.

The Street Law faculty trains and supervises the law student instructors directly. Law student instructors arrive at the Law Center each fall prior to the start of regular classes for an intensive three-day orientation in participatory educational methodology and learner-centered instruction. Additionally, the faculty conducts a weekly two-hour seminar throughout the year, in which the law students are trained in the curriculum and methodology of Street Law. More significant than the seminar instruction is the intensive supervision, formal and informal, law students receive. Each law student instructor is observed and critiqued three times each semester. In addition to period review and consultation regarding the instructors' materials, the faculty maintains an open door approach to supervision and is constantly available to assist the instructors and to consult with them on their educational progress and development as instructors.

Law students must prepare substantial lesson plans containing objectives, methods and evaluations for each class, maintain records of student attendance, assignments, and evaluations, develop or adapt Street Law lessons appropriate to the needs, interests, and abilities of their students, conduct regular assessments of their students' progress, and maintain a journal of their experiences and reflections. These materials are reviewed monthly by the clinic faculty. Additionally, law student instructors prepare self-evaluations at the end of the year and meet with Professor Roe and the Clinical Fellow to review their achievements. For the year-end review, law student instructors also assemble a twenty-five page portfolio representative of their year.

Another feature of the course is the Mentor program, in which most Street Law classes are paired with a law firm or legal organization. This additional approach raises the involvement of the broader legal community and focuses on building important and needed relationships for the students. The Mentor firm typically is involved in Street Law in four ways. In cooperation with the law student instructor, the firm first visits the class to teach about certain aspects of the law that the firm is involved in. Second, the firm may take the students on a field trip to a law-related activity it is connected to, such as a visit to a Superior Court trial, a Congressional hearing, or to the U.S. Supreme Court. Third, the firm may invite the students to a visit to the firm itself, where the students learn about the operations of a law firm, observe potential careers from legal secretary to lawyer, and perhaps examine the development of a case in some detail. Fourth, the Mentor firm helps the class to prepare for the mock trial competition.

A useful framework for organizing the value of Street Law to law students can be drawn from an ABA survey of what skills practitioners found most valuable in their work, dividing responses into Legal/Analytical and Legal/Interpersonal.[7] Some of the most common of the ones derived from participation in Street Law are described as follows:

Regarding Legal/Analytical skills, the most common response is that teaching others about a subject is one of the best ways to learn it. Law student instructors gain knowledge and insight into a wide range of legal areas and advocacy skills. Secondly, law students conduct significant study of and research into these legal topics. Third, the preparation of lesson plans and conducting of classes, which often amount to over fifty classes in two semesters, teaches formulation, organization, and clarity of expression of legal concepts. While this does not constitute legal writing or argumentation *per se*, the exposition of legal concepts with a lay audience prepares law student instructors for a range of legal expression in more conventional legal contexts, from meetings with partners and clients to court appearances and preparation of memos and briefs. Fourth, the rapid and responsive quality of discourse and interchanges in a learner-centered classroom builds skills in legal analysis and thinking on one's feet. In the course of conducting participatory classes, law students engage in literally hundreds of decisions around legal categories involving application and interpretation of legal ideas and their meaning in the contexts of their students' experiences and values. Fifth, instructors learn the value of preparation and adaptability

Practitioners reported Legal/Interpersonal skills to be equally important in the practice of law. Some of the many legal/interpersonal skills include development of abilities in communication, collaboration, administration, organization, motivation, persistence, and presentation. One of the most frequently employed skills is problem solving, from dealing with school administration, student behavior, issues with cooperating teachers, and other administrative matters. Another important value is gaining insights into the nature of people, their life experiences, their values, and their problems. On one level, law students learn how law affects people in their everyday lives. On another, they experience how a range of rules and approaches operate in a classroom to shape their students' conduct and behavior. On a third, they come to see their students not just as learners in a classroom but also as individuals influenced by a striking variety of life's forces. Reflection itself is a value, and reflection on their experiences builds law student knowledge and respect for life's variables, and shapes law students' attitudes regarding larger issues in education, law, and justice. Students also appreciate the function of public interest work. Not surprisingly, Street Law instructors learn to teach, and some become teachers either in law school, college, or K–12 settings.[8] Moreover, teaching in local schools and community settings helps law students appreciate public service and diversity. The learner-centered, due process model of instruction helps law students shift their perspectives to see how their students see and experience law, policies and values from a wide range of perspectives.

Syllabus, Curriculum, and Credits

Syllabus and Curriculum

The instructional and supervisory components of the Street Law Clinic are designed to provide participating law students with the abilities both to carry out their work as instructors in their assigned educational settings and to develop and reflect on their capacities as legal professionals. Instructional capacities include both content and methods. There are six specific learning contexts for clinic law students: orientation, seminar, planning and preparation, instruction, supervision, and reflection.

Orientation

The Street Law clinic begins with a three-day, eighteen-hour orientation. The principle goals of the orientation are to shift students toward a leaner-centered, due process model of instruction of law for laypersons and to build their knowledge and ability to conduct that form of instruction. We accomplish this principally by engaging the law students in a planned series of participatory, learner-centered lessons from which they will experience, observe, analyze, discuss, assess and distill the major components. These activities always have three stages: preparation, activity, and review. The activities develop varying degrees of substantive knowledge and skills on the one hand and thinking and expressive skills on the other. Essentially, the sequence moves from activities requiring little prior knowledge to integration of more detailed and complex legal knowledge, concepts and materials. The methodology introduces students to a wide variety of learner-centered, interactive approaches. The sequence concludes with lessons to help students create law-related lesson plans of their own design.

The second part of the orientation, in the next week, is termed "practice teaching," where students develop ten-minute lessons, which they teach to three other students and a supervisor; the lessons are then reviewed using positive feedback from the group. Each student is assigned a different method and topic. This session both applies the principles of learner-centered teaching and lesson development and also shares new methods. Additionally, students "get their feet wet" in a supportive context.

Seminars

The seminars attempt a balance among content, methods, and administration. As in the orientation, they principally are comprised of the type of learner-centered instruction that the law students are urged to employ in their own placements. Early seminars are directed toward essential topics like discipline and assessment. Typically, content is not taught separately, but rather integrated into lessons along with advanced methodology. In our experience, much of the content in Street Law may have been previously studied at the Law Center and can be readily learned or refreshed through independent study and research. The seminars also include two other types of sessions. One is "demonstration teachings," where law students teach half hour model lessons to the larger group; these are critiqued by the larger group. The other is "rounds," where students select clinic-wide or common classroom topics or issues that need addressing. These topics are then discussed in small groups or later by the group as a whole, offering diagnoses and remedies much the same as doctors might discuss patients in rounds.

Planning and Preparing to Teach

The clinic establishes a sequence of instructional topics for the year, within which the law students have wide latitude in determining the specific lessons they will teach. This is due both to the wide range of learning contexts presented in the various schools and to be consonant with the clinic's learner-centered approach as applied to the law students. The first two weeks of instruction should draw heavily on the lessons modeled in the orientation. The second two weeks of instruction focus on negotiation. The lessons in these first 3–4 weeks are highly interactive and teach, encourage, and support the high school students in appropriate styles of discourse. The remaining ten or so weeks of the first semester are devoted to criminal law, criminal procedure, and individual rights. Law students are encouraged to draw upon and adapt exemplary lessons collected in the clinic Courseware site, to use demonstrated lessons, to select lessons from the Street Law textbook, and to design their own lessons. Regardless of the source of the lessons, law students need to adapt them to the current law, innovative teaching ideas, their own students' needs, interests and abilities, and the law student's teaching style. Students are also encouraged to collaborate with each other and to consult with clinic faculty on these lessons.

In the spring semester, the first month typically focuses on housing and family law, followed by six–eight weeks on the mock trial. Law students teach their students basic trial advocacy skills, to comprehend and explore the ever-emerging intricacies and interrelated concepts of the mock trial, and have their students practice these skills and concepts for presentation in court. The challenges presented by low literacy, learning disabilities, erratic attendance, English as a second language, lack of knowledge, confidence and experience, and other forces are daunting, yet our law students insist on the work being the students' own. Law students typically devote extra classes, after-school hours, class visits to GULC, courtroom visits, help from law firms and friends, late night phone conversations, friendly calls to parents, and every other means available to bring out the best in their students. Until the end, many [if not most] law students and their own students wonder if the students will be effective and successful, but they always are.

Instruction

In the learner-centered model of instruction, a lesson plan is not a blueprint but rather a springboard for the actual lesson. The basic idea is to engage in a series of activities bringing out legal topics or themes, then to develop and advance student expression and thinking about these topics through discussion and subsequent activities. Because student reactions and responses cannot be entirely predicted, the plans need to have alternative routes, materials, and ideas, some of which may never be explored. While a lesson cannot "follow" a plan, plans are essential for successful lessons. Research and planning is the springboard for inspiration. Law students are encouraged to structure lessons in a way that has their students' thoughts and expressions connect with the substantive content wherever possible. The law students facilitate this discourse, writing, or action by injecting building blocks rich with legal ideas. Law students experience success as well as disappointment in their instruction, but they and their students learn from both.

Supervision

Clinic faculty consult frequently with the law students on every dimension of clinic work. We have an open door policy for consultation with students on both preparation and review of lessons and other clinic matters, as well as routinely scheduled sessions. Faculty observe each law student at least three times per semester, and more often if needed or requested; these observations are followed by review sessions. Students prepare monthly reports of their attendance, lesson plans, and journals. The clinic follows a model of positive support based largely on the law students' experience and insights, particularly examining what worked or was effective, and what can be improved.

Reflection

Law students are encouraged to reflect on their clinic work throughout the course. Submission of reflective journals is required monthly, and students meet regularly and as needed with the faculty. The clinic environment is intended to be supportive and collegial. At the conclusion of the year, law students assemble a representative portfolio of their work, write a self-assessment, and conduct an exit interview reviewing their accomplishments, challenges, and benefits given and gained over the year.

Credit

Students in the Street Law Clinic receive three credits per semester. They almost universally report that they spend more time on Street Law than typically devoted to other three credit courses. Of course, the value of a law course is not simply measured by the work put in but (even more so) by the value to the learner's legal professional ability that comes out. The gains in professional development from Street Law very likely could qualify a program for more credit.

Conclusions

Street Law clinics help law schools meet important educational goals in terms of developing law students' professional abilities in research, planning and preparation, advocacy, "thinking on one's feet," and written and verbal exposition of legal topics from core concepts to practical applications. Street Law also fosters a commitment to public service and diversity. For high school students and community members, Street Law not only teaches about law that can be useful in everyday life but also builds larger legal concepts such as fairness, justice, due process, and the fundamental Constitutional values that are the underpinnings of our democracy. Because students learn largely though highly participatory, high cognitive and high expressive activities, where they themselves examine topical and substantively rich law-related issues that connect with their own lives, they not only experience success in learning but also develop a wide range of ancillary civic and academic skills. Because the Street Law methodology works effectively across the full range of academic and literacy abilities, respects individual and diverse learning capacities and life experiences, and creates a positive experience of success in school for a wide range of learners, it is ideal as a pipeline program.

Replicability

Street Law law school-based programs have been replicated throughout the United States and around the world. Street Law, Inc.,[9] the national program that provides support and programming to law school and school-based Street Law programs, estimates that there are more than seventy formal law school-based Street Law programs, ranging from student organizations to fully accredited clinical programs. In addition to supporting existing Street Law programs, Street Law, Inc. publishes the textbook, Street Law: A Course in Practical Law and an accompanying teacher's manual, and provides on line curriculum support. The national program also provides teacher training and support, including two sessions of the Supreme Court summer institute for teachers each summer at Georgetown Law Center in Washington, D.C. Street Law, Inc. also provides support through a law firm mentor and pipeline program, particularly through a Corporate Counsel program. Other programs focused particularly on various aspects of the law and targeted populations include the new Street Law in Community College initiative and Street Law programs internationally.

Patrick Campbell
One Student's Success Story[10]

Patrick Campbell participated in the Street Law Clinic while he was a student at Calvin Coolidge Senior High School. "There was a time when I would not have dared to dream of becoming a lawyer. Back then, hope of survival took precedence over thoughts of success. As I was growing up impoverished in a violence-plagued ghetto in the heart of Kingston, Jamaica, my home consisted of a single room, which I shared with my mother, stepfather, sister, and two brothers. When I left Jamaica and moved to the United States at age 14, I quickly discovered that the inner city of Washington had something sinister in common with my hometown. In either case, criminal careers were more prevalent than professional ones. When I started the 11th grade, a fortuitous event led me to a Street Law class at my high school, opening my eyes to a world that I previously thought unattainable. First, learning about some of the rights that I possessed by simply being in the United States was remarkably empowering. Even more importantly, the entire Street Law experience awakened in me a spirit that had previously been asleep—the sense that I could become a lawyer—and represented a genuine turning point in my life." Street Law changed Mr. Campbell's life. He attended Georgetown University and then Stanford Law School. Mr. Campbell is currently a Partner in the Communications and Technology Department at Paul Weiss Rifkind Wharton & Garrison. Mr. Campbell's story, although unique in its particular circumstances has been retold in many forms by Street Law participants from around the country and around the world.

Chapter 12

Law School–High School

Marshall–Brennan and Moot Court
American University Washington College of Law
and Others

Maryam Ahranjani*

Pre-K	Elementary	Middle	High School	College	Law School	Profession

Marshall–Brennan Beginning

The Marshall Brennan program is a star in the catalogue of law-themed and law school partnership programs. Both rigorous and prestigious, it offers a model that law schools can readily incorporate in their curricula and that quickly becomes an important part of community outreach. Expanding yearly to more locations, it is also a great example of a strong program that is replicable, has scaled up, and has benefitted from this kind of collaboration.

"Professor Raskin, can our school censor our cable TV show about gay marriage?" What started as an innocent question by a group of Montgomery County, Md., public high school students sparked a national movement for constitutional and civic literacy. Named for the late Supreme Court justices Thurgood Marshall and William Brennan in honor of their commitment to students' rights, the Marshall Brennan Con-

---

* Maryam Ahranjani is an adjunct professor of law and associate director of the Marshall Brennan Constitutional Literacy Project. She oversees the national and international expansion of the Marshall Brennan Constitutional Literacy Project and directs the program's efforts in DC public high schools. Professor Ahranjani teaches an advanced constitutional law seminar entitled, "Education and the Constitution" to upper-level law students and designed and teaches an externship seminar entitled, "Reflections on Meaningful Lawyering." Most recently, Professor Ahranjani worked for Kaplan, Inc., serving as a regional director and product manager. She formerly served as associate director of WCL's Program on Law and Government, where she ran the SJD and LLM programs. Co-author of the textbook Youth Justice in America (CQ Press, 2005), Professor Ahranjani has appeared on C-SPAN and has authored numerous articles and lesson plans about students' rights and civic literacy. A founder of the National Youth Justice Alliance, she was also the recipient of the 2008 Alumni of the Year Award from the Latino/a Law Students Association and a 2006 American University Performance Award. A magna cum laude graduate of Northwestern University, Professor Ahranjani obtained her JD degree from WCL, and is fluent in Spanish and Persian.

stitutional Literacy Project began as an innovative experiment in the fall of 1999 with the support of both justices' widows.

American University Washington College of Law Professor Jamin B. Raskin conceived of the project after assisting a group of local high school students whose cable TV show on gay marriage was censored. In the process of assisting the students with their First Amendment question, Professor Raskin and his colleague Stephen Wermiel realized there was a dearth of meaningful learning about the Constitution in public schools. In brainstorming what to do about this problem, they realized they had valuable social capital at their disposal—a surplus of energetic law students eager to share their knowledge about Supreme Court cases.

The program started in the public high schools of Washington, DC and neighboring Montgomery County, Maryland. Washington is known as "Chocolate City" for a primarily Black population since the city's founding. The city's demographics have changed over the past ten years, with African Americans now representing 54% of the population, Whites representing 36%, Hispanic or Latinos (of any race) representing 9% and Asians representing just over 3%.[1] While the adult population reflects an increase of Whites, Latinos, and Asians relative to African Americans, the public school population remains 79% Black, 12% Hispanic, 7% White, and 2% other.[2]

In terms of the public schools, DC is known for high dropout rates and low college graduation rates, although notably we have relatively high college attendance rates.[3] The DC public schools (DCPS) have always struggled to produce college and career-ready graduates.[4] Sixty-six percent of DC public school students qualify for free or reduced lunch, 19% receive special education services, and 8% are English language learners.[5] As of 2006, only 9% of DC public school students finished high school in five years, enrolled in college, and graduated from college in a timely fashion.[6] The fact that these statistics exist in the public schools of the nation's capital heightens awareness of the tremendous need for intervention all over the country.

Nuts and Bolts

In DC, Marshall Brennan Fellows from American University Washington College of Law (AU WCL) teach alongside fellows from Howard University Law School. During the 2010–2011 academic year, 59 law students (45 new fellows from WCL, six returning fellows from WCL, and eight new fellows from Howard) taught 19 elective courses in ten regular public schools and four public charter schools across the city. We carefully select our schools with the goal of serving underserved low-income and minority students who would not otherwise have access to the information and experiences we provide.

The Fellows teach in pairs, and each classroom has two pairs of fellows. One pair teaches constitutional law "theory" (from either *We the Students* or *Youth Justice in America*) and the other teaches "lab" (moot court and other experiential learning opportunities such as visits to the U.S. Supreme Court, the National Archives' Constitution-in-Action Lab, and the Newseum). All of our high school students participate in in-class moot court competitions, and the winners from each class proceed to the citywide competition. The winners of our citywide competitions across the country compete in the spring at our National Marshall Brennan High School Moot Court Competition.

DCPS offers the elective courses we designed and teach for social studies elective credit, and they maintain our syllabi on file for students, parents, administrators, and teachers to review.[7] We have close relationships with central administrators, principals, teachers, and important community groups. We obtain substitute-teaching licenses for all of the fellows, allowing fellows to teach without close supervision, although in many instances the public schools provide a classroom liaison. In terms of our fellows' selection, we have an extremely rigorous and competitive process. Recognizing the importance of role models for our high school students, we cultivate and maintain relationships with leaders and members of diverse student organizations such as the Black Law Students' Association and the Latino Law Students' Association. Traditionally, the presidents of both organizations serve as Marshall Brennan fellows. During the 2010–2011 academic year, ten of the fifty WCL fellows were African American and ten were of Latino descent, for an overall rate of 40% of the fellows from underrepresented minority groups. The fellows commit to teach for the entire public school calendar year, from the last week in August through the third week in June, and during their exam and break periods, to the extent that they do not overlap with the public school calendar.

Professional Development

Professional development begins with the application process for law student fellows, which is rigorous and competitive.[8] In DC, we require applicants to attend an information session, submit a resume and letter of interest, conduct a "guest teach," submit a self-evaluation of their "guest teach," and do a thirty-minute interview with program staff. We collect evaluations from current fellows of the applicants' "guest teach" and also convene a committee of first-year faculty who can provide insights into each applicant's performance in constitutional law and general aptitude for teaching. Because the process is so challenging, we generally weed out applicants who are not prepared to make a fifteen to twenty hour per week commitment for an entire academic year. The rigorous application process also allows us to begin training the next year's group of fellows in terms of program expectations, school conditions, students' reading and writing levels, and other important details.

After the new fellows are selected in late March, we host a welcome reception in early April, where we distribute important information (forms and reading material) to be completed before our two-day intensive orientation in August. Early in the fall semester, program staff members visit classrooms and provide feedback to fellows after the observations. During the weekly seminar, fellows learn the nuances of the cases contained in our two textbooks and receive training on pedagogy. Content experts and pedagogical specialists join the seminar to train the fellows on a host of issues, including special education, teaching to different learning styles, effective classroom management, police complaint procedures, school disciplinary appeals, etc.

Expansion

News of our work in DC quickly spread to law schools around the country. Other communities have welcomed law students into their public schools to teach high school students about their constitutional rights and responsibilities. Twelve years after the project first began in Washington, DC, we now have chapters from coast to coast — in San Francisco, Phoenix, Camden, Boston, Philadelphia, Baton Rouge, Louisville, and U.S. chapters — ranging in size from ten law students in one school to sixty students in fourteen schools. During the summer of 2010, we secured funding to begin a spin-off project in Cape Town, South Africa.

Headquartered at American University Washington College of Law, we have a board of advisors and are developing further infrastructure for growth. There are currently six additional domestic law schools in the process of forming chapters. With the support of the Marshall and Brennan families, we designed essential elements for chapter formation, including:

- The Marshall Brennan Constitutional Literacy Project requires host law schools to foster a partnership with an underserved local public school system and/or individual local public high schools.

- The Marshall Brennan Project requires an academic component for the law students and the high school students and requires supervision of the law students by a law school faculty and/or staff person.

- Through the use of the textbooks, *We the Students* and/or *Youth Justice in America* and through participation in moot court, the Marshall Brennan Project aims to improve high school students' oral advocacy skills, critical thinking skills, and understanding of constitutional cases and concepts.

- Each Marshall Brennan Project chapter requires a commitment of staff and faculty resources from the law school.

- Each chapter must maintain regular communication with the national office at American University Washington College of Law.

- Each chapter is urged to send one or more delegates to annual Directors' meetings.

- All Marshall Brennan chapters are urged to participate in the National Marshall Brennan High School Moot Court Competition.

In theory, and in practice, a number of different stakeholders can initiate formation of a chapter. Chapters have been formed by former Marshall Brennan fellows, law school deans, law school administrators, law students, and law school faculty. The common traits of a chapter founder include patience, a focus on creating relationships, the ability to raise money, and a long-term personal and professional commitment to the project.

Costs

The largest cost related to running a project is faculty and staff time to run the program and teach the law school seminar. There are many different models for staffing, but a combination of both is required. Additional budget items include textbooks, teaching supplies, orientation expenses, moot court competition expenses, copy costs, travel stipends for fellows, brochures, social activities for fellows, an end-of-year celebration for high school students and fellows, and other miscellaneous costs. It costs approximately $250,000 per year to run our chapter in DC. These costs are primarily absorbed by WCL and grants that program staff obtain each year. Since we serve approximately 400 high school students per year, the cost per high school student for the one-semester course is approximately $625.

Results

We are often asked if we know whether or not what we do works. The truth is that it is very difficult to measure efficacy because we believe there are long-term effects on both the high school and law school participants. While increasing the number of diverse students interested in legal careers and who ultimately attend law school is an important byproduct of our work, our main mission is to teach students about their constitutional rights and responsibilities.

Improvement in Understanding Constitutional Rights

We measure progress toward this mission through administration of pre- and post-tests. Some notable results from the 2009–2010 academic year include:

Question 1 — Name the three branches of government.

Before taking the Marshall Brennan class, only **65.5%** of the students correctly answered that the Executive branch was one of the three branches of government. After the class, **87.62%** of the students knew that the Executive branch was one of the three branches of government.

Question 2 — How many justices currently sit on the Supreme Court?

Before taking the Marshall Brennan class, only **35.67%** of the students correctly answered that the nine justices currently sit on the Supreme Court. After the class, **78.1%** of the students answered correctly.

Question 3 — What does the Fourth Amendment protect?

Before taking the Marshall Brennan class, only **35.96%** of the students correctly answered that the Fourth Amendment protects privacy. After the class, **83.33%** of the students answered correctly.

Question 4 — Which amendment was involved in *Miranda v. Arizona*?

Before taking the Marshall Brennan class, only **4.26%** of the students correctly answered that the Fifth Amendment was involved in the *Miranda* case. After the class, **60.53%** of the students knew that the Fifth Amendment was involved in the *Miranda* case.

Question 5—What are the six rights contained in the First Amendment?

Before taking the Marshall Brennan class, only **37.9%** of the students correctly answered that the free exercise of religion is one of the rights contained in the First Amendment. After the class, **85.07%** of the students answered correctly.

Before taking the Marshall Brennan class, only **69.35%** of the students correctly answered that free speech is one of the rights contained in the First Amendment. After the class, **89.55%** of the students answered correctly.

Before taking the Marshall Brennan class, only **34.68%** of the students correctly answered that the freedom of the press is one of the rights contained in the First Amendment. After the class, **77.61%** of the students answered correctly.

Before taking the Marshall Brennan class, only **24.19%** of the students correctly answered that the freedom to assemble is one of the rights contained in the First Amendment. After the class, **80.6%** of the students answered correctly.

Before taking the Marshall Brennan class, only **17.74%** of the students correctly answered that the right to petition government is one of the rights contained in the First Amendment. After the class, **61.19%** answered correctly.

Question 6—True or False? Police always need a warrant before conducting a search.

Before taking the Marshall Brennan class, only **47.56%** of the students correctly answered that police do not always need a warrant before conducting a search. After the class, **72.46%** of the students knew that police do not always need a warrant before conducting a search.

Question 7—True or False? The Sixth Amendment provides every criminal defendant the right to free, effective assistance of counsel.

Before taking the Marshall Brennan class, only **58.54%** of the students correctly answered that criminal defendants are entitled to free but not effective assistance of counsel. After the class, **82.61%** of the students answered correctly.

Other Measures

Two professors from American University's School of Public Affairs, one of whom is a former fellow, are studying the effects of participating in the project on the 2010–2011 fellows in terms of their own civic engagement. Also, after amassing 500 former fellows over the past eleven years and thousands of high school students, we have countless success stories of students who would not have otherwise achieved what they have achieved. A few examples follow:

- Chanell Autrey was a high school student who decided to go to law school because the class ignited her passion for civil rights. She is in her second year at a top-tier law school and plans to pursue a career in public interest.

- Enela Zyka was a top student at a failing high school, and as a recent immigrant, the course taught her vocabulary that made her feel empowered to pursue her dream of becoming a pharmacist. She is in her first year of a Doctor of Pharmacy program.

- Greg Ongao won our citywide competition, became a semi-finalist at the national competition in 2010, and obtained a scholarship to Georgetown University thanks to the assistance of his teaching fellows.

- Daniella Schmidt was a winner of our citywide moot court competition nearly ten years ago, and was so motivated by the experience that she also decided to attend law school and just started her first year at a top-tier school.

Both Chanell and Daniella explain that their teachers served as role models, and that because of their support, they were able to aim high and understand what it took to be successful in law school.

Teachers are also impacted. One returning fellow named Heidi Sahmel wrote the following about her teaching experience last year:

> Each of my students has forever changed my life. My Marshall Brennan students have exposed me to many experiences and life lessons that I did not expect to encounter along the way. Although there have been too many lessons to address, some of the most memorable, as depicted in my previously mentioned stories, include the importance of the good role model, the rewards of selflessness, the strength of human attachment and emotions, the impact that you can make by merely showing that you care, and the undeniable fact that small changes make big differences.

Challenges

The hardest issue our organization has faced is building a national infrastructure that allows for consistency but also flexibility. The faculty and staff running the chapters are extremely busy individuals who often have full plates, excluding their Marshall Brennan responsibilities, so maintaining consistent, meaningful relationships with each chapter is sometimes a challenge. As any other non-profit, we could use additional staff and resources.

Conclusions

In the last five years, the American Bar Association has issued at least two major reports about the lack of diversity in the legal profession, and the current and immediate past president of the ABA have indicated a strong interest in civic education. The ABA has committed serious resources to investigating the problems and potential solutions.

Our movement for constitutional and civic literacy has spread like wildfire over the past dozen years. Our model works. Reasons for our success include the recognition that diversity in the legal profession does not reflect diversity in the general population, a decline in civic education in public schools, and a common desire for law students to teach about the Constitution, and high school students to learn about the Constitution from law students. Of course the learning transcends formal education. In the words of 2009–2010 Marshall Brennan Fellow Rosa Satanovskaya, "The Marshall Brennan experience is an invaluable opportunity for both the fellows and the students. I have learned things about myself that will be with me forever. I have acquired skills that will be valuable in nearly everything I do."

Appendix A

Constitutional Law Survey Course Syllabus

Course Description

The course is co-taught with a DCPS social studies teacher of record and upper-level law students from American University Washington College of Law and Howard University Law School, as part of the Marshall Brennan Constitutional Literacy Project. The Marshall Brennan teaching fellows are selected through a competitive process and become licensed substitute teachers in the District of Columbia. The course can be adapted to a sixty hour or 120 hour course. HJ1 is the code for the 0.5 credit version, and HJ2 is the code for the 1.0 credit version.

The course will introduce students to the U.S. Constitution and the role of the U.S. Supreme Court in interpreting the Constitution. Students will read excerpts of important cases in constitutional law (including, but not limited to, *Tinker v. Des Moines Independent School District*, *Brown v. Board of Education*, and *Goss v. Lopez*) and study how the Constitution affects their lives as young people and society at large. The course also involves experiential learning, including: developing a class constitution; participating in moot court competitions; engaging in voter education and registration efforts; visiting the Constitution-in-Action Lab at the National Archives; observing oral arguments at the Supreme Court; and participating in workshops at the Newseum.

Text

Jamin B. Raskin, *We the Students: Supreme Court Cases for and About Students* (3d ed. 2008)

Goals and Expectations

Students will develop the ability to:

- Understand and apply basic constitutional principles
- Read U.S. Supreme Court opinions
- Think critically about different sides of controversial issues
- Formulate an effective legal argument
- Present an appellate case before a lawyer and/or judge

Students will be expected to:

- Be on time to class
- Bring all required class materials to class
- Respect themselves, their teachers and their classmates
- Take an active role in class discussions
- Complete all activities and assignments during time provided in class

- Avoid using cell phones, iPods, and other electronic devices during class
- Observe all relevant school policies

Scope and Sequence

This course will cover:
I. The U.S. Constitution
    A. Formation of the Constitution
    B. Structure of the U.S. Government
       1. Legislative Branch
       2. Executive Branch
       3. Judicial Branch
          a. Article III Courts versus State/Local Courts
          b. Judicial Review
    C. Separation of Powers; Checks and Balances
    D. Federalism
       1. Unique Case of the District of Columbia
          a. Voting Rights
          b. Jury Service
    E. The Bill of Rights
II. Moot Court
    A. Process of Filing and Appealing Federal Cases
    B. Reading and Understanding Supreme Court Opinions
       1. Identifying and Weighing Different Arguments
       2. Case Precedent
       3. Briefing a Case
    C. Elements of an Oral Argument
    D. Preparation of an Argument
    E. Moot Court Competitions
       1. In-Class Competition
       2. Citywide Competition
       3. National Competition

Depending on student interest, prior knowledge, moot court topic, and time, this course will cover a combination of the following areas of substantive constitutional law:
I.   The First Amendment and Student Speech
     A. *West Virginia v. Barnette* (1943)
     B. *Tinker v. Des Moines Independent School District* (1969)
     C. *Karr v. Schmidt* (1972)
     D. *Bethel School District No. 403 v. Fraser* (1986)
     E. *Good News Club v. Milford Central School* (2001)
II. Freedom of Student Press
     A. *Hazelwood School District v. Kuhlmeier* (1988)
     B. *Killion v. Franklin Regional School District* (2001)
III. Religion and Public Schools
     A. *Engel v. Vitale* (1962)
     B. *Lee v. Weisman* (1992)
     C. *Santa Fe Independent School District v. Doe* (2000)

    D. *Everson v. Board of Education of the Township of Ewing* (1947)

    E. *Zelman v. Simmons-Harris* (2002)

    F. *Stone v. Graham* (1980)

    G. *Newdow v. U.S. Congress* (2002)

    H. *Wisconsin v. Yoder* (1972)

IV. School Searches

    A. *New Jersey v. T.L.O.* (1985)

    B. *Vernonia v. Acton* (1995)

    C. *Board of Education of Pottawatomie County v. Earls* (2002)

    D. *Safford Unified School District v. Redding* (2009)

V.   Cruel and Unusual Punishment in School

    A. *Goss v. Lopez* (1975)

    B. *City of Chicago v. Morales* (1999)

    C. *Ingraham v. Wright* (1977)

VI. Equal Protection against Race Discrimination:
     From Segregation to Multicultural Democracy

    A. *Brown v. Board of Education* (1954)

    B. *Cooper v. Aaron* (1958)

    C. *Griffin v. County School Board of Prince Edward County* (1964)

    D. *Parents Involved in Community Schools v. Seattle School Dist. No. 1* (2007)

    E. *Gratz v. Bollinger, Grutter v. Bollinger* (2003)

VII. Wealth, Gender, Citizenship, and Sexual Orientation

    A. *Jackson v. Birmingham Board of Education* (2005)

    B. *Plyler v. Doe* (1982)

    C. *Boy Scouts of America v. Dale* (2000)

VIII. Sexual Harassment, Bullying and the Law

    A. *Gebser v. Lago Vista Independent School District* (1998)

    B. *Davis v. Monroe County Board of Education* (1999)

IX. Disability, Privacy, Pregnancy, and Sexuality

    A. *Cedar Rapids Community School District v. Garret F.* (1999)

    B. *Owasso Independent School Dist. No. I-011 v. Falvo* (2002)

    C. *Pfeiffer v. Marion Center Area School District* (1990)

    D. *Curtis v. School Committee of Falmouth* (1995)

    E. *Planned Parenthood of Southeastern Pennsylvania v. Casey* (1992)

Course Grading

   Recognizing that students learn in different ways and demonstrate knowledge in different ways, retention and application of knowledge will be assessed by weighing a combination of the following factors:

- Attendance and Participation

- Classwork (worksheets, activities) and Homework Assignments*

- Quizzes**
- Tests***

- Final Portfolio (which may include any of the following: substantial research paper on a constitutional law topic in the news, case briefs, essays responding to fact patterns, creative expressions of constitutional knowledge in the form of poems, songs, drawings, collages, etc.)

*Classwork and Homework Assignments

Classwork will consist of all work done during class time as a part of the day's activities. Homework Assignments will consist of readings from the textbook, short assignments, and longer writing assignments.

- Reading Assignments. Completing your reading on time is important to your understanding of the class material. If students are not completing their reading, a pop quiz may be given covering the assigned reading.

- Short Assignments. These will include worksheets, tasks, and short writing assignments that can easily be completed before the next class. This may also include assignments related to Moot Court.

- Longer Writing Assignments. At times students will be assigned a longer writing assignment such as an essay or short research paper. This may also include assignments related to moot court. You will be given one to two weeks to complete each assignment. In order to make sure you have time to complete your longer writing assignment, I will only assign short readings from the textbook while you are working on your papers.

- Try your best on all assignments. Your work should be well thought out and easy to understand. Spelling and grammar always count. Whenever possible it is suggested that assignments are typewritten. If handwritten, be sure to write legibly. Assignments that are undecipherable may result in a lowered grade.

**Vocabulary, Reading, and Unit Quizzes

- Vocabulary quizzes will be given to test legal terms used in class. A list of required vocabulary will be added to daily and you will be given the complete list one week before the quiz. You will be responsible for knowing the definition of the term and how to spell it correctly.

- Reading quizzes may be given without notice if the class is not completing their assigned readings consistently. These will be short quizzes which will test the main points of the assigned reading. Students who have a 90% or above for their participation grade each term will have their lowest reading quiz score removed from their grade for the term.

- Unit quizzes may be given to assess student's understanding of concepts covered in the course. Unit quizzes serve two purposes: to keep students on track in their studies and to assess areas needing stronger review before each test.

***Tests

- Tests will be given at the end of each major unit. Tests will cover the assigned readings, material discussed in class, and terms from the vocabulary lists.

- A study guide and information on the format of each test will be provided to students well before exams, to allow for adequate time for preparation.

Appendix B

Youth Justice in America Course Syllabus

Course Description

The course is co-taught with a DCPS social studies teacher of record and upper-level law students from American University Washington College of Law and Howard University Law School as part of the Marshall Brennan Constitutional Literacy Project. The Marshall Brennan teaching fellows are selected through a competitive process and become licensed substitute teachers in the District of Columbia. The course can be adapted to a sixty hour or 120 hour course. HJ3 is the 0.5 credit of the course, and HJ4 is the 1.0 credit version of the course.

The course will introduce students to theories of crime and punishment, the U.S. Constitution, and U.S. Supreme Court cases interpreting the Fourth, Fifth, Sixth, and Eighth Amendments to the Constitution, and criminal justice policy. Students will read excerpts of important cases in criminal constitutional law and study how the Constitution affects their lives as young people and society at large. Cases covered include *New Jersey v. T.L.O., Safford Unified School District v. Redding, Miranda v. Arizona, Gideon v. Wainwright*, and *Graham v. Florida*. The course also involves experiential learning, including: developing a class constitution; participating in moot court competitions; engaging in voter education and registration efforts; visiting the Constitution-in-Action Lab at the National Archives; observing oral arguments at the Supreme Court; and participating in workshops at the Newseum.

Text

Maryam Ahranjani, Andrew Ferguson, and Jamin B. Raskin, *Youth Justice in America* (2005).

Goals and Expectations

Students will develop the ability to:

- Understand and apply basic constitutional principles
- Read U.S. Supreme Court opinions
- Think critically about different sides of controversial issues
- Formulate an effective legal argument
- Present an appellate case before a lawyer and/or judge

Students will be expected to:

- Be on time to class
- Bring all required class materials to class
- Respect themselves, their teachers and their classmates

- Take an active role in class discussions
- Complete all activities and assignments during time provided in class
- Avoid using cell phones, iPods, and other electronic devices during class
- Observe all relevant school policies

Scope and Sequence

This course will cover:

I.   The U.S. Constitution
    A. Formation of the Constitution
    B. Structure of the U.S. Government
      1. Legislative Branch
      2. Executive Branch
      3. Judicial Branch
        a. Article III Courts versus State/Local Courts
        b. Judicial Review
    C. Separation of Powers; Checks and Balances
    D. Federalism
      1. Unique Case of the District of Columbia
        a. Voting Rights
        b. Jury Service
    E. The Bill of Rights and the Rights of Criminal Defendants

II.   Structure of the Criminal Justice System
    A. What is Crime?
    B. Who Defines Crime?
    C. What are the Predominant Theories of Punishment?
    D. What is the Juvenile Justice System?
    E. How is the Juvenile Justice System Different From and Similar to the Adult System?
      1. Culpability and Brain Development
      2. Waiver to Adult Court
    F. Constitutional Limits on the Government's Power to Make Crimes
      1. Notice (*City of Chicago v. Morales*—1999)
      2. Harm (*Papachristou v. City of Jacksonville*—1972)

III. Moot Court
    A. Process of Filing and Appealing Federal Cases
    B. Reading and Understanding Supreme Court Opinions
      1. Identifying and Weighing Different Arguments
      2. Case Precedent
      3. Briefing a Case
    C. Elements of an Oral Argument
    D. Preparation of an Argument
    E. Moot Court Competitions
      1. In-Class Competition
      2. Citywide Competition
      3. National Competition

Depending on student interest, prior knowledge, moot court topic, and time, this course will cover a combination of the following areas of substantive constitutional law:

I.   The Fourth Amendment's Protection from Unreasonable Searches and Seizures
   A. *Katz v. United States* (1967)
   B. *California v. Greenwood* (1988)
   C. *Bond v. United States* (2000)
   D. *United States v. Mendenhall* (1980)
   E. *Florida v. Bostick* (1991)
   F. *California v. Hodari D.* (1991)
   G. *Illinois v. Gates* (1983)

II. Exceptions to the Fourth Amendment's Warrant Requirement
   A. Hot Pursuit
   B. Plain View
   C. Search Incident to an Arrest
   D. Automobile Exception
   E. Consensual Searches
   F. Reasonable Suspicion
   G. Exclusionary Rule

III. School Searches
   A. *New Jersey v. T.L.O.* (1985)
   B. *Vernonia v. Acton* (1995)
   C. *Board of Education of Pottawatomie County v. Earls* (2002)
   D. *Safford Unified School District v. Redding* (2009)

IV. Fifth Amendment Privilege against Self-Incrimination
   A. *Miranda v. Arizona* (1966)
   B. *Fare v. Michael C.* (1979)

V.   Sixth Amendment Right to Counsel
   A. *Powell v. State of Alabama* (1932)
   B. *Gideon v. Wainwright* (1963)
   C. *In re Gault* (1967)

VI. Eighth Amendment Ban on Cruel and Unusual Punishment
   A. *Thompson v. Oklahoma* (1988)
   B. *Stanford v. Kentucky* (1989)
   C. *Atkins v. Virginia* (2002)
   D. *Roper v. Simmons* (2005)
   E. *Graham v. Florida* (2010)

VII. The Future of Youth Justice
   A. Record Prison Populations
   B. Movement toward Decarceration
   C. Race and the Criminal Justice System
   D. Felon and Ex-Felon Voting Disenfranchisement
   E. Increase in Young Women in the Criminal Justice System

Course Grading

Recognizing that students learn in different ways and demonstrate knowledge in different ways, retention and application of knowledge will be assessed by weighing a combination of the following factors:

- Attendance and Participation
- Classwork (worksheets, activities) and Homework Assignments*
- Quizzes**
- Tests***
- Final Portfolio (which may include any of the following: substantial research paper on a constitutional law topic in the news, case briefs, essays responding to fact patterns, creative expressions of constitutional knowledge in the form of poems, songs, drawings, collages, etc.)

*Classwork and Homework Assignments

Classwork will consist of all work done during class time as a part of the day's activities. Homework Assignments will consist of readings from the textbook, short assignments, and longer writing assignments.

- Reading Assignments. Completing your reading on time is important to your understanding of the class material. If students are not completing their reading, a pop quiz may be given covering the assigned reading.

- Short Assignments. These will include worksheets, tasks, and short writing assignments that can easily be completed before the next class. This may also include assignments related to moot court.

- Longer Writing Assignments. At times students will be assigned a longer writing assignment such as an essay or short research paper. This may also include assignments related to moot court. You will be given one to two weeks to complete each assignment. In order to make sure you have time to complete your longer writing assignment, I will only assign short readings from the textbook while you are working on your papers.

- Try your best on all assignments. Your work should be well thought out and easy to understand. Spelling and grammar always count. Whenever possible it is suggested that assignments are typewritten. If handwritten, be sure to write legibly. Assignments that are undecipherable may result in a lowered grade.

**Vocabulary, Reading, and Unit Quizzes

- Vocabulary quizzes will be given to test legal terms used in class. A list of required vocabulary will be added to daily and you will be given the complete list one week before the quiz. You will be responsible for knowing the definition of the term and how to spell it correctly.

- Reading quizzes may be given without notice if the class is not completing their assigned readings consistently. These will be short quizzes which will test the main points of the assigned reading. Students who have a 90% or above for their participation grade each term will have their lowest reading quiz score removed from their grade for the term.

- Unit quizzes may be given to assess student's understanding of concepts covered in the course. Unit quizzes serve two purposes: to keep students on track in their studies and to assess areas needing stronger review before each test.

***Tests

- Tests will be given at the end of each major unit. Tests will cover the assigned readings, material discussed in class, and terms from the vocabulary lists.

- A study guide and information on the format of each test will be provided to students well before exams to allow for adequate time for preparation.

College Programs

Chapter 13

Texas Pipeline: College and Beyond

Texas Law School Preparation Institutes
El Paso, San Antonio, and Others

Jerry Polinard*, Richard Gambitta†

Pre-K	Elementary	Middle	High School	College	Law School	Profession

Born of necessity in response to the Fifth Circuit opinion in Hopwood, *the Texas Law School Preparation Institutes (LSPIs) have proven successful. Focused on college level intervention, these programs maintain consonance with rigor, relevance, and relationship. They identify and nurture interest in law and send a remarkable cohort of students on to success in law school and in practice. Two of the Texas law-prep programs are described here, one shorter version at UT Pan Am (what they themselves call LSPI Light), and a larger version, part of an extended program at UT San Antonio (LSPI Large). Both offer inspirational and replicable examples of programs, which avoid the race-based concerns initially raised by Hopwood. Both clearly work to engage diverse students, improve their academic skills, and increase their admissions to law schools in Texas and across the country.*

Introduction

History and legal development have ironies aplenty, and some may be found in the origin and continuation of the Texas Law School Preparation Institutes (LSPIs). Texas conceived, established, and has continued to execute undergraduate race-neutral and minority-supplying pipeline institutes as a consequence of the Fifth Circuit Court of Ap-

---

* Dr. Polinard is a professor of political science and the university prelaw advisor at the University of Texas Pan American Institute for Law and Public Affairs. He is a member of the Prelaw Advisors National Council (PLANC) and the Southwest Association of Prelaw Advisors (SWAPLA).

† Dr. Gambitta is Director of the Institute for Law and Public Affairs at the University of Texas at San Antonio, former chair of the department of political science, university prelaw advisor, and inaugural recipient of the University of Texas Regents' Outstanding Teaching Award in 2009.

peals decision prohibiting Texas from employing race-based affirmative action in its law school admissions process.[1] Had Cheryl Hopwood not sued to prevent race considerations, and won, today's LSPIs would likely not have been conceived, nurtured, or maturated into the minority flowing pipelines that exist today. The irony should not evade us. The case that closed down the use of racial preferences spawned new institutes that today facilitate diversity and enhance student preparation.

After the U.S. Supreme Court reversed the rule of *Hopwood* in *Grutter*, allowing some consideration of race in admissions, the LSPIs conceived as a response to *Hopwood* have blossomed even more.[2] This chapter illuminates the history and contemporary operations of two such effective offspring institutes, a compact one at the University of Texas at Pan America (UTPA), and an expanded one at the University of Texas at San Antonio (UTSA). Both institutes contribute significantly to increasing the numbers and preparation of students historically underrepresented in law schools and the practice of law.

Texas and Race and Legal History

In 1896, in *Plessy v. Ferguson*, the U.S. Supreme Court legitimized Jim Crow—the pattern of law and practice that maintained racial segregation, approving apartheid under the separate and equal principle while tolerating separate and unequal practice.[3] A lone dissenter, Justice John Marshall Harlan, declared: "Our Constitution is color-blind ..." Consistent with *Plessy*, and segregated by law, Texas forbade the admission of Blacks into White public schools and universities.

In 1946, fifty years after *Plessy*, Heman Sweatt, an African American, applied to the all-White University of Texas School of Law. Denied admission on the basis of his race, he sued UT for admission. Though Texas operated under *Plessy's* separate and equal principle, Texas had no separate law school for Blacks. The state rushed to construct two new law schools to suffice as equal. Sweatt found those unacceptable and pursued his litigation. Texas' pell-mell efforts failed to impress the U.S. Supreme Court, which observed that while the schools were separate, they were hardly equal. The Court ordered Sweatt's admission to UT, though leaving the doctrine of separate and equal intact. Texas could segregate, but only if capable of creating a school equal to UT, unlikely given the intangibles the Court included in its calculus for constitutional consent.[4]

After *Sweatt* and then *Brown v. Board of Education*,[5] Texas desegregated its schools progressively, if reluctantly. Eventually, the UT Law School sought a more diversified student body for pedagogical and remedial purposes, instituting an affirmative action plan that gave preferential admission to minorities based on race—an approach eventually and successfully challenged in the *Hopwood* litigation. For instance, in one admissions' cluster under the plan, which the Hopwood court scrutinized, "100% of Blacks and 90% of Mexican Americans, but only 6% of Whites, were offered admission."[6] Under this policy, the UT School of Law denied admission to Cheryl Hopwood, a White woman, mother of a special needs child and married to a serviceman, although she had earned a higher GPA and LSAT score than many minority students that UT had accepted. She sued, contending that UT denied her admission on the basis of race.

In 1996, 100 years after *Plessy* legitimized *de jure* segregation, and 50 years after *Sweatt* declared the establishment of a law school for Blacks did not meet the "equal" requirement and, therefore, UT law school had to admit Sweatt, the Fifth Circuit struck down the affirmative action policy of UT Law as a violation of the equal protection clause of the Fourteenth Amendment of the U.S. Constitution. The Fifth Circuit found that any racial preference activated strict judicial scrutiny. The appellate court stated that "non-remedial state interests will never justify racial classifications." Race-based classifications "for the purpose of diversity frustrates, rather than facilitates, the goals of equal protection...." and "the use of ethnic diversity simply to achieve racial heterogeneity, even as part of the consideration of a number of factors, is unconstitutional...."[7] The Fifth Circuit concluded: "we hold that the University of Texas School of Law may not use race as a factor in deciding which applicants to admit in order to achieve a diverse student body, to combat the perceived effects of a hostile environment at the law school, to alleviate the law school's poor reputation in the minority community, or to eliminate any present effects of past discrimination by actors other than the law school."[8] In 1997, Texas Attorney General Dan Morales, a Mexican American Democrat, expanded the application of the opinion beyond admission decisions to such areas as scholarships, faculty recruitment and retention, financial aid, and also beyond public universities to private ones receiving federal aid.[9]

Hopwood to the Summer Institutes

The *Hopwood* opinions had an immediate impact. Using its pre-*Hopwood* affirmative action plan, UT Law had enrolled a student body that was approximately 20% Black and Mexican American in 1995. These figures dropped to about 6% post-*Hopwood* in 1997.[10] In 1999–2000, Texas' premier law school would enroll a combined Black and Hispanic total of only 8%. By way of contrast, the 2000 Census indicated Hispanics and Blacks constituted approximately 44% of the Texas population and a majority of the primary and secondary school-aged population.

The *Hopwood* opinion, however, had provided a pathway to progress, stating: "While the use of race *per se* is proscribed, state-supported schools may reasonably consider a host of factors some of which may have some correlation with race in making admissions decisions ... To foster such diversity, state universities and law schools ... must scrutinize applicants individually, rather than resorting to the dangerous proxy of race."[11]

In this context, the University of Texas System created the Law School Partnership Task Force (LSPTF) to respond to *Hopwood* by suggesting strategies that might increase the number of minority students applying to law school in general, and to the University of Texas Law School in particular. The LSPTF was composed of representatives from the UT System, UT Law School, and the four System components with predominantly Mexican American student populations: UT Brownsville, UT El Paso (UTEP), UT Pan American (UTPA) and UT San Antonio (UTSA).

The Task Force recommended sharing system and component resources to focus on students at undergraduate institutions with traditionally high minority enrollments by creating and sustaining annual summer law school preparation institutes at these schools.

The demographics of the participating UT branches would likely guarantee that the ethnic make-up of the institutes would be primarily Mexican American at three institutes, and a majority of minorities at the fourth. These summer institutes would admit students from these locations on a race neutral basis, and offer a rigorous program to enhance their academic skills and increase the probability of their admission to and success in law school. UT Law would share its expertise, provide some of the start-up funding, lend its committed faculty for plenary sessions at the UT system schools, and assist in securing external funding.

Within this framework, UT Law facilitated the development of several innovative law school preparation institutes at UT branch campuses. UTEP proposed and implemented the first summer Law School Preparation Institute (LSPI) in 1998.[12] UTPA began its institute in 2001 and UTSA, establishing a broader Institute for Law and Public Affairs in 2001, offered its Summer Law School Preparation Academy in 2002.[13] Later, UT Brownsville established its less comprehensive but developing Filemon B. Vela Pre-Law Academy.[14] Additionally, Prairie View A & M, a historically Black university, is currently developing an institute where UT faculty play a supportive role.[15]

These programs vary in design, length, and execution, but all focus on enhancing student proficiency in analytical thinking, critical reading, legal reasoning, and writing. These institutes provide exposure to the legal profession, information about the law school application process, and access to administrators at UT and other law schools. Because Blacks and Hispanics tend to score lower than Anglos on the Law School Admission Test (LSAT), all of the programs provide intensive LSAT preparation. This kind of focused prep-course is often one to which students from lower economic environments would not otherwise have access. Given the fact that the LSAT remains the single most important factor concerning a student's chances at being admitted, the LSPIs have remained important and flourishing in this post-*Hopwood* era, at least in part because of their significant successes in enhancing academic and professional opportunities.

UTPA Law School Preparation Institute (LSPI): "LSPI Light!"

The UTPA LSPI is the smallest of the three programs that emerged post-*Hopwood*. It's the "little engine that could!" And its results are impressive. LSPI enrolls an average of 18–20 diverse students each summer and introduces them to the law and its practitioners, eventually sending almost 90% of those who apply to law school.

UTPA and the LSPI Selection Process

UTPA has almost 18,000 students, 90% of whom are Mexican American. The UTPA LSPI is open only to full-time undergraduate UTPA students. Since their inception in 2001, the ten institutes have reflected the campus demographics, both in terms of ethnicity and gender. In addition, over the ten years, there has been an average of ten different majors represented by the students selected to participate.

During the spring semester, an email inviting applications for the LSPI is sent to every full time undergraduate UTPA student who possesses at least a 3.0 GPA and 45 credit hours. On average, 40–60 students interested in a legal career apply each year, and are evaluated and selected on the basis of their application essay and academic achievement. No more than 20 students are accepted. Three UTPA faculty members make admissions decisions and conduct the institute. All three have experience in pre-law advising, as well as in teaching undergraduate and graduate courses related to legal issues.

Program Description

The LSPI takes place during Pan Am's second summer session, running for approximately five weeks. LSPI's goal is not just to prepare students for law school, but also to make them better students overall. To achieve this, LSPI has both academic and counseling and relationship components. The last week is devoted to preparation for the LSAT. The first four weeks focus on intensive development of analytical skills, including reading, writing, and speaking. The class meets from 9–4, Monday through Friday, and from 9–12, Saturday mornings, the latter including meetings with both public and private law firms.

The classes include intensive analytical reading and writing assignments. The first day is more than just an introduction to the institute. Role models are important for underrepresented groups. After the three faculty members introduce themselves and outline the expectations for the course, they leave and turn the class over to three groups of "role models." One group consists of former LSPI students who currently are practicing law. A second group includes former LSPI students currently in law school. The third group is composed of students from the previous institute who are still undergraduates. The three groups provide the current class with a handout they have labeled "Survivor Tips." They discuss the "Survivor Tips," but also discuss their experiences in law school and their current practices.

In a broad sense, the course divides into three concurrent segments. One professor focuses on developing writing and communication skills. Essays analyzing Supreme Court jurisprudence on such issues as student rights, capital punishment, and affirmative action are graded for both substance and style. Selected essays are displayed on a screen (the students have named the Elmo device used the "Elmo of Joy") where the essay is dissected virtually word for word. Another professor will focus on formal logic, with the students frequently working in groups. The third professor, who possesses a J.D., focuses on the rigors of the law school environment, including training the students in the Socratic method and the technique of outlining.

In addition, faculty and staff from various law schools from Texas and beyond Texas visit the class. They introduce the students to the admissions process as well as the way a law class is conducted. For example, a contracts professor from the University of Texas Law School will, in effect, conduct his introductory class; the LSPI students will be assigned the appropriate cases to read and discuss.

The course sequence and engagement is arguably the most rigorous academic program on the campus. The emphasis on such academic rigor is a conscious decision. It is deliberately designed to focus on student success. The intensive hands-on approach mandates limiting the enrollment. With numbers limited and expectations high, LSPI is successful in achieving exactly what it was designed to do. That is, although, as the name implies, the institute hopes to prepare students interested in a legal education, it consistently makes the participants better students, whether they pursue a legal career or alternative post-graduate work.

Following the formal completion of the LSPI at the end of the second summer session, the students and faculty meet several weekends prior to the students taking the LSAT in October and December. The three UTPA faculty members also work continuously with the students on various aspects of the application process through the fall and spring semesters, including reviewing the personal statements with the students, arranging for letters of recommendation, putting the students in contact with various law school representatives, and, in general, maintaining an on-going, supportive relationship.

Staff, Budget, Partners

As mentioned above, several members of the faculty and staff at the University of Texas School of Law participate in the LSPI. In addition, representatives from various other law schools also visit the LSPI. The local county bar association also contributes to the LSPI by providing speakers and financial aid. A representative from the Kaplan commercial test preparation corporation conducts an LSAC preparation course in the final week of the program, at a much-reduced rate compared to Kaplan's normal costs.

Each student receives a $1,000 stipend, and six hours advanced credit upon successful completion of the Institute. All materials are provided to the students and the Kaplan preparation course is paid by the university. The only financial cost to the students is the registration for six hours of university credit. However, given the success of the institute, if budgetary cuts became necessary, there is little doubt the students would be willing to assume the costs of the materials and waive the stipend. The university would still be responsible for the faculty salaries and the cost of the Kaplan preparation course.

Results

Of the UTPA LSPI students who apply to law school, 90% have been accepted to at least one law school. All but three have been accepted to more than one law school. This percentage is almost double the average overall acceptance rate of UTPA students, and exceeds the national acceptance rate by 30%. Perhaps ironically, the institutes are also a success story for those who decide not to apply. That is, it is much more desirable that a student discover they do not wish to pursue a legal education while they are still undergraduates, rather than in the middle of their first semester in law school. In virtually every one of UTPA's institutes, at least one student has said the LSPI experience convinced them they did not want to become a lawyer. Those students who do not pursue a law degree virtually always go to graduate school, and consistently note how the analytical training they have received is a major plus in the graduate school environment.

By virtually every measure, both quantitative and qualitative, the institute has been a success. Indeed, it arguably is the most successful program on our campus in terms of its goals. Students have improved their reading and writing analytical skills in general; they are not just more competitive in terms of the law school admissions process, they are better students. The participants are exposed to intellectual training they would not otherwise receive, so they are better students after completing the institute. They enhance the skills needed to be competitive in the law school application process, so they increase their chances not only of being accepted to law school, but of having more choices than they otherwise would have. Finally, they are much more prepared than their peers for the law school experience. This enhances their chances of success in law school.

The support of the UTPA administration and the University of Texas School of Law measurably contributes to the success of our institute, but, ultimately, the credit must go to the students who have responded to an intensive learning process.

The Students

The student response has been overwhelmingly positive. Undergraduate students often email or stop by during the fall semester after LSPI, commenting on how much easier their classes are after the LSPI training. One student laughed and said, "It's all downhill after LSPI." One first-year law student said in a remark echoed over and over again by other LSPI 1Ls, "Certainly, classes here at the law school are challenging, but I'm so much better prepared than some of my classmates for the challenge. And, I'm confident."

One aspect of LSPI that has emerged over the years is the impact the institute has on the personal relationships of the participants. It is clear from student comments that the students form bonds that will go with them throughout the rest of their lives. There is, in effect, a cohort. Emails from LSPI students at various law schools invariably will provide updates on their cohort.

This has emerged as one of the most important, if unanticipated, consequences of the LSPI: the shared experience continues to inform their lives.

The UTSA Institute for Law and Public Affairs and Summer Law School Preparation Academy: "LSPI Large"

At the UTSA, a "LSPI Large" has developed, where the innovative summer enhancement program is larger in enrollments and curriculum, and more diverse than the others, but also is woven into a refocused comprehensive pre-law program that provides enhanced opportunities to students throughout the academic year.

To meet 21st century pre-law educational challenges, the UTSA established a new Institute for Law and Public Affairs (ILPA) in 2001.[16] The ILPA would house a tailored LSPI, which UTSA calls its Summer Law School Preparation Academy (SLSPA), implementing its first sessions in the summer of 2002.[17] The broader ILPA has a three-part mission: education, research, and service. But, its primary charge has always been to develop and execute a premier, innovative, and comprehensive pre-law education for its students. The goal has been to enrich the academic experience and professional opportunities available to its students, including it multitude of first generation college students and those from historically underrepresented classes. ILPA's secondary missions of research and service reinforce the pre-professional preparatory mission.

Originally reporting directly to the UTSA Provost, the ILPA chose to become part of the UTSA Honors College in 2006, lending additional prestige to its endeavors.[18] Although SLSPA students do not have to be enrolled in the Honors College, the relationship now exposes SLSPA students to the additional academic possibilities that the Honors College provides, and introduces the Honors College to a highly motivated and diverse student assemblage, some of whom decide to pursue Honors degrees.

The Summer Law School Preparation Academy provides the signature experience to the ILPA's larger pre-law undertaking. By design, the SLSPA links to other ILPA initiatives including the UTSA Certificate in Legal Reasoning (a four course designated sequence), the newly developed Legal Studies Minor (21 hours), specialized legal studies coursework taught across the full academic year by adjunct specialists in a legal area (e.g. an annual course in Federal Courts taught by a federal judge), and potential student access to elevated opportunities for enhanced academic and high-status experiential learning (e.g., respectively, introduction to the UTSA Honors College or award of a UTSA "McClendon" Legislative Scholars Program)—all demonstrable credentials for a law school application.[19] The ILPA reaches out early to potential pre-law students in varied ways, ranging from providing brochures to incoming college students who express an interest in law, to receiving referrals from advisors campus wide, to expanding the pipeline by establishing a dual enrollment program that brings inner city high school students to the UTSA to take pre-law coursework, paid for by the local federal bar. All of these aspects promote opportunities for pre-law students and facilitate the academic preparation for law school.

The Origins of the Institute and Summer Program

Today, the UTSA enrolls about 29,000 students, even after raising admissions standards several times in recent years. After flagship UT Austin, UTSA has emerged as the UT system's largest university, and overall applicants' first choice. It is federally designated as a Hispanic serving institution with about 43% Hispanic students, 38% White non-Hispanic, 9% Black, and 6% Asian.[20] At the time of *Hopwood*, UTSA's diversity and high growth rate highlighted its emerging importance as a potential feeder school to UT and other law schools in Texas. Operating under *Hopwood*, if UTSA could produce a significant number of students who could compete with others nationally on a race neutral basis, the demographics and numbers at UTSA would contribute to diversity interests, while retaining race neutral law school admissions.

Significant support of this initiative came from UTSA President Ricardo Romo and then-Provost Guy Bailey (now President of Texas Tech University), UT School of Law Dean William Powers, Jr. (now UT Austin's President), and the local bar. Chief Justice Phil Hardberger, Texas Court of Appeals, 4th Circuit, (and later San Antonio's mayor) keynoted the announcement ceremonies with several state legislators in attendance. The offices and operations were strategically located at the UTSA Downtown Campus, within close proximity to the courts, large law firms, corporations, and concentrations of minority populations.

The UTSA Institute for Law and Public Affairs (ILPA) commenced on September 1, 2001 as an academic collaboration between the University of Texas at San Antonio and the University of Texas School of Law. Its mission was to develop and sustain a premier pre-law program, commence a new Summer Law School Preparation Academy (SLSPA), and enhance the academic and professional opportunities available to UTSA students, including those from historically underrepresented populations. Over time, the institute was intended to have a positive impact on the diversity of Texas law schools and the Texas Bar.

Often, university systems have resources that remain in geographic and disciplinary silos and are not shared among the system components and levels. ILPA broke this mold. The ILPA Summer Law School Preparation Academy started in the summer of 2002 with forty selected students. The institute and Academy shared UT System resources at UTSA and UT School of Law in this collaborative endeavor, with UTSA contributing SLSPA's initial curriculum design, start-up and operation costs, and faculty expertise.[21] ILPA believed that achieving its mission to elevate student performance and competitiveness depended upon the synergistic incorporation of persons from academia, business, the government, and the bar. The collaboration makes it possible to provide a small liberal-arts atmosphere within an emerging research-oriented university. In this collaborative model, undergraduate students could and did receive individual attention and seminar instruction from award-winning instructors inside ILPA. Yet, at the same time they had access to the benefits of a research university—the best of both worlds. The institute invested dollars for stipends and used its networking resources to achieve significant academic enhancement for its students. The SLSPA exposed students to the competitive rigor akin to the law school experience, to law school faculty and admissions officials, and to attorneys, judges, and role models in the field. Six students from that initial class eventually entered UT School of Law.[22] In a subsequent year, ten were accepted. The SLSPA had started to have an impact.

The UTSA Application and Selection Process

If the pipeline is to produce a greater quantity of quality law students and attorneys from historically underrepresented groups, the mission and resources need to focus not only on the academically endowed who have demonstrably performed with excellence from the start, but also on the academically endowed but "disinherited" who possess extreme talent but have had "issues"—often major—early on, and little to no guidance, family tradition, or economic support. Special attention to assisting the resurrection of the academic potential of these students is especially important to increase the flow of the pipeline. In keeping with this ideology, ILPA does not simply cream from the top echelon of GPAs. The institute prides itself in taking some significant chances, admitting students who may not possess the typical template credentials thought necessary for successful law school admissions. The SLSPA admissions committee supports admission of students whose background and interview show promise of the ability and desire to restore and build credentials sufficient to convince law schools to admit them. Furthermore, the ILPA recognizes the need to intervene earlier in students' academic careers to ward off or reverse the lackadaisical or disastrous beginnings that normally foreclose admission to law school. Hence, the ILPA is allowing initial admission to students early, at the sophomore level.

Recruitment starts around the second week of the spring semester when ILPA: (a) sends out email notices to UTSA students who possess a GPA of 2.8 or above, (b) announces the availability of the application on the UTSA Today Website, (c) asks professors teaching law-related courses to announce the availability of the application in their classes, and (d) contacts some other universities about the program and application availability.

The SLSPA application requires general demographic information, background characteristics, academic credentials, extracurricular activities, work and financial aid history, and community service. Students must submit a personal statement and at least one letter of recommendation, preferably from a professor with whom they have worked.[23]

Faculty panels review all applications and recommend SLSPA admission, probationary admission, or denial based on an assessment of each student's overall portfolio and ability to perform successfully in the program. The Director conducts interviews with marginal applicants. In 2010, the ILPA received over 150 applications. Of the admitted students, about 15% are rising or established sophomores, 40% juniors, 40 % rising seniors, and about 5% are graduate students.

Starting with the initial 40 students in 2002, the institute has grown consistently to 75 regularly admitted students in 2007, 95 in 2009, and 100 students in 2010. Each year, some students are admitted on probation, where their progress is monitored at each stage and additional counseling provided. 70 to 80% of the SLSPA students come from underrepresented groups each of last three years. Enrolling students have come from across seven UTSA colleges. Moreover, the institute admits about ten percent from other universities into its summer program, which ILPA believes raises the competitive level for all students and provides opportunity for students from our geographical region who attend other universities. SLSPA participants have come from such varied institutions as Emory, Georgetown, and Northern Iowa, nationally, and, from across Texas, including Incarnate Word, St. Edwards, St. Mary's, Texas State, Texas A&M (College Station, Corpus Christi, & Laredo International), and UT campuses including Austin, Brownsville, El Paso, and Pan American. The program now admits a few community college students transitioning to the UTSA who have strong records and commitments. UTSA is a federally designated Hispanic Serving Institution, but the SLSPA also attracts a significant Black and Asian population. The law school admissions of these students lend testimony to our program's draw and success. In 2010 alone, for instance, Black SLSPA participants enrolled in law schools as varied as Harvard, Georgetown, Washington (St. Louis), University of Texas, Oklahoma, St. Mary's, and TSU's Thurgood Marshall, among others. The number of law schools offering admission to our top Black students this year were especially extensive, the schools highly prestigious (e.g. Chicago, NYU, Duke, UC Berkeley), and the scholarship offers highly impressive. In recent years, our Black students have chosen schools stretching across the country, including Wake Forest, Kentucky, Richmond, Texas Tech, and UC Berkeley. This year, the SLSPA's Asian students have selected law schools including the University of Houston, South Texas, and Texas Tech, and in recent years the University of Texas. Diversity exists in our classrooms, and that diversity is reflected in the students gaining admission to law school. Our admissions to law school have generally reflected our SLSPA composition.

Partners, Inspiration, Support

UTSA has benefitted from its proximity to and support in mission from the UT School of Law—San Antonio is about 19 miles south of Austin. UT Law made an initial contribution to start the UTSA institute. Each year, the current dean conducts a seminar with UTSA's students on the SLSPA's opening day. Within the first three weeks of classes, UT's head writing professor, dean of admissions, and award winning contracts professor have made separate presentations for two hours to SLSPA students. Across a single summer, as many as nine UT Law professors and deans have conducted plenary sessions in their areas of expertise at the SLSPA.

The SLSPA's opening day is viewed as especially important, setting the pace and prestige of the program. Opening day begins with a motivating presentation by the Mayor of San Antonio, Julián Castro, who, now in his thirties, was raised by a single female head of household, graduated from the public schools of San Antonio, then Stanford University, then Harvard Law School. He spoke last year at the SLSPA opening day as his first official act on his first day as mayor. His twin brother, State Representative Joaquin Castro (same educational background) gave our 2010 SLSPA commencement address, where the ILPA awards the Certificate in Legal Reasoning to its graduates, a ceremony where distinguished judges have consistently given the keynote.

Role models are important, informing students that they had been where the students are now, just a few years ago. In addition to the mayor, speakers during the opening session, last year and this, offer these role models. They included the Associate Dean of St. Mary's School of Law (also a Latino, raised with eight siblings and little money, a product of Texas public schools, Stanford graduate, Harvard J.D., and White House Fellow); Congressman Charles Gonzalez (J.D., UT Law); Texas legislators (an Anglo Senator with a J.D. from Texas Tech, a female African American and a male Latino State Representative and head of the Hispanic Caucus with a BA from UTSA and a J.D. from UT; the City Attorney (UTSA alum and J.D. St. Mary's Law); the First Assistant District Attorney, the FBI's Regional Counsel (UTSA alum); two federal judges; the retired chief justice of the court of appeals (Latina); four state district or county court judges (alumni and minorities); the President of the Texas Young Lawyers Association (alumna). Also involved were practicing attorneys ranging from legal aid and MALDEF to Fortune 500 corporate counsel, to law firms including the corporate, bond, energy, immigration, criminal defense, and lobbying sectors representing the rich diversity of practices, persons, and law school educations.

Graduates from the UTSA's SLSPA return and serve on panels each opening day, explaining their diverse experiences during the law school admission process, law school, and the practice of law. ILPA presents three types of SLSPA alumni panels—fresh alumni just going to law school who explain the process and the program; those with one, two, or three years of law school experience; and those who are now practicing law. The alumni-to-student interaction is invaluable, with incoming students seeing what they could achieve and become with a few years of dedicated hard work. The first day is long, 8:00 a.m. to 5:30 p.m., exhilarating, and sends the message that long days are required, but that great rewards result for those who persevere, work hard, adhere to program, and aspire greatly. Twenty select alumni came back and spoke at both the 2009 and 2010 opening days, including those from each Texas law school, plus from schools including Harvard, Columbia, Georgetown, Oklahoma, Richmond, UC Berkeley, Washington University, and Wisconsin.

On a more academic note, during the first three days, ILPA administers an editing diagnostic test designed by UTSA and UT Law's writing faculty and a full LSAT practice test for assessment, advisement, and placement.[24] These tests allow us to fine tune the advising of students on the curricula they need most during and after the program, and to measure student progress, program effectiveness, and investment-to-benefit return.

During the summer sessions, deans, professors or admissions directors from every law school in Texas and many from across the country present to SLSPA students in plenary sessions—including from national law schools as diverse as UC Berkeley, CUNY, Utah, and Wisconsin. Getting students to envision leaving the perceived security of their hometowns and families is essential to the breadth and height of success. The venue and demographics of San Antonio assist here in various ways. Law school admissions personnel know that we constitute a pool of diversity, congregated in one place, producing quality students; San Antonio is also a nice place to visit on their recruitment tours. In this vein, UTSA also hosts an annual Law School Fair at UTSA, in conjunction with the Southwest Association of Pre Law Advisors Association, which brings approximately 100 law schools to the campus to inform and recruit students from across South Texas colleges. This provides our students with access to information about opportunities previously unexplored.

Program Description

The SLSPA started with a four-course curriculum in 2002, and now has expanded to eight discrete courses, twelve sections, plus independent research studies in six disciplines, some of which are cross-listed.[25] All UTSA SLSPA courses are designed to hone students' analytical skills, assure mastery of writing competence, improve reading comprehension, develop the capacity to outline and summarize complex material, and facilitate drawing reasoned conclusions and articulating them professionally. Case law courses are taught much as they are in law school. The set SLSPA coursework includes five-week seminars in: (1) Legal and Technical Writing, (2) Legal Research and Writing, (3) Constitutional Law, (4) Torts, and (5) Law School Studies, a "buffet course" designed to give substantive instruction in each subject area to be taken during the first year of law school. Two additional courses, (6) Legal & Philosophical Reasoning and (7) Analytic Reasoning and Logic, are aimed at enhancing the reasoning skills necessary to improve performance on the LSAT and the first year of law school.

The Institute Director or Program Coordinator place admitted students into courses based upon a review of the student's academic records, diagnostic tests, writing samples, and perceived need for improvement in a specific area. In general, students take at least one course in each of the three areas, writing and research (1 or 2 above), substantive case law (3, 4, or 5 above) and reasoning and logic (6 or 7 above.)

SLSPA classes are limited to students admitted into the program, thus raising the competitive edge and intellectual pitch level.[26] Classes are small for a public university, most at approximately 20 to 25 students, while a couple of the case law courses grow into the 30s with professors teaching these similar to law school classes, by deploying combinations of Socratic method, interactive discussions, critical examination across voluminous readings, with significant weight placed on a final comprehensive exam. Spending every day with students for five to ten weeks has dramatic positive effects on performance. Persistent focus, pressure, and feedback pay off. Students see the commitment and regimen necessary for stellar performance. This pays off in elevated performance subsequent to the SLSPA.

The SLSPA runs across ten weeks. The program requires a full-time commitment, enrollment in two courses during each five-week summer session across one summer or two, plus attendance at plenary sessions where law school deans, admission directors, and faculty present information on law school admissions, financing, personal statements, and addenda. Law school faculty known for teaching prowess also conduct substantive law school seminar sessions, with assigned readings in a wide range of subject areas like contracts, disability law, education law, torts, immigration, property, water law, civil procedure or rights, and a host of other topics. These sessions occur two to three times per week, interspersed with regular classes, and provide students with an additional feel for the preparation and thinking level required in the law school classroom.

Given that many of the SLSPA students have never even met an attorney, the ILPA supplements course work and the law school seminars by an array of speakers. ILPA brings top practitioners to its SLSPA to discuss major litigation or contemporary issues in which they are involved, supreme court cases that they have argued, the role of mediation, or the different professional positions available to JDs. With the assistance of the Texas Bar Foundation and the Bexar County Bar Association, ILPA brought former FBI director William Sessions for an open conversation with SLSPA students.

Motivating and demanding instructors are essential to the program's success. From the outset, the institute director made a special point to attract exceptionally talented instructors from multiple disciplines including English, legal studies, political science, and philosophy. By reference and appeal to mission, elevated rigor, smaller classes, the promise and delivery of dedicated and motivated students, and the chance to partake in a special enterprise, the ILPA has recruited and sustained SLSPA instructors who have won significant recognition and awards for teaching and mentoring at the college, university, system, and state levels. Six UTSA faculty members teach daily in the summer program.; two have won the prestigious UT Regents Outstanding Teaching Award (in the two years the Regents have awarded it), four have won the UTSA President's Distinguished Achievement Award for Outstanding Teaching, one has won the UT System's Chancellor's Award for Outstanding Teaching two times, and one was awarded a Piper Professor Award and the Texas Chicano Law Students Education Spirit Award. The student faculty relations are close, interactive, daily, and sustained.

These prize-winning instructors bring excellent teaching and high expectations. They motivate students to higher performances, and communicate clearly the type of work that is necessary to perform at a level sufficient for admission to and success in law school. Receiving an A is not automatic, as is the case with many preparatory programs. Compared to the normal academic year, the ILPA elevates the academic rigor of the curriculum, the classroom and cohort competitiveness, and the students' esprit de corps. The momentum carries forward after the SLSPA. Cohort cohesion emerges and continues through and beyond law school. This cohort cohesion is a signature feature of the program.

Advising plays a key role during and beyond the summer program.[27] The director of the institute serves also as the university's pre-law advisor. Students get direct counseling from the director, SLSPA faculty, program coordinator, and legal studies minor advisors in the Honors College. The director, writing instructor, and program coordinator review the applicants' personal statements, addenda, or portfolios, counsel on appropriate recommenders, and monitor progress, encouraging early application submissions.

Because the SLSPA is a summer program, the ILPA awards financial stipends to students. Some years, all students received stipends; in all years, a majority have received stipends, even as the admissions have dramatically grown. That revenue stream flows from an annual contribution of $25,000 from the UTSA President's or Provost's Office, supplemented by grants and gifts secured by ILPA (see sections below). Students have received $1,500, $1,000, or $500 scholarships or stipends, based on a combination of credentials, overall portfolio, performance in the SLSPA, and dedication to full participation in plenary sessions outside of classes.

Each student pays the normal charge for tuition and fees per credit hour. The program does not cost the student any additional charge. One might say the value added is paid by the student in sweat, academic labor, and heightened performance.

Costs, Staff, Budget

The ILPA occupies a suite of offices at the UTSA Downtown Campus, which includes two offices for the director (who is also a professor) and the program coordinator (a position historically held by an M.A., then by a J.D., and now by an Ed.D.), and a reception and work area. ILPA is allotted several work-study students (slightly over one full time equivalent (FTE)) throughout the year who act as receptionists and administrative clerks.

Second, as previously mentioned, the ILPA receives $25,000 each academic year for scholarships for SLSPA students from the President or Provost's Offices, now through the Honors College. This money is supplemented by grants (e.g. Texas Bar Foundation), private contributions (law firms), and other revenue streams explained in the section below on fundraising and grants.

For 2010–2011, ILPA received a Maintenance and Operation budget of $5,000. This allotment is to cover all costs associated with operations (e.g., charges for copying, telephones, supplies, etc.), the 12 class sections of the SLSPA, the eight sections of legal studies coursework conducted during the academic year, and the many functions conducted throughout the year.

The only budgeted staff salary for the ILPA or SLSPA is for the program coordinator. Under the ILPA director, the program coordinator administers program, budget, and operational details. The director gets a two-course reduction during the academic year, plus an episodic one course payment during the summer for the program administration.

Traditionally, faculty in the SLSPA were all paid entirely from the departments in which the courses academically fell, e.g. English for Technical Writing, POL for Constitutional Law, etc. Moreover, those departments got the student enrollments. No problems developed because the department chairs and ILPA director were mutually accommodating, and the SLSPA classes benefitted department summer enrollments. Because of SLSPA demand and popularity, conventional departments could fill summer courses at the downtown campus where otherwise they might not be able to, even finding that the SLSPA courses would have the largest enrollment among their upper-division summer offerings. As the SLSPA grew, the ILPA became part of the Honors College, the courses became more tailored to mission, and the ILPA now has a budget for summer coursework that pays the per course salaries of most summer program faculty. The courses are cross-listed between LGS and other disciplines (e.g. Torts with Business Law, Legal and Philosophical Reasoning with Philosophy, etc.) Therein, cooperating departments continue to allow their students to enroll in the SLSPA, and still progress toward graduation in their majors and minors. Moreover, the transfer of per course, tenured faculty summer salaries to the ILPA is revenue neutral for the university. Four of the summer sections are taught or team-taught by adjunct specialists, at about $3,000 per five-week course.

Each year, the ILPA hires a law school student, an alumnus of the program, as an "education specialist" who assists with the operation of the SLSPA. The law student acts as a teaching assistant, reader, grader, tutor, mentor, and liaison, or conduit of information flow, between faculty, students, and administration. Approximately $3,000 is paid to this program alumnus. Initially, UT School of Law provided one of its law students for one summer for this role, and subsequently ILPA has paid for this important person.

So, in summary budgetary terms, the ILPA and SLSPA cost the university office space, a program coordinator's modest salary, $25,000 in scholarships, a $5,000 maintenance and operations budget, and a professor's two-course reduction. Classroom space and faculty salaries have a cost, of course, but are not add-ons; courses easily fill, and the returns of the coordinated program become apparent. Moreover, as the grants and fundraising section below show, the ILPA raises significant money for student programs, as well as defraying operating costs.

Finally, ILPA also receives $24,000 appropriated for the faculty who teach the eight special legal studies courses during the fall and spring semesters—an average of $3,000 per course. This amount has not increased since 2002, when the legal studies minor take-off period began.[28] Obviously, the professionals hired as adjuncts do not depend on their adjunct salaries for their survival, but rather enjoy the experience of teaching and sharing their expertise in a respected program, providing opportunities to diverse students with aspirations.

ILPA students have been admitted to over 150 law schools in the U.S., including 18 of the top 20. Presently, students are enrolled in such prestigious law schools as Harvard, University of California-Berkeley, Columbia, Georgetown, NYU, University of Texas, and Washington University (St. Louis), among many others. For the Fall 2010 admission cycle, UT School of Law accepted seven SLSPA students, with others on the waitlist. Over 50 SLSPA students have been accepted to law schools for the Fall of 2010. Combining other UTSA students with the institute's students, projections indicate that over 65 will receive admission, a remarkable increase from the past. Before opening the institute, the initial benchmark year indicated that only eight UTSA students had been admitted to law school nationally, and only one to UT Law. UTSA President Romo has repeated the story that when UT Law Dean Powers and he first discussed starting a UTSA pre-law preparatory program, he was informed that not a single UTSA student had been admitted to the UT School of Law that year. Progress has been meteoric. Moreover, when assessing impact and admissions, one must remember that some from the 2007 class and many from 2008 and 2009 have not graduated due to the multi-year admissions policy of the ILPA and many others, including the first and fourth highest LSAT scores who chose not to apply this cycle.[29] Hence, a multi-year lag exists.

As mentioned, the SLSPA admissions committee takes "risks," but counts some remarkable success stories to its credit. Some students come into the institute with a 2.6 GPA or worse, after lackluster or tragic early academic careers. These students are able to enhance their academic skills and performance, and significantly increase their GPAs and LSAT skills. They impress their professors, who then support them with testimonial letters of recommendation. With expert advice from these professions and others, they eventually gain entrance to and succeed in law school. To mention only two cases of many, a Latina and a Black woman entered the institute with particularly low GPAs, gained focused and renewed aspirations, enhanced their skills, and subsequently gained admission to tier one public and private law schools. One ultimately attended a public tier-three law school on scholarship, and the other a private tier one law school, both outside of Texas. After completing law school, they both returned to pass the bar and are practicing law in Texas today.

The SLSPA achieves positive results through a complex combination of factors:

(A) Students engage completely in an academically enhanced environment, building relevant skills, a propensity for hard work, substantive knowledge, confidence, credentials, and an elevated morality of aspiration. Students demonstrate their capacity to perform well in a competitive, rigorous program akin to the law school experience. As former UT Law Dean William Powers stated in an address to SLSPA students: "What is the most important thing you can do to elevate your chances of going to law school? You are doing it by enrolling in this program; now excel in it."

(B) Student academic skills increase, elevating subsequent coursework performance, interest, and GPA. The daily intensity of the program pays off. Many students realize that they must develop new skills just to complete the assigned readings, workload, and preparation for class each day. The SLSPA measures student skill enhancement in several ways, but one example relating to the writing course may suffice. At the beginning of the summer, students take a pre-test to measure their editing competency.[30] During the semester, students use *The Handbook of Technical Writing* to learn and practice editing conventions, and they directly apply what they have learned to their own writing. At the end of the semester, students take an editing post-test covering the material. In 2010, every student showed improvement. Often the progress is dramatic. In one case, a student improved from a pre-test score of 54% to a post-test score of 88% (out of 100%). In 2009, when students entered with lower pre-test scores, one student increased from a 38% to a 70% and, another student's score improved from 46% to 82%.[31]

One 2010 student's unsolicited comments capture the impact of the SLSPA overall on the elevation of writing skill and the accumulation and retention of substantive knowledge:

> The skills that I had learned in just a few weeks of the program surpass those that I had learned my entire college experience. The legal technical writing class taught by Professor Abdo, transformed my skills in writing from grossly obsolete before the program, to writing clear and concise papers that were worthy of submission to even the harshest critic. The knowledge from your Constitutional Law class is perhaps the most extensive and personally valuable

information I had received in my college experience. Any time I am asked what constitutional case created a certain situation in America, if we covered it in your class I can give the name of the case, the number of justices that voted certain directions, and the holding of the case that created the situation. I have taken no other class where I can recall such things from memory in such detail.

(C) SLSPA students become prepared and motivated for the LSAT, certainly one of the most critical components of the law school application portfolio, and one where Hispanic and Black students, on average, do not fare well. One important result of the program is that SLSPA students make significant progress in preparation on the LSAT. In 2010, the average increase on the LSAT score for all students from the three sections of the analytic reasoning and logic course was 6.0 points, a 16% increase from the initial pre-test to the final test. In LSAT conversion scores, the percentile increase resulting from a six-point raw score increase varies depending on where one starts. For example, a six-point increase from a 144 starting point (a score that ranks in the 22.8th percentile) to a 150 end point (44.1%) would constitute a 21.3% point increase or rise; from a start of 148 (36.3%) to 154 (60%) is a 23.7% point rise; 150 (44.1%) to 156 (67.9%) is a 22.8% point rise; or 158 (75.1%) to 164 (90.4%) is a 14.3% point rise.[32] These average increases indicate effectiveness in the learning of logic and sharpening of analytical abilities. Moreover, students in a controlled two-course sequence of "legal and philosophical reasoning" followed by the analytical reasoning and logic course, which contextualizes the learning materials in the manner in which the LSAT asks questions, have averaged as high an increase as 7.2 points. Students in the SLSPA take at least three practice examinations each summer, in addition to the coursework. Then, practice LSAT exams are offered in simulated conditions every other week until the actual October test. For virtually all of our students, the academy is their initial exposure to the LSAT. The instructor goes over their practice scores with them, following test administration. These positive results have made differences in law school admissions.

Again, the same 2010 student quoted above wrote: "I personally increased 15 points, and have used the notes and [excess exercises] from the class since the end of the program. This has increased my points further, and I now have been close to approaching the score of 160 and hope to push that to 170 by the time I take the LSAT." On the other hand, some students recognize that the law school environment, rigor, intensity, educational style, or substance are simply not right for them, or right for them at this time in their lives (e.g. with child rearing, support options, etc.) After consultation, several choose not to apply to law school. Most of these students select graduate school environments and pursue that option, often part-time. Others elect to start businesses or enter the labor force, even though accepted to tier one schools. It is better to learn now that other options are more appealing than law school than to enter law school and hate it, to end up with a huge financial aid debt, indentured to work in an area which one does not love, or to flunk out because of lack of time or passion or distaste for the style, process, or substance of law school. Hence, our students who choose graduate schools, including public administration, biology, history, and business administration, find that the honed academic skills acquired at the institute are propaedeutic to their preferred professional fields, a secondary positive effect of the pre-law program."

Whatever their destination, the institute has a lasting impact on students. They rise to the occasion and it changes their lives. The program is intensive but the rigor pays off in multiple ways. Four comments from former students will suffice to show the impact of the program on their lives.

- A student enrolling at Harvard Law School wrote recently: "The time spent at the Summer Law School Preparation Academy fostered in me not only a deeper understanding of the law and law school, but also a deep appreciation for the field of legal studies. The mentorship and education I received [from particular, identified SLSPA professors] were instrumental in my development not only as a pupil or a writer, but as a man as well. I feel that my admittance into Harvard Law School would not have been made possible if not for the Summer Law School Preparation Academy."

- One UT student wrote: "The [SLSPA] program was not easy and I would sometimes feel overwhelmed by the material, yet I knew my efforts would only make me stronger and more prepared.... The program introduced me to more than the law school curriculum. It exposed me to the all-important law school application process, it trained me how to handle a rigorous course load with complex material, and much more."

- A student, who is now a 3L at Columbia, wrote: "As a result of the ILPA training, I saw my LSAT pre-test scores go from 42% to over 90%. Now, I've been admitted to law school at Berkeley, Chicago, Columbia, Cornell, Duke, Georgetown, and UT, among others."

- And a former student who is now very successfully practicing law wrote during her 1L year: "The skills and knowledge that I received at the institute allowed me to excel in my first year of law school at the University of California, Berkeley, Boalt Hall. I was stunned by how far my knowledge exceeded others with undergraduate degrees from prestigious schools like Brown, Princeton, Stanford, and Harvard."

The Expanded Program: A Legal Studies Minor, Legislative Scholars

Related to the SLSPA, the ILPA developed a legal studies minor to sustain and complement an enriched pre-law curriculum throughout the year. The minor requires 21 academic hours across multiple disciplines, including courses in writing, research, and substantive law. The legal studies courses are taught by practitioners, for example, a federal judge teaches federal courts. The FBI's regional counsel and the first assistant district attorney team up to teach public integrity and governmental corruption. A diverse set of attorneys teach such courses as Blacks, Chicanos and the law, women and the law, regulatory law and enterprise, legal research and writing, and immigration law. During the time of the institute's existence, the legal studies minor has grown from zero students to over 90 active minors, ranking among the top ten minors at the university.[33]

Thought important to its mission and for the enhancement of the credentials of its students, ILPA has initiated several innovative programs linking the community and the institute to provide additional opportunities to enhance the academic and professional experiences of SLSPA students. One such program is the UTSA Legislative Scholars

Program, commonly referred to as the "McClendon Scholars," at the Texas state capitol. The program is named after State Representative Ruth Jones McClendon, who teamed up with the ILPA director to conceive, launch, and sustain the program.[34] The program started with the 2005 legislative session when students were placed as legislative assistants. In 2009, the ILPA program placed seven legislative scholars in the Texas House of Representatives, awarding each $10,000 to live in Austin and perform professional duties as legislative assistants at the capitol during the Texas legislative session. ILPA is increasing the number of scholars for the 2011 legislative session to nine. All student stipends are raised from sources external to university funding from the state. Selected by a university committee, each legislative scholar is assigned to a participating state legislator, including one student to the speaker's office as a policy analyst. The scholars work the 140 day legislative session, which coincides with the university's spring semester. Each scholar earns up to 12 credit hours through internships, independent studies, or streamed distance learning classes, generally focused on the policy issues with which they deal on the job.[35]

These experiences constitute important credentials and contacts relevant to the development of a law school or graduate school admissions portfolio. Six of the seven 2009 participants had been SLSPA graduates, eight of the nine for 2011. Five of the seven from 2009, all that applied to law school thus far, have been admitted to law school.[36] This pipeline-related program has been exceptionally successful from a variety of perspectives. Besides law school admissions, the Heinz College at Carnegie Mellon University has recently extended up to ten scholarships to UTSA Legislative Scholars to pursue their MSPMP degrees at Carnegie Mellon. The first is exercising that option this year, deferring law school until completing his master's degree. During the past two years, four other top-ten schools in the public affairs, administration, and policy arena have recruited at UTSA through ILPA, focused on minority outreach. The linkage of law and public affairs in the ILPA is becoming a reality.

Creating Other Opportunities, Fundraising, and Grants

Over time, the ILPA network is providing opportunities in additional ways including jobs, mentoring, and funding. Students are interning in the law offices of former ILPA graduates, not just in San Antonio. This summer, one student secured a paid clerkship with a Houston firm. Quality internships are a staple, and some students are serving in the legal departments of corporations (e.g. Valero), nonprofits (e.g. MALDEF and Legal Aid offices), government entities (e.g. federal, state, and local legislative offices), district and city attorneys' offices, judicial offices (e.g. federal, state and local, including the U.S. Supreme Court), and many different types of private law firms.

To support its programs, the ILPA raised over $80,000 in external funds in 2009, and anticipates doing about the same in 2010. Fundraising is the necessary ingredient in providing opportunities for our students. In addition to supporting work opportunities, alumni have contributed handsomely to ILPA for scholarships and operations. One alumna established an annual $5,000 individual contribution and a matching contribution from her law firm. Another set up a scholarship for an ILPA student to attend his law school alma mater, and one UTSA alumna attorney has given a total of $15,000 to this enhanced training and pipeline cause.

The local bar has also supported UTSA's effort in increasing the quality and number of its law school admissions. The ILPA has secured generous contributions from many San Antonio law firms, large and small, as well as from firms ranging from Laredo to Dallas. The local Mexican American Bar Association has contributed funding. Moreover, several San Antonio corporations have contributed generously to the ILPA, including energy, telecommunications, beverage, and banking corporations. As only one example of creative fundraising, a state senator sponsored a chili cook-off and auction for the SLSPA.

The ILPA has won generous grant support from the Texas Bar Association for its students and programs. The Bexar County Federal Bar Association has sponsored an annual program that helps bridge the divide between inner city high schools and universities, by providing tuition and fees for selected students from a magnet center-city high school to enroll in undergraduate law courses through ILPA for dual credit, i.e. simultaneous high school and college credit. This creative partnership between the federal bar and ILPA has extended the pipeline further to the high school level. The program has been successful and is going into its fourth year, 2011. This provides linkage from an enhanced law-related high school curriculum, to an enhanced law-related college curriculum, to law school admission.

Finally, UTSA and ILPA students have benefitted from a series of especially generous and helpful annual grants from the Law School Admission Counsel. LSAC has financed up to 50 pre-law students to attend the annual Law School Forums in Dallas or Houston, where over 150 law schools professionals provide recruitment information and conduct seminars on financing, applying to, and coping with law school. These grants have enriched the information given to and horizons of our pre-law students, and have encouraged our minority and financially poor students in ways hard to fully articulate.

In 2006, the ILPA became part of the UTSA Honors College (HC), moving the legal studies minor, Legislative Scholars Program, and other components with it. Students do not have to be a member of the Honors College to enroll in any of the ILPA programs, including the SLSPA, legal studies minor, or "McClendon" Scholars. This relationship has expanded opportunities for ILPA students and, reciprocally, the ILPA has provided fertile ground for recruiting top minority students for the Honors College and its programs. Two examples will suffice to show the benefits of combining the ILPA with the Honors College. First, the Archer Fellows Program, administered by the Honors College, provides high achieving, public spirited students with opportunities to go to Washington, D.C. for a semester, earn seminar credits in political science, and serve in quality D.C. internships. Many SLSPA students have served as Archer Fellows, including one at the U.S. Supreme Court, another at the Civil Rights Division of the U.S. Department of State, others with members of Congress, one with NPR, and others with the Heritage Foundation and UNITE HERE. This contributes to the students' admissions portfolios and to the extension of the pipeline. Second, two of our ILPA students, an African American and Mexican American, utilized the services of the Honors College's scholarship advisor, a faculty member who nurtures students to apply for major national and international fellowships. Through efforts of the Honors College and ILPA, they became simultaneous regional finalists for 2010 Rhodes Scholar Awards, and, ultimately, chose to attend Harvard and the University of Texas law schools, their top choices.

The UTSA's ILPA is fulfilling its initial pre-law mission and succeeding beyond original expectations. The ILPA executes a multilevel premier pre-law program that incorporates: a productive summer law school preparation academy, a skills-enhancing legal studies curriculum executed across the academic year, and multiple new programs reinforcing academic education with experiential training and opportunities. The SLSPA has enhanced the quality and rigor of law school preparatory coursework, exposed students to law school admission processes and expertise, and created a special environment containing escalated rigor, individual student assessment and attention, and induced a morality of individual and cohort aspiration. As a consequence, ILPA has exponentially raised the number of students gaining admission to law school, increased the number and quality of law school choices that students have, and elevated students' chances to succeed and excel when enrolled in law school because the students have elevated their preparation, experiences, confidence, motivation, and professional focus and aspiration.

As with LSPI, much of the credit for SLSPA's success must go to the students who have responded remarkably to the enhanced and intensive learning environment. ILPA's credit comes from providing opportunities that its students would not have had to gain adequate preparation and access to law school. Given the opportunity, they have delivered. The lesson lies there. The success of ILPA and SLSPA contributes to the pipeline, that is, to the increase in the number and quality of students from historically underrepresented classes. The SLSPA has great diversity and this contributes to its success in many ways, including in the preparation of its students. ILPA has alumni practicing law who are Native, Latino, African, Asian, Anglo, and physically impaired Americans. The large number of veterans and non-traditional students contribute to the diversity as well. This, ILPA contends, adds to its strength in adequately preparing students for law school and practice.

Conclusion

The Texas experiment in creating LSPIs at selected universities has contributed to the Texas pipeline, while avoiding the legal and constitutional questions raised by preferential admissions. The *Hopwood* decision's challenge to diversity stimulated the creation of the LSPIs to assist UT and other law schools in preserving and expanding—at a point prior to their seeking entry to law school—the pool of students from underrepresented minorities interested in and qualified for admission to law-school under the extant admissions standards, including the LSAT. The LSPIs have consistently contributed to the Texas and national pipeline to the profession by elevating the preparation of students from disproportionately minority and poor groups, and producing students prepared for success who have matriculated and graduated not only from Texas law schools, but also from other schools around the country. This chapter described the history and operations of two of these programs, UTPA and UTSA; both are quite different in breadth and specifics, but similar in substance and spirit. Both have effectively worked for diversity. As UT Law Dean Sager stated: "Our commitment to diversity is steadfast."

As part of our ongoing efforts, we helped create law school preparation institutes at UT-El Paso, UT-Pan American, UT-San Antonio and Prairie View A&M. Members of our faculty continue to teach at each of these institutes. Our South Texas Program with the UT-Brownsville, UT-Pan American, Texas A&M Corpus Christi, Texas A&M Kingsville, and Texas A&M International seeks to remedy historic underrepresentation from south Texas and the Rio Grande Valley. I am proud to report that our efforts have borne fruit—these programs together have yielded 243 offers of admission.[37]

Necessity is the mother of invention. Ingenuity finds a better way. The UTPA LSPI and the UTSA SLSPA are not increasing the number of lawyers, but securing the number of law school seats that students from historically underrepresented classes occupy. This achievement contributes to a more diverse profession and to fair and representative justice.

Multiple-Level/ Overarching Programs

Chapter 14

Mentoring: All Levels

The Pacific Pathways Mentoring Program
University of the Pacific McGeorge School of Law
Sacramento, California

Melissa Keyzer*, Torie Flournoy-England†

Pre-K	Elementary	Middle	High School	College	Law School	Profession

Mentoring—focused on the third of the new 3Rs, relationship—is an established and well-documented approach to supporting students' persistence and success in school. This chapter illustrates a second law school approach, one that started with a neighboring high school and now works with high school, middle school, and elementary school students on campus in Sacramento. Written by a former director and school partner principal, the chapter offers a journal-type view of how the program truly works.

---

* Melissa Keyzer received her JD from the University of the Pacific McGeorge School of Law in 2007. She earned her LL.M. in 2008, and is admitted to practice in California. In her first two years of law school she worked with McGeorge's America Reads program tutoring and mentoring neighborhood elementary school students off-site. In 2006 she became involved with McGeorge's Pipeline efforts, and helped create the McGeorge mentoring program, which would be the first to bring "mentees" to the McGeorge campus on a regular basis. In 2008 she was selected as one of McGeorge's three Downey Brand Education Law Fellows, heading up the mentoring program while earning her LL.M. She plans to pursue a career in education law, and to continue to work toward making the goals of the Pipeline Initiative a reality.

† Dr. England began her career as a high school counselor working with inner city, at-risk youth. She quickly became interested in site leadership and administration. Her career has led her to many schools all in need of vision, leadership, and academic growth. She has worked at K–12 school sites to increase student achievement as much as 80 points a year, as well as working to close the current achievement gap apparent in the California education system. There is never an excuse for lack of student success when working with Torie. Her experiences include inner city gang mediation, serving students in transition, homeless families, and students currently involved with social services. Educating students on breaking the cycle of poverty, violence, and drugs is a common theme. Dr. England graduated from California State University, Sacramento in 1997 with a BA in Psychology. She earned a Pupil Personnel Services credential and Master's degree in Education Counseling from Chapman University. Most recently, Torie earned her Ed.D. from the University of LaVerne in Organizational Leadership. Her dissertation explored character education and the impact such programs have on student achievement and in creating a safe learning environment.

Historical Introduction

In 2004, the Dean of the University of the Pacific McGeorge School of Law joined forces with future Sacramento mayor Kevin Johnson to support an emerging law-themed charter school at Sacramento High. The joint work of the law school and the new high school was multifaceted and also involved other professional schools. Along the way, this program changed to a many-partner effort called Pacific Pathways, which included, among early partners, not only the law school but also the University of the Pacific's Liberal Arts and Education Deans, Downey Brand, a major area law firm, and schools and school leadership in Sacramento and Natomas. This chapter focuses on the Pacific McGeorge mentoring program that had its genesis in this relationship and has since grown to other locations and age groups.

Why a Mentoring Program?

The mentoring program at University of the Pacific McGeorge School of Law (Pacific McGeorge) is loosely based on the BYU mentoring program, which brings students to campus for weekly mentoring sessions with first year law students.[1] In the Pacific McGeorge program, participating students from grades 3–12 come from partnering elementary, middle, and high schools. They visit the Pacific McGeorge campus once a week after school to spend time with their first, second, or third year law student mentors. McGeorge provides food and drinks, and the students find their law student mentors and retreat to various parts of the campus to spend the hour. The elementary school students are encouraged to bring homework to work on with their mentor's help. The older students sometimes bring schoolwork, but most often spend the hour playing board games or walking the campus and talking with their mentors.

The immediate goal of the McGeorge program is simple but profound. It seeks to introduce young students, the majority of whom are both minority and disadvantaged students, to the world of higher education. We seek to make them comfortable in the law school environment, and to help them connect personally to someone currently pursuing a higher education goal. The elementary and high school students in the program are those who might not otherwise have had any contact with the world of higher education, and may not have considered college or graduate school a personal possibility. We simply seek to give them some meaningful exposure to a place of higher education, hopeful that if they feel comfortable on our campus, and with their law student mentors, they might then begin to envision themselves walking the campus as future college and perhaps law students. To our young mentees, law school likely becomes less mysterious than it is to most adults. For the mentees, law school is a real place, full of friendly, focused people, who truly care about the mentees' education and plans for the future. No mentee participates in our program without hearing the message that a higher education is waiting for them if they choose to pursue it, and that there is a large group of lawyers and future lawyers, including their personal mentor, who truly hope to see them become college graduates and perhaps return to the Pacific McGeorge campus as law students.

The secondary, though no less important, goal of the mentoring program is the enrichment mentoring offers the law student mentors. From Pacific McGeorge's perspective, legal education is evolving. It's becoming globalized. It's becoming more holistic. It's no less rigorous or daunting—the Socratic method won't be threatened—but the world is requiring more of attorneys, and law schools like McGeorge are responding. The Bar needs more lawyers sensitive to pipeline issues, and advocating for change in the demographics of the legal profession. Every law student on the Pacific McGeorge campus is now aware of the pipeline initiative, and a significant number are participants in pipeline programs. Mentoring involves the law students personally in caring for the pipeline, connecting them with the young students whose futures we hope to inspire. McGeorge sends out into the world law students who carry pipeline concerns with them into their legal careers, to big law firms and small firms, to their clerkships and to the bench. With the graduation of class after class of pipeline mentors, Pacific McGeorge does its part in seeing that the pipeline initiative is slowly infiltrating all areas of the legal profession.

The Role of Pacific McGeorge's Education Law Fellows

To enable its pipeline initiative work, Pacific McGeorge has come up with a creative and effective way to bring in a small staff devoted to pipeline work, with minimal cost to the law school. Pacific McGeorge has partnered with local law firm, Downey Brand, to create a unique opportunity for select law school graduates to obtain their LL.M. degrees while serving as the frontline of the law school's pipeline efforts. Downey Brand funds full scholarships for the "Education Law Fellows" who sign on as full time LL.M. students and part-time pipeline devotees, working on various pipeline projects. Students applying for the fellowship are interested in studying education law in furtherance of their legal educations, and at the same time see the value in helping students in the pipeline along the way. For the LL.M. candidate truly interested in education issues and in furthering young students' access to higher education and the legal profession, the fellowship provides the perfect opportunity for both service and study. In this way, Pacific McGeorge is able to maintain a devoted pipeline "staff" without adding full-time employees to the payroll, or adding to the duties of current full-time faculty and staff. The fellowship also works to turn out LL.M. graduates year after year, who, like McGeorge's graduating law students, bring their enthusiasm for pipeline programs back to their law firms and other contacts in the wider legal world. The mentoring coordinator who organizes and runs the Pacific McGeorge mentoring program is an Education Law Fellow whose sole Pipeline duty is to keep the mentoring program running efficiently, and to train in the next mentoring coordinator.

Partnering with Hagginwood Elementary School

The partnership between Hagginwood Elementary's K–6 campus and the Pacific Mc-George campus came about through a direct networking relationship between the elementary school principal and the law school dean. The mentoring component of the pipeline concept had been a vision the dean carried for many years. Since the law school already had the high school piece in place, the meeting was perfect timing. After discussion of the details of the pipeline program, a local junior high school campus was brought in as a perfect final piece to the puzzle, creating a complete K–12 pipeline system.

Hagginwood is an inner city, high-poverty, gang-infested neighborhood with much history. The community is stable in the sense that many generations live and stay. However, the economic status never seems to improve, making growth for students wanting to break the cycle of their family history a challenge. As the school where many young neighborhood children receive their educations and spend their days, Hagginwood Elementary became a hub for the community. Personal safety was never an issue for those working at the school because community members understood our role, as we did theirs. It was a partnership that grew into something built on trust and boundaries. Families began to understand that breaking the cycle was not a bad thing for their young children, but an opportunity for those children to learn and grow in order to give back later in life. The McGeorge campus opened many eyes to the possibilities for all students.

When looking for the perfect school partnership, both sides need to be fully invested in the program. A school partnership will not be successful if a common vision and understanding has not been established. Educating the mentors about their group of students is critical. Before the mentors ever meet their mentees, the school principals speak at the mentor training session to give the mentors information about the neighborhood and general background of the schools from which their students come. They explain demographics, average GPAs, and any particular challenges the majority of students might face. While it is important not to generalize too much as each student has an individual story, it is important for the mentors to know this basic background, and how their efforts fit into the overarching goals of the pipeline project as a whole. It is also important for the mentors to have some idea of how to generally interact with the students and what they might expect from students in their mentee's grade level. Students from Hagginwood, for example, begin attending the mentoring program as young as the third grade, and Hagginwood's principal warned that the law students should not be afraid of the younger students, as they are the ones that often gain the most from mentoring and structure. And often it is the Pacific McGeorge mentors who state at the end of each year just how much the third or fourth grader taught them.

Mentee Selection

Students selected from Hagginwood were mostly self-selected, although many were placed in the mentoring program based on potential versus current success. Students are usually already participants in the school-wide after school program, making the logistics of getting students to the Pacific McGeorge campus every week manageable. Twenty students were initially selected to participate.

Mentee attrition has been a struggle at times for both partners. As mentees move and create openings, new students are placed in the program, as there is never a shortage of students eager to join the program. As students learn about the program, they too request to join. Students see the excitement on the faces of their peers when leaving and returning from Pacific McGeorge, making the program marketable on its own. However, a new relationship between the mentor and the new mentee needs to be established, making the goal of a long term mentoring relationship difficult to achieve, and detracting from the benefits for both mentor and mentees. A waiting list was created and communication between the McGeorge coordinator and school site coordinator regarding mentee attendance is a must. In the event that a mentee slot does open, the best match can then be made from the waiting list of potential mentees to the available mentor. Once the program was established, the coordinator at Hagginwood better understood which families maintained stability etc., helping to head off mentee attrition from the program as well as to make the mentee transition process go as smoothly as possible when it does occur.

Recruiting Law Student Mentors

One week before the first day of classes, first year students—1Ls—fill the grassy quad in the center of the McGeorge campus. It's orientation week, and in addition to the mock classes, assignments, campus tours and class scheduling, all of the campus clubs and organizations are invited to introduce themselves to the incoming students. Tables are set up in the quad and 1Ls roam from table to table learning about the clubs, special programs, and organizations eager to consume any free time they might have left in their new schedules.[2] A 1L approaches the pipeline mentoring table. "I'd like a mentor, how do I get one?" he asks. We tell him that while McGeorge does have a peer mentoring program (I point to another table), in this program it's law students who mentor high schoolers. Before he can walk away I launch my pitch. "This program provides law student mentors to elementary, middle and high school students. The kids are bussed here once a week, so you don't even need to leave campus. We've scheduled the hour-long meeting between classes, so you won't have a class conflict, and we always provide free pizza and drinks. It's a really nice way to get your head out of the books for a little while each week, and do something really meaningful for someone else, and for you. The kids know how busy we are, and are so appreciative of the time we take to spend with them." "Just think about it" I say, as he smiles, takes a brochure, and heads off to another table.

Recruiting already overburdened law students is no simple task. A few are enthusiastic from the start, and commit without hesitation. Many more want to sign up, but the recent shock of their new reading load gives them pause. Others seem to be concerned only with extracurricular activities that will directly further their legal careers, and don't see a connection between mentoring and lawyering. To convince the interested but reluctant students, and to attempt to broaden the seeming tunnel vision of the students who don't initially see the importance of mentoring, we launched a full-scale recruitment and information campaign to "market" the program to the entire law school.

We had a window of about four weeks between the first day of class and the first scheduled mentor-mentee meeting, during which time we had to recruit, train, and match mentors to their mentees. Considering that training mentors and getting all of their background checks and paperwork in order would take significant time, and also that after the second week of classes most students would be inundated with reading and other assignments and less likely to take on another activity, we did our major campaigning prior to and during the first week of school.

While it is, of course, the hope that students from every year will volunteer, for several reasons, it is best to make a special effort to recruit 1Ls to the program, particularly during the first year of the program. The hope is that each mentor-mentee relationship will last the entire time the law student is in school, and perhaps beyond. The earlier a law student is introduced to her mentee, the more time she will be able to spend mentoring him or her within the program. In the first semester of our inaugural year, we had the most success recruiting 1Ls, likely because they had not filled all of their available time with other commitments. In our second year we found that those who had mentored with the program in the first year were the easiest to recruit. Most of these students were eager to resume the campus visits with the same mentee, and many even volunteered to help recruit more law students to the program. It was getting many of the law students to buy in to the program initially that proved to be the real challenge.

On the McGeorge campus there are several methods of communicating messages to the student body, and we took advantage of all of them. In addition to setting up an orientation day table to be visible to all of the 1Ls, we also got permission from several professors to address their 1L classes briefly at the beginning of class to tell them again about the program. This way we were sure we spoke to all of the 1L students who may have missed our table, either deliberately or inadvertently, and we handed out fliers to all students with information about the program and how to sign up. I suggest choosing a particular subject like torts and sending a representative to the first or second meeting of each torts class so that all of the 1Ls hear the message. This has the added benefit of demonstrating to the students that their law professors support the program, which can help remove the hesitation to act. Some of the more enthusiastic professors even offered their personal endorsement of the program, which seemed to further improve our recruitment numbers. We also assured that all 2Ls were aware of the program, by making the same speech for each of the three sections of the writing class that all 2Ls must take.

We put program brochures in each student mailbox the first day of classes, and also manned a table in the cafeteria with brochures and a signup sheet during the first, second, and third week of classes. As we added new names and email addresses to the signup sheet, we would email each volunteer with a thank you and a reiteration of the time and place of the mentor training, and the time and place of the first mentor-mentee meeting. As the mentor training date approached, we made flyers that we put in all student mailboxes and posted around campus. We also wrote messages with the same information on the classroom chalkboards, making sure that it was clear that we were still in need of volunteers. On the day of the mentor training, we again posted signs all over campus with the time and location of the training, as well as the offer of free pizza to all attendees. By then, we had collected over 100 names and email addresses. Of those, over 80 attended the training (including some who followed the signs to the free pizza), and over 60 became mentors.

In the second semester, we launched a second recruiting effort, attempting to recruit some of the many law students who claimed that they would have participated in the first semester, but for a personal scheduling conflict. We used most of the same recruiting tactics, but on a somewhat smaller scale, and of course we did not have the benefit of the orientation day table, or the fall semester enthusiasm that gave us such good results the first semester. We did gain some mentors at the beginning of the semester, though we also lost a few to new class and work schedules, so after our second semester recruiting we essentially broke even.

After the inaugural year, recruiting became somewhat easier, though our efforts remained intense. Because we had the benefit of a 2L class full of students who had mentored during their first year, the 2L participation was very high. Most continued to mentor the same mentees, and some had even kept in touch with their mentees over the summer. We launched the same heavy campaign for the entering 1L class, with even better results since we also had the assistance of former and current mentors to help sell the program to the new students. In the program's third year, the success of the recruitment effort grew proportionally, as at this point the whole student body was familiar with or involved in the program.

It is true that there are still many students who simply cannot be recruited because they find the program irrelevant to their resumes. We're optimistic, however, that an attitude shift is on the horizon for this type of student, as law schools like Pacific McGeorge and the legal profession as a whole continue to increase the legal community's awareness of the importance of pipeline efforts.

Mentor Training and Screening

The mentor training session is the first time a law student must show up for a mentoring-related event. We held the training session at the same time, Wednesday afternoon, as future mentoring sessions would be held, since we knew that only law students with that hour free could be mentors. We held it just a few weeks into the semester, once we felt the recruiting effort had been exhausted, but before the enthusiasm of our volunteers had waned.

Many of the mentors had worked with students before, but most had no experience mentoring. To help them feel comfortable and confident as mentors, we brought in a representative from a professional mentor training organization to go over basic mentoring skills and ethics. To help the law students choose what age mentee they would like to mentor, we had the principals from the partnering schools speak about their students so that the mentors could get a sense of whom they would be mentoring. The principals also gave the mentors their personal contact information so that the mentors would be able to have direct contact should it become necessary. We went over the mentoring timeline, going over all of the program logistics, such as where and when the busses would drop the kids off, where to come to pick up their food, and when to have them back to the busses. We also talked about the first day of mentoring, explaining how the mentors would be introduced to their mentees, and suggesting some icebreaker activities.

There were also a lot of logistical matters to deal with. We handed out the mentor-mentee matching survey to fill out, asking the mentors some questions about themselves and for their mentee grade level preference. We also had to get all of the mentors fingerprinted per the partnering schools' requirement,[3] so that the school districts would have the prints on file before the mentees were left in the mentors' care. We brought a fingerprinting service to campus the day of mentor training, and we emailed the mentors in advance letting them know that the service would be on campus that afternoon before and after the mentor training. By bringing the fingerprinting service to campus, we were able to get this potentially deal-breaking requirement out of the way as easily for the mentors as possible. In addition, all of the mentors had to be TB tested, again due to the partnering schools' requirement. Fortunately, there is a clinic located nearby, and after committing to the program and being fingerprinted, most volunteers found the time to visit the clinic both for the injection and again to have the site checked and to get their clearance certificates. Luckily, the schools were willing to accept the TB clearance for up to three years from the date of testing, so once in the program, mentors do not need to worry about TB testing or fingerprinting the following years.

After the training, we maintained contact with the volunteers via email messages to make sure that the program didn't drop off their radar between the training day and the first mentoring session. Even after the training there were a few law students on the emailing list who emailed that they had missed the training, and we held several additional, abbreviated training sessions for these students, and brought the fingerprinting service back to campus at a time when they could all meet to be fingerprinted. Prior to the first day of mentoring, we made sure that the mentors knew the names and grade levels of their mentees, even giving some mentors some background information about their mentees if it was available. Of the over 100 names and email addresses on the mailing list, over 60 fulfilled all of the necessary requirements to become pipeline mentors. We considered this a great success, and of course held on to the contact information of the 40 or so who had not been ready to commit, hoping that they might decide to become mentors in the spring, or the following year.

Mentor-Mentee Matching

Matching mentors with mentees was probably the most daunting part of setting up the program. We had both the mentors and mentees fill out surveys attempting to get a sense of their interests and personalities in order to make appropriate matches, but of course, there is no formula that can predict whether that magical element necessary for friendship will spark.[4] It was extremely beneficial to sit down with the high school counselor who knew all of her students personally to select their mentors from the pile of mentor surveys. Not knowing all of the law students personally, prior to mentor matching, was a disadvantage. While there were questions in the mentor survey asking about the type of mentee they thought they would like to be paired with, in retrospect it may actually have been even better to let the mentors themselves select their mentees from the mentee surveys. While such a process would have been much more cumbersome, perhaps it would have yielded even better matches and promoted bonding, since a mentor could tell a mentee that she chose her specifically.

Program Support from the Mentoring Coordinator

Once the program was off the ground, training and paperwork completed, mentors and mentees paired up, and the first day underway, it was then up to the program coordinator to help keep the program running smoothly. The first day, which in the first year involved simply introducing the mentors to their mentees, has since evolved into a grand event, complete with group icebreaker activities in the quad. This is not only fun for the mentors and mentees, but helps promote the program once more to the whole law school. During the subsequent mentoring sessions the coordinator would meet the kids and mentors in the cafeteria where we would have the pizza and games set out for them. She would monitor attendance of the mentees (and the mentors) and check in with the teacher who accompanied them to the campus to make sure any absentees were accounted for, and to keep a record of attendance for reporting purposes.

Occasionally, there would be an issue that required some minor troubleshooting. If a mentor could not make it to the mentoring session, we would find a substitute mentor for his or her mentee for the day. There was also the occasional mentee who for one reason or another would need to leave the program, so we would arrange with their mentor and the school for a new mentee to enter the program. We would also face occasional issues with the students that required coordination with their school principals to remedy, such as frequent absences, or failure of the younger mentees to bring their homework as their teachers required. We reported with program status updates on a regular basis at our pipeline partnership meetings to keep all partners abreast of program issues, difficulties, and successes.

Sustaining an On-campus Mentoring Program — Hands-on Support from the Law School

The commitment Pacific McGeorge has made to the pipeline is an example of how a law school can attempt to integrate pipeline philosophy into the education of future lawyers. By keeping the pipeline initiative in mind, while shaping the school's pedagogic philosophy and designing the academic calendar for the school year, McGeorge demonstrates its commitment to the young students in the pipeline and to producing graduates accustomed to making the pipeline a priority. The following suggestions can help sustain an on-campus mentoring program with minimal sacrifice from law students' rigorous academic schedules.

Most importantly, class scheduling must be taken into consideration. A weekly one hour block of time, free of any courses, scheduled roughly one half hour after the partnering school lets out, is ideal, since it frees all law students from the possibility of a course schedule conflict preventing them from mentoring. If this is not possible, and classes must meet during this hour, the next best scenario is that no 1L classes be scheduled during this hour, since 1Ls are the ideal recruits as discussed below.

Help from law professors during the first weeks of class can also give a great boost to the recruitment effort. If a professor is willing to make an announcement about the program, allow a mentoring spokesperson to address the class to promote the program, hand out flyers, or write a recruiting message on the board, the students are much more likely to seriously consider volunteering. As stated above, even a brief, public show of support by a professor can go a long way.

Setting aside an area for mentors and mentees to meet up, pick up their food, choose a board game, or simply sit and talk, shows the mentees and mentors that the program is important to the law school. It quietly sends the message that the law school is supportive of the mentoring relationship, which is a very important part of the overall goal of the mentoring program—to welcome the mentees to the campus and show them that they matter to us. In addition to this all-important message, the fact that the mentees come to us (as opposed to the mentors going to the mentees' schools) makes the program infinitely more practical for the law students. Squeezing in an hour of mentoring right on campus between classes is much less complicated and far more appealing to the law students than traveling to and from the mentees' schools. For these reasons it is imperative that some campus location be designated for the program for at least one hour each week.

At the end of the year, McGeorge hosts a dinner and celebration for the mentors and mentees in the program. For some, it is a way to cap the entire mentoring experience because they are graduating and will not return to the program the following year. For others it is a way to celebrate the year they have spent with their mentor or mentee and an enthusiastic show of support from the law school that helps convince them to return to the program next year. Mentees bring their parents to the campus for the celebration and feel a great sense of pride showing them around and introducing them to their law student mentors. On this day the mentees own the campus—the place of higher education is theirs, and we celebrate them for it.

Once the program is in place, it doesn't take much work for a law school to send the message to its students that its pipeline initiative is a priority. What it does take is a dedicated effort to keep the program in mind as the law school goes about its regular business. Even if the class schedule cannot be ideally manipulated, hosting a mentoring program in any form can be invaluable to the students it serves.

Program Support from the Partner Schools

Ensuring the program runs smoothly and effectively each week can be a challenge if there is not good communication between the mentees' schools and the mentors. For example, the elementary school students were required to bring their homework as a condition of participation in the mentoring program, and so some communication between teachers and mentors was necessary. We learned that the "golden ticket" was the best form of communication between mentors of the elementary school students and elementary school teachers. A golden ticket is a half sheet of gold paper that the student has his or her classroom teacher complete each Wednesday before visiting the McGeorge campus. The core classroom teacher checks that homework assignments to be completed during the mentoring session are accurate. Students who do not have homework during mentoring are assigned things such as reading to the mentor for twenty minutes, working on an art project, doing research on a college they might want to attend, or career exploration. The tasks take approximately half of the mentoring time, leaving the other half for a sports activity, games, or other activities decided upon by mentee and mentor. For the younger students, the golden ticket has become a critical piece of communication.

Another form of communication takes place between the McGeorge mentors and the site administrator at Hagginwood. If the mentor has concerns regarding a conversation they have had with the mentee, mentors know from the training session what steps to follow. Because of the population served at Hagginwood, it is best to have mentors fully trained on Child Protection Services issues. Mentors are always encouraged to visit the mentee's school, if possible, in order to gain a better understanding of the mentee's world. Mentors contact the site administrator via email or phone for approval prior to the visit. Often the mentor will choose to keep the visit a secret from the mentee as a nice surprise lunch or classroom visit. This relationship was a wonderful way for mentors to learn and grow from the partnership as well.

Perhaps the biggest challenge faced from the K–12 schools' perspective in creating a pipeline mentoring program was obtaining start-up funding. Transportation for mentees was an issue every year without fail. Funding difficulty, especially in 2008–2012 speaks for itself, although we discovered ways around this speed bump. Obtaining donations from large and small law firms who also support the pipeline vision was much easier than first anticipated. Once being educated on the costs of transportation and the benefits of the pipeline to the profession, many law firms never had an issue with providing financial support for the students. Support from cabinet level administrators helped in allowing some funding to support the cause. It all adds up if the organizers can get small pots of money to put together.

Devoting ample time to planning at the start of the program is also immensely important. Each step of the process requires communication between the law school mentoring program coordinator and the participating K–12 schools. Small issues, such as where to send the fingerprint records and distribution and collection of the mentees' pre-program surveys, must be worked out ahead of time. We began the planning process months before the fall semester began, ensuring that each detail could be worked out well in advance of its execution, ultimately resulting in a smooth and successful start-up.

An Update — The View from 2010

It is hard to capture all of the results from this mentoring program. The short version is that it has been good for the University of the Pacific, good for the law school and its students, and good for the communities it serves. The schools which Pacific McGeorge mentees attend continue to show strong progress academically, and young lives have been changed. A short story illustrates. At an end of the year banquet for the mentors, mentees, and their families, a Black father approached Judge England (a mentor partner and himself Black) and told the judge that his elementary school daughter had visited the judge's courtroom and told her family about it. But it wasn't until the dinner that the father realized that Black men could be judges. This anecdote offers commentary and education on many levels!

Appendix A

Mentor Surveys

Pacific Pathways Pipeline Project Mentorship Program

Mentor Pre-assessment

As a pre-assessment of your involvement in the Pacific McGeorge Mentorship Program, we would like to gather some information *before* you meet your mentee. We will also try to gather some comparable information during and after the program is completed. Some of this information will focus on the impact of the program for mentees and mentors; other information will help us improve the program in the future.

Name: _____

(Your responses will be kept confidential, but this will allow us to track your responses during the year.)

1. **Motivation:** Why have you volunteered to be a Mentor?

2. **Desired Impact:** What are the 2 or 3 specific things you most hope to achieve as you work with your mentee?

3. **Concerns:** As you begin the program, what is your biggest concern or uncertainty about being a mentor?

Mentee Pre-assessment

As a pre-assessment of your involvement in the Pacific McGeorge Mentorship Program, we would like to gather some information *before* you meet your mentor. We will also try to gather some comparable information during the program and also when it ends next spring. Some of this information will focus on the impact of the program for mentees and mentors; other information will help us improve the program in the future.

Name: _____ School: _____

(Your responses will be kept confidential, but this will allow us to track your responses during the year)

1. **Motivation:** Why do you want to work with a mentor from Pacific McGeorge Law School? That is, how do you hope to benefit from this program?

2. **Desired Activities:** What kind of activities would you like to do each week with your mentor?

3. **Attendance:** Are you willing to come every week?

    _____Yes   _____No   _____Maybe

4. **Concerns:** As you begin the program, what is your biggest concern or fear about being a mentee?

5. What part of the program are you most excited about?

Mentor Matching

Pacific McGeorge Mentor Information Form

Thank you for your interest in becoming a mentor. In order to ensure you and your student will be a good match, please take the time to complete this information sheet.

Name: _____ Year/Div.: _____

Address: _____

E-mail: _____

Home Phone: _____ Cell Phone_____

We will use the following interest survey to match you to your mentee.

I would prefer to tutor/mentor a:
  3rd–6th grade student
  7th–8th grade student
  9th–12th grade student
  Any grade
	I am interested in receiving work-study for my mentoring and/or tutoring service. (Mentoring can supplement other work-study as long as your total work hours do not exceed 20 hrs./wk.)
	I would like to volunteer my time.

Please indicate any particular reason(s) you have for working with the grade level you chose above:

_____

Your gender: _____Your ethnicity: _____

College(s)/University you attended prior to law school:

_____

Undergraduate major:

_____

Any additional degrees held:

_____

What are your favorite pastime activities/hobbies?

_____

What are your favorite movies?

_____

Who are your three favorite actors/actresses?

_____

What are your favorite television shows?

_____

Do you like to listen to the radio? _____   If so, which stations/DJs?

_____

Do you like to read for fun? Check one:
   __a little   __a lot   __not at all   __an average amount

What are the three best novels you have ever read?

_____

What are the three best nonfiction books you have ever read?

_____

Did you know how to read before you started school?

_____

Did someone read to you before you entered school?

_____

If so, did they read to you: ___a little   ___a lot   ___an average amount

How many books (other than law school books) do you read a month?

_____

Check the kinds of things you like to read about (as many as you wish):

__Love stories	__How to make things	__Cookbooks
__Crafts	__Baseball	__Football
__Basketball	__Other sports	__War stories
__Teenagers' problems	__Famous people	__Murder mysteries
__Mathematics	__Historical tales	__Mythology
__Adventure	__Poetry	__Essays
__Dictionaries	__Nature stories	__Space travel
__Scientific experiments	__Westerns	__Travel articles
__Politics	__Encyclopedias	__Legal fiction
__Biographies		

If you could buy as many books as you want, what would they be?

_____

What do teenagers read about?

_____

If you wrote a book, what would the title be?

_____

What books have you disliked very much?

_____

What newspapers, magazines, or websites do you like to read?

_____

What are your favorite comic strips in the newspaper?

_____

What do you like about them?

_____

What three living men and three living women do you admire most in the world?

_____

What were your favorite and least favorite subjects in high school?

_____

What type of law do you think you might want to practice?

_____

Have you been a mentor in the past? (If so where?)

_____

If you were a tutor/mentor last year, and would you like to be paired with the same student, please indicate:

_____

Any additional information you believe will be relevant, i.e., prior occupations, special interests.

_____

Is there anything about your schedule or commitments that we should know about?

_____

Mentee Matching

Pacific McGeorge Mentee Information Form
   We will use this interest survey to match you to your mentor.

Name: _____ Age: _____ Grade:_____

School: _____

Gender: _____ Ethnicity: _____
College(s)/University you might want to attend:

_____

Jobs you are most interested in:

_____

What are your favorite pastime activities/hobbies?

_____

What are your favorite movies?

_____

Who are your three favorite actors/ actresses?

_____

What are your favorite television shows?

_____

Do you like to listen to the radio? _____   If so, which stations/DJs?

_____

Do you like to read for fun? Check one:
   __a little   __a lot   __not at all   __an average amount
What are the three best novels you have ever read?

_____

What are the three best nonfiction books you have ever read?

_____

Did you know how to read before you started school?

_____

Did someone read to you before you entered school?

_____

If so, did they read to you: ___a little   ___a lot   ___an average amount

How many books (other than law school books) do you read a month?

_____

Check the kinds of things you like to read about (as many as you wish):

__Love stories	__How to make things	__Cookbooks
__Crafts	__Baseball	__Football
__Basketball	__Other sports	__War stories
__Teenagers' problems	__Famous people	__Murder mysteries
__Mathematics	__Historical tales	__Mythology
__Adventure	__Poetry	__Essays
__Dictionaries	__Nature stories	__Space travel
__Scientific experiments	__Westerns	__Travel articles
__Politics	__Encyclopedias	__Legal fiction
__Biographies		

If you could buy as many books as you want, what would they be?

_____

What do teenagers read about?

_____

If you wrote a book, what would the title be?

_____

What books have you disliked very much?

_____

What newspapers, magazines, or websites do you like to read?

_____

What are your favorite comic strips in the newspaper?

_____

What do you like about them?

_____

What three living men and three living women do you admire most in the world?

_____

Who are your favorite heroes from the past?

_____

What are your favorite and least favorite subjects in school?

_____

Have you had or been a mentor in the past? (Where?)

_____

Anything else you would like to add?

_____

Is there anything about your after school schedule or commitments that we should know about?

_____

Appendix B

Accounts of Two Pacific McGeorge Mentors

(Names are deliberately left out to protect student privacy.)

Mentor Account #1

For me, mentoring was a 1 hour opportunity every week to give back to the community, have an impact on someone whose life I could help shape, and to be a kid again. A law school environment can be very intense and by being around the playful laughs of children, it helped me open myself up to that child-like energy. Also, I saw how quickly the younger kids look up to us. Many of them may not have had the same opportunities, but I can tell how much they value us and our opinions. Also, I learned a lot from my mentee. His perspective of the world and the way he questioned it was free and unrestricted from the judgments and set thinking that is found in many adults. I felt I learned from him about life just as much as he may have learned from me.

Mentor Account #2

Just when I thought I was not getting through to my mentee, his teacher approached me to compliment his improvement in class and how his staying out of trouble, she believed, was directly related to the time that we shared each week. The euphoria from hearing that good news helped me realize how my mentee had affected me.

In one of our early meetings, I asked "Frank" (real name withheld), my mentee, what I thought was a facile question: "So, what do you think about gangs?" Even though I knew that he lived in a troubled environment, I never expected him to answer saying, "Gangs are cool!" I though he was being facetious, until he told me why: "Everyone in my family is in a gang." My jaw dropped.

He went on to tell me how everyone in his family was presently involved in a gang. His uncles, cousins, even his mother were in some way gang affiliated. As most boys in his situation, his father was not around, but he knew that his mother had met his father through the gang. He believed that his future was limited to the possibilities that a gang could offer.

I tried to think he was exaggerating, but then he described certain experiences about gang life; things that I knew because of being exposed to a similar environment at that age. Frank's situation was much worse than my experience.

My confidence as the "experienced and all-knowing elder" vanished. I became a mentor thinking that I had all of the answers a kid like Frank might ask. But after that short meeting, I was speechless. How could I help guide this kid away from gangs and that life when everyone he looked up to pushed him towards it? Then, I remembered that the mentoring directors suggested not to try to change the kids' lives. Instead, just be a friend. If I could just be his friend, maybe he'll see, through my actions, that staying away from gangs was what is really cool.

When I learned that Frank had improved in school, I was reminded how effective being a friend can be. I remembered that when I was his age, I wished to have someone who would not give up on me, even if enduring meant that someone would just be there. By the end of the year, Frank seemed increasingly inquisitive about being a lawyer. Giving Frank the idea that being a lawyer was a real possibility for him, if he made the right decisions, means the pipeline mentoring program gave him something that his world did not have: hope.

Account of a Hagginwood Elementary School Administrator

Pedro was a Hispanic male in the fourth grade at Hagginwood when the program took flight. Historically, he was a student with poor attendance, failing grades, and multiple suspensions for fighting. When you had Pedro one-on-one with an adult, he was the most amazing student. His potential for learning was far beyond what he ever believed. Pedro had supportive parents and family members, but because he was the oldest of five siblings, he had many responsibilities. Pedro learned at an early age that fighting was a way of survival to and from school each day. He knew that "reputation" on the streets would keep him alive and keep him safe. What he did not understand at eight years old was the fact that fighting would eventually get him kicked out of school. Pedro did not care if he was kicked out of school because he still had his "good name" on the street which kept him alive and out of gangs. As he began to grow and mature, the gangs from the community started approaching Pedro. They were asking him to join in order to insure additional safety. As Pedro's behaviors drastically became worse, his attendance slipped by the day, and his grades sank to all F's ... we knew it was time for additional interventions. Pedro loved attending the after school program but never felt a connection to anything academic. He knew the program kept him off the streets but the only adults he connected with at the school were the principal and his teacher. As the principal saw Pedro's potential versus his current output, it was decided that the McGeorge campus would be presented to Pedro as a way for him to learn and see what his future could be all about.

The principal approached Pedro with a plan. He would attend the program for four weeks straight in lieu of a suspension for fighting. Reluctantly, Pedro agreed. He attended the first two sessions positively but skeptical. He was unsure about how this partnership could make him a better student when all he knew was that school was a constant struggle because English was not his first language. He knew that gangs and fighting would keep his good name on the streets, but how would McGeorge help him?

By the end of the four weeks, Pedro had changed his attitude about school. His attendance began to improve, as did his attitude in general. He was paired with a first year law student who enjoyed many of the same things. They would do homework and then play soccer. He would confide in his mentor about the challenges he faced day in and day out both at home and at school, knowing he was safe to speak freely. Pedro's sprit came alive!

By the spring of Pedro's first year in the pipeline program, he had B and C grades, almost perfect attendance, and had not received any suspensions since before the winter break. He was smiling, helping others, and confident. One afternoon while playing soccer at recess, Pedro came to the office frantic. There were only 45 minutes left in the school day and he insisted on calling home to get a clean pair of pants. He had slipped on the field and was covered in mud from his shoulders to his toes. The office staff could not figure out why Pedro was suddenly being so disrespectful by yelling at them that he needed to call home. The principal heard a commotion in the front office and went out to see what it was about. There was Pedro crying, hardly able to speak, begging her to call home. The principal too explained that by the time his was able to get there with clean clothes the school day would be over and he could go home to change. Pedro looked up at the principal and said, "But I have to get clean clothes … today is McGeorge. It is the day I go there to be a lawyer and I cannot look like this. I need clean clothes to be professional." Without a thought, the principal hugged Pedro and took him to the phone to call his parents. It was at this moment that we all knew the program was more of a success than even we had believed or dreamed.

Chapter 15

Hispanic National Bar Association Mentoring: High School to the Profession

The HNBA Multi-Tier Mentoring Program[*]
Arizona State University and Others

Charles Calleros†

Pre-K	Elementary	Middle	High School	College	Law School	Profession

This chapter revisits and updates an earlier article by Professor Calleros about the Hispanic National Bar Association multi-level mentoring program. The program reaches out to high school students, pre-law students, law schools, and practitioners, bringing them together in an extraordinarily coordinated initiative that forms and supports mentoring teams or tings. It's an elegant program, which has turned out to be multi-ethnic, and most important replicated and replicable. Special thanks is extended to the Journal of Legal Education for their gracious permission to reprint the earlier work.

Introduction: Awakening to a Need

For many years, the legal profession has been painfully aware of disparities between the ethnic composition of the legal profession and that of our general population.[1] In response, state and local bar associations and private organizations affiliated with the law have become increasingly interested in educational "pipeline" programs. These programs are designed to provide student populations with the information, guidance,

* We express our great appreciation to the American Association of Law Schools for their generous grant of permission to reprint this article by Professor Calleros; Copyright © 2008 by the Association of American Law Schools; Charles R. Calleros. [Footnote numbers have been changed to conform to this publication.]

† Charles R. Calleros is Professor of Law, Sandra Day O'Connor College of Law at Arizona State University. I wish to thank Diane Murley, Reference Librarian at the College of Law, for her assistance with research and analysis.

and inspiration needed to keep them engaged in school, and to encourage them to aspire to higher education.

For example, the State Bar of California created a Diversity Pipeline Task Force in September 2005, with the goal of raising student aspirations and providing them with the necessary support.[2] Two months later, the American Bar Association (ABA) and the Law School Admissions Council (LSAC) collaborated to host and fund a national pipeline diversity conference at Rice University in Houston, Texas, entitled "Embracing the Opportunities for Increasing Diversity into the Legal Profession: Collaborating to Expand the Pipeline (Let's Get Real)."[3] A recurring theme of this conference was the need for collaboration among members of the bar, private foundations, members of the community, supportive governmental entities, and educators throughout the pipeline, from elementary school to graduate school.[4]

At a more local level, law schools and local bar associations across the country are engaged in programs that reach out to youth. My school, the Sandra Day O'Connor College of Law, for example, regularly hosts visiting high school classes for interactive legal method exercises, and other programming designed to give the students the confidence and motivation to seek higher education.[5] The Bronx Bar Association has implemented the national Thurgood Marshall Junior Mock Trial program, in which junior high school students play the roles of attorneys, witnesses, and jurors in simulated trials.[6]

These pipeline programs typically target communities whose members are underrepresented in the legal profession and are most in need of assistance: low-income communities, largely composed of ethnic minorities, with few role models from the professions and higher education. Unfortunately, these communities often are short-changed by the public school system. In March 2006, for example, a joint report issued by two organizations affiliated with the University of California commented on the manner in which low-income minority communities have disproportionately borne the impact of inadequate resources devoted to K–12 education in California:

> The roadblocks to college loom larger for students living in low-income communities of color. Every California community feels the effect of the state's educational crisis, but all communities do not suffer equally. Schools with high concentrations of students of color, many of whom are poor or learning the English language, report the highest rates of unqualified teachers and shortages of college preparatory courses in the state. These students are not given a fair and equal opportunity to learn.[7]

Mentoring programs or other pipeline programs cannot fully compensate for serious systemic problems in public education. However, they can make a difference with students who have talent and ambition, but might lose hope or focus without the encouragement and guidance of a role model. Lawyers who promote or work in these programs obviously hope that some of the assisted youth will one day enroll in law school and become leaders and role models in the legal profession. They recognize, though, that every such student who enrolls in college and pursues a college or graduate degree in any discipline represents success for these and other pipeline programs.

The Hispanic National Bar Association National Mentoring Program

Upon assuming the presidency of the Hispanic National Bar Association (HNBA) in October 2005, attorney Nelson Castillo appointed HNBA officers Jose Perez and Norma Garcia to co-chair a committee on pipeline programs, including a national mentoring program. Over the next year, this committee conceived of citywide programs that would organize mentoring teams, each team consisting of at least one attorney, one law student, one pre-law college student, and one high school student. On September 1, 2006, the Hispanic National Bar Association launched its National Mentoring Program at the HNBA's National Meeting in San Francisco, California.[8]

Over the following year, HNBA members organized mentoring programs in several cities, including Miami, Phoenix, New York, and Tampa, joining the program that was launched in San Francisco at the September meeting. Most of these programs, however, went no further than pairing attorneys with law students, affecting the pipeline only at the point where it flowed directly into the profession. In Phoenix and New York, though, the HNBA mentoring programs encompassed at least four levels in the pipeline.

The Pilot Mentoring Program in Phoenix, Spring 2007

Administrative Resources for Organization

One advantage of the HNBA mentoring program is the relatively low cost of implementation, as described later in this section. Organizing a program, in contrast, can be a complex, time-consuming process.[9] Without administrative assistance at the program's inception, the burdens of organization fell on volunteers in each of the cities promoting mentoring programs.

In the Phoenix area, the organizational efforts have been contributed by the Sandra Day O'Connor College of Law at Arizona State University in Tempe. My light teaching load in the 2006–07 academic year fortuitously corresponded with the launching of the HNBA mentoring program, allowing me to devote substantial time to the project.

Recruiting Participants

High school participants were drawn primarily from the Law Magnet Program at South Mountain High School, and from a community organization for college-bound Latino students, called Aguila. In both cases, the directors of those high school programs recruited and selected the high school participants. Similarly, pre-law and student group advisors at Arizona State University spread the word among pre-law students, resulting in adequate numbers of college applicants.

Two affiliate organizations of the HNBA provided natural pools of potential participants at the attorney and law school levels: Los Abogados, an organization of Hispanic attorneys in Phoenix, and the Chicano/Latino Law Students Association at the Sandra Day O'Connor College of Law, for which I am a faculty supervisor. Although largely Hispanic in membership, both organizations are open to any attorney or student interested in the organizations' activities and goals. Perhaps unsurprisingly, neither group's members responded in significant numbers to general e-mail solicitations. Instead, I recruited attorneys through individual solicitations, and recruited students largely through passing around a sign-up sheet at a student organization meeting. After a viable program was assured through adequate participation of HNBA affiliated organizations, I recruited additional participants from other bar and student organizations.

Forming the Mentoring Teams

Ultimately, seventy-five participants were recruited and were organized into fifteen mentoring teams, sometimes called mentoring rings, or "mento-rings" for short. Each team included one or more participants from each of the four tiers of the HNBA program.

Because of the demographics of the community served by South Mountain High School, most of the high school students were Hispanic; however, one was Anglo American, two were African American, and one was Native American. Among the college, law school, and attorney participants all ethnicities were represented, including several Asian and Asian-American students. Thus, the program was multi-ethnic at all levels, although it was of particular interest to Hispanic students and attorneys because of its HNBA affiliation.

In organizing students into teams, I took several factors into consideration. Two teams, for example, were organized around subject matter preferences stated by some of the college and law students, intellectual property law for one, and business law for the other; indeed, I recruited the intellectual property attorney especially to provide guidance in that legal field.

The emphasis on the early end of the pipeline, however, led me to organize most of the thirteen teams around the needs of the high school participants. The director of the high school law magnet program identified a few of the female high school participants as ones who would respond best to a female mentor, leading to their placement on a team that had a least one female mentor at the college or law school level. The ethnicity of attorney mentors was a consideration in three other teams that included students at various levels who might respond particularly well to role models from their own ethnicity, culture, or community. These teams were led by African-American, Asian-American, or Native-American attorneys, to help create critical masses and provide role models for the relatively small numbers of student participants from those communities.

Yet, for the most part, the teams were organized randomly. Some of the most successful mentoring partnerships in the program crossed gender and ethnic lines as well as subject matter interests.

Special Requirements for Working with High School Students

In telephone and e-mail correspondence with the Assistant Superintendent for human resources for the Phoenix Union High School District, we soon learned that the school district would not permit our mentoring program to work with their high school students unless all mentors were fingerprinted at the district office so that they could be cleared by law enforcement agencies. This requirement represented either an implementation of state legislative requirements designed to protect students from harm, or a more demanding school district policy authorized by state law, though not required by it.[10] Clearance is not required when students, supervised by a certified teacher, welcome a one-time guest speaker to the classroom or take a field trip to visit the speaker at another setting.[11] The possibility of off-campus mentoring team meetings involving a high school student not accompanied by a teacher, however, raised the necessity of clearance for all the college students, law students, and attorneys participating in the program.

The fingerprinting process required substantial processing of forms, facilitated by the staff at the Sandra Day O'Connor College of Law. Then the fun began. In the two weeks prior to the scheduled kick-off dinner on February 3, 2007, fifty-seven student and attorney mentors visited the district office to fill out more forms and to get fingerprinted. Aside from these formal requirements for working with K–12 students, we recognized that high school students would thrive academically only with parental support. Accordingly, we took care to invite their parents to most mentoring events.

The Launching of the Phoenix Program

It was important for all members of the mentoring program to attend the first group meeting, so that everyone could absorb and reflect the group energy, and so that the members of each mentoring team could develop a working relationship. Accordingly, we spent some time with e-mail messages confirming a date that ended up working for nearly everyone.

During the morning and afternoon of Saturday, February 3, staff from Arizona State University joined with two visiting attorneys to hold a workshop on higher education for a few dozen students from the South Mountain High School Law Magnet Program and from the community group, Aguila. Like other programs of its kind, the cost of busing and lunch for this outreach program was sponsored by the Law School Admissions Council and by the ASU Undergraduate Admissions Office.

That evening, eighteen of those high school students, some of them with their parents, joined the other participants of the mentoring program at the Sandra Day O'-Connor College of Law to launch the Phoenix version of the HNBA mentoring program. Two law firms provided funds for a light dinner for more than eighty guests, to allow general mingling for the first hour.

In the meeting's second stage, the participants moved to a large classroom to receive instructions on the program and on suggested team mentoring activities. The new HNBA President, Jimmie Reyna, had altered his flight schedule to provide his encouragement to the program, and the room was alive with excitement. The ethnically diverse high school students, already immersed in pre-law studies, looked around the room and saw dozens of college students, law students, and attorneys who looked like them, some of whom came from their communities. The high school students and their parents were invited to recognize that this path was open to all who displayed the requisite determination and devotion to their studies.

In this group meeting, law student Alba Jaramillo and her attorney mentor Alexander Navidad spoke about their early mentoring activities. They had met as mentoring partners at a Los Abogados luncheon earlier in the semester, and Mr. Navidad had invited Ms. Jaramillo to shadow him for a few weeks over the semester break. Ms. Jaramillo told the group how much she had learned from accompanying Mr. Navidad to office strategy sessions, meetings with other attorneys, and court hearings. Although we all agreed that this full-time shadowing went well beyond the activities that were feasible for team mentoring during the spring semester, the testimony of these two participants helped to set an inspiring tone for the evening.

In the meeting's third stage, each mentoring team gathered as a small group a suitable meeting place at the law school, to exchange contact information, develop a rapport, and begin planning mentoring activities. At the end of the evening, one Asian-American law student, Estelle Pae, told me of her "bonding" with the Latina high school student in her group, whom I will call Sara. Ms. Pae told of Sara's pride in recently being accepted to ASU and then her tearful confession that her parents did not want her to attend college, any college. Sara's parents, relatively recent immigrants from Mexico, had traditional views about the proper place for their daughter after graduating from high school, and higher education was not on their agenda. Sara's parents, however, had cared enough to attend this meeting, and they had seen their daughter sitting with dozens of Latina college students, law students, and attorneys. We may never know whether this role modeling helped to increase the level of support that Sara's parents provided to Sara in her quest for higher education, but Ms. Pae reported later that Sara did enroll at ASU.

Mentoring Activities, Spring 2007

During the plenary session, I requested that each mentoring team engage in at least one educational meeting during the semester, and that pairs or trios within the team stay in touch more regularly. Below, are examples of the kinds of mentoring activities that took place:

- Attorney mentors arranged for their team members to attend oral arguments in court in interesting cases and then either had lunch with the attorney member to discuss what they saw, or meet with the judge and/or the advocates to discuss advocacy.

- Team members met for brunch or dinner (usually paid for by the attorney mentor) to exchange information and ideas about lawyering, law school, and getting into college.

- An attorney mentor on a team that had an interest in intellectual property law, took the team on a trip to a high-tech firm to speak with the firm's attorneys about their work.

- An attorney mentor took her team to the closing of a major transaction providing financing for construction at ASU, so that the team could get a view of transactional work, and could discuss it later over lunch.

- A college team member took her high school counterpart on a tour of ASU and then out for coffee to talk about college life and academics.

- Law school team members invited their college counterparts to events at the law school, such as guest speakers or moot court arguments.

- An attorney mentor, a criminal defense attorney, took the two college student members of his team to the state trial courthouse and arranged for short conversations with a number of attorneys, staff members, and judges.

- An attorney mentor invited all high school participants and their parents to an evening reception at his firm, including a Mexican buffet, a brief welcome to the group, and then small-group tours and discussions with an attorney from the firm. A university admissions representative was also on hand with information about college admissions and financial aid.

- On Sunday, June 3, many of the mentoring participants met as a group again, this time to assess the program. Although the program was generally a great success, we focused our attention during this meeting on the problems encountered by some mentoring teams and on brainstorming ways to overcome those problems and improve future programs. Below, are some of the issues that arose:

- Communication among team members—Some teams experienced difficulty in getting four to six team members to respond quickly to e-mails or phone messages so that they could schedule team activities. We concluded that, at the first group meeting each year, we should underscore the importance of each team developing a strategy for communication.

- Large group meetings—Many participants enjoyed the plenary group sessions, as supplements to team meetings, and they requested that we add one or two group meetings in addition to the kick-off and closing dinners each year. Under our new approach, moreover, the group meetings will be opportunities to meet with classes of high school students.

- Sub-meetings within a mentoring team—At the other end of the spectrum, some team mentors confessed that they relied too heavily on efforts to organize team meetings that fit every team members' schedule. More mentoring could have taken place had pairs or trios within a team made efforts to meet at an attorney's office or on campus for some enlightening event.

- Starting date—Team members found that the months passed quickly and that team meetings were difficult to fit within busy schedules when the program was compressed between the months of February and June. They hoped that the 2007–2008 program could begin sooner in the academic year. Because of some restructuring of our program, we did not meet this goal in the 2007–2008 program, but held our kick-off dinner on January 26, 2008, in conjunction with a mock trial and outreach program for high school students. In Fall 2008, we achieved continuity by continuing the teams and activities of the Spring 2008 program, filling gaps created by departures from teams.

Changes in the Phoenix Mentoring Program, Spring 2008

New School District Restrictions on Working with High School Students

By the fall of 2007, the Director of Admissions, Zarinah Nadir, and the Director of Pro Bono Programs, K Royal, at the College of Law expressed interest in helping to administer the program, thus relieving me of organizational responsibilities while I handled a heavy teaching load during the fall semester. Nadir, Royal, and our law library staff organized a very successful law library tour and exercise for thirty students from the South Mountain High School Law Magnet Program, which took place in October. They encountered a substantial roadblock, though, in creating the fourth tier of the HNBA mentoring program.

In the 2007-2008 academic year, the Phoenix High School District implemented a requirement that undermined our ability to place high school students on mentoring teams. A district official determined that HNBA mentors could not meet with South Mountain High School students unless a certified teacher was present even if the mentors were fingerprinted and cleared by state officials for work with K–12 students.[12] This issue had arisen in the school district's Office of Business and Operations, which is responsible for risk management, when the mentoring program came to their attention near the beginning of the fall 2007 semester. It was the topic of numerous discussions during that semester.[13]

The policy posed no obstacle to a major field trip, such as a high school class visit to the College of Law or a law firm, which would be routinely supervised by at least one teacher. But it was not realistic to expect certified teachers to attend every meeting of an individual mentoring team in which a high school student was present.

As the fall semester drew to a close, we realized that further correspondence and negotiations would not change the district's new policy pronouncement, and it was clear that the Law Magnet Program at South Mountain High School was free to work with our program only within the parameters defined by the district. True, we could bypass some district policies by working with high school students through private community organizations. The Law Magnet Program, however, was an invaluable partner in the mentoring program. Accordingly, in early December our organizing team set a January date for launching a new model for the program. The new mentoring teams would include ninety attorneys, law students, and college students, while the program would provide K–12 students with programming and mentoring in group settings in which at least one certified teacher was present.

In some ways, this new approach worked well for high school students, and on one occasion for younger students as well. By hosting group field trips, we could ensure participation of a critical mass of K–12 students in programming tailored to their needs. On January 26, 2008, for example, we combined three outreach and mentoring events, each of which targeted different segments or combinations of segments of the educational pipeline. During the afternoon, while a team of law students and faculty coached mock trial competition teams from several high schools, another law student and I provided introductory lessons in legal method and trial practice for students from several middle schools. The K–12 students, accompanied throughout the afternoon by several of their teachers, then met for an hour-long panel presentation on college admissions and academic life. Finally, these K–12 students briefly overlapped with the college students, law students, and attorneys on the mentoring teams while all mingled over pizza at the kick-off dinner for the mentoring program. As the K–12 students later boarded buses for their home schools, the mentoring teams received instructions in a group meeting before breaking into team meetings for their first mentoring sessions.

On other occasions, mentoring attorneys and their law firm associates hosted groups of high school students, accompanied by a few teachers and parents, for tours, dinner, and presentations at their law firms. Thus, we managed to continue the mentoring process for high school students in group settings, often featuring presentations by attorneys participating in the mentoring teams.

Nonetheless, the absence of high school students on individual mentoring teams represented a lost opportunity for more individualized mentoring. During the pilot program in 2007, a few of the high school students developed solid friendships and mentoring relationships with attorneys and with college or law students. In these more personal mentoring relationships, the high school students gained access to lawyers or university students to whom they felt comfortable directing questions and expressing concerns. Some of these mentoring relationships endured beyond the 2007 mentoring program season. Accordingly, in the fall of 2008, we began to restore these opportunities for individualized mentoring by working with some high school students through community organizations and with parental consent. Thus, in the 2008–2009 program, we are reaching K–12 students both in group field trips and by including high school students on several of our mentoring teams.

Other Lessons from the Second Year of the Program

Two law firms contributed several attorneys to the program in the spring 2008 program. This provided the firms with some advantages in mentoring. The Phoenix office of the law firm of Quarles and Brady, for example, scheduled monthly presentations at its firm, each on a different field of practice, and invited all of its teams to each presentation. Quarles and Brady even had enough attorney mentors to provide two attorney mentors for three out of four of their mentoring teams, pairing a senior attorney with a relatively junior one. Another law firm with multiple mentors in the program, Gust Rosenfeld, noted that the mentors could cover for each other when a conflict prevented one of them from meeting a mentoring program responsibility.

Perhaps these advantages of coordination among mentoring teams could be extended to teams that are not affiliated with the same law firm. In addition to encouraging individual team activities, as well as scheduling occasional group meetings of all the teams, the program organizers could assign three or four teams to intermediate-sized mentoring groups, so that they can be encouraged to plan activities together and to cover for one another in mentoring responsibilities.

Launching the Mentoring Program in Las Vegas

From February 2007 to September 2008, I served as HNBA Regional President for Arizona and Nevada, and sought to generate interest in the HNBA mentoring program in the sister communities of Tucson, Arizona, and Las Vegas, Nevada. In the fall of 2007, members of the student organization La Voz, in their second year of operation at the William S. Boyd School of Law at the University of Las Vegas, began to organize a four-tier HNBA mentoring program. Under the leadership of their President, Leslie Niño Fidance, members of La Voz launched such a program with ten teams on March 1, 2008. Those teams engaged in activities similar to those in the Phoenix program including activities such as tours of the district court and county government offices, a mock courtroom exercise, a tour of a private law firm, a meeting with the managing partner and associate attorneys at a law firm, team gatherings for lunch, dinner, bowling, and even a hike at Red Rock Canyon. The program celebrated the success of its pilot program in a closing dinner in May, with plans to repeat the program during the full 2008–2009 academic year.[14]

Plans for the Future: Reaching Further Back in the Pipeline

By meeting with middle school students at the January 26 outreach program, the Phoenix program addressed a segment in the pipeline to higher education where many students may lose their academic focus unless inspired and guided by influential role models. We hope to include this segment more frequently in the mentoring or outreach events open to high school students.

Moreover, even students in earlier grades, such as third or fourth grade, can find inspiration in creative demonstrations of law and higher education. Accordingly, I hope to organize mentoring team trips to primary schools so that teams can present outreach programs to younger students. For example, available materials could help young students imagine Goldilocks' trial for her trespass against the home of the Three Bears.[15]

Expanding the HNBA Mentoring Program to Other Communities (Including Yours)

The HNBA mentoring program is a grassroots program that runs largely on the volunteered time of committed persons and the collaboration among professional organizations and educational institutions at several levels. If this program can spread to most major cities in the country, students who most need a helping hand may be enabled to realize their dreams for higher education on a more level playing field. Indeed, if reached early enough, some students may develop that dream when they otherwise might not envision a college or graduate level of education.

In some communities, a citywide or regional mentoring program may draw from a number of universities.[16] The HNBA encourages other communities to follow suit and bring cooperative pipeline programs to life throughout the nation. Although mentoring programs such as these cannot single-handedly solve the problems of underfunded schools and under-appreciated, overworked K–12 teachers, they can help. They can help students adopt academic goals that, in turn, lead the students to take their current studies more seriously. In the best of cases, they may even form lasting partnerships that can bring long-term benefits to all participants. Whether the mentored students ultimately turn to law school or some other productive pursuit matters little. The mentoring program will succeed if it helps guide and inspire youth who might otherwise fall through the cracks of our educational system.[17]

Conclusion

The HNBA mentoring program is a successful pipeline program that can make a difference for students who lack professional and academic role models, and can benefit from guidance, inspiration, and other mentoring from professionals and from older students. If readers of this chapter take the first step toward implementing this program in their communities, in collaboration with other individuals and institutions, we stand a chance of spreading this worthwhile program throughout the nation, taking advantage of the goodwill, time, and valuable experience of thousands of professionals and students in higher education, collaborating with community leaders and with dedicated K–12 and college teachers and counselors, all to the benefit of our youth.

Postscript

The College of Law has continued its partnership with the Law Magnet Program at South Mountain High School. Law students teach Street Law and Marshall Brennan Constitutional Literacy courses at South Mountain, and two law school graduates continue to organize a day-long annual Mock Trial Academy for students from South Mountain and other high schools and middle schools. Law students also help to teach summer institutes for high school students, conducted at the university. In addition, the College's law library staff annually lead a class from South Mountain in a research exercise at the law library.

The Phoenix HNBA mentoring program has successfully maintained a critical mass of high school students on its mentoring teams. They attend high schools from various parts of the Phoenix metropolitan area, and typically learn of the program when they or their parents or teachers visit the mentoring program's website.[18] The Phoenix law firm of Gust Rosenfeld is a leading participant in the mentoring program, fielding six lawyers, and leading five mentoring teams in the 2010–2011 academic year. The program continues to run on the volunteer work of students, attorneys, and otherwise fully employed law school staff, supported by modest grants from LSAC, the HNBA, and the Arizona State Bar's Office of Diversity.

The College of Law's Junior Law program organizes visits to middle schools. In those visits, law students provide general information on careers in the law or prepare eighth grade students for mock trial exercises in the annual Court Works exercise at the United States District Court.

In 2010, the College of Law's Indian Legal Program received a grant that will enable it to operate a summer program designed to assist college students in preparing their applications to law school and preparing for the LSAT.

The various outreach and mentoring programs at the law school have become increasingly interrelated, building on one another, and building networks for each other. Challenges remain, including coordinating student schedules to facilitate maximum attendance at mentoring team events. Moreover, the mentoring program is unlikely to grow beyond its current size of approximately 100 participants until funding enables creation of a full-time staff position dedicated to administering the program. In the meantime, however, the combined efforts of dozens of volunteers ensure that multi-level mentoring and outreach to youth continues in Phoenix.

Notes

Chapter 1

1. Sarah E. Redfield, DIVERSITY REALIZED: PUTTING THE WALK WITH THE TALK FOR DIVERSITY IN THE LEGAL PROFESSION (2009).

2. *U.S. Minorities Will Be the Majority by 2042, Census Bureau Says*, AMERICA.GOV, Aug. 15, 2008, http://www.america.gov/st/diversity-english/2008/August/20080815140005xlrennef0.1078106. html.

3. E.g., Emily Barker, *Diversity Scorecard 2010: One Step Back*, AMLAW DAILY, Mar. 1, 2010, http://amlawdaily.typepad.com/amlawdaily/2010/03/onestepback.html (Observing that "[f]or the first time in years, the population of minority lawyers at big law firms is shrinking").

4. Recent Bureau of Labor of data confirms this. *See, e.g.,* Sarah E. Redfield, Professor of Law, University of NH, Presentation, *The Educational Pipeline to the Legal Profession*, Chapman and Cutler LLP, Slide 3 (May 2011) (on file with the author).

5. Despite decades of task force studies, reports, and summits, the bar has not found an approach to change these numbers in a meaningful way; indeed the American Bar Association (ABA) itself reports that "the proportion of minorities in the legal profession is not likely to attain parity with that in the general population in the foreseeable future." ABA, Leadership, *Office of Diversity Initiatives*, http://www.abanet.org/leadership/ diversity.html.

6. Redfield, *supra* note 1 at 10 and at Chapter 1 (discussing current demographics, admissions, and related issues and providing citations for all references and data in this paragraph).

7. Redfield, *supra* note 1 at Chapter 5 (describing history of the bar's involvement).

8. ABA Presidential Advisory Council on Diversity in the Profession, *Pipeline Diversity Directory*, http://www.abanet.org/op/pipelndir/home.html (providing a searchable directory of pipeline programs). *See also* The State Bar of California, *Report & Recommendations from the Diversity Pipeline Task Force* (2006), http://calbar.ca.gov/calbar/pdfs/reports/2006_Diversity-Pipeline-Report.pdf (outlining in the recommendations of the California Task Force on pipeline programs at various levels of the continuum).

9. *See, e.g.,* Leonard M. Baynes, Professor of Law & Director, The Ronald H. Brown Center for Civil Rights and Economic Development, St. John's University School of Law, The Ronald H. Brown Law School Prep Program, Presentation, *Law School Shut Out Rates from 2000–2009*, Slide 3, ABA (Aug. 2010).

10. *Marine Mentoring*, http://www.tecom.usmc.mil/mentoring/. *See also* e-mail correspondence from Kimberly Greely to author quoting Major Samuel E. Jackson, USMC, Jul. 26, 2009 (describing importance of diversity).

11. *See, e.g.,* DENNIS MCGRATH ET AL., THE COLLABORATIVE ADVANTAGE: LESSONS FROM K–16 EDUCATIONAL REFORM (2005); H. Thomas Wells, Jr., Eduardo Roberto Rodriguez, Sarah E. Redfield & Lee Arbetman, *LRE Meets Diversity*, Keynote Presentation, Wingspread IX (Portland, ME July 2008).

12. *See, e.g.,* The Bill & Melinda Gates Foundation, *The 3Rs Solution*, http://www.gatesfoundation.org/Education/RelatedInfo/3Rs_Solution.htm (on file with author); International Center for Leadership in Education, *Rigor/Relevance Framework*, http://www.leadered.com/rrr.html; Willard R. Daggett, *How Brain Research Relates to Rigor, Relevance and Relationship* 5–8, http://www.leadered.com/pdf/Brain%20Research%20White%20Paper.pdf); National Academies, *Relationships, Rigor, and Relevance: The Three R's of Engaging Students in Urban Relationships, Rigor, and Relevance: The Three R's of Engaging Students in Urban High Schools*, http://www8.nationalacademies.org/onpine ws/newsitem.aspx?RecordID=10421.

13. *See generally* William M. Sullivan, Anne Colby, Judith Welch Wegner, Lloyd Bond & Lee S. Shulman, Educating Lawyers 2–3 (The Carnegie Foundation for the Advancement of Teaching 2007) (describing a signature pedagogy); Dr. William Sullivan, Senior Scholar, The Carnegie Foundation for the Advancement of Teaching, Presentation, *The Future of Legal Education*, Wingspread VI, Monterey, CA (Oct. 6, 2006).

14. Calvin Sims, *What Went Wrong: Why Programs Failed*, 258 Science 1185, 1185–86 (Nov. 13, 1992) (describing lack of assessment and follow up in science and engineering). See, e.g., Karen Mitchell, Jamie Shkolnik, Mengli Song, Kazuaki Uekawa, Robert Murphy, Mike Garet & Barbara Means, Am. Insts. for Research, *Rigor, Relevance, and Results: The Quality of Teacher Assignments and Student Work in New and Conventional High Schools* (July 2005), http://smallhs.sri.com/documents/Rigor_Rpt_10_21_2005.pdf.

15. The book does not extend to programs, such as academic support, which come into play after admission to law school.

16. One obvious example here is the 2010 ABA Sadie Alexander winner, Len Baynes and his college pipeline program, the Ronald H. Brown Law School Prep Program in New York. I have every hope of having a chance to include Len's chapter in the next book.

17. For more information on all of these programs, please visit their current websites.

Chapter 2

1. John F. Kennedy: "As they say on my own Cape Cod, a rising tide lifts all the boats and a partnership, by definition, serves both partners, without domination or unfair advantage. Together we have been partners in adversity—let us also be partners in prosperity." Public Papers of the Presidents of the United States: John F. Kennedy, 1963, at 519.

2. Young low-income children have smaller vocabularies than their middle-class counterparts do. By age three, they know about 525 words compared to 1,116 words. Betty Hart & Todd R. Risley, *The Early Catastrophe: The 30 Million Word Gap by Age 3*, Am. Educator (Spring 2003) http://www.aft.org/pubs-reports/american_educator/spring2003/catastrophe.html. These early differences correlate with later IQ measurements. Betty Hart & Todd R. Risley, Meaningful Differences in the Everyday Experience of Young American Children 128, 155–58, 252, (1995). This "linguistic cultural capital" that starts accruing so early often predicts the trajectory for learning and the achievement gaps that follow. *See* Paul E. Barton & Richard J. Coley, Educ. Testing Serv., *Windows on Achievement and Inequality* 9–10 (2008), http://www.ets.org/Media/Research/pdf/PICWINDOWS.pdf (reviewing achievement gap from child development to global comparisons).

3. U.S. Dep't of Educ., National Center for Education Statistics (NCES), *Common Core Data, Latin America Youth Bilingual Montessori*, http://nces.ed.gov/ccd/schoolsearch/school_detail.asp?Search=1&City=Washington&State=11&SchoolType=1&SchoolType=2&SchoolType=3&SchoolType=4&SpecificSchlTypes=charter&IncGrade=-1&LoGrade=-1&HiGrade=-1&SchoolPageNum=5&ID=110003200247.

4. Forty-one students are eligible for free lunch and five for reduced-price lunch. *Id.*

5. "Founded in 1968 and incorporated as a non-profit 501 (c)(3) in 1974 for the purpose of serving immigrant Latino youth, LAYC has grown from a small grassroots recreation center to a nationally recognized organization serving all low-income youth and families across the District of Columbia and in Maryland's Prince George's and Montgomery Counties.

LAYC achieves its mission by operating a regional network of youth centers and public charter schools with a shared commitment to meet young people where they are and help them make a successful transition to young adulthood. LAYC provides multi-lingual, culturally sensitive programs in five areas; Educational Enhancement, Workforce Investment, Social Services, Art + Media, and Advocacy." Latin American Youth Center, About, http://www.layc-dc.org/index.php/about-us-intro.html (last visited Jul. 22, 2011).

6. Latin American Montessori Bilingual PCS, *History*, http://www.lambpcs.org/history.html (last visited Jul. 22, 2011).

7. *Id.*

8. LAYC, *About, supra* note 24.

9. *Id.*

10. *Montessori education*, http://en.wikipedia.org/wiki/Montessori_education, (last visited Aug. 22, 2009).

11. LAMB, *Philosophy*, http://www.lambpcs.org/philosophy.html (last visited Jul. 22, 2011).

12. *Id.*

13. *Id.*

14. See note 140 *infra*.

15. Marco's mother, present during the discussion part of the book session, wanted Marco to add two smaller circles as wheels. We explained that his drawing was good the way it was, that it did not have to be a perfect numerical correspondence at the age of three. In a subsequent detailed drawing, he depicted six smaller circles as wheels for James.

16. *See* American Education Research Council, *Research Points*, (Winter 2009). This newsletter details strategies and activities that can be used to foster early literacy skills.

17. Catherine Snow, *What Counts as Literacy in Early Childhood* in The Blackwell Handbook of Early Childhood Development 282 (Kathleen McCartney & Deborah Phillips, eds., 2006).

18. Although listing can be thought of as lower on the cognitive scale, like stating or describing, here this listing is combined with a higher cognitive skill of categorization and assessment i.e., whether a thing is good or bad.

19. How Students Learn 16 (Nadine M Lambert & Barbara L. McCombs, eds., 1998). This is the first of 14 "learner-centered psychological principles." Corollary principles are: #2, "Goals of the learning process. The successful learner, over time and with support and instructional guidance, can create meaningful, coherent representations of knowledge" and #3, "Construction of knowledge. The successful learner can link new information with existing knowledge in meaningful ways." *Id.* at 16–17.

20. National Research Council, How People Learn: Brain, Mind, Experience and School, Expanded Edition 10 (John D, Bransford, Ann L. Brown & Rodney Cocking, eds., 2000).

21. Preparing Teachers for a Changing World 41 (Linda Darling-Hammond & John D. Bransford, eds., 2005).

22. National Association for the Education of Young Children, *Overview of Learning to Read and Write: Developmentally Appropriate Practices for Young Children: A joint position of the International Reading Association (IRA) and the National Association for the Education of Young Children (NAEYC)* (1998). *See also* Preventing Reading Difficulties in Young Children (Catherine E. Snow, M. Susan Burns & Peg Griffin, Eds., 1998). Both of these works contain summaries of research and recommendations for best practices for the literacy development of young children.

23. Bransford, *supra* note 36, at 3818.

Chapter 4

1. See Brett G. Scharffs, *Starting a Law School Youth Mentoring Program*, 2002 BYU Ed. & L. J. 233–254. If you would like to talk further about starting a youth mentoring program, feel free to contact Professor Scharffs at 801-422-9025, or scharffsb@law.byu.edu.

Chapter 5

1. *Ed-Data*, http://www.ed-data.k12.ca.us/welcome.asp, (follow link for District Reports).

2. Number of students in grades 7–8. California Dep't of Educ., Educational Demographics Unit, *California Public School Enrollment–School Report, 2008–09 School Enrollment by Grade, Smythe Academy of Arts and Sciences*, http://www.cde.ca.gov/index.asp (follow link "School Directory"). Calculated using data on enrollment in grades 7–8 at California Dep't of Educ., Educational Demographics Unit, *California Public School Enrollment–School Report, 2008–09 School Enrollment by Gender, Grade & Ethnic Designation, Smythe Academy of Arts and Sciences*, http://www.cde.ca.gov/index.asp (follow link "School Directory").

3. This includes Smythe Academy Elementary School. California Dep't of Educ., http://www.cde.ca.gov/index.asp (follow link "School Directory").

4. California Dep't of Educ., *2009 Base Academic Performance Index (API) Report, School Demographic Characteristics*, http://www.cde.ca.gov/index.asp (follow link "School Directory").

5. Calculated using data on grades 7–8 at California Dep't of Educ., Educational Demographics Unit, Number of English Learners by Language, 2008–09, Smythe Academy of Arts and Sciences, http://www.cde.ca.gov/index.asp (follow link "School Directory").

6. This includes Smythe Academy Elementary School. *2009 Adequate Yearly Progress (AYP) Report,* at California Dep't of Educ., http://www.cde.ca.gov/index.asp (follow link "School Directory").

7. Smythe Academy of Arts and Sciences is composed of two separate schools — an Elementary School (K–6) and a Middle School (grades 7–8) — at different locations with separate administrations. The Peer Court was established at the middle school.

8. *Smythe Academy*, http://www.twinriversusd.org/schools/smythe_academy_78/.

9. For a brief description of other reasons specific to Smythe that lead the parties to select this design option, *see* Recommendations *infra*.

10. Maternity-leave and school administration personnel changes the subsequent year disrupted the court's operation, so no results were tallied.

11. E-mail communication with Vera Morris, Leadership Class teacher, Smythe Academy of Arts and Sciences Middle School (on file with author).

Chapter 6

1. ConnectEd, Career Academy Support Network, *A Profile of the California Partnership Academies 2004–2005* (2007), http://www.connectedcalifornia.org/about/downloads/CA_Partnerships. pdf. *See generally* Betsy Brand, *Rigor and Relevance: A New Vision for Career and Technical Education* (2003), http://www.ecs.org/html/offsite.asp?document=http%3A%2F%2Fwww.aypf.org%2Fpublications %2Faypf_rigor_0004v.3.pdf (discussing the value of rigor in career and technical education).

2. Cal. Educ. Code § 54690 (West).

3. The Appendix to this chapter provides the full text of the California eligibility standards for Partnership Academies. These standards are remarkably similar to the attributes described for the Legal Studies Academy at First Colonial in the next chapter.

4. West Oakland Demographic Profile compiled from various sources by Margot Lederer Prado, AICP City of Oakland http://www.planning.org/communityassistance/2005/pdf/WestOakland DemographicProfile.pdf.

5. CrimeView Community Incident Map, http://gismaps.oaklandnet.com/crimewatch/wizard. asp.

6. Oakland/Berkeley Asthma Coalition, *Oakland/Berkeley Asthma Hospitalization Report Vol 1 2004* at 5, http://www.ci.berkeley.ca.us/council1/images/asthma%202004.PDF.

7. See Chapter 5 *supra*.

8. Center for Youth Development through Law, www.youthlawworks.org. See Chapter 10, *infra*.

9. For further discussion of Mock Trials, *see* Chapter 11, *infra*.

10. *Alameda County Mock Trial Competition*, www.acoe.org/acoe/EdServices/ProgramsandServices/ YouthDev/MockTrial.

11. *Urban Debate League*, www.urbandebate.org/mission.shtml.

12. *Rose Foundation*, www.rosefdn.org.

13. Anna Kuchment, Into the Wilds of Oakland, California: Young Pollution Sleuths and Community Activists Fight for Healthier Air, NEWSWEEK 49, Aug. 1, 2008.

14. *Yosemite Institute*, http://www.naturebridge.org/yosemite.

15. *See* ConnectEd, *supra* note 52.

16. Cal. Educ. Code § 54692 (West).

Chapter 7

1. Legal Studies Academy Program Proposal, as presented to the Virginia Beach City Public Schools, VBCPS School Board on January 8, 2002 (on file with author).

2. Virginia Beach City Public Schools, www.vbschools.com/compass/index.asp.

3. *Id.*

4. Heidi Janicki, Legal Studies Academy at First Colonial High School Summary of Academy Exit Survey Results — 2010 (2011).

5. *Id.*

6. *Id.*

7. 2010–11 Legal Studies Academy Student Demographics.

8. Virginia Beach City Public Schools Professional Development Manual.

9. Heidi L. Janicki, Academy and Advanced Academic Programs Longitudinal Study: Survey Results Update for High School Programs, (Research Brief Number 6, 2010).

10. First Colonial High School Guidance Records.

Chapter 8

1. Legal Outreach, http://www.legaloutreach.org/.

2. For FAQ regarding the mentoring program, see the Appendix to this chapter.

3. If you are interested in licensing the Life Skills curriculum, please e-mail ssantana@legal outreach.org.

4. Legal Outreach offers its curricula, training, and strategic planning to others interested in this model. Fees are based upon a menu of services which the organization provides. Anyone who is interested should contact James O'Neal, Executive Director, at 718-752-0222 ext. 105 or e-mail him at joneal@legaloutreach.org.

Chapter 9

1. University of California Irvine's Center for Educational Partnerships (CFEP), http://www.cfep.uci.edu/.

2. The research base is clear on the intransigence of the achievement gap in reading. *See, e.g.,* Nat'l Center for Educ. Statistic, U.S. Dep't of Educ., Digest of Education Statistics 2007 [hereinafter Digest 2007], Table 112. *Average reading scale score, by age and selected student and school characteristics: Selected years, 1971 through 2004,* http://nces.ed.gov/pubs2008/2008022.pdf (showing, *e.g.,* on average, Black and Latino 17-year-olds read at the same level as White 13-year-olds.).

3. The research base is also clear on the intransigence of the achievement gap in writing. *See, e.g.,* Nat'l Center for Educ. Statistics (NCES), U.S. Dep't of Educ., *The Nation's Report Card: Writing 2007,* at 39 fig. 22 (2008), http://nces.ed.gov/nationsreportcard/pdf/main2007/2008 468.pdf; Digest 2007, supra note 96, *Table 119. Percentage of students attaining writing achievement levels, by grade level and selected student characteristics: 2002,* at 186.

4. Dr. Sara Lundquist, Vice President of Student Services, Santa Ana College, *The Santa Ana Partnership,* Presentation, CaliforniaALL Symposium, Irvine, Calif. (February 5, 2010).

5. CaliforniaALL was itself an innovative nonprofit organized under the auspices of the State Bar of California, the California Public Utilities Commission, the California Retirement System (CalPERS), and the California Department of Insurance. CaliforniaALL obtained grant funding from Verizon, which was the underlying funding for the Saturday Academy of Law. CaliforniaALL ceased operating in 2010.

6. *Charles Drew University Science Academy,* http://www.cdrewu.edu/pipeline-programs/saturday-science-academy/about.

7. See CFEP Research & Evaluation, UC Irvine Saturday Academy of Law Session I & II Evaluation Report (Sept. 2010) (full text on file with authors. See also Appendices C & D to this chapter.

8. The research base supports the focus on the so-called new 3Rs. *See, e.g.,* The Bill & Melinda Gates Foundation, *The 3Rs Solution,* http://www.gatesfoundation.org/Education/RelatedInfo/3Rs_Solution.htm; *see generally* Geoffrey D. Borman, Gina M. Hewes, Laura Overman & Shelly Brown, *Comprehensive School Reform and Student Achievement: A Meta-Analysis* (2002), http://www.csos.jhu.edu/CRESPAR/techReports/Report59.pdf (reviewing research on comprehensive, whole school reforms).

9. *SAL,* http://www.cfep.uci.edu/SAL (last visited Sept. 27, 2010).

10. The Oversight Committee is chaired by Dr. Stephanie Reyes-Tuccio, Director of CFEP. Participants included UCI staff with extensive experience in educational outreach programs as well as representatives from partner institutions such as Santa Ana College and the Delhi Community Center as well as representatives from funding partners such as the Verizon Foundation and from the legal community. *See SAL–UCI,* http://www.cfep.uci.edu/sal/oversightcomm.html. The Curriculum Committee included UCI faculty for undergraduate programs and the UCI School of Law, high school teachers, and outside expertise. *See id.,* http://www.cfep.uci.edu/sal/curriculumcomm.html. Members of the Curriculum Committee also serve on the Oversight Committee.

11. The research base supports the focus on critical skills and specifically finds these skills consistent with the demands of employers in the 21st century. *See generally, e.g.,* The Conference Bd., Partnership for 21st Century Skills, *Corporate Voices for Working Families & Soc'y for Human Res. Mgmt., Are They Ready to Work? Employers' Perspectives on the Basic Knowledge and Applied Skills of New Entrants to the 21st Century U.S. Workforce* 26–29 (2006), http://www.21stcenturyskills.org/documents/FINAL_REPORT_PDF09-29-06.pdf.

12. The mission of the Delhi Center is to "increase the leadership capacity and participation of Latinos for the construction of their own health and social well-being. Our vision is to be a model for the development of leadership and a center of service strengthened by the unique and diverse characteristics of the Latino community in Orange County." *Delhi Center,* http://delhicenter.com/ index.htm.

13. Santa Ana College (SAC) itself serves a diverse student population (including 1% Native American, 2% African American, 2% Filipino, 12% Asian, and 47% Latino. Santa Ana College has been recognized as one of the top associate degree producers for Hispanic students in the nation. *See Santa Ana Fact Sheet,* http://www.sac.edu/Projects/10/FactSheet_SAC_062509.pdf. Delhi and SAC have also been active partners with UCI, the SAUSD and others on innovative and collaborative initiatives under the banner of the Santa Ana Partnership; *see Santa Ana Partnership and Partners,* http://sac.edu/community/partnerships/sapartnership/, http://sac.edu/community/partnerships/sapartnership/partners.html.

14. This chapter was written before the beginning of the January 2011 session.

15. The research base supports emphasizing parent involvement. *See, e.g.,* Anne T. Henderson & Karen L. Mapp, *A New Wave of Evidence: The Impact of School, Family, and Community Connections on Student Achievement* 7, 38 (Southwest Educational Development Laboratory, National Center for Family & Community Connections with Schools 2002), www.sedl.org/connections/research-syntheses.html; Cori Brewster & Jennifer Railsback, *Building Trust with Schools and Diverse Families: A Foundation for Lasting Partnerships* (Northwest Regional Educational Laboratory 2003), http://www.nwrel.org/request/2003dec/trust.pdf.

16. The research base supports such an approach. *See generally, e.g.,* Karen Mitchell, Jamie Shkolnik, Mengli Song, Kazuaki Uekawa, Robert Murphy, Mike Garet & Barbara Means, The Nat'l Evaluation of High Sch. Transformation, Research, Rigor Relevance, and Results, *The Quality of Teacher Assignments and Student Work in New and Conventional High Schools* 9 (2005), http:// smallhs.sri.com/documents/Rigor_Rpt_10_21_2005.pdf; ACT, *Ready for College and Ready for Work: Same or Different?* 1 (2006), http://www.act.org/research/policymakers/pdf/ReadinessBrief.pdf; The Am. Diploma Project, *Ready or Not: Creating a High School Diploma that Counts* 8 (2004), http://www.achieve.org/files/ADPreport_7.pdf.

17. Other programs follow a similar philosophy and reach successful student outcomes. *See, e.g.,* Meyers Institute for College Preparation, *About MICP,* http://cmea.georgetown.edu/precollege/ prep/about/; Laura Cavender, *High Aspirations: Center Helps D.C. Students Prepare for Higher Education, Hughes Pre-College Scholars,* Blue & Gray Vol. 12 #1, Aug. 26, 2002; Shelley Dubois & Cori Vanchieri, *Reaching Across the Divide,* HHMI Bull. 32, 34, Feb. 2008, http://www.hhmi.org/bulletin/ feb2008/pdf/Divide.pdf (all describing MICP outreach and success); *Thurgood Marshall Academy Public Charter High School,* http://www.thurgoodmarshallacademy.org/ (reporting excellent results in open enrollment in one of the District of Columbia's most

challenged school districts: test scores are "more than 6.5 times higher than the DC CAS scores of other high schools in Wards 7 and 8 to which our students would traditionally be assigned" and higher than "the average scores of all DC open-enrollment high schools by 17% in reading and 26% in math"); ENLACE New Mexico, http://enlacenm.unm.edu/; Email from Karen Griego, Principal, Atrisco Heritage High Sch., Former Dir., ENLACE Albuquerque to author (Mar. 30, 2009) (on file with author) (reporting successful results in open program for Latino youth in Albuquerque).

18. The research base supports the emphasis on teacher qualification and quality. *See generally, e.g.,* Linda Darling-Hammond, Doing What Matters Most: Investing in Quality Teaching 8 (1997), http://www.nctaf.org/documents/DoingWhatMattersMost.pdf. William L. Sanders & June C. Rivers, *Cumulative and Residual Effects of Teachers on Future Student Academic Achievement* ii (1996), http://www.mccsc.edu/~curriculum/cumulative and residual effects of teachers.pdf.

19. The job description provides: "Under the direction of Santa Ana Unified School District teachers and UCI staff, SAL Teaching Assistants will provide academic support for ninth-grade students who are interested in learning about the legal profession. Each TA will be assigned to 5 students, leading discussions, assisting with written assignments, and aiding in the preparation of a final project. TAs will also assist teachers with set-up and clean-up for each Saturday session."

20. TA recruitment materials and handbooks were created as part of SAL–UCI and are available on request to the authors.

21. The curriculum is aligned with the California content standards for ninth grade language arts, and could be revised as needed to align with other state standards.

22. The emphasis on engagement is consistent with the research base. *See, generally, e.g.,* Comm. on Increasing High Sch. Students' Engagement and Motivation to Learn, Nat'l Research Council, *Engaging Schools: Fostering High School Students' Motivation to Learn* 10 (2004); Stephen Peters, *Capture, Inspire, Teach,* in *Engaging Every Learner* HOPE, AASA, NAESP (Alan M. Blankstein, Robert W. Cole, Paul D. Houston, eds., 2007*).*

23. The research base supports the focus on self-competence and confidence. *Consider, e.g.,* Claude Steele, *Stereotype Threat and African-American Student Achievement,* in Young, Gifted and Black 109 (2003).

24. Beth Bulgeron, Chief Academic Officer, Chicago Legal Prep, Chicago, Ill.

25. A sample of the curriculum is set forth in Appendix B to this chapter.

26. These tests were carefully customized by the evaluation team at CFEP to reflect the California content standards for ninth grade language arts, and could be revised, if needed to align with other state standards.

27. The Survey is attached as Appendix A to this chapter.

28. The UCI Evaluation Department analyzed the results of the pre- and post-tests as part of its evaluation, *see Evaluation Protocol and Results.* Evaluation materials are attached as Appendices C and D to this chapter.

29. The approach is consistent with the research base on aspirations. *See, e.g.,* Janice Ollarvia, *Breaking Ranks II: Strategies for Leading High School Change Georgia Conference on High School Improvement* (March 2005) ("Students need to make a strong connection to an adult they can see themselves becoming."); Barbara Schneider & David Stevenson, The Ambitious Generation: America's Teenagers, Motivated but Directionless 108 (1999).

30. The SAL-UCI population was drawn from Santa Ana Unified School District. See CFEP, *Research & Evaluation, UC Irvine Saturday Academy of Law Session I & II Evaluation Report* (Sept. 2010).

31. *Id.*

32. For example, SAL-UCI arranged a special session for these TAs with the Dean and Assistant Dean of Admissions from UCI School of Law who offered advice and assistance on the law school application process and another session with UCI faculty on writing personal statements. Similarly, SAL–UCI arranged for some of the TAs to attend the Orange County Hispanic Bar Association Annual Black Tie Dinner where they had the opportunity to network with area legal professionals.

33. The research base supports these aspects of the program as very significant and capable of producing long-term opportunities for networking, mentoring, access, and individual support. The Cleveland 3Rs program is another example of this. *Cleveland Metropolitan Bar Association,* http://www.clemetrobar.org/probono.asp?id=176; Interview with Louise Dempsey, Assistant Dean for External Affairs, Cleveland-Marshall College of Law Cleveland State University, Bd. Member, Cleveland Metro. Sch. Dist., in Portland, Maine (July 27, 2008).

34. This protocol is illustrative from first year SAL-UCI.

35. The evaluators also noted, "This provides some validity to the object test even though the items on the test are aligned with the Writing Strategies standards for 9th grade. Students in the second session had significantly higher scores at the end of the program on the test ($p < .05$). Although students in the first session did not improve overall on this test of recognition of writing strategies by the time of the posttest, some students increased their ability to evaluate and revise writing to improve logic and coherence."

Chapter 10

1. This curriculum was created by Urana Jackson, MA.

2. Those interested in replicating or learning more about this program are invited to contact Nancy Schiff at nschiff@youthlawworks.org or 510-642-4520 and to view our website at www.youthlawworks.org. A short film with glimpses of this program's activities and participants speaking candidly about their experiences is available at www.youthlawworks.org/movie.

Chapter 11

1. The legal and educational value and methodology of the Street Law Clinic parallel clinical legal education generally. In the D.C. Street Law Clinic at GULC, law student instructors teach about the law in high school and community settings as one of Georgetown's thirteen clinical courses. In the early years of clinical legal education in the US, clinics were primarily characterized as, and justified on the grounds of, providing practical legal training as a supplement to law schools' academic focus. While a major value of clinics has continued to be practical legal experience through hands-on client representation, clinics have evolved to provide the full range of legal professional development advanced by legal education generally. Clinical faculty use client representation as an entry point to teach both the practical and policy dimensions of legal doctrine, process, analysis, writing, ethics, and jurisprudence. While live client service and hands on learning through case preparation are major *ends* of clinical legal education, at the same time these are the *means* of engaging students in the full set of learning outcomes desired by the whole of legal education.

2. For an in depth presentation of this idea, *see* Richard Roe, *Valuing Student Speech: The Work of the Schools as Conceptual Development*, 79 Cal. L. Rev. 1269 (1991). *See also* Chapter 2 of this book for a discussion of the learning theory that underpins learner-centered education.

3. Its highest enrollment was 1984, when, in the Street Law: High Schools Clinic, we enrolled 33 law students in the year-long course. In 1984, we also enrolled 18 law students per semester in the one-semester Street Law: Corrections Clinic, making a total of 69 law students taking Street Law. In the 1990s, DC prisons were closed except for the DC Jail and the adjoining Correctional Treatment Facility; long term prisoners are now housed outside of DC. This greatly diminished the scope of the Street Law: Corrections Clinic, which morphed into the Street Law in the Community Clinic with a broadened set of settings: homeless shelters, rehabilitation centers, adult education centers, and other community sites for mostly adult populations.

4. In 2009, Street Law provided 16 classes in 14 high schools. Attendance ran from 8 to 10 in 5 classes, around 15 in 2 classes, and 20 or more in 9 classes, totaling 420 high school students (enrollment figures are significantly higher than attendance figures). Some of the DC high schools hosting Street Law classes are academically strong [three of the ten public non-charter high schools are not "in need of improvement," the highest of the five categories on the Federally Mandated School Improvement scale], while others are characterized by low levels of literacy and low academic skills [six are in the "restructuring" level, the lowest on the scale]. Moreover, in most of the schools, a majority of the students are below the poverty line (more than 50% of students in nine of the 15 schools we serve are eligible for free and reduced price lunch).

5. See the section below on Value to Law Students.

6. The Street Law Handbook.

7. See generally American Bar Association, The MacCrate Report: An Education Continuum Report of The Task Force on Law Schools and the Profession: Narrowing the Gap (, July 1992), http://www.abanet.org/legaled/publications/onlinepubs/maccrate.html#Part%20II.

8. See the section below on Value to Law Students.

9. *See* the Street Law, Inc. website at www.streetlaw.org for details on programs and services provided. Street Law, Inc. began as the National Street Law Institute (NSLI) in 1975, growing out of the Georgetown Street Law program to replicate Street Law in other law schools and communities. I began my Street Law career after graduating from law school in 1977, when I joined NSLI as an Assistant to the Director as a grants writer. NSLI became the National Institute for Citizen Education in the Law for a period of time, and then reincorporated Street Law in its name when it later became Street Law Inc. The Georgetown Street Law Clinic and Street, Law Inc. have collaborated throughout their histories. Persons interested in more information about Street Law may contact this writer or Street Law, Inc.

10. From the Georgetown University Law Center Clinical Fellowship Brochure for 2012 (on file with author).

Chapter 12

1. U.S. Census Bureau, *Fact Sheet for the District of Columbia*, http://factfinder.census.gov/servlet/ACSSAFFFacts?_event=Search&_state=04000US11&_lang=en&_sse=on (last visited on Nov. 30, 201011/30/2010).

2. District of Columbia Public Schools, *Facts and Statistics for 2008–2009 academic year*, http://dcps.dc.gov/DCPS/About+DCPS/Who+We+Are/Facts+and+Statistics (last visited Nov. 30, 2010).

3. The District reported its 2009 graduation rate as 72.3% but *Education Week* used the more strenuous calculation formula used by other states and computed a figure of 49%. *See* Bill Turque, *High School Graduation Rates Rise in D.C.*, http://www.washingtonpost.com/wp-dyn/content/article/2010/01/08/AR2010010802102.html (last visited Dec. 22, 2010).

4. Parents United for the D.C. Public Schools and Washington Lawyers' Committee for Civil Rights and Urban Affairs, *Separate and Unequal: The State of the D.C. Public Schools Fifty Years After Brown and Bolling* 2, Mar. 2005, http://www.washlaw.org/pdf/Separate_and_Unequal_Report.pdf.

5. See Census, supra note 130.

6. District of Columbia College Success Foundation, Double the Numbers Coalition, http://www.doublethenumbersdc.org/who-we-are (last visited on Nov. 30, 2010).

7. See Appendices A and B to this chapter.

8. Marshall Brennan Constitutional Literacy Project, *Application Process*, http://www.wcl.american.edu/marshallbrennan/application_process.cfm).

Chapter 13

1. Hopwood v. Texas, 78 F.3d 932 (5th Cir. 1996).

2. *See* Grutter v. Bollinger, 539 U.S. 306, 346 (2003).

3. Plessy v. Ferguson, 163 U.S. 537 (1896).

4. Sweatt v. Painter, 339 U.S. 629 (1950).

5. Brown v. Bd. of Educ., 347 U.S. 483 (1954); Brown v. Bd. of Educ., 349 U.S. 294 (1955).

6. Hopwood, 78 F.3d 932, *overruled in part by* Grutter v. Bollinger, 539 U.S. 306, 320 (2003).

7. The Court admitted: "No one disputes that Texas has a history of racial discrimination in education.... [P]ast discrimination in education, other than at the law school, cannot justify the present consideration of race in law school admissions." Hopwood, 78 F.3d at 951. Texas had not recently discriminated against Blacks or Hispanics, so such preferential treatment was neither remedial nor constitutional. Hopwood, 78 F.3d at 962.

8. *Id.*

9. Texas Attorney General's Opinion L097-001, issued on February Feb. 5, 1997.

10. State Bar of Texas, Department of Research & Analysis, *Survey of Texas Law Schools: The Racial/Ethnic Composition of First Year Classes, 1996–97, 1997–98, 1998–99, 1999–2000*, Austin,

Texas 2001. The data reported by Douglas Laycock for the law school had enrollments dropping even more drastically. He states: "Black enrollment dropped more than 90% in the first year, from 38 to 4. Mexican-American enrollment dropped nearly 60%, from 64 to 26." http://tarltonguides. law.utexas.edu/content.php?pid=98968&sid=742830; source of data: American Bar Association, 1992–1998, Table C3-9899. Douglas Laycock, June 25, 2001.

11. Hopwood, 78 F.3d at 947.

12. UTEP, http://academics.utep.edu/Default.aspx?tabid=49400).

13. UTPA, http://ur.utpa.edu/publications/read/7de1c71ebf2ff37b273; UTSA, http://www.utsa. edu/ilpa/).

14. *Filemon B. Vela Pre-Law Academy*, http://blue.utb.edu/vpaa/prelaw.htm.

15. *Prairie View*, http://www.pvamu.edu/pages/1.asp.

16. The ILPA website appears at http://utsa.edu/ilpa/, which covers ILPA programs.

17. A LSPI, by any other name, is a LSPI, as is UTSA's SLSPA. The SLSPA website appears at http://www.utsa.edu/ilpa/.

18. The UTSA Honors College website appears at http://utsa.edu/honors/?page=strategicplan.

19. The Certificate in Legal Reasoning and the SLSPA curriculum are explained at: http://www. utsa.edu/ilpa/?pg=SLSPACurriculum. The Legal Studies Minor appears at: http://utsa.edu/honors/? page=programs.mls.

20. *See* http://www.utsa.edu/ir/pdf/factbook/2009/StudentEnrollment.pdf, Student Enrollment, The UTSA Fact Book Office of Institutional Research (last visited, accessed May 16, 2010).

21. Plus, the UTSA benefitted from the expertise of Professor Bob Webking who headed UTEP's LSPI, initially.

22. Though some were circuitous, for instance, going to UC Berkeley that first year, then back to UT Law, another getting her MPA at the Maxwell School at Syracuse, then to UT Law, and another who spent time in China, deferring admission then entering UT Law the following year.

23. The SLSPA application appears at: http://www.utsa.edu/ilpa/?pg=SLSPA_App.

24. Administration and analysis of this test is administered by the head of the San Antonio Kaplan Test Prep Offices. ILPA thanks and acknowledges them him (her?) for this contribution.

25. Disciplines have included Business Law, English, History, Legal Studies, Philosophy, and Political Science.

26. With permission of the ILPA Director, students not enrolled in the SLSPA can take a particular course, such as Constitutional Law or Legal Technical Writing, if necessary for graduation or to complete a major or minor.

27. Examples of ILPA advice is available to others through CLEO Edge, see ILPA Director Gambitta's piece on advising juniors at: http://www.cleoscholars.com/_data/global/images/2011EDGE-Junior.pdf) or at *"The College Years. The Junior Year,"* CLEO Edge, American Bar Association, Winter/Spring, 2011, (Sept. 2010). published 9/2010

28. See The Expanded Program section *infra*.

29. Some students also take advantage of other undergraduate opportunities available through ILPA or the Honors College, also, such as travel abroad or the national or state capitol programs discussed herein. These activities sometimes prolong graduation slightly in return for enriched educational experiences.

30. The test covers areas including punctuation, subject-verb agreement, capitalization, possession, sentence structure, spelling, restrictive and nonrestrictive clauses, pronouns, parallel structure, modifiers, word choice, redundancy, and wordiness. It was designed as a collaboration between the writing instructors for UT Law and the UTSA SLSPA.

31. Thanks to Diane Abdo, who teaches the writing course for retrieval of this most current information.

32. Versions of conversions are available on the Web, *see, e.g.,* see http://www.alpha-score.com/resources/lsat-score-conversion/ ("Scores represent the analysis of 429,816 LSAT scores from June, 2006 to February, 2009. The mean scaled score for this period was 150.72 and the standard deviation was 9.89.").

33. The traditional disciplines at UTSA offer minors, so LGS operates without a traditional base.

34. Ruth Jones McClendon, an African-American woman, has served as a Member of the Texas House since 1996. *See* http://www.house.state.tx.us/members/dist120/mcclendon.php).

35. See overview of the UTSA Legislative Scholars Program at: http://www.utsa.edu/ilpa/?pg=LS.

36. The other two have accepted jobs with the Texas Democratic Party and the Heritage Foundation, but plan to apply to graduate school and law school, respectively, in the future. The majority of the students in 2009, as has been the case each time with McClendon Scholars, have been from

underrepresented groups. Fs—for 2011, seven of the nine students were from underrepresented groups.

37. *Commitment to Diversity*, http://www.utexas.edu/law/depts/admissions/studentlife/diversity.html/).

Chapter 14

1. *See* Chapter 4, *supra*.

2. One clear advantage of the BYU program is that mentoring appears as a block on students' schedules from the registrar, that is, a time is officially preserved for students to register for mentoring.

3. *See e.g.,* Cal. Educ. Code §45125 et seq.

4. See Appendix to this chapter.

Chapter 15

1. In 2004, for example, *American Lawyer* reported that "[m]inority attorneys make up 14.2 percent of U.S. lawyers," and "only 4.4 percent of U.S. partners," even though members of minority groups made up 37.3 percent of the U.S. general population in the 2000 census. "Slow rise to the top: despite formal efforts to recruit and retain minority lawyers, large firms continue to be overwhelmingly White, a new study finds." Am. Law., June 2004, at 103. Table of percentages of lawyers and the general populations by ethnicity, from the 2000 census can be found online at ABA Commission on Racial and Ethnic Diversity in the Profession, "Statistics about Minorities in the Profession from the Census," http:// www.abanet.org/minorities/links/2000census.html (last visited Dec. 8, 2008).

2. Diversity Pipeline Task Force Courts Working Group Final Report and Recommendations, Feb. 15, 2007, at 1, http:// calbar.ca.gov/calbar/pdfs/reports/2007_Courts-Working-Report.pdf (last visited Dec. 8, 2008).

3. Links to information about, and reports from, this conference and follow-up conferences can be found at the home page for the ABA Presidential Advisory Council on Diversity in the Profession, http:// www.abanet.org/op/councilondiversity/home.html (last visited Dec. 8, 2008).

4. This theme is underscored in the Post-Conference Report, Embracing the Opportunities for Increasing Diversity into the Legal Profession: Collaborating to Expand the Pipeline (Let's Get Real) at 12 (Executive Summary), 24–26 (2006), http:// www.abanet.org/op/pipelineconf/Pipeline PostReport.pdf (last visited Dec. 8, 2008).

5. The legal method exercises are set in familiar, non-legal settings that are accessible to the students and that engage them in legal reasoning by analogy. For a full description, see Charles Calleros, *Law School Exams: Preparing and Writing to Win* 37–41, 49–52, 121–22 (New York, 2007).

6. The program is described in the bar association's application for an ABA award, http:// www.abanet.org/barserv/partnernominees2007/local/bcba.pdf (last visited Dec. 8, 2008). For its efforts, this bar association earned an ABA 2007 Partnership Award. The awards are announced online at http:// www.abanet.org/barserv/partnership/ (last visited Dec. 11, 2008).

7. John Rogers et al., Univ. Cal. All Campus Consortium on Research for Diversity and UCLA Institute for Democracy, Education, and Access ("UC/ACCORD and UCLA/IDEA"), *California Educational Opportunity Report 2006: Roadblocks to College at 1*, available under the "publications" tab at http://www.edopp.org (last visited Dec. 8, 2008). The 2007 report once again highlighted greater shortages of highly qualified teachers, especially among those teaching college preparatory courses, in schools with high concentrations of African-American, Latino, and Native-American students. UC/ACCORD and UCLA/IDEA, *California Educational Opportunity Report 2007*, at 2, 5–11, http:// www.edopp.org (last visited Dec. 8, 2008).

8. I joined the committee just prior to the program's launch and have knowledge of many of these events. The history in the accompanying text, however, is set forth in the HNBA's application for the American Bar Association's 2007 Partnership Award, http:// www.abanet.org/barserv/partner nominees2007/national/hnba.pdf (last visited Dec. 8, 2008).

9. In 2008, the foundation of the HNBA, the Hispanic National Bar Foundation ("HNBF"), received a substantial grant from the Law School Admissions Council (LSAC) to help organize new mentoring programs in Los Angeles and Chicago from its offices in Washington, D.C. The program is now commonly called the HNBA/HNBF National Mentoring Program. For simplicity, however, this article refers more generally to HNBA as the founder and sponsor for the program implemented in Phoenix.

10. An Arizona statute provides, in part, that:

"Noncertificated personnel and personnel who are not paid employees of the school district and who are not either the parent or the guardian of a pupil who attends school in the school district but who are required or allowed to provide services directly to pupils without the supervision of a certificated employee and who are initially hired by a school district after January 1, 1990 shall be fingerprinted as a condition of employment.". ARIZ. REV. STAT. ANN. § 15-512(A) (2002).

This section appears to apply only to those seeking "employment," but that term likely applies broadly to anyone who provides services, volunteer or otherwise, because the first line of the statute distinguishes those who are "paid employees of the school district" and because another subsection refers to paying the cost of finger-printing for "personnel of the school district who are not paid employees." Moreover, the primary purpose of the statute is to screen out those who would represent a criminal or moral threat to children. *See* ARIZ. REV. STAT. ANN. § 15-512(D) (2002) (requiring disclosure of conviction or open-court admission of various kinds of crimes, most of them relating to sexual abuse of minors or other risks to minors). Those risks, of course, apply to volunteers who work with children through a school program such as the Law Magnet Program at South Mountain High School. *See also* ARIZ. REV. STAT. §§ 36-425.03(A & (K)(2)), 36-883.02(A & H), 36-897.03(A) (date) (fingerprinting requirements for child care personnel and child behavioral health care personnel apply to "volunteers"). In one way, the school district's policy may have exceeded the state law requirements. The school district required fingerprinting even though the mentoring would occur off-campus pursuant to a program for which parents of high school students had given written consent through forms I drafted and that were administered by the director of the high school law magnet program. The statute appears to provide an exception to the fingerprinting requirement in such circumstances:

"Subsection A of this section does not apply to a person who provides instruction or other education services to a pupil, with the written consent of the parent or guardian of the pupil, under a work release program, advance placement course or other education program that occurs off school property."

ARIZ. REV. STAT. ANN. § 15-512(I) (2008).

The statute contemplates, however, that school districts may impose fingerprinting requirements that go beyond the minimum required by the statute: "A school district may fingerprint any other employee of the district, whether paid or not," so long as the district does not charge the cost of the fingerprinting to the "nonpaid employee." ARIZ. REV. STAT. ANN. § 15-512(G) (2002). As illustrated by an even more demanding district policy implemented in the 2007–08 school year—requiring a certified teacher to be present at all mentoring team meetings—the school district erred on the side of providing maximum protection to its students.

11. See, e.g., ARIZ. REV. STAT. ANN. § 1583(C)(4) (2002) (in charter schools, excepting from fingerprinting requirements a "volunteer or guest speaker who is accompanied in the classroom by a person with a valid fingerprint clearance card").

12. This policy does not appear to represent an implementation of state statutory requirements, because a state statute excludes from fingerprinting requirements "a person who provides instruction or other education services to a pupil, with the written consent of the parent or guardian of the pupil, under … [an] education program that occurs off school property." ARIZ. REV. STAT. ANN. § 15-512(1) (2008); see *supra* note 119.

13. These requirements were discussed in several phone conversations and e-mails between Lorrie Drobny, Assistant Superintendent for Business and Operations at Phoenix Union High School District, and K Royal, who attempted to analogize the mentoring program to other community partnerships to which the district policy had not been applied. E-mail from K Royal, former Director of Pro Bono Programs, to Professor Charles Calleros (June 26, 2008) (on file with author). The Director of the Law Magnet Program at South Mountain High School also made numerous attempts to persuade the district office to modify its requirements. E-mail from K Royal to Charles Calleros, (June 27, 2008) (on file with author).

14. A short videotape description of the Phoenix and Las Vegas programs can be seen at http://media.law.asu.edu/Law/HNBAweb.wmv (last visited Dec. 8, 2008).

15. Richard D. Torpy, Am. Bar Ass'n, Mock Trial, A Script and How-To Guide for the Case: Goldilocks and the Three Bears, Kindergarten–6th Grade (1998).

16. The HNBA mentoring program in New York has, in the past, formed up to 30 mentoring teams with students from a single high school, but with college and law students from Barnard College, Cornell University, CUNY Honors College, Hunter College, John Jay College, Albany Law School, Brooklyn Law School, Cardozo Law School, Cornell Law School, Fordham Law School, New York University School of Law, St. John's University School of Law, and Touro Law Center.

17. If you advise or teach a law-related program in high school, college, or law school and would like to start a four-tier mentoring program in your community, contact the HNBA for information about which law schools and lawyers might be available to help you organize a program. You can start by going to the HNBA website at hnba.com, roll your cursor to the right side of the block labeled "About HNBA" and then click on "Board of Governors." Look for the Regional President in your region, or look for the National Mentoring Committee Co-Chairs, and ask for guidance in linking up with attorney or student organizations that can collaborate with you in starting a mentoring program.

18. See *Hispanic National Bar Association Mentoring Program*, law.asu.edu/hnba.

Index